An American Homecoming

by Brian Swartz

Photos by Brian Swartz

For Phyllis, Joyce, Susan and Francis --
who all believed in this project...

and for Richard "Dick" Shaw...
we made history this time

Copyright 1996

Bangor Publishing Company, Book Div.
P.O. Box 1329, Bangor, ME 04402-1329
207 - 990-8000

INTRODUCTION

"An American Homecoming" ironically originated from a TV broadcast on March 8, 1991. I had learned the previous evening that paratroopers returning from the Gulf War would land at Bangor International Airport, about two miles from my home. I decided to watch the TV report rather than meet the flight, which landed by 7 a.m.

The excitement immediately caught my attention. The son of WWII vets, I had never served in Vietnam, but I recalled the terrible homecomings that returning veterans received then. On March 8, I watched mesmerized as Maine residents, mostly civilians, raucously welcomed home combat-hardened soldiers they did not know.

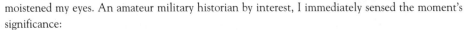

Then Sgt. Kevin Tillman plucked that saxophone from a high school musician and played a solo "Star-Spangled Banner." His proud, haunting rendition shivered my spine and goosebumped my arms; tears moistened my eyes. An amateur military historian by interest, I immediately sensed the moment's significance:

This was not Vietnam; this was not circa-1969 America. We had flipped the page historically by welcoming home our veterans, not by castigating them for obeying their civilian superiors' orders and policies, but by honoring them for what they were: the best of the best, American men and women who had gone into harm's way for the rest of us.

I rounded up my children and caught a troop flight after lunch. I went back – and back – and back. The sweeping emotional outbursts, the intense emotional displays by civilians and soldiers, the sheer excitement initially snagged my attention. I volunteered to help staff the greeting table. I brought relatives and friends to share the moment. I was there every moment possible.

Then the reporter's instinct kicked in, probably a week into the flights. I work as the advertising staff editor for the Bangor Daily News, the largest daily newspaper in Maine. By mid-March, I realized that someone should record what was happening; I started wielding a pen and camera.

The goal was to develop material for a special section the BDN subsequently published in July 1991. Then one day in late March, Elizabeth "Scottie" Bell, the Chamber of Commerce director, locked eyeballs with me and quietly said, "Someone should write a book about this, Brian."

So "An American Homecoming" was born.

I owe much to the people who supported the concept. My gratitude goes to Richard "Dick" Shaw, the BDN employee and local historian who initially read the rough copy; Kent Ward, the retired BDN assistant managing editor who tightly edited the copy and made it work; Wayne Lawton and J. Michael Kearney, who granted me free rein to pursue material for the July special section; Scottie Bell for the inspiration; Bob Jones of Cablevision for taping the flights and broadcasting them hours later; Gary Leighton and other BIA staffers who granted me access to the troops; Earle and Bernadette Rafuse for providing a veteran's viewpoint on the flights; Valerie Bellomy and Sylvia Thompson for keeping the faith; Richard J. Warren for agreeing to publish "An American Homecoming"; John Bishop for running with the project; and Martha Lostrom, who brought it all together on deadline.

Hampden, Maine
October 1996

CONTENTS

AN AMERICAN HOMECOMING

Its gleaming white fuselage sporting the citrus-colored symbols found in a warmer environment, a Hawaiian Airlines L-1011 descended through the drizzly, overcast sky while making a final approach to Bangor International Airport.

The newspaper secretary glimpsed the L-1011 as it passed northwest-bound over Interstate 395, a short stretch of pavement connecting Interstate 95 with Down East Maine.

Peering through her eyeglasses at the airliner framed by her office window, the secretary asked, "Is that one of them?"

Yes, a reporter replied, the HAL L-1011 was "one of them," one of the many airliners that beginning in late winter 1991, had formed an air bridge between the Persian Gulf and the airport in Bangor, Maine. Since the planes ferried troops returning from the Gulf War, the public decided that the phrase "troop flights" accurately described the planes and their passengers.

On Thursday, April 11, HAL Flight 7844 carried soldiers destined for Fort Bliss in El Paso, Texas. As the L-1011 landed at 9:27 a.m., anticipation stirred the soldiers and other military personnel who'd endured the long transatlantic flight from a refueling stop in Europe. Many soldiers had not touched American soil since August 1990, when Saddam Hussein had bullied Kuwait into submission.

Seven months earlier, some of the L-1011's passengers had kissed their families good-bye and flown off to the international nervous tic called the Gulf Crisis. Loneliness had been their lot. Only letters and tenuous phone calls had linked the soldiers with home since that long ago August day.

Suddenly, the soldiers sat just yards above tarmac belonging to the United States. The flight attendants had spread the word, "We're deplaning here." The men and women clad in desert fatigues tensed in anticipation.

American soil, at last!

Men and women who had forgotten the joys of hot showers hurriedly ran their fingers or combs through their hair or applied makeup. Soldiers fumbled with their wallets to find enough money for a payphone call home.

Actually, money presented few problems for most soldiers aboard HAL Flight 7844: Where could they spend their checks in the desert?

A Customs official boarded the plane and asked perfunctory questions: No plants? Check. No firearms? Great. "You cleared customs in Saudi Arabia, so, welcome to the U.S., ladies and gentlemen."

Cheers and applause thundered through the aircraft.

Then the senior officer on the L-1011 released the soldiers for a short visit to Bangor, an unknown city located in a state that so many people could not point to on a map. Hey, what the heck. It's still the U.S.A., the troops reasoned.

The first desert-fatigued passengers disembarked through a forward hatch and trudged through the elongated jetway leading to the international terminal, shivering in the New England cold. Definitely not the desert!

The uniformed vanguard entered the terminal, where some airport personnel suddenly flanked them. As the soldiers trudged along a security corridor leading toward blue metal doors, someone yanked the doors open.

The soldiers didn't realize that the doors formed a last barrier between war and peace, delineating what had been in the desert from what would be at home.

The lead troops noticed a gray-haired woman - "gosh, she reminded of my grandmother," a young soldier assigned to a Patriot battery later observed - standing beyond those last open doors. She grasped a pole that mounted a large American flag.

Then the soldiers stepped through the doors and turned right. The grandmotherly flag-bearer hastened to lead the troopers farther into the terminal.

No words can ever express the wonder that the war-weary soldiers experienced the moment they swung right through the door...and met the thunderous applause, throaty cheers, and general noise that echoed up the ramp connecting the international terminal to the domestic terminal.

A few short yards from the open doors that separated peace from war, the soldiers met their audience, the people who had turned out on this cold, windy morning to welcome them home.

Even as HAL Flight 7844 flew toward Bangor that day, people arrived at the airport from towns throughout Maine. Yellow buses discharged schoolchildren, family sedans jockeyed for parking spaces on Godfrey Boulevard, the two-lane road leading to the terminals, and a few people wondered if this time a loved one would step off the L-1011, a wondrous aerial chariot of peace.

The L-1011's arrival would push the number of military personnel who'd passed through Bangor while en route home to more than 35,000. By 9:40 a.m. that Thursday, about 110 flights had unloaded their U.S.-bound passengers at the international terminal.

With 109 prior troop landings under their collective belts, BIA employees knew the routine by heart. Hard-worn experience had determined who would meet the soldiers first and where most people would stand to witness the arrival.

Red, vinyl-covered ropes linked the stanchions that marked the passageway for troops entering BIA. On April 11, the stanchions ran from the passenger-service desk atop the ramp to the domestic terminal, where the designated corridor hooked left beside the duty-free shop.

As the troops deplaning from HAL Flight 7844 followed the flag-bearer onto the ramp, they passed through metal-framed glass doors adjacent to the passenger-service desk. The ramp began here, where the troops could proceed into the domestic terminal or go downstairs to use the phones or restrooms.

At the ramp entrance stood an official greeting party, with nary a politician or bureaucrat in its ranks.

The people whom the soldiers encountered as they swung right beyond the Doorway to Freedom wore the full or partial uniforms belonging to the veterans of other wars. Middle- or older-aged men and women sporting VFW or American Legion hats waited quietly behind the stanchions.

Among greeters standing along the rope barrier, which a local wag would dub the "wire" - a name that stuck - stood several older veterans clad in powder blue uniforms. These men and one woman comprised the honor guard from American Legion Post No. 84 in Orono, a college town eight miles north of Bangor on the Penobscot River.

Tossing out their personal schedules, these Legionnaires had met every arriving troop flight since the first one on Friday, March 8.

So the returning Gulf vets met vets from World War II and Korea as they stepped onto American soil. No age barrier existed between the generations, however, as the Fort Bliss soldiers soon discovered.

As sustained applause and cheering washed up the ramp, the troops reached out to shake hands with the people who had fought other wars. Then the initial nervousness gave way to relieved smiles and laughter as the Texas-bound troops recognized the genuine joy awaiting them.

Comments like "welcome home, soldier" and "I'm glad you made it back" echoed through the ramp. Young and old veterans alike pressed flesh, smiled at each other, and occasionally hugged while the now-not-so-weary soldiers worked their way down the ramp.

After clearing the official receiving line, the soldiers walked down the ramp. As they passed through another set of blue doors and approached a level floor, the startled Patriot missileers suddenly saw who else waited for them.

Civilians, more American civilians than the soldiers had seen in one place in seven months or more. Civilians, young babies asleep in cradled arms, toddlers perched atop their parents' shoulders, young people, old people. Civilians, most of whom could not differentiate between Marines, sailors, soldiers, and airmen.

There, pressed firmly against the stanchioned wire, stood 400 to 500 people stacked rows deep, all wildly cheering and applauding.

American flags waved in mid-air as patriotic music swelled about the soldiers. Faces that had witnessed ecological disaster in Kuwait or wartime carnage in Iraq split into infectious grins, and at least one soldier raised his hands high above his head, jumped up, and let loose with a Midwestern screech of joy.

The crowd responded in kind. Hands, many, many hands reached out to touch the returning soldiers. Eyes that would not have met except for the Gulf War blinked in recognition of this moment, of this time and space in history, when Americans finally honored the men and women who'd served them so well.

More soldiers poured down the ramp and into the terminal. No matter how many came, the civilians cheered and yelled and welcomed home their heroes, the very men and women who had wondered if America had forgotten them in the desert.

The wire guided the troops to the left as they entered the domestic terminal. Here, the full impact of their greeting struck home. As far as the wire stretched, and on both sides of the artificial aisle, people edged forward to shake hands, exchange hugs, and occasionally kiss a stubbled cheek.

The aisle also guided the soldiers toward the telephones, a busy lounge, a small cafeteria, and a few gift shops. Some soldiers bolted for the phones. Others headed for the Red Baron Lounge and a cold beer, the first they'd tasted in many months. Countless troops paused to talk with strangers who acted like they had always known the boys and girls from Arkansas, California, and elsewhere.

Schoolkids wearing Desert Storm T-shirts sought autographs from the happy soldiers. Within minutes, some soldiers wore out their dominant hands while writing with indelible markers.

Sometimes, children traded a flower or a small teddy bear for an autograph. Soldiers long gone from their own children hugged a child who reminded them of a son or daughter back home.

Uniform accouterments started disappearing as the soldiers pinned chevrons to civilian lapels or ripped off their highly coveted shoulder patches and handed them to adoring children. In the future, many Maine kids would remember the day they obtained a captain's bars or a master sergeant's insignia.

And so that Thursday morning passed, until a final boarding call brought the last Tail-End Charlie running up the ramp toward the international terminal. For 90 minutes or so that April 11, homebound soldiers experienced an American homecoming in Bangor, the city that that ABC-TV's "Inside Edition" called "Hometown USA."

For a space of 10 months, from March to January 1992, thousands of people turned out at BIA to welcome about 60,000 troops returning from the Gulf. With little official organization, civilians threw together the longest homecoming celebration in American history.

There had been nothing like it since World War II, not for Korean vets, not for Vietnam vets, not for Grenada or Panama vets. Operating with a shoestring budget, Maine residents united to show their appreciation for their troops, the very people whom a previous generation had vilified on the streets and in the media.

Those 10 months wrote an important, yet overlooked page into the nation's history. For the first time since late 1945, Americans had risen to welcome home their own. The fact that the homecomings took place in Bangor, a city cursed with an inferiority complex caused by a proximity to Portland and Boston, surprised everyone, particularly Bangor residents.

During those 10 months, many events coalesced into the historical fact known as the troop flights. Poignant reunions, tearful departures, impromptu comedy all took place on the ramp or in the domestic terminal. History passed through BIA as troops related their stories about their war. For 10 months, the military and civilians mingled easily in a joyous American homecoming that began on Friday,

March 8, 1991.

Through geographical and historical quirks, Bangor would become the refueling point for a troop flight returning from the Gulf. Being in Maine, Bangor was naturally nearer to Europe and the Middle East than Boston or New York. The Army recognized this geographical reality during World War II, when it built Dow Field in Bangor as a refueling point for warplanes headed for Iceland and Great Britain.

After the war, Dow remained open as Dow Air Force Base. Strategic Air Command bombers, tankers, and jet fighters flew from Dow until 1968, when the Pentagon closed the base and sold it to Bangor.

The city paid $1 for the best real-estate deal since Manhattan went for $24 and some beads.

Over the years, Bangor International Airport developed a reputation for efficiently handling international traffic. By stopping at BIA, transatlantic airliners could refuel and clear customs (usually) faster than at Logan in Boston or JFK in New York.

And, unlike those two international jetports, a snowstorm seldom closed BIA.

During Operation Desert Shield, many outbound troop flights put into Bangor to refuel. Those flights went unnoticed by the local media and the public, except when a smoke grenade detonated in an aircraft shortly after its departure from BIA.

No harm done, no casualties inflicted.

When a ceasefire ended the Gulf War in early March 1991, Bangor area residents never imagined the war would come to them. BIA officials, including Airport Director Robert Ziegelaar, received advance warning that American Trans Air Flight 7254 would land about 7 a.m. on March 8.

Word got out, of course; you can't keep a secret in Maine. Officials organized a welcoming party, airport crews spruced up the international and domestic terminals, and New England Telephone crews installed additional pay phones. Even the few businesses serving the flying public in the domestic terminal geared up for what Maine residents figured was a one-shot deal.

Elizabeth "Scottie" Bell, the executive director of the Greater Bangor Chamber of Commerce, suggested that the soldiers arriving on AMT Flight 7254 might like some small gifts. In late 1990, when the Iraqis still held many American civilians as "guests," Bangor residents had prepared to receive any released civilians who might pass through the airport. Local businesses had donated countless merchandise, which had been stored at the Chamber office on Main Street.

Since no ex-hostages ever reached BIA, Bell wondered if the teddy bears and other items could be given to the troops instead. Board members enthusiastically approved her suggestion.

Excitement rippled through the community. People discussed going to BIA to meet the troops. Since Channel 2 promised live coverage on Friday morning, many people opted to stay home and tape the news. Other people decided to go.

Some local officials wondered if anybody other than the invited guests would show up. There was little warning about the event, just the blurb on the Thursday evening news and a writeup in the morning's Bangor Daily News.

Perhaps the powers-that-be need not have worried. A month earlier, about 2,500 people had paraded for two miles through Brewer and Bangor to show their support for the troops. Obviously, the men and women on duty in the Gulf had their fans in central Maine.

Taciturn Mainers don't tend to wave the flag or demonstrate outside their federal buildings to boast their patriotism. Oh, a yellow ribbon here, a bumper sticker there, but no grandiose demonstrations to back the troops. In fact, the February march had been organized by the Exiles, a local motorcycle club. The cheering accompanying that march had marked the closest point that local residents came to getting emotional.

So the powers-that-be organized an official welcome for the paratroopers aboard AMT Flight 7254. The band from John Bapst Memorial High School in Bangor would provide music for AMT Flight 7254. With more flights added to the schedule as Friday approached, Bangor High School agreed to send its band later in the day.

Still, two or three troop flights. What was there to get excited about?

No one envisioned that the few troop flights would exponentially increase to more than 220 by January 1992.

Preparations were well underway on March 8 when AMT Flight 7254 landed an hour early. About 4 a.m., Chamber of Commerce volunteers loaded three cars with "goodies" and transported the merchandise to BIA, where Ziegelaar had instructed his employees to set up two tables at the lower ramp entrance. Volunteers packed these tables with the teddy bears, post cards, magazines, and other donated items.

When the AMT L-1011 touched down about 6 a.m., not all the musicians from John Bapst had arrived, nor had some local dignitaries. A fundamental truth applied to this first flight and the hundreds that followed. Get there early, else the plane might beat you.

Despite the early arrival of AMT Flight 7254, a few hundred people already thronged the domestic terminal. As paratroopers from the 82nd Airborne Division reached the upper ramp, civilians cheered.

Cheered? According to Marc Blanchette, a Bangor Daily News photographer who covered the morning flights, "the crowd went bananas. I've never seen anything like it."

Dignitaries shook hands with the deplaning troops and welcomed them to Maine. Suspicion gradually faded as the adrenaline-pumped paratroopers worked their way along the official receiving line. "Hey, man!" a soldier blurted. "This is for real!"

More civilians reinforced the homecoming crowd as the John Bapst band played a patriotic medley to match the emotional mood. Directed down the ramp, soldiers poured into the domestic terminal and threw themselves into the outstretched arms that reached out for them. Any pretense at dignified behavior dissolved in those tender moments, as Americans tearfully expressed their appreciation.

5

The paratroopers, too, went nuts that morning. They laughed and guffawed while encountering American women, beer, phones, and fast food in quantity for the first time since August 1990. Brawny troopers who'd bested Saddam Hussein's best tenderly kissed babies, then hugged their older siblings. Many Maine women, from teen-agers to their grandmothers, tasted lips still sand-blasted from dust storms.

According to Renee Ordway, a newspaper reporter, some paratroopers rubbed snow on their faces and shouted, "God bless America!" Yet other soldiers mugged for the TV cameras by waving and yelling, "Hi, mom!"

The John Bapst band kept playing as soldiers and civilians discussed the war, the news, sports, any subject at all, as long as it centered on the good old U.S. of A. Some soldiers drifted away from the phones and lounge to listen to the well-rehearsed musicians.

Gary Eckmann, a Bapst senior and a drummer from Holden, watched as the band director indicated another number. Sticks in hand, Eckmann tensed. Then someone tapped his shoulder.

About 7 a.m. on March 8, 1991, Army Sgt. Kevin Tillman (seen here performing during the July 4 parade in Bangor) borrowed a saxophone and played the "Star-Spangled Banner" at Bangor International Airport. His impromptu performance epitomized the emotions that would surround the Gulf flights landing at BIA.

He turned to deal with the interruption.

There stood his brother, paratrooper Mark Fleigelman. Just like that. One moment gone to war, the next moment home. Eckmann dropped his sticks and warmly hugged Fleigelman.

The crowd cheered. In the days to come, other families would reunite at BIA, but today belonged to a drummer, a soldier, and their mother, Beth Eckmann, who arrived late only because AMT Flight 7254 had landed early.

Emotions ran wild that morning. Maine civilians hugged uniformed and battle-hardened strangers who melted beneath the attention. Soldiers cried and dabbed at tears, they were so overcome that so many people would turn out to welcome them home.

Many older people, both military and civilian, who'd kept their frustrations bottled up since Vietnam vented their true feelings as they celebrated a return to peace. A generation ago, the press and its allies in academia had frowned upon patriotism, especially the flag-waving, soldier-hugging variety that burst across America when the troops returned from the Gulf. People pressured by American society to keep quiet in 1968 or 1969 spoke forcefully in winter 1991. Nowhere did they speak louder than in Bangor.

Older soldiers who had served in Vietnam responded enthusiastically to the homecoming celebration. "I can't believe this is happening," a multistriped sergeant wept on a woman's shoulder. "We didn't get anything like this coming back from Southeast Asia. Is this real, or am I dreaming?"

"This is real," the Maine woman assured him.

"Oh, oh, thank you so much," the soldier blurted, swiping at his tears with his right forefinger.

About 7 a.m., Sgt. Kevin Tillman asked a Bapst saxophonist if he might borrow the student's instrument. Expertly fingering the keys, Tillman stood near the expansive terminal windows and eased into the "Star-Spangled Banner."

What happened next would forever capture the essence of the BIA homecomings.

As Tillman soulfully played the "Star-Spangled Banner" a capella, his slow-paced notes rolled across the terminal. People stopped talking and turned toward the music. Paratroopers stood ramrod-straight. Veterans from other wars searched the terminal for the nearest American flag, then raised their hands in salute. Civilians who had never served in the military respectfully faced Tillman. Some people spread their hands over their hearts.

Soldiers started crying and singing as Tillman reached "o'er the ramparts we watched, were so gallantly streaming." TV cameramen and still photographers, even amateur videotapers, jostled close to the sergeant and tried to capture the moment on film.

"Oh, say, does that Star-Spangled Banner yet wave, o'er the land of the free, and the home of the brave," people sang as Tillman concluded his impromptu performance. When the last note faded into history, Americans cheered, and a comrade whose face glistened with tears clutched the startled Tillman.

Tillman's unrehearsed musical salute eloquently expressed what people felt that day - and would feel in the months to come. Columnists would expend their energy trying to explain what happened across the country in March 1991. Commentators would speculate why Americans from Bangor to San Antonio to San Francisco mobbed returning Gulf vets.

Sgt. Kevin Tillman said it all with a borrowed saxophone.

By mid-morning, AMT Flight 7254 and its jubilant human cargo had exited BIA. Minutes after the blue-and-white L-1011 lifted off for a two-hour flight to Pope Air Force Base in North Carolina, Continental Flight 7253 landed with 400 sailors from the USS Mercy, a Navy hospital ship.

Troop greeters threw another homecoming party for the sailors, as they did the 1st Infantry Division soldiers who landed at 11:12 a.m. aboard AMT Flight 7246. Momentum built toward the afternoon, when AMT Flight 7244 would stop while en route to McGuire Air Force Base, New Jersey.

Reports filtered to the newspaper throughout the morning. "You've got to see this," Blanchette phoned anyone who'd listen. Editors scrambled to rearrange reporters' schedules. "Get people out there!" became Friday's watchword in the newsroom.

When AMT Flight 7244 landed at 3:28 p.m., the crowd intensified its cheering and applause. As the L-1011 taxied to the international terminal, many troop greeters readied their cameras.

Stepping to the lectern placed beside the duty-free shop, Robert Ziegelaar addressed the crowd. He explained some basic rules intended to keep a corridor open for the troops, thanked everyone for coming out for the flight, and announced its arrival.

The crowd cheered.

Then soldiers appeared atop the ramp.

The crowd thundered its approval.

Soldiers hooted and hollered as they walked past the gift table. Three women soldiers - a fourth companion must have been a Marine, as she wore no tags on her uniform - bounced down the ramp and into the terminal, where they hugged civilians, shook hands, and let loose in celebration.

By now, the Bangor High School band had replaced the Bapst band. The director guided her sweater-clad musicians through various numbers. The disciplined students remained in their seats, for a while, at least, until the director finally released them to join the homecoming.

Soldiers and a few airmen moved along the wire, where Maine women grabbed uniform lapels and hauled startled troops forward for a friendly kiss. Women soldiers wept as they hugged each person standing in line.

Then a tall, incredibly young soldier whose black moustache did not conceal his age emerged from the ramp and threw his arms around a troop greeter. The men embraced as the soldier sobbed on the civilian's right shoulder.

The youth lifted his tear-streaked face and whispered, "My God, this is absolutely incredible! You don't know how I feel!" Slightly embarrassed by his tears, he stiffened his upper lip before working his way farther along the wire.

The soldier traveled perhaps 10 feet before a grandmother hugged him. His reserve shattered, the trooper cried as the woman held him.

The afternoon blurred into disparate images...

...a soldier talking on a pay phone noticed that he was being photographed and said long distance, "Some guy with a camera's trying to take my picture. Should I smile?"...

...a dark-haired woman soldier blurted into a pay phone nearer the restrooms that "I'm in Bang-ger, Maine! No, I don't know where it is, but I'm in the U.S.!"...

...an Army sergeant using an adjacent phone quietly told someone on the East Coast, "I'm back in the States, babe...Yeah, that's right, up in Maine...Yeah, I missed you, too"...

...Robert Ziegelaar introduced a Lt. Col. Floyd, who stood behind the lectern and thanked the crowd for the kindness extended his soldiers...

...the four servicewomen spotted people equipped with cameras. "Take our picture!" the soldiers (and one possible Marine) laughed as they hammed it up...

...schoolkids chased autographs across the terminal. Soldiers obliged every request, no matter the child's age...

...civilians chatted with soldiers whom they'd never met. Conversations flowed like those between old friends...

...a soldier who identified himself as a Vietnam vet shook hands with every civilian he could find and thanked them for welcoming him home.

All too soon, Robert Ziegelaar announced the first boarding call for AMT Flight 7244. Soldiers reluctantly disengaged from their warm reception and reversed their movement along the wire. By 5 p.m., the last troops vanished into the ramp, leaving behind some 500 people who couldn't believe what had happened this afternoon.

I've got to come back again, many of them vowed.

THE WRONG GENERAL

Rumors move fast in central Maine.

About 5 a.m. on Tuesday, March 12, American Trans Air Flight 7262 and Hawaiian Airlines Flight 7342 landed just minutes apart at Bangor International Airport. Even at that time of the morning, about a hundred people had gathered to greet the troops.

On the fourth morning since the 82nd Airborne had sent its first detachment through Bangor, informal disorganization still reigned at the airport. The greeting techniques had not yet been refined. Civilians could still walk up the ramp, stand beside the Legionnaires, and shake hands with the returning military personnel.

That would change after this morning.

The people who'd come to BIA before sunrise this Tuesday closely resembled dorm students who'd been rousted for a midnight fire drill. Informally dressed in jeans and baggy sweatshirts, with the occasional "Desert Storm" T-shirt draped across someone's body - a decidedly older woman wore a bath robe - civilians sprawled half-asleep across the vinyl airport chairs, drank hot coffee, or chatted quietly while struggling to remain awake.

AMT Flight 7262, bound for Charleston, S.C., landed at 5:15 a.m. Two minutes later, HAL Flight 7243 spun its wheels on the pavement while en route to Cherry Point Marine Corps Air Station in North Carolina.

Just before the troops started unloading from the two aircraft, Margaret Warner, a reporter from the Bangor Daily News, appeared on the ramp and stood near the assembled Legionnaires. Not known as a "morning person," Warner exchanged pleasantries with people around her.

"I did not willingly choose to get up at four today," Warner told another off-duty reporter who had come to greet the troops. Keeping her voice low, she explained that a reliable source had tipped the newspaper that General H. Norman Schwarzkopf might be aboard one of the planes.

A conversation with the police sergeant commanding the BIA security detail revealed that the Bangor Police Department had received a similar tip from a source at the airport. Jeff Strout, the city editor at the BDN, had buzzed Warner awake about 4 a.m. He told her about the tip and asked her to check it out.

The two airliners disembarked their passengers minutes apart. The troops pouring into the ramp seemed primarily Marines, with soldiers and airmen scattered among their ranks. Perhaps 700 uniformed Americans occupied BIA for less than two hours that Tuesday before flying off to their respective destinations.

The troops dutifully walked down the ramp to cheers and applause from the adoring crowd. Military fashion designers had dictated desert fatigues for the Marines and soldiers; Air Force personnel stood apart in their jungle fatigues.

Legionnaires and other troop greeters shook hands and welcomed the troops home. Uniform after uniform poured past the people standing on the ramp, until one rank blurred into another. Even the happy faces, although differentiated by color and age, gradually melded into an American montage.

The alert reporters kept searching for Gen. Schwarzkopf. He certainly wouldn't get past unnoticed...or would he?

Then, a gap developed between some Marines, and the off-duty reporter looked up into the dark eyes of a three-star Marine general. His name tag proclaimed him as "Waller."

"Welcome home, General," the journalist said, to which Waller, second in command to Gen. Schwarzkopf, replied his thanks.

Other Marines, soldiers, and airmen passed down the ramp, until only a few stragglers wandered down from the phones in the international terminal. By waiting to greet the Tail-End Charlies, the people standing on the ramp set a precedent. In the future, someone always waited to greet the last arriving troop. Everyone received the welcome they deserved.

Finally, the last Marines reached the domestic terminal, so the greeters on the ramp joined the crowd within the building. Gen. Waller vanished, apparently spirited away to a quiet office, and a few people expressed their disappointment that Gen. Schwarzkopf had not arrived with the incoming flights.

Later that morning, TV reports indicated that the Bear had gone to Kuwait City instead of Bangor.

A half hour later, Air Force Senior Master Sgt. Harold Billings, who hailed from Sumter, S.C., spoke about his work on the CENTCOM staff in Riyadh, where he helped plan bomb strikes against the Iraqi infrastructure.

Billings stopped to ask questions about Bangor author Stephen King and his wife, Tabitha, then deviated into conversation about the Billings family.

The senior master sergeant explained that since his flight terminated in Charleston, he would probably rent a car for the two-hour drive to Sumter. No, his family did not know that he had returned to the United States. "They think I'm still in Riyadh," he said.

In fact, his wife had left for a business trip to Florida, and his sons, ages 11 and 15, would be in school by the time he arrived home. Billings planned to surprise the boys when they got home from school.

"I'm looking forward to pulling into my front yard," he said.

Who could blame him, considering that he had missed every family holiday since August 1990?

AMT Flight 7262 departed BIA by 7 a.m., taking Billings, Waller, and their comrades home to South Carolina. The general's unannounced visit to Bangor made the March 13 edition of the Bangor Daily News, since Margaret Warner knew a story when she saw one.

In her article, Warner noted that Brig. Gen. Schwartz had flown into Bangor with Waller.

Schwartz, but not Schwarzkopf. Close, but no Bear.

PARTY TYPES

During Tuesday, March 12, airport officials refined their crowd-control techniques. The changes were evident to the people who caught the 5 a.m. flights and returned to meet an evening flight on its way to Gulfport, Mississippi.

Sometime that day, the powers-that-be set up more stanchions in the domestic terminal and aligned them to create a wider entry corridor for the returning troops. The idea made sense, since the unrestrained crowd usually collapsed upon the troops attempting to enter the domestic terminal.

If the troops dallied too long at BIA for any reason, the ferrying airline disrupted its schedule and possibly incurred higher operating expenses.

A packed terminal also meant that passengers who disembarked from international flights must remain in a secure holding area within the international terminal. Foreign visitors wouldn't appreciate an American attempt to teach them the herding instinct, so they might not fly with a particular airline again. This would equal lower revenues.

Of course, if stopping in Bangor upset its passengers or cost it too much money, a foreign-flag carrier could move down Interstate 95 to Logan in Boston. Bangor would lose business and tarnish its reputation. From an economic sense, this was not permissible.

Crowd control otherwise, airport officials still let people into the ramp on March 12. As they gained experience in shepherding the rowdy, but friendly crowds, airport officials gradually weaned "unauthorized personnel" from standing on the ramp. Legionnaires, members of the press, VFWers, and the volunteers working the gift table were OK, the BIA staff said.

So were people waiting for relatives landing on a troop flight, Robert Ziegelaar said.

His decision led to many poignant reunions there on the ramp.

Unfortunately, some people attempted to abuse the system established by the airport. When Gary Leighton or Richard Myrshall would announce that family members could wait on the ramp, a few unscrupulous characters would occasionally identify themselves as relatives and stand with people whose sons or daughters had survived Scud attacks or battles with the Republican Guards.

The experienced troop greeters learned to discern the non-relatives. Several times during the next few months, the wolf-in-sheep's-clothing waiting on the ramp heard a whispered "get your butt outta here" from someone who didn't appreciate fakes.

This Tuesday evening, however, such internecine tensions did not exist at BIA. How could the troop greeters find fault on a sunny and fairly warm winter's day, when five airliners carrying soldiers, Marines, sailors, and Air Force personnel had passed through Bangor?

And with the sixth aircraft still to arrive?

By 6 p.m. on March 12, people started lining the wire in the domestic terminal. Phyllis MacKinnon, a 90-year-old woman from Brewer, arrived about 5:45 p.m. with a grandson and two great-grandchildren. "I haven't seen any excitement like this since World War II," she said just minutes after riding the escalator to the second floor.

Citing his grandmother's age, the grandson finagled MacKinnon a place along the wall across from the gift table. "She's 90," he told the police officer who arched an eyebrow at the intrusion.

"All right, she can stay there," the police officer acknowledged. "This her first flight?"

"Yep," the grandson replied.

"Just make sure she doesn't get bowled over in the rush," the officer suggested. "What about the two kids? They related to her?"

"Great-grandchildren," the grandson answered.

"Yours, I take it?" the cop inquired.

"Ah, yeah," the third-generation MacKinnon said.

"They can stay, too, but don't block the ramp," the cop said.

"No problem," MacKinnon's grandson replied.

More than 300 people joined MacKinnon and her relations to greet Hawaiian Airlines Flight 6402. From the familiar faces spotted along the wire, tonight must be Old Home Week at BIA, someone observed. A longtime Bangor resident could walk through the crowd and chat with friends or relatives...almost like shopping at the Bangor Mall.

The HAL L-1011 landed at 7:06 p.m. and taxied to the international terminal. Despite the glare from the interior lights, the "scouts" who plastered their noses to the windows in the domestic terminal detected the airliner as it dropped from the night sky.

"Is that the plane?" a child called.

A man who'd apparently met an earlier HAL troop flight recognized the citrus-fruit color scheme applied by HAL and yelled, "There they are!"

People applauded and cheered.

After the L-1011 landed, the troop greeters pressed closer to the wire. Like soccer fans cramming nearer the match, the people standing a few rows from the wire shoved toward the troops. By evening's end, the people aligned on the wire found the stanchions and vinyl-coated wire crushed into their guts.

By now, the troops aboard the L-1011 had received a lecture from Customs before exiting the plane. The people awaiting them down the ramp wondered which service branch rode the homeward-bound airliner.

"Let's see," a veteran reasoned, "if they're going to Gulfport, it's gotta be Navy."

"Naw, you got it all wrong," a buddy chided him. "Keesler's over in Biloxi. They gotta be Air Force."

Shadowy figures appeared by the double-glass doors atop the ramp. "What is it?" an elderly Legionnaire asked as he squinted against the lights reflected in the glass.

"Air Force!" a friend hollered.

"They're here!" another Legionnaire shouted down the ramp. Taking their cue, the people packed along the wire went wild.

Men and women clad in jungle fatigues laughed and shook hands as they worked their way along the receiving line formed by the Legionnaires and the VFWers. "Welcome home!" and "welcome back!" the veterans of other wars cried. Especially resplendent in their powder blue uniforms, the honor guard from Legion Post 84 received particular attention from the Air Force veterans.

Joe King Sr., the oldest member of the honor guard, didn't realize that the pretty women whom he hugged and the tall men whose hands he shook were more than just Air Force types.

When 90-year-old Phyllis MacKinnon caught her first troop flight in early March 1991, she received a pleasant surprise: a kiss from an Air Force enlisted man named Owings. MacKinnon could remember watching Canadian troops bound for Europe pass through Maine during World War I.

They were also party types!

Belonging primarily to medical units scattered across the South, the Air Force personnel went absolutely nuts by the time they got to the wire. Hooting and hollering and clapping as frenziedly as their greeters, the troops unabashedly responded to the warmth and affection that flooded the terminal that night.

For the next hour or so, nurses, doctors, and technicians wearing everything but Air Force blue danced, sang, signed autographs, and celebrated their return to American soil.

As she squeezed through the jammed ramp, an Air Force nurse turned toward a camera-toting troop greeter, smiled, and ripped open her fatigue jacket to reveal a white T-shirt emblazoned "I Survived Desert Storm (in) Firford-England."

"England?" the startled volunteer asked. "Weren't you folks over in the Gulf?"

"Heck, no," the nurse replied. "Some of us were stationed at a reactivated Air Force hospital in England."

The civilian never got the chance to ask the nurse about her war stories. A friend called to her from farther along the ramp. The nurse whirled, laughed, and cried, "I'm coming!" Then she dematerialized into the crowd.

Outside the Red Baron Lounge, a Sgt. Wood led a jubilant melange of civilians and Air Force personnel. A 16-ounce Coke clasped in her left hand and three small American flags grasped in her right, Wood clambered onto an airport lounge chair and cheered her comrades. She whirled the flags faster and faster over her head and laughed as her friends clapped and roared their approval.

Overwhelmed by the human chaos surrounding her, MacKinnon sought refuge by the entrance to the duty-free shop. She shook hands with a few airmen and told one man about seeing the troop trains carrying Canadian soldiers through Vanceboro during World War I.

Beside MacKinnon stood a young, moustachioed airman who bore the name Owings, an Air Terminal Command patch, and a staff sergeant's stripes on his jungle fatigues. He chatted with MacKinnon for a few minutes, then slid his left arm around her shoulders, leaned down, and planted a kiss on her cheek.

Her jaw fell open.

The first boarding call sounded all too soon. Reluctant to leave such a warm reception, the Air Force visitors knelt to autograph T-shirts or pose for photo ops with Maine kids. Local youngsters already knew the social value of a Desert Storm T-shirt adorned with indelible-ink autographs. Tonight, many a school-ager went home wearing a shirt with signatures from the Deep South.

The Air Force personnel gradually passed along the ramp and into the international terminal. MacKinnon remained by the duty-free shop, where she hugged young men and women not much older than her great-grandchildren. She watched as volunteers handed them newspapers, a few teddy bears, and other goodies.

"I think this was better than watching the boys come home after World War I," MacKinnon commented, tears glistening in her eyes.

A YELLOW RIBBON

So many photos taken during the homecoming celebrations at Bangor International Airport captured the troops wearing tiny yellow ribbons pinned to their uniforms.

No, the Pentagon hadn't declared yellow ribbons to be service issue, but the troop greeters at BIA had.

The tradition probably began with Carl and Kathleen Lindh of Mariaville, a town located among the hills and lakes southeast of Bangor. The news that a troop flight would land in Bangor on March 8 inspired the Lindhs to travel the wintry roads from home. They remained at BIA that Thursday, then returned on Friday.

Carl and Kathleen Lindh of Mariaville, who greeted most troop flights at BIA.

On March 9, Kathleen pinned a yellow ribbon on a soldier returning from the Gulf. By then, she and Carl had committed themselves to a difficult task: They would continue greeting the troops until the last homeward-bound American military personnel passed through Bangor.

At first, the Lindhs scrambled to make ribbons between each troop flight. Other people soon volunteered to help them, and the tradition snowballed into yellow-ribbon derivatives. While other people pinned ribbons on all the returning troops, the Lindhs concentrated their efforts on Vietnam veterans who still wore the nation's uniform.

The Mariaville couple heat-sealed a red, white, and blue streamer to a ribbon's lower edge, then stamped the phrase "Welcome Home Vietnam Vets and Persian Gulf Troops" on the ribbon and the word Maine on the patriotic streamer.

During more than 200 flights, the Lindhs sought the Vietnam vets among the returning troops and pinned ribbons to their uniforms. At times, friends among the troop greeters worked the crowded terminal by holding aloft signs that read, "Vietnam vets, please see me."

Why did the Lindhs emphasize the Vietnam veterans? Carl explained that he'd spent 20 years in the Air Force, including a year in Vietnam.

He'd grown up in Manchester, N.H., a city linked to Bangor by United Airlines. He met Kathleen while stationed in England in 1953. She grew up in High Wycombe in Buckinghamshire.

Married in May 1954, the Lindhs later had three children: Susan, Janice, and Mark. In January 1965, Lindh landed in South Vietnam for a year's tour of duty with Advisory Team 95, assigned to Headquarters, III Corps, in Bien Hoa.

He retained no bad memories of the war, although "the attitude of the official military bothered me the most in Vietnam. I can't say that the military brass was living in a dreamworld, but I sensed early on that the people actually fighting the war were forgotten.

"The brass living it up back in Saigon quickly lost touch with the guys in the field. When we reduced the war to body counts and so many American KIA (killed-in-action) each week, the war was impersonalized.

"And I think the American public sensed that. Suddenly, we were no longer `their boys' fighting and dying, but some kind of nameless, faceless entities to be feared and reviled," he recalled.

"I could feel it even when waiting for him in '65," Kathleen Lindh remembered. Years spent in the United States had mellowed her soft English accent, which still fell pleasantly on a listener's ear.

"There was so little support for the boys over in Vietnam," she said. "I don't know why the people at home forgot about them. Looking back now, I still don't know why."

Lindh wrote a letter home almost every day until he left Vietnam in January 1966. He described his return from Southeast Asia "as very quiet, since no one seemed to know there was a war going on."

Kathleen and the children met him at Logan International Airport in Boston. Lindh had never met Mark, who was six and one-half months old. "Susan thought I had changed skin color, because I had such a dark tan," he recalled. "It took some time to reassure her that `yes, this is Daddy.'"

In May 1988, the Lindhs moved to Maine and bought a house at Goodwin Bridge on Route 181 in Mariaville. Most of the time, life passes quietly there beside the Union River. In fact, visitors will find little excitement in Mariaville, unless a fully loaded logging truck turns over, or someone hits a deer or moose. The town appears very quiet to outsiders, and the residents prefer it that way.

Then in March 1991, the media announced that a troop flight would land at BIA.

"We had to come," Kathleen said. She, her husband, and the other people who went to the airport that day anticipated a few flights, not the onslaught that brought more than 50 planeloads of troops into Bangor in March alone.

Until the troop flights slowed in mid-May, the Lindhs practically lived at the airport. During those hectic initial weeks when flights landed around the clock, they tried to drive home to sleep, but the effort exhausted them. A local businessman, Danny Lafayette, let them use a room at his White House Inn in Hampden free of charge, a gesture that the Lindhs will always appreciate.

"We go home when we can, and read the front page of the paper, and that's about all we do," Lindh said.

"We don't watch TV. We're either sleeping or making ribbons," a weary Kathleen smiled as the BIA public-address system announced the arrival of a United Airlines 747.

"Even our dog doesn't know us any more," Lindh chuckled.

Referring to the hesitance that some Vietnam veterans felt about turning out for the troop receptions, he said, "I've told other Vietnam vets that we're in the history books now...it's time to get on with the future. We as a nation can't afford to repeat the mistakes we made with the troops in Vietnam. It's time to welcome home a new generation of veterans. No matter how long it takes, I wouldn't miss it for the world."

"It's so rewarding to see the expressions on their faces as they come down the ramp. Oh, I can't really describe how it makes you feel," Kathleen said.

AN APPOINTMENT WITH DESTINY

Lillian Crowell of Bangor gambled with destiny before sunrise on Good Friday, March 29.

She gambled - and she won.

Shortly before sunrise that Friday, United Airlines Flight 6426 greased its tires at BIA and rolled some distance before turning onto a taxiway. The 747 carried soldiers assigned to the 4th Battalion, 41st Field Artillery Regiment, 197th Infantry Brigade, a component of the 24th Infantry Division (Mechanized).

Although preceded by paratroopers and Marines during the last six hours, the soldiers of the 24th entered BIA in grand style. A helmeted soldier wearing more stripes than many troop greeters could count led the procession that packed the ramp. Behind him marched a soldier carrying a regimental flag bearing crossed cannons and the number 41.

The multistriped soldier attempted to mask his delight as civilians greeted his men, but a grin twitched the corners of his mouth by the time he reached the bottom of the ramp. Within moments, any semblance of a military formation collapsed as the soldiers and civilians met along the wire.

The crowd numbered perhaps a few hundred people that cold March dawn. Just a short distance beyond the point where the wire hooked a right turn stood three women. One of them, Lillian Crowell, held a sign that spelled in red letters "Sgt. Chris Brown."

Known as "Tillie" to her friends, Crowell had lived most of her life in Eddington, a town northeast of Bangor. She had moved to Bangor when her husband died about 10 years earlier.

In fall 1990, Crowell read a particular Ann Landers column in the Bangor Daily News. The column mentioned that military personnel serving in the Persian Gulf sought mail from the United States. Landers then listed an APO address and asked people planning to address their mail to "any soldier" in the Gulf to indicate a preference for the branch of service.

Crowell decided to write. "I picked the Army because my late husband was in the Army during World War II," she explained her decision to write to a ground-pounder.

Crowell's letter and hundreds of thousands of others went to Saudi Arabia. Somewhere in the featureless Saudi desert, a Sgt. Christopher Brown assigned to B Battery, 4th Battalion, 41st Field Artillery Regiment, 197th Infantry Brigade, selected Crowell's envelope from a pile of mail.

He wrote her immediately.

Brown dated his first letter to Crowell Nov. 20, 1990. Writing in a clear, concise hand, he indicated that he was 28 and hailed from Charleston, S.C. His unit was "the first heavy unit to hit the ground," landing in Saudi Arabia on Sept. 1, 1990.

Even in November 1990, just two months before the air war began, Brown desired a peaceful solution to the Gulf crisis. He wrote that "hopefully by then a settlement has been reached and we all can come home to our love (sic) ones. Nobody wants to fight, but we are well prepared if we have to. The Lord guides us all…"

Crowell and Brown continued writing through the winter. His second letter to Maine was misplaced by an acquaintance of Crowell's.

In his third letter, dated Jan. 25, 1991, Brown wrote, "As you know by now, the war has started…At the moment, the Air Force is pounding them day and night. Hopefully, Saddam Hussain will realize he is in a no-win situation and (will) spare his soldiers and his people the terrible suffering they are experiencing at the moment."

Besides her letters, Crowell sent Brown some fresh baked cookies. The artillerymen of B Battery enjoyed the goodies. "We can never complain about not getting any homemade cooking out here, because the fudge and the cookies surely had the taste of home all over them," Brown wrote in his fourth letter, dated Feb. 6, 1991.

When the ground war started on Feb. 23, 1991, Crowell worried for Sgt. Brown. Would he survive uninjured? Had his battery gone into action? Her fears eased slightly with the ceasefire.

Then the troops started coming home through BIA. Crowell read the daily schedule in the newspaper on March 28. As usual, the boxed column printed the projected arrival times and destinations for the next day. That Thursday, the column indicated some airliners on their way to Fort Benning, Ga., where Sgt. Chris Brown was stationed.

"Maybe, just maybe, I'd get to meet him," Crowell recalled thinking at the time. "But, what were the odds? I figured I didn't have a chance."

Although the troop flights were scheduled to arrive very early on Friday, Crowell asked Doris Davis and a niece, Ree Wells of Wilton, if they would like to meet the troops.

The women arrived at BIA about 1:30 a.m. to find UAL Flight 6426 delayed until 6 a.m. "We were already up, so we decided to spend the night at the airport," Crowell said. She, Wells, and Davis helped to greet the troops aboard American Trans Air Flight 7548, which landed about 4 a.m.

Then the three women took a short break and went to Dunkin Donuts on Union Street for coffee. They returned to BIA "just as the sun was rising," Crowell said, and positioned themselves across from the pay TVs in the center of the domestic terminal.

As artillerymen wearing the divisional patch of the 24th flooded the terminal, Crowell stood nervously holding a white cardboard sign on which she'd printed with red paint the words "Sgt. Chris Brown."

Crowell held the sign up where the troops could see it. Suddenly, a soldier looked at the sign and announced, "Oh, Chris is coming right back there!"

"I thought, `Gee, I don't know what he looks like,'" Crowell recalled.

Then a soldier stopped by her and introduced himself. "I'm Sgt. Chris Brown," he said, a big smile on his face. He hugged Crowell, then stepped from the line of troops to chat with his fans for a few minutes.

"The time went by so fast," Crowell said, expressing her disappointment at having only 15 minutes or so to visit with Brown. "A boarding call came so soon," she said, "and we didn't have enough time."

Before he left, Brown asked for Crowell's sign. "We gave him big hugs and kisses" before he vanished into the thronged soldiers heading for their 747, Crowell said.

Minutes before the first boarding call, and less than 100 feet from where Brown chatted with the three women, the multistriped sergeant snapped to attention outside the Red Bar Lounge and bawled his men into a semblance of a formation.

Then the definitely senior sergeant riveted his steely gaze on a Spec. Mitchell, a soldier who stood at attention with the regimental flagbearer a few paces behind him. Did Mitchell know what was happening to him? If not, he soon learned.

As a few dozen surprised civilians watched, the multistriped sergeant read aloud a Pentagon order proclaiming that Spec. Mitchell had been promoted to Sgt. Mitchell. Still wearing his helmet, the multistriped sergeant and another soldier replaced the specialist's insignia on Mitchell's collar with a sergeant's three chevrons.

His eyes relaxing their vigilant stare, Mitchell snapped a salute as the assembled soldiers and civilians wildly cheered. "Welcome home, Sgt. Mitchell!" a man shouted.

The newly pinned sergeant grinned from ear to ear.

The soldiers soon reboarded their airliner and took off for Fort Benning. Crowell wondered if she'd ever hear from Chris Brown again.

She did.

Another letter arrived in the mail a few days later. Dated March 3, 1991, and mailed from Saudi Arabia, this letter was written from somewhere in Iraq after the ground war ended.

"As I sit here now because of the ceasefire, I was just reflecting over the past few days and months..." Brown wrote. After noting his pride in his country and in his troops and what they had accomplished, Brown wrote, "We rumbled across the desert at a furious pace for two days to reach our objectives and cutting off their (the Iraqis) escape route..."

He initially pitied the Iraqi POWs. Then his feelings toward them changed after thinking about what the Iraqis had done to Kuwait.

"But after we came down a highway and saw so many burning cars and trucks with bodies everywhere, the real horrors of war really set in on me. Mainly because I felt a sense of guilt because we were the ones that unloaded the barrage of artillery rounds at this particular convoy..." Brown wrote.

He wondered "how do you justify killing?" and tried to answer this thorny question in his letter. "I guess I am thankful that the bodies and destruction I have witness(ed) is not me or my crew."

"I think that letter contained his heart and soul," Crowell said as she neatly folded the piece of paper and placed it with the other letters.

"He tried to explain the war through his eyes. For that reason alone, I'll always treasure what he wrote," she said. "I'm just so glad that he came back all right, that nothing happened to him."

Brown and Crowell maintained their correspondence long after he came home through Bangor. "I'm very glad that he chose my letter to answer," Crowell later commented.

AN EARLY EASTER MORNING

About 1:30 a.m. on Sunday, March 31, the 3rd Battalion, 502nd Infantry Regiment, 101st Airborne Division, "occupied" Bangor International Airport. Their arrival marked the earliest troop flight into Bangor on Easter, the holiest day in the Christian calendar.

When the 1st Engineering Battalion, 1st Marine Division landed at BIA at 5 p.m. on Saturday, March 30, the bands from the Bucksport Junior High and High Schools turned out to greet the weary Marines with patriotic songs. The paratroopers from the 101st had intended to land about 8:40 p.m. that Saturday, but their jet didn't touch down until early Easter morning.

Undaunted by the late hour, some young musicians from Bucksport lingered past midnight to serenade the 300 to 400 soldiers who swept into Maine history that night.

Representing the Greater Bangor Chamber of Commerce, Les Stevens returned to BIA about midnight to set up the gift table. Assisted by other volunteers, Stevens piled cookies, brownies, fresh fruit, Red Cross gift packages, and other assorted merchandise on the table.

He'd done the same thing just seven hours earlier for the arriving Marines. As he rearranged the table to make room for yet another platter of fresh-baked cookies, Stevens wearily asked, "Why'd we ever bother to take it all down?"

About 1:40 a.m., someone standing among the Legionnaires on the ramp shouted, "Here they come!" The 200 people awaiting the "Screaming Eagles" of the 101st Airborne Division cheered, then redoubled their efforts as the lead soldiers walked into view.

While the jubilant paratroopers bounded down the ramp and melted into the arms of the waiting civilians, a sandy-haired sergeant wearing sand-scoured combat boots halted at the base of the ramp. Placing his hands on his web belt, he studied the absolutely crazy crowd and muttered, "Great! This is great! This is real great!"

The sergeant, who named Glens Falls, N.Y., as his hometown, said that he'd honeymooned at Old Orchard Beach, Maine's equivalent of the French Riviera for Canadians living in Quebec. "It was warmer weather then, but I don't care how cold it is outside tonight," the sergeant commented. "You folks are fantastic! I'm just so happy to see Maine again!"

The jubilant groundswell inside the domestic terminal crested as more paratroopers mobbed the gift table or reached into the crowd to kiss pretty girls or hug their mothers and grandmothers. Everyone's mood suddenly shifted.

The artificial wire that the troop greeters so scrupulously tried to maintain between themselves and the soldiers collapsed as men and women hauled the ecstatic paratroopers into their ranks. The soldiers still entering the terminal saw their comrades swamped by winter-clad civilians. The paratroopers caught the joy sweeping the terminal and responded in kind.

The battalion commander stepped to the lectern, leaned into the microphone, and thanked the crowd for welcoming his troops home. He struggled to make his voice heard over the din.

As the officer spoke, "George Bush" stepped into the domestic terminal and warmly shook his hand. Laughing soldiers drew themselves to attention and saluted their commander-in-chief. The president spoke a few encouraging words to the battalion commander, then turned to wave to the crowd.

The paratroopers and the civilians applauded the president's appearance so far north from his summer home in Kennebunkport. Only a few people mentioned the fact that

President Bush bore a striking resemblance to a United Airlines attendant wearing a presidential mask.

The young Bucksport musicians stopped playing around 2 a.m. and set down their instruments to mingle with the paratroopers. Moments later, three soldiers seized the opportunity that they had awaited.

One soldier grabbed an alto sax, and two others went for a tenor sax and the snare drums. The first soldier launched into an impromptu jazz fest, working the saxophone through music that he created in his mind as he played.

Taking their cues from their comrade, the other two paratroopers whirled into 15 minutes of jazz that set other soldiers to swaying and dancing on their tired feet. People crowded about the chairs where the uniformed musicians sat and clapped to the music.

Beyond the people clustered about the desert-fatigued musicians, a soldier and a Maine girl danced to the music. The jazz fest later broke up to sustained applause from appreciative soldiers and civilians.

Paratroopers eagerly chatted about life in the desert and about coming home. "Yeah, that's where I wanna be," a youthful Pfc. said to anyone listening. "I can't wait to get home. Yeah, home!"

Emotions ran high even as the PA system announced the boarding call. "Not now!" a soldier yelled. "We're having too good a time!"

By 2:30 a.m., paratroopers began filing up the ramp toward their plane. Chamber of Commerce volunteers implored the soldiers to "take anything you want" from the donated food and souvenirs piled high on the gift table.

One volunteer, a woman, reached into the paratroopers and yanked a young private out of line. "Here, take some cookies and whoopie pies," she told the soldier while handing him homecooked food. "It's all free, it's all for you. Please, take some home with you."

Paratroopers stuffed their multipocketed uniforms with souvenirs. Faced with a half dozen chocolate-chip cookies, a soldier asked for a plastic bag. He slid the cookies into the bag, spun it while holding the top, and gingerly worked the plastic-enclosed goodies into a deep pocket.

GUARDING HEAVEN'S STREETS

The last stanza of the Marine Corps Hymn brags that "if the Army and the Navy ever get to Heaven's scenes, they will find the streets are guarded by United States Marines."

When the Marines got to BIA about suppertime on Wednesday, April 10, they found the terminals already guarded by Army paratroopers.

Word got out during the day that two troop flights would land at BIA that evening. Thirty-three days into the flights, and the novelty remained: Before United Airlines Flight 6447 touched down at 4:53 p.m., between 500 and 600 people had gathered to meet the plane.

On that drizzly Wednesday afternoon, people started arriving at 3 p.m. to find a good place on the wire. Tom Dean bounced upstairs early with his trusty camcorder in tow. A PI (private investigator) by trade, Dean had vowed to videotape every troop flight and send a copy to each aircraft commander. This afternoon, he passed down the ramp and greeted the Legionnaires already gathered there, including Everett Steele of Brooksville. A member of Legion Post No. 85 in Blue Hill, Steele would ultimately catch most troop flights. He would meet his 200th on Sept. 15, when the official count reached 205 flights.

Troop greeters milled about the terminal, elbowed onto the wire, or sat in the vinyl chairs. These chairs differed in color depending on where you sat: a blighted pumpkin by the street, or a faded Chevy blue toward the runway. A row of black plastic TV seats divided the chairs by color.

At the gift table, volunteers heaped teddy bears between the plattered cookies, muffins, and other goodies still pouring in from Maine women. Until the past few days, troop greeters had given what teddy bears they could afford to the arriving troops.

Then Russ Berrie and Co. Inc. of Oakland, N.J., sent 1,400 cartons, or 25,000 teddy bears, to the Greater Bangor Chamber of Commerce. Give these bears to the troops, Russ Berrie instructed the recipients. Give them all to the troops.

So the American homecomings received an official teddy bear. The stuffed critters resembled the "Snuggle Bear" seen on TV ads for the dryer sheets by the same name. For tens of thousands of troops landing at BIA, the little cream-colored bear with its black eyes, plastic "Russ" ornament in its right ear, and its yellow neck ribbon became the most desired souvenir to take home from Maine.

Today, the donated teddy bears would go to soldiers and Marines alike. Even as UAL Flight 6447 began its final approach to BIA, Hawaiian Airlines Flight 7842 trailed just minutes behind. The UAL 747 had as its final destination Fort Campbell in Kentucky. The HAL jet would unload its passengers at Cherry Point Marine Corps Air Station in North Carolina.

As people gathered for the arriving flights, the young musicians from the Leonard Middle School "Braves Band" (Old Town) played several songs. Experienced troop greeters had noted how musical quality varied from band to band. For seventh- and eight-grade students, the Old Town kids weren't bad. In fact, they were rather good.

Members of the press were waiting, too, for the incoming soldiers and Marines. A camera crew from the McNeil-Lehrer Hour hoped to film extensive footage of tonight's events. The three major networks, CNN, and USA Today had already covered the troop flights.

By 4:45 p.m., people crowded the domestic terminal, and families waiting for relatives edged into the ramp. Sharon Selwood of Bangor, a musician with the 195th Army Band, Maine Army National Guard, had brought a pile of relatives to wait for her brother, Glenn Selwood of Portland. A corpsman in the Navy Reserve, Selwood had left for the Gulf on Dec. 3, 1990. He'd gone into Kuwait with the Marines and later treated some captured Iraqi prisoners-of-war.

Other sisters - Corinne Smith of Eastport and Sheila Ziegler from Newport, R.I. - also waited for Selwood. Two more relatives who lived in Eastport stood against the wall near the gift table, while Sheila held her 5-month-old son, Evan.

He'd never met his uncle.

At 4:50 p.m., a Sterling Airways jet landed to resonant cheering from the people packed along the wire. "Wrong plane! Wrong plane!" the knowledgeable people shouted.

When a UAL 747 gracefully descended from the sky three minutes later, the troop greeters got it right. The terminal walls vibrated to the cacophonous din that lifted from several hundred throats.

Minutes later, the paratroopers belonging to the 8th Battalion, 101st Aviation Regiment, 101st Airborne Division, encountered a wild and joyous welcome on the ramp. Clad in their web gear - and in many instances, still wearing their helmets - the soldiers politely shook hands along the official receiving line.

The paratroopers held their formation until they reached the bottom of the ramp. Then all military discipline collapsed as the civilians mobbed the soldiers, who eagerly reached into the crowd to shake hands, exchange hugs, and gather young children into their arms.

CWO4 Mike Mannion, a member of the 8th Battalion, said that he'd served in Vietnam and had not received such a homecoming. "I've never seen anything like this in my life!" he hollered over the din. "I think the people here are great! Tell 'em I said so!"

Paratroopers kept pouring into the terminal for several minutes. Then a lull developed, only to be broken by the paratroopers who had slipped away to use the phones in the international terminal. These soldiers dribbled down the ramp alone or by two's and three's. They, too, were surrounded by cheering civilians.

"Hey, the Marines are landing!" someone yelled from his vantage point at the terminal windows. The colorful HAL L-1011 touched down and rolled along the runway as some people cheered.

Minutes later, as if enough chaos did not already fill the terminal, the Marines belonging to the 1st Battalion, 6th Marine Regiment, 2nd Marine Division, flooded the ramp. The troop greeters, already wound up from the greeting they'd given the paratroopers, went wild as the Marines and Navy corpsmen crowded into the terminal.

A young Marine limped down the ramp on crutches. "A war wound?" an onlooker asked.

When she landed in Bangor on April 10, 1991, Army Specialist Christina Rhodes of Missouri plucked 11-month-old Rebecca Smith of Hampden from the welcoming crowd and held her a while. Rhodes later said that Smith reminded her of her own daughter.

"No, football," the Marine grinned.

Glenn Selwood didn't arrive on HAL Flight 7842.

The film crew from the McNeil-Lehrer Hour calmly and professionally went about their business. As Marines and soldiers signed T-shirts, notebooks, and "Welcome Home" signs at his elbows, the bearded McNeil-Lehrer reporter interviewed Spec. Christina Rhodes of Desloge, Mo.

While passing through the terminal, Rhodes had met 11-month-old Rebecca Smith of Hampden. Bedecked in a plaid dress with white ruffles at her throat and shoulders, Rebecca happily sucked a pacifier. Three teen-age girls sat atop the vinyl seats behind them.

As the camera whirred, the pacifier slipped from Rebecca's mouth, and she grinned at the TV reporter.

Swamped by all the attention, Rhodes took a moment to talk about her own 2-year-old daughter, Rhendi, whom she had not seen in seven months. "I miss her so much, I can't tell you how much, and I bet she's changed so much," Rhodes quietly said. "I'll see her in a few days, though, and everything will be all right."

Although known for their legendary animosity, particularly when intermingled in bars, the soldiers and Marines got along well that evening in Bangor. With paratroopers and leathernecks jostling one another around him, Navy Corpsman William Dukes of Griffin, Ga., talked about his war.

A sailor since 1988, he'd been assigned to Bravo Co. of the 1st Battalion during that unit's six-month deployment to Okinawa. Bravo Co. had gone from the Far East to Saudi Arabia and had opened a main breach in the Iraqi defenses for the 2nd Marine Division.

"Yeah, the war definitely disrupted my marriage plans," Dukes said. He and his fiancee, Annette Velez, had anticipated a March 1991 wedding in Puerto Rico. Then he'd gone to the Gulf, and Annette had worried about him, especially when the Marines attacked Kuwait on Feb. 23.

As soon as he could, Dukes called Annette from Kuwait to tell her that he was "a-okay. It was great hearing her voice. I couldn't wait to get back home. You can keep Kuwait and Iraq and Saudi Arabia. I hate that place. All I want to do is get home and get married."

Boarding calls soon summoned the paratroopers to their airliner. The soldiers cleared the teddy bears from the gift table, so the volunteers unpacked more bears and heaped them high for the Marines.

As he ascended the ramp, a Col. Gerald from the HHC DISCOM of the 101st Airborne Division heard someone yell, "Where's your home, Colonel?"

"I am home!" he responded. "I'm a Maine boy. I'm from Belgrade!" Nearby Legionnaires slapped his shoulders and eagerly shook his hand.

True to their hymn, the Marines remained to guard the BIA terminals as the paratroopers reboarded their aircraft. Bangor may never qualify as Heaven's scenes by Marine standards, but for a brief hour on April 10, both soldiers and Marines guarded the city's airport.

THE CONVOY FROM HELL

Despite the chill, the soldiers preferred the flight to freedom to the convoy from hell when they landed in Bangor on Friday, April 12.

Hawaiian Airlines Flight 7846, which touched down at 5:53 a.m., discharged more than its share of officers, but the lieutenants, majors, captains, and occasional lieutenant colonels striding down the ramp soon explained why: Most of them belonged to the 5th Mobile Army Surgical Hospital out of Fort Bragg, N.C.

That sunny, but cold Friday morning brought a special passenger into Bangor. Among the 75 people awaiting the L-1011's arrival were a well-dressed middle-aged couple, Fred and Elaine Rice of Brewer.

They had anticipated this day since Oct. 1, 1990, when their 29-year-old son, Fred Rice II, shipped out with the 5th MASH. A registered nurse actually stationed at the Trippler Army Medical Center in Honolulu, Hawaii, Rice had been assigned to the 5th MASH through the so-called "professional filler system."

He had stayed in touch with his parents since leaving for Saudi Arabia, but occasional letters and phone calls did little to dispel parental anxiety. The Rices followed the progress of the war, especially after the ground troops crossed the Iraqi border on Feb. 23 - their son's 30th birthday.

A phone call came after President Bush declared the ceasefire; Fred had toured southern Iraq the hard way, but he'd survived, and he'd be home as soon as possible.

About 11 p.m. Thursday, April 11, the phone rang again in the Rice home. "Hello from Shannon, Ireland," Fred happily said to his mom and dad before giving them his flight number and anticipated arrival time at Bangor International Airport.

Scheduled to land his aircraft at 6:35 a.m. on April 12, the HAL flight captain made good time across the Atlantic and landed the jet about 40 minutes early. Fred and Elaine stood watching from the terminal as the homeward-bound airliner rolled down the BIA runway.

Minutes later, as the L-1011 taxied past the windows, people applauded, cheered, and waved their hands. Despite FAA admonitions to the contrary, two soldiers popped open the planes's upper hatch and lifted a large American flag high so the colors could stream in the cold northwest wind.

Fred Rice II had returned to Maine in grand style, hardly letting the cold bother him as he and Spec. Kirk Jones, assigned to the Fort Bragg-based 46th Support Group, proudly held the American flag aloft.

"Wave, honey," a woman said to her young blond-haired daughter as the L-1011 made the 90-degree turn toward the terminal.

Separated from the windows by the corridor left open for passengers embarking on a United Airlines flight, the little girl lifted a hand and waved at the L-1011.

"See, they can see you waving to them," her mother told her. Rice and Spec. Jones struggled to hold onto the billowing oriflamme while waving at the domestic terminal.

A graduate of Winthrop High School in central Maine, Rice earned his lieutenant's bars the hard way. After serving as an enlisted soldier, he had attended the University of Maine and graduated with a bachelor's degree in 1987.

According to the official records, the L-1011 disembarked about 220 soldiers and airmen at 6:15 a.m. Though the PA system warned the airport shops and employees that the jet had arrived, the welcoming crowd apparently wondered how they should respond to the troops.

Perhaps most people in the crowd were greeting the troops for the first time. The "regulars" - those people who returned time and again for different landings - knew the routine: As soon as the first troop appears at the top of the ramp, everyone applauds and cheers.

Unfortunately, there weren't many regulars in the crowd that Friday morning.

When the first soldier from Hawaiian Airlines Flight 7846 walked onto the ramp, only the dozen or so Legionnaires and four Chamber of Commerce greeters standing there actually clapped and cheered. Surprised by the relatively quiet greeting, a Chamber volunteer turned and shouted into the terminal, "Start cheering! Let's hear it!"

Silence reigned within the domestic terminal.

Not until the soldiers reached the lower ramp did a man standing along the wire suddenly blurt, "Are they inside yet?"

"Yes! Can't you see them?" responded the irritated greeter from the Chamber. "Start cheering!"

The crowd finally broke into as much applause, cheers, and noise as 75 people can make.

The soldiers apparently never noticed the initial subdued greeting. A major or two, a full bird colonel, and three or four captains shook hands with the people from the Chamber, and a moment later, a nurse passed by with tears streaming down her cheeks.

A lesson learned that morning: Noise alone did not guarantee a warm homecoming, but it sure helped.

More and more military personnel strode down the ramp. Most of them took the time to shake every hand in sight, smiled from ear to ear, and invariably said, "Thank you," "Thank you so much," or "I'm so glad to be here."

The Rices carefully scanned the uniformed horde for a glimpse of their son. Yes! He's home! Right there among 300 wildly celebrating people, the Rices held their own homecoming, the parents hugging and touching the son who towered over his mom and dad, and the son graciously accepting the adulation that was rightfully his.

Other soldiers entered the terminal. Having deployed to the Gulf with the 46th Support Group in September 1991, Staff Sgt. Edwin Jusino-Vega was pleased to walk on American soil again. He spoke briefly about his version of the war before moving off to find a quiet place to gather his thoughts.

Army Capt. Rod Christoffer spoke about his hometown of Clarksville, Tenn. He and Rice served together in the 5th MASH and also worked together at Trippler. Happily chug-a-lugging the first cold beer he'd tasted in months, Christoffer bounced on the balls of his feet. "I haven't been asleep for at least 30 hours, and I'm still pumped up!" he exclaimed.

Grinning widely, Spec. Jones listed Macon, Ga., as his hometown. He had shipped out eight months earlier to a place called Dragon City, then had gone to Dhahran. Some weeks before the ground invasion, Jones saw the Iraq border for the first time.

The 46th Support Group had traveled at least a hundred miles into Iraq before finally stopping at the Euphrates River. After spending about a month in Iraq, elements of the 46th Support Group started leaving for the States. Jones patiently waited for his orders, which finally granted him a seat aboard HAL Flight 7846.

As the jet approached BIA, Col. Eugene Wilson (commander of the 46th Support Group) tapped Jones to help Fred Rice II fly the flag from the cockpit hatch. "He's the greatest CO there ever was," Jones said about Wilson. "He took us all the way to the Euphrates and back again without losing a man. He's fantastic!"

The cockpit crew held off popping the hatch until the L-1011 had taxied to a point opposite the international terminal. Then Rice and Jones clambered through the open hatch, thrust the flag and its pole into the frigid air, and stuck their heads and torsos out where they could see.

Definitely a Southern boy, Jones imitated a shiver as he remembered that initial bracing contact with cold Maine air. "We were all right until we turned off the taxiway," he said.

"That crosswind was a shock!" Jones commented, chuckling at the memory. "I thought, `This ain't Saudi Arabia any more!'"

Yet Jones didn't mind the cold wind a bit. Landing at BIA placed him less than 1,500 miles from Macon and his fiancee, Monica Jones. "I miss her, I miss her an an awful lot," he said.

No wives or girlfriends would meet Fred Rice II or Capt. Christoffer. Both men proclaimed themselves bachelors, but Rice hinted that his marital status could be negotiated sometime in the future. For a few minutes, though, Rice forgot about his civilian relationships and talked about the war.

Assigned to Dhahran until December 1990, Rice and the 5th MASH then traveled westward to King Khalid Military City, the so-called "Emerald City" near Hafr al-Batin. This movement occurred weeks before the epic flanking maneuver by coalition forces that took them even farther west beyond the Iraqi defense line.

Rice recounted that between Sept. 17, 1990 and Dec. 10, 1990, the time he spent in Dhahran, the 5th MASH treated 11,000 patients. When this figure raised a few eyebrows, he explained that "just like in civilian life, people still get sick and need medical care."

The military patients, most of them American, suffered ailments ranging from the common cold to emergency appendectomies. "I think the desert had something to do with a lot of colds," Rice said.

He did not find Saudi Arabia to be an exotic country, with its blowing sand, hot days, and cold nights. "I don't think I'll ever go back," he confided.

From Dhahran, the 5th MASH rode westward in the long truck convoys that Rice said raised so much dust. The soldiers stayed at KKMC (in typical fashion, the Army reduced the Saudi city to an acronym) for almost two months, then moved up to the sand berms that separated Saudi Arabia from Iraq.

When the 5th MASH finally kicked off its part in the ground war, the unit split in two. Rice went with the FSE (Forward Surgical Element) for an interesting 100-mile truck ride into Iraq, to a point where the medical personnel set up a tent hospital.

Soldiers rode packed into the cargo compartments of 5-ton trucks. During the week preceding their cross-border excursion, the medical personnel had watched the B-52s fly north into Iraq and listened to the distant thuds as the bombers and Army artillery pounded Iraqi positions.

Now they saw the devastation close at hand. Rice described traveling past destroyed Iraqi armor and defensive positions. Iraqis were missing their legs, arms, or heads.

One hundred miles deep in Iraq, the FSE stopped advancing, unloaded its trucks, and set up a small field hospital. Rice chuckled as he recalled riding in "the Convoy From Hell" for 26 hours across the desert.

"Bouncin' and jouncin' all the way across lower Iraq - that's my memory of the Convoy from Hell!" he laughed. "It wasn't funny at the time, barreling through dust storms and rainstorms and dust, dust, and more dust."

The desert environment definitely affected living conditions in Iraq. The Army medical personnel lived in tents, ate in tents, and worked in tents. No solid walls kept out the wind or the sand - or the winter storms that plagued southern Iraq.

A memorable "hurricane-force storm that we called 'Stormin' Norman'" swept through the camp one day and blew away the tents covering the laboratory and x-ray department, Rice said. Even as enlisted personnel and officers alike scrambled to drive extra tent pegs into the ground, surgery continued in the operating room.

By the time that they rejoined the 5th MASH another 100 miles farther into Iraq, the soldiers assigned to the FSE longed for hot showers. Rice improvised one day by heating water one liter at a time in a microwave and then dumping it into an Australian shower.

"It wasn't a nice, white porcelain tub, but it was great," he said. "It was the first shower I'd had in three days."

During their advance into Iraq, the 5th MASH treated only a few American casualties and examined 45 Iraqi EPWs (enemy prisoners-of-war). The medical personnel performed surgery on 11 EPWs.

"All the Iraqis kept saying was 'thank you, thank you' when they found out that we were a hospital," Rice said.

By 7 a.m., the PA system summoned the soldiers for a second time to the L-1011. As usual, the volunteers from the Chamber of Commerce implored the troopers to help themselves to the gifts and food piled high on the gift table. Other volunteers passed out newspapers.

In the domestic terminal, Rice and Capt. Christoffer applauded the welcoming crowd. After hugging his parents a last time and kissing his father's cheek, Rice raised his right hand above his head and cheered. Onlookers enthusiastically responded.

HAL Flight 7846 lifted off from BIA shortly after 7 a.m.

The next two inbound flights coming into Bangor that day were also headed for North Carolina. Both planes carried Marines en route to Cherry Point Marine Corps Air Station.

United Airlines Flight 6449 put down to a wild greeting at 10:07 a.m. Many people who'd met Fred Rice II and HAL Flight 7846 lingered at the airport to catch the mid-morning flight, then left for the day. They figured they'd return that night to catch UAL Flight 6450.

No one envisioned meeting some troops flying the other way.

By 8:30 p.m. that Friday, probably 600 or 700 people had crowded into the domestic terminal to meet UAL Flight 6450, which was carrying elements of the 1st Battalion, 8th Marine Regiment, and the 3rd Battalion, 6th Marine Regiment. The evening called for a typical airport greeting, with two glitches: Someone forgot the music, and until 15 minutes before touchdown, no one knew about the Navy people going the other way.

Airport employees granted the official welcoming committee a few minutes' advanced warning, but the crowd remained blissfully ignorant about the additional military personnel they would meet.

The homecoming for the 400 Marines aboard the UAL 747 went off as planned. The civilians cheered and hugged the leathernecks.

Then several green fatigued-sailors filled the upper ramp.

A Hawaiian Airlines jet had landed to refuel at BIA. Aboard were the Navy Reservists belonging to Cargo Handling Battalion 9 from Columbus, Ohio.

A Chamber volunteer enthusiastically greeted the sailors, repeatedly telling them "welcome home" until the Chamber employee supervising the gift table gently informed her companion that "they're going over, not coming back."

The several hundred people mixing it up with the leathernecks in the domestic terminal didn't care which way the sailors flew. People joyfully reached out to the Navy Reservists as they had to the absolutely wild Marines.

Surprisingly, some sailors felt embarrassed at receiving such a welcome and retreated into the ramp. Legionnaires and VFWers chased them out again into the waiting arms of the crowd, "where you guys belong" as one World War II veteran succinctly told a sailor young enough to be his grandson.

Later, two women sailors stopped by the gift table. Storekeeper Third Class (SK3 in Navy parlance) Cherie Walker said that she had been called to active duty on April 5, almost six weeks after the Gulf War ended. A full-time student at Ohio State University, she'd left behind her studies, her husband of 12 years, and two sons.

Despite leaving her family in Ohio, Walker didn't mind the call to active duty. "I'm real excited," she said, "and I'm real proud to get the chance to be a part of this. We'd wondered if we'd ever get overseas."

"We are definitely going overseas," said SK2 Brenda Thomas, who also lived in Columbus. The first destination for CHB 9 was Rota, Spain, but "from there we'll be assigned all over," she explained. "They haven't told us where, yet."

Thomas, who was married in September 1990, left behind her husband and two children, a son aged 6 and a daughter aged 9. As with Walker, she would miss her children's birthdays, since the Navy Reservists had orders keeping them on active duty for a year.

The Navy Reservists reboarded their HAL L-1011 long before the Marines received a boarding call. As green fatigues packed the ramp, Electrician's Mate Steven Kerst, another Columbus resident, stopped by the gift table.

In civilian life a circuit-board test technician for ABB Process Automation, Kerst welcomed the challenge presented by active duty. A guaranteed job awaiting his return to Ohio eased the transition into uniform; Kerst also made other changes in his life.

"I ended the lease on my apartment, packed up all my furniture" and safety stored it, and "basically broke all the connections with the way I'd been living before," Kerst said.

He mentioned a friend who had been discharged from the Navy and had returned home to Maine. Kerst couldn't recall the name of his buddy's hometown, "a bigger city near a lake that's popular as a resort."

No matter. "It's great being in Maine, anyway," Kerst said.

LEATHERNECK ARTILLERY FIRE

Either side of midnight on April 13, distant blasts from Marine artillery echoed faintly through Bangor International Airport. United Airlines Flight 6452 staged through BIA at 11:35 p.m. on Saturday, April 13, less than an hour before an American Trans Air L-1011, Flight 8063, landed on Sunday, April 14. The UAL 747 ferried the 1st Battalion, 12th Marine Regiment, 1st Marine Division, on the long journey to Hickam Air Force Base in Hawaii. The AMT L-1011 was taking the 2nd Battalion, 10th Marine Regiment, 2nd Marine Division, home to Cherry Point Marine Corps Air Station in North Carolina.

Between 400 and 500 people had gathered in the domestic terminal before the UAL 747, its beacon lights glowing red and white, dropped from the night sky and rolled down the runway. As with previous estimates of crowd sizes, the April 13 figure could be disputed. A police officer estimated 800 people; others figured lower.

Right on cue, the young man operating the sound system started playing Lee Greenwood's "God Bless the U.S.A." as soon as the 747 flashed down the runway. Some people sang along or waved an American flag in time to the music; other people waited expectantly for the military personnel to appear.

With more than 110 troop flights under their belts, experienced greeters had learned to predict the service branch of an airliner's passengers by the plane's final destination. Pope Air Force Base in North Carolina usually meant the 82nd Airborne; with March Air Force Base in California, you took your chances.

The same guessing game existed with UAL Flight 6452. Hickam Air Force Base might be anybody.

The crowd didn't care, of course. Anyone wearing an American uniform deserved a homecoming, no matter the destination or branch of service.

Just before midnight, the people positioned where they could see up the ramp broke into wild, sustained applause and cheers. Minutes later, the American flag made the left turn into the terminal as a gray-haired woman from the American Legion led about 400 Marines to meet their adoring fans.

A woman reporter-cum-photographer from "People Magazine" stood on a borrowed chair to snap photos as the Marines poured into the terminal. Intent on pursuing her assignment, an article and photographs on the homecoming crowd, she missed a tearful reunion that occurred just a few feet behind her.

A young Marine standing about 5 feet, 11 inches tall and sporting a regulation hair-cut emerged from the avalanche of incoming Marines. He looked anxiously into the crowd. Suddenly, a middle-aged man burst through the wire and wrapped himself about the Marine's neck.

Other people, an older woman and a younger man, followed the middle-aged man. Within touching distance of a reporter from a national magazine, a Marine hugged his family for the first time since September 1990, but the story passed unnoticed in the national media.

More Marines rounded the corner into the terminal. Most followed the stanchioned corridor leading to the phones. Some quick-thinking civilians motioned other Marines toward the Red Baron Lounge.

One glimpse of the lounge was all those Marines needed.

As Marines broke simultaneously for the lounge and the cafeteria, Cpl. Thomas Clemons of Americus, Ga., stopped a moment to talk about the Gulf War.

He'd shipped with the 1st Battalion last September, fought with it all the way to Kuwait City, then gladly packed his gear when the order sending the First of the 12th home came a week ago.

Clemons said that he felt "exceptionally happy" about returning to the States. "What else can you think about when you've been gone so long?" he asked.

Before the official welcoming ceremonies (not always a standard practice) began, many Marines reappeared in the terminal with beer bottles in their hands. Coors, Miller, whatever: the brand did not matter as much as did the taste - and the temperature.

A brunette wearing a red sweater shouted across the wire to a Marine chuga-lugging on a beer, "How's it taste, soldier?"

The civilians and Marines gathered about the two people fell silent as the Marine's eyes widened. Lowering the beer bottle from his lips, he pointedly responded, "Soldier?"

"Marine!" someone yelled.

"Yeah! Yeah!" other Marines roared before breaking into the distinctive guttural cheer that earned American infantry the nickname "grunts."

Along the wall near the duty-free shop, two other Marines played out different roles. The airport employee manning the microphone repeatedly called for the parents of a young Marine to meet their son by the lectern.

A graduate of Mount Blue High School in Farmington, Maine, the Marine said he'd called his family from Jubail, Saudi Arabia, to let them know he was flying home through Bangor. The flight had delayed en route, however, but he'd hoped to meet his loved ones at BIA.

The Marine would have called his family from a refueling stop in Belgium, but the troops were not permitted off the plane. This practice applied to refueling stops else-where, including Rome, Athens and Cairo, but not to Shannon, Ireland.

The Farmington Marine anxiously scanned the crowd while sipping his beer. Would his family make the airport in time to catch his flight? He really hoped so, yet doubt crept into his conversation.

Meanwhile, an airport employee leaned over the microphone mounted on the lectern and announced that another Marine, a tall, spectacled boy who grinned from ear to ear, "claims that today's his birthday! Let's all sing him `Happy Birthday'!"

Civilians and Marines alike broke into a discordant refrain of "Happy Birthday to You." The young Marine's face glowed from embarrassment and joy.

Then the airport employee introduced Capt. Bruce Kowalski, the commander of Fox Battery, 1st Battalion, 12th Marine Regiment, 1st Marine Division. The speaker announced to the crowd that Fox Battery "was the first American artillery unit to engage the Iraqis."

After speaking briefly to the cheering crowd, Kowalski detailed his battery's adventures in Saudi Arabia.

As the air war started, Fox Battery positioned itself just south of Khafji, the captain said. Charlie Battery, also aboard UAL Flight 6452, dug in nearby "so that we could provide each other with supporting fire."

On the night of Jan. 21-22, "we rolled forward of the Saudi Arabian forces so the only ones in front of us were Iraqis," Kowalski recalled. Fox Battery aimed its 155-mm. cannons at a preplanned target and sat quietly until early morning, then opened fire so "we could get in, fire them up, and get out before they could fire back."

"Our basic philosophy was to 'shoot and scoot,'" Kowalski said.

Since some Iraqi artillery could outrange the Marine guns, Fox Battery delayed its raids "until 3 or 4 in the morning, when the enemy was the sleepiest," he said.

While conducting border raids against Iraqi positions, the captain received an escort comprising vehicle-borne TOW missiles and a heavy weapons detachment. "We could fight a retrograde, and Charlie Battery could shoot to cover us while we disengaged," he said.

Fox Battery's Iraqi depredations didn't pass unnoticed in Baghdad, Kowalski said. He heard from other Marines "who lived closer to a radio" that "Baghdad Betty had promised that Saddam Hussein would come out and remove us.

"Well, he didn't," the captain smiled.

Fox Battery went all the way to Kuwait City, he said, his voice softening so he could hardly be heard over the joyful din surrounding him.

"We were blessed on this," Capt. Kowalski said. "We didn't have a man injured. I can't tell you how much that means to me, to bring every one of my Marines home safe and sound."

The January border raid marked the captain's third time in combat. As a lieutenant stationed in the mountains east of Beirut, Lebanon, in February 1984, he spotted targets for naval guns. His activities earned him a writeup by a national wire service.

During the invasion of Grenada, Kowalski served as a forward air controller and naval gunfire spotter attached to Alpha Co., 3rd Battalion, 325th Regiment, 82nd Airborne Division. He remained with the paratroopers during the first 11 days of the invasion.

Sometime after returning to his base at Kaneohe Bay Marine Corps Air Station in Hawaii, Kowalski would be promoted to major and would be reassigned as the fire support coordinator for the 3rd Marine Infantry Regiment.

The captain looked forward to a reunion with his wife, Ann-Marie, and their 2-year-old twin sons. As he stepped away from the lectern, Kowalski again watched the friendly interaction between civilians and combat-hardened Marines and said, "I hadn't expected this. Thanks for everything you've done."

By the time that the last Marines from the 1st of the 12th began to file into the ramp, the first Marines from the 2nd of the 10th entered the domestic terminal. The two groups intermingled, much to the chagrin of the officers and senior sergeants of the 1st Battalion who were charged with getting their men aboard the United Airlines jet.

At 12:50 a.m. on Sunday, April 14, the crowd didn't care. No matter which direction a Marine moved, no matter if he'd fought with the 1st Division or the 2nd, he received a warm greeting.

LARRY ROSE?

When Patricia Berg dialed a phone number in Fresno, Calif., in 1986, she never envisioned the family reunion that would happen at Bangor International Airport on April 15, 1991.

By now, exhaustion stalked many troop greeters who attempted to catch as many flights as possible at BIA. Returning troop-laden airliners seemingly landed around the clock, as the times for the last four flights indicated: 11:35 p.m. on April 13 and 12:24 a.m., 9:53 a.m., and 10:40 a.m. on April 14.

Fortunately for the people determined to meet the troops, these four flights had landed in pairs just a few minutes apart. That exasperating American advertising slogan, "buy one and get the second one free," could read "see two for the time of one" at BIA.

Dual landings occasionally meant that the tired troop greeters could grab some shut-eye before the next solitary flight. This happened with the four flights between Saturday night and Sunday morning.

It did not happen with the two flights that landed less than an hour apart at noon-time Monday. United Airlines Flight 6455 and Hawaiian Airlines Flight 7852 approached Bangor that fairly warm day. Both aircraft were going to Cherry Point Marine Corps Air Station.

While en route to Fort Hood, Texas, UAL Flight 6454 touched down at 2:05 p.m., more than two hours after UAL Flight 6455 reached BIA. No one ever asked why Flight 6455 beat Flight 6454 into Bangor. Did the general's presence on Flight 6455 spell the difference?

Probably. Generals can do things like that.

As people gathered in the domestic terminal about 11 a.m. that Monday, BIA employee Gary Leighton said that "we're expecting this to be a big week, with the children out of school." For those children whose families didn't flock to Disneyworld this April vacation, the troop flights offered a diversion from boredom, Leighton explained.

He'd regret those words by week's end.

The problem began on March 8, when schoolkids first sought and received autographs from the returning troops. What the youngest troop greeters received as a gift from a homesick father or mother in military uniform, older siblings wanted for themselves. By late March, collecting as much military paraphernalia as possible from the troops became de rigeur with Bangor-area teens, especially those in the middle-school grades.

Where a teen-ager had once patiently waited an offer of a patch or insignia, the youth now asked or demanded a memento. Adult troop greeters noticed the brazen requests and quietly expressed their shock to each other, then complained quietly to BIA management, then complained louder to whomever listened.

The souvenir-grabbing problem peaked between April 15 and April 22, when the underworked and bored teen-agers returned to school.

But on this Monday, Gary Leighton only suspected the headaches that lay ahead. We've had no complaints so far from the troops, he said.

In fact, one soldier had said, "It was a joyful experience to share with them (the children). I didn't mind giving away my insignia."

Many children circulated among the people who'd gathered to meet the two troop flights this noontime. By mid-week, too many children spent too much time at BIA, where the employees learned that certain parents dropped their children off at the airport in the morning and picked them up after work.

The BIA staff later addressed this problem, too.

As he waited for UAL Flight 6455 to land, Leighton stood by the lectern and asked for a show of hands "from those who are attending their first troop flight." A rough estimate pegged 25 percent of the 400 people as newcomers to the American homecomings.

"Well," Leighton said into the microphone, "let me welcome you to BIA. There are a few ground rules for you to follow."

Some people listened attentively as Leighton outlined the five or six BIA commandments. Then he announced the arrival of UAL Flight 6455 (the glistening 747 touched the runway at 11:54 a.m., even as Leighton spoke) and its destination: Cherry Point Marine Corps Air Station in North Carolina.

All right! the crowd enthusiastically responded. Marines!

Clad in a white pullover blouse, a dark-haired woman in her 30s stood near the newspaper-vending machine beside the duty-free shop. Joy and a tinge of doubt etched on her face, Patricia Berg held up a white sign that spelled in black letters, "Larry Rose?"

Berg's nephew, Sgt. Larry Rose, had shipped for the Persian Gulf with the 5th Battalion, 10th Marine Artillery Regiment, 2nd Marine Division. Rose, a Marine Corps Reservist, lived with his wife, Suzanne, in Knoxville, Tenn.

Before the Gulf War started, Pat Berg of Brewer discovered that she had relatives whom she never knew existed. Taking a chance that she would encounter Larry Rose, a long lost nephew, she greeted returning Marines on April 15, 1991.

Rose's departure for the Gulf made the subsequent war extremely personal for Pat Berg. When Marines started returning home through BIA, she checked the daily flight schedule printed in the newspaper and tried to welcome those aircraft traveling to North Carolina, her nephew's destination.

When Berg read the April 15 paper, she noted the two flights going to Cherry Point. Then Suzanne Rose called and told her aunt-in-law that Larry had departed the Gulf less than a day earlier.

"Based on his tentative departure from Saudi Arabia, I figured he would pass through Bangor that day," Berg said. "That is, if his plane didn't go directly to North Carolina. I had no idea which airline he would be on. I just assumed he would be on one of those flights."

Today marked the 12th birthday for Berg's twin sons, Zachary and Shawn. They'd invited their friends to the birthday party, so she'd bundled all of them into the car and brought them to the airport.

Before the Marines from UAL Flight 6455 entered the domestic terminal, Leighton quietly told the press (one newspaper reporter, plus video specialists Tom Dean and Bob Jones) that a high-ranking general traveled aboard the 747. He wasn't sure just who.

Then the Marines from UAL Flight 6455 flooded the ramp, leaving Leighton no time to speculate on the general's identity. The people in the domestic terminal roared their approval as the tired leathernecks reached the gift table and finally realized that the reception was for them.

Wearing an insignia-laden desert-camouflage hat, Sheila Dean sat in her wheelchair beside the gift table and warmly shook hands with the Marines. Across from Dean, a nervous Pat Berg shifted her "Larry Rose?" sign to her left hand and extended her right hand to the incoming leathernecks.

More Marines poured into the terminal. Three stripes, a silver bar, double silver bars, a confusing single stripe with a hash mark that indicated a lance corporal: All sorts of insignia passed by.

So did two silver stars.

Whoa! Two silver stars! A major general!

Maj. Gen. Bill Keys, the commanding officer of the 2nd Marine Division, strode past the gift table and into the terminal.

Comfortably wearing a ring-toughened prizefighter's muscular physique and pug nose, Bill Keys grinned as he shook hands with the women Red Cross volunteers at the gift table. Then, after Gary Leighton introduced him to the adoring crowd, he stepped to

the microphone and thanked the Maine residents for supporting his Marines.

Keys said that the 2nd Marine Division had heard about the troop greetings in the Gulf, but knowing the often hostile receptions given to troops returning from Vietnam, "I wondered what sort of reception we'd receive."

People listened attentively as the general mentioned how much importance the Marines had placed on

Marine Maj. Gen. Bill Keys, commander of the 2nd Marine Division, spoke to troop greeters at BIA on April 15, 1991.

support from home. When he thanked the crowd for their warm welcome, Marines and civilians alike started cheering and applauding.

Keys then signed autographs for a few minutes. Sheila Dean edged into the people clustered about the general and handed her autograph book to the general. He took the book, scribbled a few lines and his name, and smiled as he returned it.

Originally from Fredericktown, a town of 1,052 people on the Monongahela River in southwestern Pennsylvania, the general had spent 31 years in the Marines. Before the Gulf War, he'd been assigned to Camp Lejeune in North Carolina.

According to Keys, most of the 16,000 men and women assigned to the 2nd Marine Division shipped for the Persian Gulf in early December 1990. The division spent several weeks in a tent city outside Jubail, a town on the Persian Gulf coast of Saudi Arabia. The Marines subsequently moved until they occupied a position just two kilometers south of the Kuwait border.

From this region, which was west of Khafji, the 2nd Marines found themselves sandwiched between the 1st Marine Division on the east and the Egyptian Army on the west.

The division invaded Kuwait on Feb. 24, 1991, "fought magnificently and far into Kuwait," and overcame all Iraqi resistance, Keys said.

The initial plan of attack into Kuwait called for the 1st Marine Division to breach the Iraqi minefields, then for the 2nd Marine Division to leapfrog through the breach and hit the Iraqi defenses. A major concern arose among divisional planners. If an assault stalled at the breach or at the two parallel minefields that the Iraqis had placed beyond the berm, the traffic-jammed Marines would be sitting ducks for Saddam Hussein's artillery.

Early in February, Keys asked Lt. Gen. Walter Boomer, the senior Marine commander in the Gulf, permission for the 2nd Marine Division to breach the berm elsewhere. This would halve the potential for creating a dangerous logjam at the border, while splitting the Iraqi defenses.

Boomer told Keys, "Okay, do it."

Opening a second breach required the 2nd Marine Division to move 60 miles farther west from its initial staging area. Supply columns rolled around the clock to a site called Khanjar. By Feb. 23, a veritable city had mushroomed in the desert, complete with a hospital, a runway, a 760-acre ammunition dump, and storage capacity for five million gallons of fuel. The Marines even trucked in about one million gallons of water, then discovered an abandoned well just a few miles away. Constructed by the Saudi government, the well provided the 2nd Marine Division with 100,000 gallons of water a day.

When his Marines hit the second breach on Feb. 24, Keys commanded a division comprising three major components. The 6th Marine Regiment, led by Col. Larry Livingston, breached the minefields before the division tore loose into Kuwait.

On the right flank, Col. Larry Schmidt and his 8th Marine Regiment watched for Iraqi counterattacks and probed north toward Kuwait City. On the left flank rolled the Tiger Brigade, the ad hoc armored outfit drawn from M-1A1s, Bradleys, and personnel belonging to the Army's 2nd Armored Division. This brigade, which sent many soldiers home through BIA, replaced the third Marine regiment assigned to the 2nd Marine Division. That regiment spent the war aboard ships in the Gulf, waiting for the amphibious assault that never came.

The 10th Marine Regiment provided artillery support for the 2nd Marine Division.

Keys tracked his leathernecks as they punched into the Iraqi defenses. Marines equipped with tanks (M-1A1 Abrams) and TOWs battled Iraqi armor as far as Kuwait City, where the Marines waited for Arab forces to bypass them and enter the Kuwaiti capital. Press accounts detailed the often extremely close and deadly encounters between the American and Iraqi armor.

Recalling that he'd served two tours in Vietnam, the general remembered that his first homecoming from Southeast Asia had assumed a patriotic flavor. Asked to describe his second homecoming, which occurred after the antiwar movement intensified in the United States, Keys looked at the happy Marines and civilians who surrounded him in Bangor. He flashed a smile and said, "Well, it was nothing like this."

"I really appreciate what you people have done here for us," Bill Keys stated. "It feels really good, knowing that the people back home were pulling for us."

By now, Pat Berg realized that Larry Rose was not aboard the 747. Trying to conceal the disappointment evident in her eyes, she mingled with the Marines and tried to locate her sons and their friends.

Lt. Col. Mary Lowery, a 19-year Marine veteran who called Virginia her home state, had been assigned to the 2nd Marine Division staff at Camp Lejeune to handle personnel and administration. She left for Saudi Arabia on Jan. 13, 1991, after remaining stateside several weeks longer than most other 2nd Marine Division personnel "because I had to close out the division, so to speak, personnelwise," she said.

Lowery estimated that by this Monday, perhaps 5,000 Marines from the division had returned home. The pace would probably accelerate in the next week or two, she said, but some people would remain to clean our equipment and load it aboard ships.

As a young girl asked Lowery to autograph her T-shirt, Leighton leaned into his microphone and called attention to Debbie Hambrock, a student at Augusta College in Augusta, Ga. Her parents, Tom and Ann Hambrock, lived in Orono.

"Today's Debbie's birthday!" Leighton announced. "I'd like to invite some Marines to sing `Happy Birthday' to this lovely young lady, who has come all the way from Georgia to say `hello' to you guys!"

Debbie Hambrock blushed as several young Marines surrounded her and bellowed the first stanza to "Happy Birthday."

The singing inspired Cpl. Rick Messa of Harrison, Ohio, to sing "God Bless the USA" to excellent accompaniment from Bill Trowell and Rick Aiken, the musicians du jour. The bespectacled Messa exhibited good voice as he competed against the occasional squeal from the music system.

When Messa finished singing, the crowd went wild.

Gary Leighton soon recalled the Marines to their aircraft. Bill Keys had already bid good-bye to Bangor, where people would remember him for his gracious appearance at the lectern. The general and his Marines shortly left BIA for Cherry Point.

Within a few months, Keys would receive his third star.

By the time the UAL Marines reboarded their plane, the HAL L-1011 had touched down. The jet carried about 220 Marines, most of whom belonged to an artillery unit: the 5th Battalion, 10th Marine Regiment, 2nd Marine Division.

As the first dozen Marines reached the upper part of the ramp, Pat Berg returned to her position beside the newspaper-vending machine. Holding up her "Larry Rose?" sign, she shook hands with the incoming Marines and scanned all those desert fatigues for a familiar face.

Then she momentarily looked away to speak to an older woman sitting beside her in a wheelchair. "I heard someone ask, 'Larry Rose?,' and I looked up, and he was standing right there looking at me," Berg said.

She no longer needed her sign.

Berg and Rose flew into each other's arms near the gift table and quietly hugged for a few moments. Tears welled in Berg's eyes, and - despite the Marine reputation for toughness - Rose, too, blinked back some tears.

The people standing nearby applauded Berg and Rose. Marines especially savored this moment, which they would share with their own families by late afternoon.

Then Berg and Rose slipped into the crowd and found a quieter location to visit with Zachary and Shawn.

A typical family reunion at BIA? Well, no: Those people who witnessed the reunion did not know about the 11-year search that precipitated it.

Berg grew up the youngest of two daughters of a Wisconsin couple. All her life, her father had refused to discuss "any relatives on his side of the family," Berg said.

"It was like no one existed in half of my family," she commented. "I always wondered if I had aunts, uncles, and cousins I didn't know about."

In 1975, Berg initiated a search to find her father's relatives. She pieced together from hints that her father had dropped that he'd once worked on farms in California. Scant evidence suggested the farm country around Fresno.

For the next 11 years, Berg contacted every imaginable source of genealogical research in the Central Valley of California. "I'd do it for a year and pump it real hard, and then I'd give it a year off out of discouragement," she described her intensive search.

Her husband, Richard, "was very supportive," Berg said. "He kept after me to keep trying, even when I wanted to give up."

Despairing of success by 1986, and having expended a large sum of money for an apparently fruitless search, Berg finally obtained a library copy of the Fresno phone directory. She photocopied the directory and followed her husband's advice "to start calling people with my maiden name, Shepherd."

Many expensive phone calls later, Berg almost hung up the phone for good. "I'd gone through two smaller towns outside Fresno with no luck. I wanted to quit," she said.

Eventually, Berg discovered a half-sister and a half-brother, aunts, uncles, and cousins whom she never knew existed. Her half-sister proved to be Laurie Rose, the mother of Larry Rose.

"I call her my `new sister,' since I've known her only the last five years," Berg said. "We've struck it off so well. We talk to each other at least once a week."

Berg and her sister soon flew to California to meet their "new" family. They learned that their father had left his family in 1945 and moved to the Midwest after severing all communications with his past. His first wife divorced him, leaving him free to remarry.

Berg also discovered an amazing physical resemblance between herself and Laurie Rose. The resemblance astonished Larry Rose on April 15.

"He told me that when he saw me standing there, holding my sign, he thought, `What is my mother doing here?' Then he realized that his mom couldn't be here in Bangor, so it had to be me!" Pat Berg said.

THE HITCHHIKER

History records that no Southern unit ever occupied Bangor during or after the Civil War. That all changed, however, at 4:06 p.m. on Tuesday, April 16, when another United Airlines 747 touched down in the Queen City.

What the Rebels didn't realize, however, was that some Yankees weren't far behind them.

New York Yankees, that is.

UAL Flight 6456 swirled tire smoke in its slipstream as the red-and-white 747 dropped from the afternoon sky and greased its wheels on the BIA tarmac that Tuesday. Most of the 400 soldiers aboard the plane belonged to Army Reserve and Army National Guard outfits from the deep South, a place warmer outdoors than Bangor that day.

If the men and women living below the Mason-Dixon Line noticed the chill in the air, though, a warm greeting from several hundred Yankees dispelled the natural cold.

While soldiers and civilians celebrated inside the domestic terminal, Chief Warrant Officer 3rd Class Richard McMullen stood on the upper ramp, where few civilians ever bothered the troops. A burly, softspoken guardsman from Jackson, Ala., McMullen belonged to the 778th Maintenance Company of the Alabama Army National Guard. This outfit, which mustered about 215 men and women, was divided between armories in Jackson and Monroeville, about 50 miles away.

Although the Pentagon activated the 778th on Sept. 27, 1990, CW3 McMullen had already prepared his family for a possible call-up. "I'd been in and around it (the Army and the National Guard) long enough, so I told my wife that when this thing breaks, I know we're going, but I just don't know when," he explained.

His wife, Sophia, and their son Richard Jr. knew what was coming. McMullen's daughter, Lynne, lives with her husband in Greensboro, N.C. "She wasn't aware of the day-to-day worries, but we told her what was happening," he said.

McMullen said good-bye to his job as a mechanical maintenance foreman for the Ciba-Geigy Chemical Corp. in McIntosh, Ala. He joined other members of the 778th at Fort Rucker, Ala., for orientation into full-time military life. The 778th left Alabama on Nov. 6, 1990, and landed in Saudi Arabia the next day. The Alabama National Guardsmen moved into the desert on Nov. 26, 1990.

Throughout the Gulf War and the months leading into it, "our mission was to provide maintenance of the equipment and what we call the Class 9 repair parts," McMullen said.

This assignment took the 778th across northern Saudi Arabia to a point about 260 miles out in the desert northwest of Dhahran. "I'll tell you, out there everything looks like everything else, and all I could tell at times was that we weren't far from the border," McMullen recalled.

He traveled to Khafji after the battle there ("no pretty sights in that town," he said) and ultimately went to Kuwait City after its liberation.

When the "go-home" order arrived, the men and women of the 778th spent a week in the desert washing their equipment, including some 170 pieces of rolling stock (trucks, trailers, etc.). The 778th returned to Dhahran on April 7, 1991, to spend almost four days hosing off their gear again.

The thoroughly cleaned vehicles would return to Alabama by ship. "We don't intend to wash them again, but, who knows?" McMullen speculated. "They say there isn't water out there in the desert, but we improvised. There's a lot more water back home."

As the boarding call sounded for his flight, he said that he was glad to be going home. "It's been an experience I won't forget, and I'm proud of what we accomplished. I feel we went over there and did what we were charged to do, but we're ready to go home," McMullen said while watching soldiers surge up the ramp, hug the women Legionnaires good-bye, and race for the plane.

"They did an outstanding job over there," he said as more soldiers vanished toward the 747.

Suddenly, only a surprised McMullen remained in the international terminal. "Guess it's time to go," he observed, pausing to shake hands.

As he stepped over the wire, a child asked him for an autograph. "Haven't I signed your shirt before?" he asked the little girl. When she shrugged her shoulders, he chuckled, took her pen, and wrote his name with a flourish.

"Hey, I don't mind," McMullen said in his gentle Alabama drawl. He bolted for the plane, whirled once in mid-trot, and waved to the Legionnaires. "Thanks again!" he called before vanishing through the metal detector.

Later that night, the 747 would land McMullen and the other 400 soldiers at Fort Benning in Georgia. From there, the Alabama National Guardsmen and reservists would travel by bus to Fort Rucker, where their families awaited them.

With McMullen's disappearance, the Confederacy temporarily withdrew its troops from Bangor.

Two more flights were on tap for tonight, including a plane going to Syracuse, N.Y. That would be the Boys From Syracuse, the New York Yankees who brought a hitchhiker with them that night.

The 1st Cav beat them to Bangor, though.

UAL Flight 6457 touched down at 8:20 p.m. while en route to Fort Hood, Texas. The 747 carried soldiers from the 13th Signal Battalion and the 2nd Battalion, 8th Cavalry Regiment, 1st Cavalry Division.

As the 1st Cav troopers entered the domestic terminal, more than 800 people waited to greet them. Marking perhaps the largest weekday crowd during the troop flights, the civilians waved flags and homemade banners and thunderously cheered to show their appreciation for the soldiers wearing the horsehead patch.

The cavalrymen worked their way along an enthusiastic reception line on the ramp. Joe King Sr. and Jr. and other Legionnaires warmly shook hands and exchanged greetings with the soldiers.

Perhaps the troop greeter most touched by tonight's flight was George Nye, a 50-year-old Bangor resident who'd fought with the 1st Cav in Vietnam. For UAL Flight 6457, he wore a black jacket adorned with various patches, including a replica 1st Cav patch that heralded the 1965 Battle of the Ia Drang Valley, the first major engagement between the armies of North Vietnam and the United States.

Later, after the 1st Cav troopers entered the domestic terminal, Nye traded his Disabled American Veterans' headgear for a campaign hat, complete with gold crossed sabers. He talked to attentive soldiers about Vietnam and asked them about their war.

Cpl. Dell Drake of Columbia, S.C., was a gunner on an M-1A1 Abrams tank assigned to the 2nd Battalion, 8th Cav. Leaving behind his wife, Linda, and their 5-year-old son, Aaron, he shipped for the Gulf in early October 1990.

"Most of the time, we were staying out in the desert. We didn't get close to any cities except KKMC and Hafr al-Batin," Drake said. During the ground war, the 2nd Battalion was initially used as a decoy along the berm, then plunged into the fighting with the rest of the 1st Cav and wound up outside Basra, he recalled. Crossing the sandy stretches of desert proved particularly difficult in a tank.

When the Army finally decided to send him home, Drake said, the brass moved quickly. Drake and his comrades were rousted from their cots at 2:30 a.m. (Saudi time) on April 15 and were told, "You're leaving here in an hour."

While Drake talked about his war, Hawaiian Airlines Flight 8109 touched down at BIA. The L-1011 carried about 250 personnel from the 174th Tactical Fighter Wing, New York Air National Guard. Since the 174th was based at Hancock International Airport, Syracuse, N.Y., the Air Guardsmen called themselves "The Boys From Syracuse."

The L-1011 also carried a hitchhiker who was thumbing a flight to Delaware.

The Boys From Syracuse received a welcome similar to that extended the 1st Cav troopers. Unlike the soldiers, the Air Guardsmen wore jungle fatigues, so there was no mistaking either service as soldiers and Air Force personnel mingled with the civilians in the sardine-packed terminal.

Later, before the inadequate PA system announced the first boarding call for UAL Flight 6457, Lt. Col. Dan Peterjohn of the 1st Cav took time to thank the troop greeters for their warm welcome. He had already met Nye during the unfurling of a divisional flag.

Peterjohn said that he had deployed to Saudi Arabia on Oct. 3, 1990. His command wound up "about a hundred miles deep into the desert, I'd say."

Before the ground war began, Peterjohn formed Task Force 2-8 by trading a tank company for a rifle (infantry) company and adding other elements. Task Force 2-8 ultimately included about 700 men and women, although the women medics "were pulled back before we went into action," Peterjohn said.

During the two to three weeks before the ground war started, "it was our job to fight the counter-reconnaissance battle while screening the 7th Corps' westward movement," he recalled. Task Force 2-8's introduction to combat before Feb. 23 was limited to probing attacks and artillery duels along the berm dividing the Neutral Zone. The unit suffered no casualties during the preliminary probing operations.

When the Allies invaded Iraq, "we were part of the big sweep," Peterjohn said. Task Force 2-8 plunged 290 kilometers into Iraq and stopped just south of the Euphrates River near Basra.

Peterjohn humorously described an incident that didn't seem so funny at the time. During the war, the M-1A1 tank that his S-3 was riding in struck a mine at the berm. The tank lost a track, but its crew escaped unscathed.

Later, "we supposedly captured the guy who mined the tank," said Peterjohn. "The Iraqi was bragging (in hearing range of interpreters) that he'd destroyed an American tank.

"Well, he described the tank, and his description matched that of the S-3's damaged tank. We showed it to him (the Iraqi braggart), and his jaw just dropped," Peterjohn laughed.

Task Force 2-8 "picked up many prisoners who surrendered willingly," he said. "Many Iraqis had a severe morale problem. Most of them had no reason to fight."

Peterjohn soon excused himself to herd his excited cavalrymen to their plane. As he walked up the almost deserted ramp - most civilians were celebrating with the Boys From Syracuse - a very young soldier unfurled a captured Iraqi flag and held it as cameras flashed.

Not too long after the UAL 747 departed BIA, the Boys From Syracuse started talking about getting home themselves. Unfortunately, their aircraft required mechanical attention. For an hour or so, no one could predict when the L-1011 would leave for New York.

Staff Sgt. Peter O'Kussick, a weapons loader with the 174th TFW, said that the wing had been activated on Dec. 29, 1990. Most of the guardsmen left for the Gulf in early January. O'Kussick, in civilian life a state corrections officer from Auburn, N.Y., flew out on Jan. 4.

He landed at a central Saudi Arabian airfield that boasted only a single runway. Someone had already erected tents, but the guardsmen had to build temporary hangars for their aircraft.

According to O'Kussick, the 174th TFW took 18 F-16A Fighting Falcons to the Gulf. In the few weeks remaining before the air war began, ground crews worked long hours preparing the planes for combat.

As Allied aircraft launched attacks against Iraqi targets, O'Kussick and other specialists put in eight-to-12-hour shifts, loading munitions aboard the F-16s at night and trying to catch some rest while the jets flew missions during the day.

The New York F-16s launched in the second wave of Allied aircraft that went after the Iraqi military on Jan. 17, 1991. Before their war ended, the Boys From Syracuse flew more than 1,000 sorties to Kuwait and Iraq and dropped some 3 million pounds of munitions.

The bombing raids continued day-in, day-out. Ground crews worked around the clock, O'Kussick said, as the 174th TFW averaged eight to 12 aircraft flying missions each day. "Yeah, we got really tired," he said, "but all the airmen wanted the war to start so we could get it over with and get on home."

The daily sandstorms made both flying and ground work hazardous. "They're (the sandstorms) just like snowstorms," O'Kussick said. "At times, I couldn't see 50 yards in front of me. Geez, it would get almost like a whiteout in a blizzard. Believe me, I prefer the snow."

The Air Guardsmen lived 10 men to a tent. "It wasn't as bad as I thought it would be. Some guys would always be at work, so you'd have room to spread out and sleep," O'Kussick said.

O'Kussick enjoyed the Saudi nights the most "because it would get cooler, and I could see all those stars shining so brightly. It was like you could reach out and touch them."

Although the Boys From Syracuse suffered no casualties during the war, they lost two F-16s to mechanical problems. Both pilots bailed out safely and lived to return home to New York.

The HAL L-1011 had brought home only half the wing's personnel, O'Kussick said. Plans called for the remainder, including the pilots and the surviving F-16s, to return later in the month.

As O'Kussick talked about landing at Shannon, Ireland, while on his way home, passenger-service supervisor Heidi Suletzki announced that the L-1011 had been towed from the gate. The plane's crew wanted to do an engine runup a safe distance from the terminal.

The Boys From Syracuse collectively groaned.

O'Kussick speculated that he'd still get home that evening to see his wife, Pamela, and their daughters Kelly and Leeann. In fact, said O'Kussick, he'd be home in time for Kelly's fifth birthday.

As the men and women who comprised the Boys From Syracuse grudgingly accepted their fate, the hitchhiker took a walk up the ramp to chat with the people at the passenger-service desk.

Maj. John Schneider, a pilot with the 142nd Tactical Airlift Squadron, Delaware Air National Guard, had thumbed a ride as far as Bangor with the 174th TFW. "I hope we get home tonight," he said, "but it really doesn't matter to me. I've still got to make a connection to Delaware, so if we stay here an hour or two, I don't mind."

An amiable, soft-spoken man, Schneider leaned against the passenger-service desk and watched the restless New York Air Guardsmen pack the ramp.

Major John Schneider, a pilot with the 142nd Tactical Airlift Squadron of the Delaware Air National Guard, hitched a ride home via Bangor with the New York ANG.

According to Schneider, the Pentagon activated the 142nd on Jan. 18, 1991, a day after the air war started. Flying from the Greater Wilmington Airport, the C-130 Hercules transports and their crews from the 142nd landed in Saudi Arabia on Jan. 25, 1991, and went to work immediately.

Schneider flew from the airport at Al-Kharj (Asad Military City), located southeast of Riyadh, the Saudi capital. The C-130Hs ferried supplies to various airfields in the Saudi kingdom, even flying supplies to (Allied bases at) the front line before the ground war began, Schneider said. No squadron aircraft ever saw any triple-A (antiaircraft fire), much less took a hit from Iraqi defenses, he said.

Once the Allies breached the Iraqi defenses, the 142nd crews flew missions into Kuwait and Iraq, including the airfield at Talil, Iraq. While flying over the war zone, Schneider could see burned-out Iraqi T-72 tanks.

Later, when he flew a mission to Kuwait, he discovered that American soldiers who were worried about unmarked mines "wouldn't take me for a ride to see the sights."

He mentioned an incident that occurred near the burning Rumaliah oil fields, where "some Army guys had captured two Iraqi jeeps, or whatever they were. They were treating people to rides in them, nothing dangerous, just a short hop where the minefields weren't.

"Well, the soldiers parked them (the Iraqi jeeps) by their tents one night, and early the next day, some Army engineers came along and blew them up," Schneider said.

Although "Kuwait City looks like a beautiful city, approaching it by air was difficult at times," he remembered. Flying into the smoke from burning Kuwaiti oil wells was especially difficult, he said.

The 142nd occasionally hauled more than supplies or soldiers. One crew on its way to Kuwait City took along some politicians, including Senators John Glenn and John Warner and Rep. Les Aspin. Schneider refused to comment when asked how the Delaware Air Guardsmen felt about risking a plane and people to take politicians on a tour. "Senators, bombs, food, ammo: Whatever it is, you take it where it's gotta go," he explained.

Schneider remained on duty in the Gulf through Ramadan, the Moslem holy month. During this time, when Moslems fast from sunrise to sunset, the Americans were restricted to their bases by day. Schneider and his comrades could go shopping after dark.

He sometimes saw his wife, Virginia, while flying about the Gulf. A major and a nurse in the 142nd, Virginia Schneider flew with Saudi crews manning C-130 hospital aircraft. Before the air war began, the Saudis flew with nurses contracted from Great Britain. All the shooting sent those nurses home, so some American nurses replaced them.

Virginia Schneider had nothing but nice things to say about the Saudis, especially the crews with which she flew. "Despite stories you probably heard to the contrary, these Saudis were professional and polite in all their dealings with American women," her husband said.

Virginia flew home from Saudi Arabia on March 18, about a month before her husband hitched a flight with the Boys From Syracuse. He intended to "thumb" a flight to Delaware, process out of the Guard, and resume his work as a landscape architect.

Schneider had been surprised by the reception in Bangor. Referring to all the autographs he'd signed, he laughed and said, "I've got my name on a lot of coats and T-shirts in Bangor."

About 10:30 p.m., the PA system announced the first boarding call for HAL Flight 8109. The Boys From Syracuse quickly packed the ramp, where they formed columns of two's and patiently waited for the order to board their aircraft.

The L-1011 left BIA later that evening and landed at Hancock International Airport at 12:47 a.m., April 17. About 1,500 people, including many families, threw an enthusiastic greeting for the New York Air Guardsmen. Although the Boys From Syracuse arrived perhaps three hours late for their official reception, the people waiting in Syracuse didn't mind.

Neither did John Schneider, the hitchhiker, who needed to catch only one more flight home himself.

PURSUING THE SOUVENIR HUNTERS

A crowd similar to Tuesday night's packed the BIA domestic terminal Wednesday, April 17. Lined rows deep along the wire, between 800 and 1,000 people met American Trans Air Flight 8145, which landed at 10:10 a.m. while en route to Andrews Air Force Base, Washington, D.C. Since United Airlines Flight 6458 planned to land at 11:08 a.m., the civilians hung around for that flight, too.

The AMT L-1011 carried the soldiers belonging to the 201st Military Intelligence Battalion, a unit that helped provide important information for Allied forces during the Gulf War. With the Shiite rebellion in southern Iraq finally quashed by Saddam Hussein's thugs, the Army began dismantling its intelligence apparatus. The 201st was among the larger intelligence formations sent home in April. Perhaps 10 minutes before the UAL 747 touched down at BIA, Gary Leighton stepped to the lectern, adjusted the microphone, and spoke to the crowd. He listed the so-called airport ground rules that were later dubbed the "Riot Act."

As outlined by Leighton, the Riot Act included such injunctions as:

* Don't stand on the airport furniture or on the window ledges.
* Family members who are waiting for relatives on this plane can stand at the entrance to the ramp.
* Let the troops enter the terminal before hugging them or asking for their autographs.
* No child under the age of 16 will be permitted to remain in the terminal without an adult who's responsible for them.
* Don't ask for souvenirs. Anyone caught asking the troops for their insignia, patches, or whatever will be removed from the terminal.

Leighton later acknowledged that he'd had complaints about kids bothering the troops for their insignia or patches, even their hats. "Seems with all the kids in here during the school vacation, they're sort of overwhelming the place," he said.

And some parents had been using the airport as their babysitter.
"We strongly disapprove, because this is an international airport, not a babysitting service. When we catch up with the kids, we tell them so, but with several hundred people in here every day, we can't always tell who comes without their parents," Leighton explained.

People standing near the terminal windows cheered as UAL Flight 6458 touched down at 11:08 a.m. Passenger-service listed the 747's final destination as Riverside, Calif. This meant that the aircraft probably carried Marines, always a favorite with the homecoming crowds.

Then the Marines exited UAL Flight 6458 and, flowing in a loose, disorganized formation, occupied the ramp and swept into the domestic terminal. The three-piece band providing the music that Wednesday greeted the Marines with a rousing, percussion-accentuated rendition of the "Caissons Go Rolling Along," the official song of the United States Army! A retired Marine standing nearby winced and cried, "Wrong song!"

Innocently adding insult to injury, the band whirled into "Anchors, Aweigh," the official song of the United States Navy. The retired Marine feigned a heart attack, then laughed and reached out to shake hands with his leatherneck descendants. As the music called the Navy to enjoy "our last night on shore, drink to the foam," the dam broke far up the ramp, and Marines, Marines, and more Marines overwhelmed the receiving line and poured into the terminal. Finally, the band got its signals right and hit the opening chords to the Marine Hymn. By this time, unfortunately, the din raised by the Marines and the civilians effectively drowned the music. Since they sat closer to the music, the three men on drums, bass, and keyboard never noticed the intense competition from loud and happy human voices.

Pauline Covert, a flight attendant with United Airlines, watched the celebration unfolding in the terminal. A wide smile on her face, she recalled that she'd flown her first troop flight into Bangor on Easter night. The flight crew had warned their military passengers about the reception waiting for them. "We say, `they're going to welcome you here,' but the troops are always amazed at the welcome they receive," Covert said.

A generation ago, she had flown soldiers into Vietnam. "The difference between now and then is the difference between night and day," Covert stated. "No one cared back then about the boys who were coming home. Even when flying into an Air Force base like Travis, no one was there to meet them."

Covert appreciated the effort made by Maine residents to welcome home the returning Gulf vets. "I think the people of Bangor are unbelievable," she spoke louder to make herself heard over the cheering, music, and laughter. "This wouldn't happen in another city." Covert described an incident that had occurred within the hour. The van bringing the UAL relief crew from their motel on the Odlin Road in Bangor had accidentally shed some baggage. The vehicle's occupants rode on to the domestic terminal, unaware of the incident. A motorist traveling behind the van stopped, grabbed the luggage, and hustled after the disappearing van. The baggage arrived about the time the flight crew discovered it missing.

"There are other cities we go into, where that luggage would have been picked up, and it would've been gone," Covert said.

Col. Jack Holly, the deputy chief of staff for operations for the 1st FSSG (Force Service Support Group), said the Marines were based at Camp Pendleton, Calif. He explained that the 1st FSSG coordinated the logistics that supported all the Marines (particularly the 1st Marine Division) who were in Saudi Arabia and Kuwait.

According to Holly, the 6,000 Marines ultimately assigned to the 1st FSSG started leaving the United States during the first week in August 1990. Many Marine Corps Reservists "are integrated into our ranks," he said. "They served admirably in Saudi Arabia, fulfilling the same functions as active-duty Marines."

Before the Gulf War ended, the 1st FSSG spread its forces over a 350-mile area extending from Sheikh Issa in Bahrain to a point north of Kuwait City, Holly said.

Within a few weeks after President Bush declared a ceasefire, the Marines from the 1st FSSG started heading home. Some Marines will remain in the Gulf until May, Holly said, "but most of us are back or en route."

A native of Corning, N.Y., who graduated from the U.S. Naval Academy, the colonel described the reception at BIA as "pretty overwhelming. I spent two years in Vietnam. That was a lot different war, a lot different reception. I thank everybody who turned out today. And we accept any of the thanks on behalf of the Vietnam vets, too. We never anticipated a welcome like this."

"You know, Marines are supposed to be rough and tough and unsentimental. There's the phrase, `once a Marine, always a Marine.' That implies you'll always display the traits, the toughness of a Marine. Well, taking it from one leatherneck who's been off to two wars, you can't imagine how this homecoming makes me feel," Holly said, blinking hard.

As the three-man band struck up "California, Here I Come," Lance Cpl. William Sanders of Phoenix, Ariz., and Blance Campbell of Orrington danced beside the lectern.

People gathered to take photos or clap their hands.

Throughout the crowd that noontime, certain young people badgered the Marines for souvenirs. A few airport employees circulated in the terminal that day and caught perhaps three or four souvenir-hunters.

A boy sporting a razor-cut appeared beside a Marine and asked for an autograph. Perhaps 8-years-old, the boy waited until the Marine finished writing, then asked, "Can I have the stripes on your collar?" A civilian standing beside the Marine reprimanded the boy, "You know you're not supposed to be asking for souvenirs. Didn't you hear the announcement before the plane landed?"

The civilian turned to the Marine and apologized for the child's behavior. The Marine shrugged his shoulders as if wondering, "What's the big deal?"

Months later, when he reviewed his notes from that week's work at BIA, a newspaper reporter who had witnessed the exchange wondered, too, just what the problem was. Whether it's sports figures, movie actors and actresses, or even such real-life heroes as the Gulf War vets, American kids always chase after autographs and souvenirs. So a few kids embarrassed their elders by bugging the troops at the airport. So what?

Though they'd deny it, and rightly so, the returning troops certainly deserved the adulation, whether feigned or real. The American homecomings at BIA granted the troops their moments in the sun.

If the young souvenir hunters played a role in that moment, then let them. No soldier, sailor, Marine, or airman ever wrote the reporter's newspaper to complain about losing uniform components in Bangor.

Cpl. Robert Gill, an air-traffic controller stationed at El Toro Marine Corps Air Station in California, didn't mind the souvenir and autograph hunters he met in Bangor that day, either.

In August 1990, Gill had volunteered for Gulf duty with his unit from El Toro. "We had a high percentage of people volunteer that day. I was working a part-time job, and Marines were being recalled from leave, and there were too many volunteers for everyone to go," Gill said. "I was left stateside, which was tough to take. The Gulf was where everyone wanted to be." He got his wish. Originally from Tallahassee, Fla., Gill left for Saudi Arabia on Feb. 5, 1991, with other combat replacements. He did mostly paperwork at Jubail, where he was assigned to Marine Air Traffic Control Squadron 38. That outfit controlled the air traffic at seven airfields in Saudi Arabia and Kuwait.

Gill arrived at Jubail in time to witness at least one Scud attack. The incident "didn't seem all that threatening, but it quickly reminded me that I was in a war zone," he recalled.

He expressed his pleasure at not fulfilling his original assignment to the Gulf. "The Marines anticipated far more casualties than we actually had," Gill said. "I was supposedly sent over to replace someone who was shot.

"Obviously, he wasn't shot, because they had to search to find me a job. That was real good news. It meant that someone was going home who wasn't expected to do so," Gill commented. "Whoever the lucky Marine was, I'm glad he made it."

WHO'S HANDICAPPED?

A thick, cold fog rolled into Bangor before sunrise on Thursday, April 18. People driving to the airport to meet American Trans Air Flight 8147 wondered if the fog had reduced visibility below the FAA minimums for safe landings.

It had.

Scheduled to land at BIA at 4:57 a.m., the AMT L-1011 diverted to Logan International Airport in Boston. Noting that that airliner was scheduled to stop at Pope Air Force Base in Fayetteville, N.C., a bleary-eyed man muttered, "Well, there goes our chance to meet some paratroopers." "But, chin up", a woman commented. "American Trans Air has another plane confirmed for 6:27 a.m." "This fog looks pretty thick," the man mumbled. "I doubt it'll lift before then."

"I can't figure this out at all," said a woman who'd driven to the airport from Dedham, a town set in the hills about 10 miles east of Bangor. "The sun was coming up at home. I didn't hit the fog until I got closer to Bangor." As the troop greeters wandered into the coffee shop or plopped into the lounge chairs, Sheila Dean of Orono parked her wheelchair nearby.

Among all the troop greeters later designated as the "regulars," Dean overcame the greatest obstacles to welcome home the 60,000 men and women who passed through BIA. Yet she never sought or accepted sympathy, an emotion that she once described "as the very thing you can feel that will insult me."

Born with spina bifida, a medical condition that confined her to a wheelchair all her life, Dean had her driver's license, but lacked an appropriately equipped car and depended on other people for transportation.

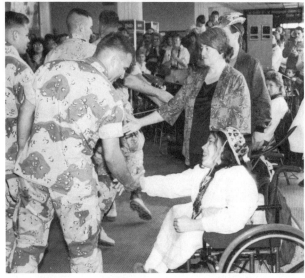

Handicapped by spina bifida since birth, Sheila Dean traveled to Bangor almost daily to meet returning Gulf War veterans. She greeted Marines on April 15, 1991.

When troop flights started landing in Bangor, she tried to get to as many flights as possible. Patriotic enthusiasm aside, she had a special reason for meeting the troops.

"I have two brothers, an uncle, and a boyfriend in the military," Dean explained that damp April morning.

Her brother, Ron, had served in the Army, while another brother, Don, joined the Marines. Both men left the military before the Gulf War started, but were called back in January (1991) within two weeks of each other, Dean said.

Folding her hands in her lap, she leaned forward and looked down at the well-worn terminal rug. "Ron was in the Army about six weeks, and they sent him home, but Don's still in the Marines. He was promoted to sergeant. He thinks he may still be in when this is all over." Her uncle, Michael Dean, "is a career guy in the Navy. He loves it, in fact, and can't imagine himself as a civilian," she laughed. "You know, when all the shooting started over there, I worried about all our people who are stationed there," Dean said. "Watching the war on TV really brought it home. It was like `hey, my family could be fighting there.'"

Before the troop flights stopped nine months later, Dean would travel frequently from Orono to Bangor. She often caught rides with friends, including people whom she

44

met at the airport, or spent $30 at a time for roundtrip cab fare. In mid-April, the Greater Bangor Chamber of Commerce sent her $100 to help defray her transportation costs.

To her immense delight, Dean was hired three months later as a switchboard operator at the Bangor Air National Guard Base. By fall, she had obtained a properly modified car that gave her a freedom of movement that other people took for granted.

Today, however, her improved fortunes remained unseen in the future. She talked about the troops whom she'd met and befriended and about the attitudes that she'd encountered here at BIA.

Dean adored the troops. "I like men," she laughed, "especially men in uniform. You didn't know that's why I was coming out here all the time, did you?"

She grinned, then said, "No, of course, that's not the only reason. It's had to do with my family and my boyfriend, too, and with all those other boyfriends and girlfriends, moms and dads who went off to war."

Before the troops disembarked from each incoming flight, the Orono woman habitually parked her wheelchair near the gift table or somewhere along the wire. As the troops entered the terminal, she would extend her right hand and shake hands with the people who noticed her sitting there.

"I've shaken hands with just about everybody who's come through here," she said on April 18. Just three days earlier, she'd met Marine Maj. Gen. Bill Keys, who signed her autograph book, exchanged a few words with her, and shook her hand.

Dean admitted that her height - perhaps waist-high to the average Marine - prevented many troops from seeing her. "I've noticed how their eyes are level with the crowd, and I can't blame them for that. When they come down that ramp, they don't know what to expect," she said. "They're trying to take it in all at once."

Yet countless times during the troop flights, a Marine, a sailor, an airman, or a soldier saw Sheila, leaned down, and took her hand. A broad smile rewarded those troops who did. The same smile awaited the troops who did not.

The troops stopped to talk, too. A willing listener, Dean heard stories about the war that "would curl your toes," yarns about desert life, and confessions once reserved for a priest. By concentrating on the troops and not talking solely about herself, Dean let many people unburden their hearts before flying to their final destination. Then there were the souvenirs.

By today, she had collected more than 1,000 signatures, enough to fill three or four notebooks. Without her ever asking, troops gave her their dog tags (more than 80), a few hats, and a camouflage jacket.

Beyond the souvenirs, there was the hat. Dean often wore a desert-camouflage hat, to which she pinned insignia she'd received from the troops. Stripes, bars, the curved triangles that denoted a specialist, a wide-winged eagle: the hat fairly bowed under the heavy weight of all those metal insignia.

Referring to her hat, she would smile and say, "That's something I'll always, always cherish.

"You know," she'd say, leaning forward and whispering conspiratorially, "I've got everything in the Army but a general's star, and I'm working on that." She sat back in her wheelchair and laughed.

Within a few weeks, Sheila Dean would have her star.

"I didn't know a soul here until I started coming out to meet the troops," she reflected as the PA system spread the news that the AMT flight had been diverted to Boston because of fog. "Now, we've formed some good friendships that I hope will last.

"Most people treat me just like they do everybody else," Dean said. "Especially the troops. To them, I'm not handicapped, I'm not in a wheelchair, I'm just a woman. I'll be here until they all come home, no matter how long it takes."

THE DOCTOR, THE GUNNERY SERGEANT, AND AMERICAN WOMEN

As the disgruntled troop greeters predicted ("it figures, doesn't it?" one woman growled), the heavy fog that diverted the two American Trans Air L-1011s to Boston on April 18 lifted not long after dawn.

"At least we've got another flight coming in later," a man said before he left the terminal early that morning.

Perhaps 400 people gathered at BIA later that Thursday to meet a 747 belonging to United Airlines. Irena Alley of Beals Island, a town on the coast about a 90-mile drive southeast of Bangor, came to the airport "for what I think is the 20th time. I think all this is absolutely fantastic, getting out here and meeting the troops."

She had brought her 3-year-old daughter, Amy, who was wearing the desert-camouflage outfit that Irena had bought her at Ames in Bangor. "She wears it about every time we come," Irena said.

Incoming troops had definitely noticed the pretty 3-year-old brunette. Her "uniform" sported the dogtags and insignia that troops had given her, and she also wore a cross, a present from another grateful soldier.

As Amy snuggled in her mother's right arm and waved a hand at the smiling mothers and grandmothers who stopped and chatted with her, a gleaming red-and-white 747 gracefully descended onto the BIA runway. United Airlines Flight 6460, carrying almost 400 Marines and sailors on their way home to Cherry Point Marine Corps Air Station, landed at 11:10 a.m.

The plane taxied along the tarmac and swung toward the terminals. Cheering swelled from a few hundred throats as a Marine thrust himself through the open hatch above the cockpit, slid a pole through his hands, and unfurled an American flag that caught in the breeze. The troop greeters went crazy with joy as the plane taxied past the terminal windows and buried its nose behind the obstruction afforded by Gate 2.

The noise gradually subsided as the civilians waited for the Marines to deplane. Perhaps 15 minutes passed before the official flagbearer standing beyond the double-glass doors shifted her position and moved toward the ramp.

Paul Revere could not have spread the word faster as the phrase, "The Marines are coming! The Marines are coming!" rippled through the domestic terminal. Barely had the first few desert "cammies" hove into view before people roared their approval.

The cheering extended even to those civilians standing at the far end of the wire. They could not see into the ramp.

In typical leatherneck fashion, the Marines ambled down the ramp and swept along the human barricade separating them from the airport chairs. Amy Alley received ample attention from the Marines, one of whom later explained that "she reminded me a whole lot of my own little girl."

A brave, but foolhardy, young, dark-haired woman ventured across the terminal carrying a box clearly stamped "Old Town House of Pizza." Four hungry Marines, their young faces beaming their happiness, spotted the box and shouted, "Pizza! Pizza!" Before the woman could reach her destination, the Marines zeroed in on her and her cargo.

She grinned from ear to ear and opened the box to reveal a hot pepperoni pizza.

The Marines took no prisoners.

UAL Flight 6460 brought home an Ellsworth boy, Sgt. Kenneth Wescott. A 1981 graduate of Ellsworth High School, he'd joined the Marines in November 1981. The day after Christmas 1990, he left for the Gulf with the Marines from the 2nd Amphibious Assault Vehicle Battalion.

"Yeah, we were really into the fighting," Wescott confirmed as his mother, Dorothy Lilly of Ellsworth, hugged him again and touched his cheek to remind herself that her son had come back, safe and whole.

"We went through Kuwait all the way to the border with Iraq," the sergeant said. His sisters, blond-haired Addie Wakefield and Debbie Pinkham, a brunette, both from Ellsworth, kissed his slightly fuzzy chin. Like their mother, they occasionally hugged their brother real tight, real close.

Another relative of Westcott's, his 5-year-old niece Jaime Pinkham, bashfully hung near her mother and didn't venture too close until her uncle reached out for a hug. Then the little girl dissolved into smiles and rushed into Westcott's arms.

"I knew they would be waiting for me." Westcott raised his voice above the din. "Oh, man, it's fantastic to be home! It feels great to be alive!"

Westcott knew that he'd land in Bangor before his plane left Jubail. As his family surrounded and continually touched him, he introduced a friend to his mother.

The unidentified Marine told her, "He talked about you the whole flight."

Trading his scalpel for an indelible pen, Navy Lt. Mike DelTerzo found himself swamped by autograph-seeking youngsters. The grinning, moustachioed doctor from Manhattan swirled his signature across one T-shirt, turned, and gladly signed another proffered shirt. DelTerzo had signed for a four-year tour with the Marines to pay off his medical scholarship. Assigned to the 2nd AAV Battalion, he'd left for the Gulf on a commercial airliner on Dec. 15, 1990. The plane landed at Jubail two days later.

"I spent about two weeks there," DelTerzo said. "Then we went into the desert. I can't tell you exactly where, but it was some place on the Saudi-Kuwaiti border."

His assignment probably handed DelTerzo the most homogenized patientload he would ever see in his life. "I had to make sure everyone was medically fit before we left the States," he said, "and I had to take care of them medically over there."

"Yeah," DelTerzo spoke louder to make himself heard over the din, "it's not every doctor who gets 400 or 450 healthy young men as his entire list of patients. That kind of eliminated some of the medical conditions I'd see in a stateside hospital."

The 2nd AAV Battalion accompanied the 2nd Marine Division during the war. The battalion pushed into Kuwait and remained about a month outside Kuwait City. Despite the fighting, DelTerzo treated no Americans at his aid station.

Reporting to DelTerzo were a Navy Reserve doctor and some 25 Navy corpsmen. During the second day of the ground war, "we checked out a group of Iraqis, who were later sent to the rear. Some line corpsmen treated Iraqi EPWs, too, about 20 in all."

DelTerzo later took a ride through the outskirts of Kuwait City. "The people were very happy and appreciative of us being there," he recalled. As their aircraft approached BIA that Thursday morning, "we had no idea about the greeting waiting for us here," he said, pausing a moment to autograph a young girl's sweatshirt. "We were told we'd hang out at the airport an hour or so," Del-Terzo commented. "At first, we didn't see anybody when we came into the terminal, up that corridor, I guess. Then we turned the corner, and everyone in Bangor must've been here, cheering for us. The enthusiasm gets you the most. People you don't even know meeting you, it's impressive."

Gunnery Sgt. Roy Boiette of Sarasota, Fla., had served in the Gulf as a platoon sergeant with the 2nd AAV Battalion. He contrasted the pleasantly wild greeting that he received in Bangor with a notso friendly homecoming at Los Angeles International Airport.

From 1966 to 1967, Boiette had served in Vietnam with the lst Marine Division. His year's tour completed, Boiette returned stateside through El Toro Marine Corps Air Station. "No one was there, no reception when we came in on a military flight," he recalled.

1st Lt. Susan Mitchell, an Army Reservist from Lanagan, Mo., went to the Gulf with the 129th Transportation Co.

Boiette went on leave through LA International, where his uniform attracted "some (antiwar) protesters (who) were scattered through the airport. We got into a discussion, a verbal disagreement, no physical stuff."

A generation later, a civilian airliner brought him home from his second war. "Just before we landed (in Bangor), the flight attendants told us there would be some sort of greeting," Boiette said.

"We were quite surprised, really surprised," Boiette admitted as he and Gunnery Sgt. Charles Adams of Jackson, Mich., stood in the safety zone provided by the entrance to the coffee shop.

Together, the Vietnam vets watched schoolchildren pursue Marines for their autographs, rank insignia, and dogtags. The powers-that-be still insisted that the kids not pester troops for souvenirs, but no one could catch the crafty children.

And no Marine could deny a wide-eyed 12-year-old an autograph or a souvenir. Signatures were free for the asking, and rank insignias could be found at the nearest BX.

"This is a helluva surprise," Boiette said. "We didn't expect this at all. We had no idea over there about this type of greeting at home."

UAL Flight 6460 soon reclaimed its human cargo and trundled down the runway for the flight to North Carolina. Yet another troop carrier, American Trans Air Flight 8152, landed at BIA at 3:35 p.m. The L1011 brought home a soldier who'd missed everything about life in the United States.

But she'd missed her family most of all.

The three-engined L-1011 taxied to the international terminal and disembarked about 250 passengers. They represented such diverse units as HHC, 18th Airborne Corps; HHC, 1st COSCOM; and the 507th Support Group.

The 129th Transportation Co. (Army Reserve) came from Osage, Kansas. 1st Lt. Susan Mitchell, a senior platoon leader with the 129th, hailed from Lanagan, Mo. She and two other soldiers formed the advance party for their company. Mitchell anticipated that if everything went well, the remaining 130 members of the company should fly home in a week.

Although the L-1011 would take them only as far as Pope Air Force Base in Fayetteville, N.C., Mitchell and her comrades would fly to Fort Riley, Kansas. "You know," Mitchell said, "home isn't too far from there."

The Pentagon activated the 129th Transportation Co. on Sept. 27, 1990. Warned about a month earlier that the company might see active duty, Mitchell reluctantly cancelled her plans to teach a second grade class scheduled to begin in September.

The job would have marked her first year as a teacher.

Instead, Mitchell flew to Saudi Arabia and ultimately went to war with Iraq. She sweated in the hot desert sun and shivered in the cold Saudi nights, wrote long letters home, and served her country well.

So did the other American women, perhaps 50,000 in all, who went to the Persian Gulf. For the first time in America's history, women fought and died in greater numbers than in past wars. While the news media detailed their stories, and amateur strategists who were safely barricaded in fireside armchairs debated their military worth, women repaired jet fighters and helicopters, attached bombs and rockets to those expensive aircraft, drove trucks on the MSRs, patched Americans who'd been injured in traffic accidents, flew helicopters and tankers and transports, and generally did their duty.

As she spoke about military life in Saudi Arabia, Mitchell waved aside any discussion about her military responsibilities. An attractive blond with a pleasant smile, she focused on life in Saudi Arabia as experienced by an American woman.

Mitchell savored the freedom that returning to the United States meant for her. "I missed America for several reasons, and one of them was because women are treated so different over there (in the Saudi kingdom)," she said.

Explaining that she intended no criticism of the Saudis, Mitchell detailed the culture shock encountered by American women soldiers. "A woman isn't allowed to talk to Saudi men, who wouldn't believe a woman's words without verification," she commented.

As a transportation company, the 129th naturally included trucks among its heavy equipment. Women soldiers could not travel together in a truck without a male soldier riding with them, if not driving, at least riding in the truck cab. "The Saudis don't permit their women to drive. A man must do the driving for them," Mitchell said.

"I think that seeing an American woman driving a truck with an American man in the front seat beside her was a difficult adjustment for Saudi men to make," she observed. "And seeing two women soldiers traveling alone was incomprehensible and just wasn't acceptable. We were also told that not letting women travel without a male soldier for company was a safety precaution."

She recalled an incident when a woman soldier from the 129th went into a Saudi town to buy parts and hardware. The woman wore a T-shirt and fatigue pants in public, not an unusual clothing arrangement in the United States, but a style forbidden in Saudi Arabia, where the women never appear in public without an escort, usually a male relative.

The religious police, the mutawa, came running within minutes and hustled the woman soldier out of sight, lest her appearance place inappropriate thoughts in the minds of Saudi women. The incident caused no lasting damage to the Saudi psyche, Mitchell chuckled, "because an American woman being picked up for wearing 'indecent' clothing wasn't an item that made the Saudi news."

"Ice cold milk, that's what I miss," Mitchell said, a smile brightening her face. "There was no real refrigeration over there, at least not where we were. Everything's just lukewarm.

"Oh, yeah, and there's no Coke, only Pepsi," she laughed. During the Gulf War, American commentators paid little attention to the fact that several years ago, some Arab countries (including Saudi Arabia) had initiated a boycott of Coca-Cola because of that company's trade relations with Israel.

Then Mitchell blinked several times, as if she fought back tears. "More than you will ever guess, I missed my family," she quietly said despite the racket surrounding her as she stood beside the gift table at BIA. "Oh, how I missed them."

Married for eight years, Mitchell and her husband had two daughters. Although she missed her oldest girl's fifth birthday on April 1, Mitchell intended to throw a combined bash for both children when the youngest turned two on May 24. "You bet it's going to be a big party!" she laughed.

Mitchell shook hands and bounced up the ramp after the PA system announced the first boarding call. She hoped to muster from the Army in a week, possibly before the 129th Transportation Co. came home en masse.

While soldiers poured up the ramp, the Red Cross volunteers manning the gift table introduced Mary Carter to the press. From Keesler Air Force Base in Mississippi, Carter was an American Red Cross staff member who'd left the United States in November 1990.

Assigned to do casework "somewhere out in the desert; to tell the truth, I'm still not sure where," Carter lived with American soldiers and provided a vital link with home.

She handled about 200 cases a week, from incoming requests for a loved one to return home on emergency leave, to meeting with lonely men and women who just wanted to talk. "I'm a civilian," Carter said. "We had to wear military uniforms with Red Cross emblems attached to them, but we're still civilians."

"For all those boys and girls over there, talking to someone who wasn't in the chain-of-command was important," she said. "You can't unload on your command sergeant or your captain - that's not the way the military does things - but you sure can unload your thoughts on a civilian who's sharing life in the desert with you.

"And it wasn't only men who needed to talk. The women did, too. They missed their husbands, their boyfriends, their kids. They just needed someone who'd listen," Carter stated. "That's what we were there for."

CONSIDER THE COST

Sometimes, you pay a high price to serve your country.

That price isn't always your life.

Early on Friday, April 19, Hawaiian Airlines brought a planeload of Marines into Bangor International Airport. The leathernecks, headed for Camp Lejeune in North Carolina, included many combat veterans, both active duty and Marine Corps Reserve.

On Nov. 30, 1990, the Pentagon activated the Marine Corps Reservists belonging to the 2nd Combat Engineer Battalion. The men from Bravo Co. reported to their reserve center in Roanoke, Va.

Staff Sgt. Muncie Hawks joined them there.

Hawks, who was employed at a state-operated mental health and retardation center, had completed a four-year tour with the Marines in 1978. Nine years later, he re-enlisted as a reservist and ultimately became a platoon leader in Bravo Co.

When the Pentagon summoned Bravo Co. to active duty, the Marines placed their civilian lives on hold. Hawks had no problem in leaving his state job. His farm presented a challenge, though.

For the last 10 years, Hawks had raised Herefords at his farm in Fancy Gap, Va. He relishes farming. Talking about soil, crops, and planting ignites a gleam in his eyes.

"I've lived in the city, but my preference is the country," Hawks explained. "Life's so different there, I can't describe it to you. My God, how I do love the country."

He asked his brother-in-law to look after the cattle and the farm while he was gone to Saudi Arabia. "I found out the day before I left that he had cancer," Hawks said. "That was bad news for the entire family."

Scheduled to leave Roanoke within 24 hours, Hawks "made a deal by phone with a certain buyer who'd already seen the cattle, to buy them. He knew the quality cattle they were." With that one call, Hawks bid good-bye to a decade's work in cattlebreeding.

Within a few weeks, Hawks arrived in Saudi Arabia, where the 2nd Combat Engineer Battalion was attached to the 2nd Marine Expeditionary Force. He described the battalion's mission as "the destruction or construction of whatever the infantry needs destroyed or built so it can advance."

The night the ground war started, the battalion was sent to blow holes in concertina wire and Iraqi minefields. Bravo Co. received the explicit mission to clear three lanes through the Iraqi defenses.

Hawks was assigned to the 3rd Platoon, a mechanized unit equipped with amtracs. These ungainly, but valuable vehicles carried single-shot line charges that, when fired across a minefield, would explode a clear lane through the mines.

Staff Sergeant Muncie Hawks of Fancy Gap, Va., was a Marine Corps Reservist sent to Saudi Arabia with the 2nd Combat Engineer Battalion.

Bravo Co. crossed into Kuwait after its four platoons fulfilled their assigned objectives. One platoon blew lanes through concertina wire; other platoons hit the minefields. According to Hawks, an amtrac in another platoon hit a mine. The explosion injured the crew. "I understood it (the mine damage) was a broken axle," he said. "The concussion coming through the metal tossed the Marines around a bit."

Marine engineers had tagged the minefields, so the 3rd Platoon knew where to fire its line charges. Hawks remembered the noise, a din shattered by whooshing rockets and the explosions from the line charges and incoming Iraqi artillery. The latter, fortunately, was notoriously inaccurate.

"Time was meaningless that night and the next day," Hawks said. "We knew our mission, but at each point in time (during the battle), the situation changed and was fluid...so you had to be flexible.

"The experience was more deadly when artillery shells were hitting 200 meters away," he recalled a particular moment in the struggle to breach the Iraqi defenses.

"We crossed into Kuwait and headed for Kuwait City," Hawks said. The Marines soon encountered the oil fires, a fiery hell "that was so bad, at times you couldn't see three feet in front of you.

"Most of that night, we breathed the musty, smoke-filled air. You could feel the black soot in the air or on your skin. There was nothing clean about it," Hawks vividly described the chaos out in the Kuwaiti desert.

A day or two later, "when we could finally see daylight, we could see the buildings of Kuwait City at least a thousand meters away," he remembered. "But, God Lord, all that oily smoke rising to the heavens over there. You really don't know what it's like until you've touched and smelled it."

By the time it reached the Kuwaiti capital, the 3rd Platoon captured some Iraqis and blew up damaged Iraqi tanks, armored personnel carriers and other tracked vehicles, and abandoned bunkers.

The 2nd Marine Expeditionary Force, comprising the 2nd Marine Division and its attached support elements, refrained from entering Kuwait City. The 1st Marine Expeditionary Force - the 1st Marine Division and its ancillary units - "occupied" the capital practically under the eyes of the 2nd MEF Marines. Arab troops, including ecstatic Kuwaiti tankers and infantry, followed the 1st MEF into Kuwait City.

Hawks and his comrades passed through the capital after they were recalled to Saudi Arabia in early March. As Bravo Co.'s amtracs rumbled along the streets, "we got to experience all the refugees there, the civilians, the kids, especially the kids standing there and waving to us," Hawks recalled.

Shifting his position in a vinyl airport chair, he tapped a finger on the chair's metal arm. "The experience...made you feel like you'd served a purpose. I'm not an emotional man, at least not emotional in the sense that I was that day.

"I'd never experienced anything like that in my life, the Arabs lining the streets and waving Kuwaiti and American flags," he said.

"Yeah, we realized that we'd done right, that maybe it was worth it all. I still feel that way, because the sight of those kids cheering and waving is strong in my mind," Hawks commented. "Did I get a lump in my throat? You bet."

Bravo Co. arrived in Jubail on March 4, 1991. Hawks lived there in a tent for the next six weeks, until an airliner flew him and 27 comrades home in mid-April. The battalion commander "had recognized us as an outstanding outfit and let us return early to Jubail. What ticked us off later, we were the advance party to Jubail, but we were the last ones to leave," Hawks growled.

"The regulars showed us a negative side of themselves, to praise us in one sense, and then to send us home last. We didn't appreciate that, not a bit, because it sort of reflected what the regulars, or some of them, at least, thought about reservists," he said.

On March 14, a Virginia court declared Hawks a single man and his wife a single woman. As he sat in the BIA domestic terminal, Hawks talked about the divorce and its implications without rancor or selfpity.

"Family life, sometimes it doesn't work out," Hawks sighed while leaning his head against his fisted right hand. He described returning home from a drill weekend in November 1989 and discovering that "everything was gone," including his family.

The divorce became final as Hawks passed his time in the Saudi desert and thought about home. "I came over here married, and I'm going back single," he said.

There remains the farm. The rich Virginia soil beckoned Hawks to come home, where the fertilizer should have been spread on the fields by March 1991. He did find someone to watch the farm and keep vandals off the property, but no one started the tractor and other equipment to keep the engine components lubricated. "I'm planning to buy more cattle," Hawks said, "but I'm afraid I'll have to pay big bucks for young heifers.

"Going home to an empty farm is a weird experience...I'm so used to all those cows standing out there in the fields. Hell, the grass will be knee-high by now, and it'll take a whole lot of work to cut it down," he groused. His glimmering eyes betrayed his excitement, however. If all went well, he'd be out of uniform within a week or two and be heading out to mow that tall grass.

"With the cattle gone, it's like 10 years of my life have gone down the tube," Hawks stated, "yet I've got the experience to start all over again."

SILVER STAR

His comrades saw only one set of footprints in the sand.

Lance Cpl. Mark Schrader believes the footprints didn't belong to him, but to God.

No matter who claimed the footprints, Schrader soon learned that he would possibly receive the Silver Star for the incident that happened where the footprints stopped in the Kuwaiti desert. A softspoken, self-effacing 24-year-old Tennessean blessed with an infectious grin, Schrader dismisses any honors due him. He points to his comrades and God as the true heroes that February night when the young Marine risked his life in a minefield.

The same Hawaiian Airlines L-1011 that brought Muncie Hawks into Bangor on April 19 also carried Mark Schrader, Marine Corps Reservist with Delta Co., 2nd Combat Engineer Battalion. While awaiting word on the HAL L-1011, which in airline parlance had suffered a "mechanical malfunction," Schrader talked about the events leading to the recommendation that he receive the second highest military honor afforded by the United States. On Dec. 2, 1990, Schrader and the other Marines from Delta Co. left their reserve center in Knoxville, Tenn., for Camp Lejeune in North Carolina.

"I'm straight out of boot camp almost," Schrader said, explaining that he'd joined Delta Co. less than a year earlier. He had graduated from boot camp at Parris Island in June 1990 and then completed combat training at Camp Lejeune. He stayed there for a combat engineering school, which he finished on Sept. 5, 1990.

"While I was in (engineering) school, the (Gulf) crisis started," he recalled, "and I wasn't

A Marine Corps Reservist called to active duty with the 2nd Combat Engineer Battalion, Lance Corporal Mark Schrader of Knoxville, Tenn., was nominated for the Silver Star for his actions during the opening phase of the ground attack against Kuwait.

sure if we were going to go or not."

The unit did, flying from the United States in December. "That was my first Christmas away from home in 24 years," Schrader said. He landed in Saudi Arabia before the year ended.

Delta Co. deployed with the 2nd Combat Engineer Battalion to support the 2nd Marine Expeditionary Force. By nightfall on Feb. 23, the Tennessee Marines knew they were going to war. The order had come down from Centcom in Riyadh to invade Kuwait and Iraq.

Schrader and his platoon deployed aboard amtracs to the sand berm marking the border between Saudi Arabia and Kuwait.

The engineers would fire line charges to breach Iraqi minefields. Each amtrac towed a trailer that mounted several line charges. Basically a glorified rocket, a line charge drags a chain of explosives across a minefield. After the explosives detonate, vehicles cross the minefield in the narrow lane blasted by the line charge.

The Tennessee Marines discovered a problem with their equipment. "The line charges we were using had dates on them of 1968 through 1970. They were still functional, but everyone had their doubts," Schrader described the slightly outdated explosives.

Just in case a line charge failed to detonate, a Marine must explode it by hand, the officers informed their men. Any volunteers?

Schrader thought about the older Marines who had families, and the younger Marines still in college with their whole lives ahead of them.

"I figured I'd already had a good 24 years of life, and I didn't have any family to worry about," he said, shrugging his shoulders. "I decided that if someone had to run out and prime a line charge by hand, it should be me." He volunteered, but hoped that the line charges would work.

"When we got to the line of departure, it really hit me that this isn't going to work," Schrader said, referring to the antiquated line charges, "and I realized I might die."

Other Marines shared similar thoughts that Saturday. The members of Schrader's squad held an impromptu prayer service beside their amtrac. Their platoon guide, a Catholic, "had brought some holy water with him, and he sprinkled everybody," Schrader said. A Southern Baptist himself, Schrader found the Catholic rite meaningful.

"I don't think anybody slept that night," he said. "We were doing a whole lot of thinking. I guess everybody does that before the battle starts."

By 4 a.m. on Sunday, Feb. 24, the Marines had moved their amtracs to the berm. Despite the light protective armor afforded by the vehicles, the Marines wore their MOP suits, but left the helmets off. Everyone expected to encounter chemical weapons.

Then the ground war opened with a terrifying barrage from artillery and rocket tubes.

The amtrac next to Schrader's fired its line charge. As the crew expected, the rocket flew from its trailer, arced straight over the amtrac, and landed in the minefield. The resulting explosion cleared a path through the hidden mines. Then amtrac 4-4, which sheltered Schrader and his squad, fired its line charge next.

The explosives didn't go off.

A Marine inside the track pumped the detonator by hand. When the line charge didn't blow on the third pump, Schrader sensed his comrades looking at him. He believes that he swallowed real hard before stepping through the rear door of the amtrac to search for the line charge. He discovered that not only had the line charge failed to detonate, it had angled to the left after it fired. Even worse, it had landed outside the zone previously cleared by another line charge.

Schrader remembers crossing about 10 feet of the blackened sand that marked the cleared zone. Then he dashed across 30 meters of undisturbed sand, where mines awaited a careless foot.

By the dawn's early light, Schrader spotted what he described as "bean cans" sticking up through the sand. Since these "cans" marked Iraqi mines, he avoided them and safely reached the line charge.

Schrader poked a hole in a brick of C-4 (an explosive) that was attached to the charge, stuck two blasting caps "and 30 seconds worth of timed fuse in it, pulled the igniter - and then you have to run for your life."

Schrader ran back across the Iraqi minefield to Amtrac 4-4, where his adrenaline gave out. "My legs suddenly went so weak I couldn't climb inside," he recalled. Other Marines hauled him into the amtrac just before the line charge exploded. At the time, Amtrac 4-4 could not move forward or backward. Too wide a gap in the minefield lay between the amtrac and the passage cleared by the faulty line charge. During the opening barrage, an M60 tank equipped with a plow had driven along a cleared passage behind, and then around, the amtrac. The "snow bank" left by the plow tank contained unexploded mines and effectively sealed Amtrac 4-4 in place.

"We were boxed in," Schrader said. A while later, another M-60 plow tank passed by and tried to clear a path through the minefield to the passage left by Schrader's line charge.

That plow tank promptly hit a mine, shed a tread, and rumbled to a halt. No crewman was injured by the explosion.

While they waited for someone to tow them from the minefield, the tankers studied the terrain and noticed where Schrader's footprints crossed the sand. Meanwhile, two other Marines used C-4 and blasting caps to blow a hole in the mine-laden dirt bank behind Amtrac 4-4, which soon went on its way.

The crewmen from the damaged M-60 caught up with Schrader later. "They told me I was either the stupidest or luckiest Marine alive," he said, smiling shyly. "They said they counted seven mines and some trip wires along my footprints." The grin vanished as Schrader said, "I didn't see any trip wires."

Afterwards, the squad members talked about the incident. Someone mentioned the poem "Footprints in the Sand," in which God walked beside the writer on a beach. Looking back, the writer noticed only one set of footprints at times and asked God why He'd left him alone in times of trouble. God reminded the poet that the single set of footprints marked the times "when I carried you." "It was obviously not my footprints that went through there," Schrader said, referring to the minefield.

A deeply religious Christian who disagrees with his denomination only on the issue of occasionally drinking a beer or two, Schrader said that he prayed for God's protection after volunteering to detonate a defective line charge - even after dark, when he could not see the mines.

"Hopefully, the Man Upstairs would look after me in the same way, and everything would be all right," he said. His bravery soon brought Schrader unaccustomed acclaim. A Capt. Cunningham, Delta Co.'s executive officer, subsequently recommended him for a Silver Star, and a reporter from Time Magazine interviewed the young Marine. He was also interviewed for a documentary to be shown later that year on national public television. An actor portrayed him in a made-for-TV movie called "The Heroes of Desert Storm."

When his unit landed at BIA, Schrader was not sure that he would be awarded the

Silver Star. "It's medal enough for me being here in one piece," he said, with a smile.

Within a half hour, the airport PA system announced that because of the mechanical malfunction, the HAL L-1011 could not leave Bangor for several hours. The troop greeters who'd remained at the airport cheered as the tinny voice speaking over the PA told the Marines to anticipate a 10-to-12-hour delay in the Queen City.

Local officials scrambled to find sufficient motel rooms for the Marines. Luxuriant motorcoaches from Cyr Bus Line in Old Town lined up outside the international terminal and soon transported the leathernecks to motels scattered across Bangor.

Although many tired Marines slept that Friday away between clean sheets - an amenity seldom found in the desert - other Marines took to the roads as guests of local residents. A lucky few went to Acadia National Park and even sampled lobster, a delicacy by local standards.

By midafternoon, many Marines staying at the Bangor Motor Inn on the Hogan Road drifted to the Bangor Mall and shopped its myriad stores. Delighted civilians treated the pleasantly surprised leathernecks to all the ice cream and soda they could consume, until, as one Marine commented when he returned to the airport, "I felt I could burst."

The civilians who welcomed the Marines at the Bangor Mall included Canadians from New Brunswick and Nova Scotia. Proud that their air force and navy had gone into action alongside the other Allies during the Gulf War, the Canadians greeted the Marines as warmly as did the American shoppers.

Later that afternoon, Muncie Hawks, Mark Schrader, and the other Marines flew home to another warm welcome at Camp Lejeune.

MOVING THE MAIL

Soldiers always grouse about mail delivery. 2nd Lt. Rhena Williams did something about their complaints.

At 4:40 p.m. on Friday, April 19, a rare World Airways jet landed at Bangor International Airport. Bound for Wright-Patterson Air Force Base in Ohio and the airport at Milwaukee, Flight A18239 carried home more than 200 Midwesterners who'd served their country in the Persian Gulf.

Between 400 and 500 people packed the wire to greet the soldiers. As the WOA passengers poured into the domestic terminal and plugged the ramp, a soldier formed a V with his fingers and held them aloft. Roaring its approval, the crowd drowned out the two-man band providing the music for the occasion. Startled by the thunderous din, the musicians stopped playing. The crowd cheered again.

More soldiers worked their way along the wire. Here and there, a soldier surreptitiously slipped from the line and made his way to a pay phone or the Red Baron Lounge. Those first words spoken long distance by a loved one, or that first sip of a cold beer drunk on American soil: Everyday pleasures in the United States, but not in Saudi Arabia.

Responding to their camouflage-clad fans who chug-a-lugged beers and cheered the music, the two civilians playing the electronic keyboard and the drums enthusiastically performed "In Kuwait, there is no beer, so that's why we drink it here."

The soldiers shouted, lifted Budweisers and Millers ceilingward, and bellowed, "In Saudi, there is no beer, so that's why we drink it here." Later verses added the words, "In Iraq, there is no beer..." Someone later claimed to hear references to no beer in Iran or an obscure town in Wisconsin. The soldier who allegedly sang the alternate verses never identified himself, the civilian explained.

As the soldiers sang with the band, 2nd Lt. Rhena Williams and a few other soldiers stood outside America To Go, the shop nearest the skywalk to the Bangor Hilton. Young girls who had identified Williams as a woman officer sought her autograph. Beseiged by children ranging in age from kindergarten to middle school, Williams slowly moved back against the wall, until she encountered a stamp machine.

Brought up short by a symbol of her military profession, Williams talked about her war as she diligently signed another autograph. Assigned to the 1015th Postal Unit of the Indiana Army National Guard, Williams was attending a postal supervisor's course at Fort Benjamin Harrison, Indiana, when Iraq invaded Kuwait in August 1990. Life immediately changed for the National Guardsman.

The course director "told us about the invasion and said that we could expect to be getting some calls soon," Williams recalled. "You could hear a pin drop in that room after he said that."

The call that came for Williams on October 19, 1990 took her far from her home and family in Gary, Indiana, and her civilian job as a computer programmer for the Veterans Administration. The 1015th processed into the Army at Fort Benjamin

Harrison, left the States on November 2, 1990, and landed in Dhahran two days later.

The 120 members of the 1015th Postal Unit supported the 82nd and 101st Airborne Divisions and the 3rd Armored Cavalry Regiment. Of the unit's five platoons, three went with the 101st; a detachment of 1-1/2 platoons went to the 82nd; and a half platoon followed the 3rd Cav.

Williams commanded the detachment - the only postal detachment assigned to the 82nd Airborne Division, one

Second Lieutenant Rhena Williams of Gary, Ind., a member of the illinois Army Guard's 1015th Postal Unit, faced the daunting task of matching mail with troops all over Saudi Arabia.

of the first combat units sent to Saudi Arabia. From Dhahran, her detachment "went up north to right on the border, then went into Iraq where we could watch the enemy walk up to us," Williams said.

Along the way, the Indiana Guardsmen handled thousands of tons of mail. "We got a lot of mail; boy, did we ever," Williams said, sighing deeply and shaking her head at the memory. "We were averaging a couple of tons of mail a day."

Occasionally, four or five semi-trailers delivered incoming mail for the 82nd Airborne Division. "Our workdays depended on how much mail we got. We worked until all the mail was processed," Williams said. Twelve- to 14-hour days were not uncommon.

The volume of outgoing mail varied. Before the air war started in January, the paratroopers of the 82nd Airborne were told that "anything they couldn't carry when we moved up north had to be shipped home," Williams recalled. The mail volume immediately increased; the postal detachment soon shipped four or five truckloads a day.

The 1015th functioned as a full-service post office, cancelling and sorting outgoing mail, delivering incoming mail, and even selling stamps. Williams recalled a two-or three-day period just as the air war started when she sold $120,000 in stamps. Since the paratroopers paid postage only for outgoing packages and sent their letters home free of charge, those "stamps covered a lot of stuff going out in cardboard boxes," Williams said. "Not that they didn't write home. When the bombing started, the soldiers got real serious about their letter-writing," she said. "There was another upswing (in outgoing mail) the closer we got to crossing the border (in late February)."

Incoming mail presented a separate challenge from homebound mail. After sorting the mail by units, the Indiana soldiers had to find the outfits; given how often the various components of the 82nd Airborne shifted position, finding the paratroopers often meant sending trucks all over the desert.

Various transportation companies, including some solely dedicated to carrying mail, did the roadwork for the 1015th. "The mail trucks would usually roll in three times a day," Williams said. "We never knew how many trucks were coming in. We'd expect three, maybe, and then we'd stand outside and count three, four, five, or six trucks rumbling towards us. The more the trucks, the more the work for us, but we sorted every bit of mail that came to us."

Williams occasionally dispatched postal teams to serve as temporary post offices for 82nd Airborne units that "were on the move and couldn't get back to us."

The paratroopers eagerly awaited their mail. Williams described the deep disappointment that she saw in a soldier's eyes when he received no mail from his family. "I could just feel his hurt, it was so obvious," she said.

Yet, thanks to countless American civilians, no soldier ever went long without mail. "We received a lot of `Any Soldier' mail, too," Williams said. To answer the myriad letters that arrived from strangers, the Army provided a standard reply form. A paratrooper answering an "Any Soldier" letter would write a personal message on the form, address it, sign it, and give it to the postal detachment. "We shipped them (the reply forms) in the thousands," Williams said.

Yet a stranger's words never fully substituted for those written by a loved one. Many mail shipments dallied en route to the Gulf. "If they (the military) had equipment, replacement parts, or food that had a higher priority, the mail would be bumped off the plane and left at whatever airport along the way," Williams said.

From the helter-skelter manner in which letters arrived from the States, a soldier might read a reference to a previous letter that he had not received. The soldier would file a claim for the missing letter, only to see it arrive later. And some mail arrived addressed to the wrong APO.

"It's just like back home," Williams explained. "If you send a letter to the wrong address, it won't arrive on time, if at all."

Williams brought her soldiers back to Dhahran in late March. The Indiana Guardsmen learned that they would fly home on April 6. That date was postponed to April 15, moved to April 20, and finally confirmed for April 19. Williams and her comrades flew out aboard the WOA jet, which refueled in Rome, Shannon, and Bangor. As she shook hands with people standing along the wire at BIA, Williams caught a Butter Bar tossed to her by someone in the crowd. She suspected the gift came from a military-wise teen-age girl. The candy "obviously referred to my second lieutenant's bar, which we call a `butter bar,'" Williams said.

"I won't be wearing it much longer, though. I'm being promoted to first lieutenant in May," she pointed out.

While an airport official announced the first boarding call, Williams signed an autograph and said that the 1015th would deplane at Wright-Patterson Air Force Base before boarding a bus for Fort Benjamin Harrison.

"We couldn't imagine when this day was coming; we couldn't wait. I just missed my third wedding anniversary in January over there," Williams said. The mother of a 12-year-old, she explained that she took care of her brother's son.

"I've missed them all," Williams quietly said.

Near Williams sat Spec. Angie Freeland, another member of the 1015th. As the airport employee announced the second boarding call, Freeland struggled to rise from her seat. Once upright, she leaned on her crutches and limped to join Williams. A combat wound? "No, oh, no!" a smiling Freeland replied. Less than two hours before the Indiana soldiers boarded their airliner, "I injured myself in a game of combat volleyball," Freeland said. "It's just a hairline fracture and sprain in my right ankle."

"Combat volleyball!" Williams laughed. "We almost left her behind, we wanted to leave so badly. But, she made it to the plane in time, not that we would actually fly out without everyone along."

APACHE WARRIOR

When the United States sent more than 500,000 troops to fight in the Persian Gulf, their ranks included people drawn from most racial and ethnic groups found in the country. Troop greeters would one day recall the black soldier named Blue, the white soldier named Green, and the other troops whose facial characteristics and name tags attested to a magnificent multicultural diversity.

American Indians, called "Native Americans" by politically correct thinkers, also went to war with their anglo, black, and hispanic comrades.

About 50 sleepy-eyed civilians wandered into Bangor International Airport about 4 a.m. on Saturday, April 20, a day that promised warm sunshine and breezes. The half-awake visitors had come to meet people arriving on two flights.

According to schedule, United Airlines Flight 3858 landed at 4:30 a.m. while en route to Cherry Point Marine Corps Air Station. Hawaiian Airlines Flight 860 would supposedly land about 5:10 a.m. while on its way to Pope Air Force Base.

Separate destinations, but found in the same state: North Carolina. The first destination spelled Marines; the second destination indicated soldiers - probably.

Yawning and stretching, the troop greeters parked their cars out on Godfrey Boulevard and entered the domestic terminal beneath God's handiwork. Stars sparkled in the cold, clear night sky.

"Good morning, how are you," the civilians mumbled to each other. The smart ones found a spot on the stanchioned wire that still separated civilians and military. Other people wandered into the coffee shop for a jolt of caffeine.

Eyes snapped wide open when 400 Marines and sailors left the UAL 747 and occupied the domestic terminal. For an almost hour, the leathernecks and their Navy corpsmen mingled easily with the civilians who really could not explain why they'd awakened so early on a spring Saturday. "Anyone in their right mind would still be sleeping," a woman said.

Navy Hospital Corpsman 1st Class Tom Bradford didn't think these civilians were crazy. Having stopped about 1,000 miles northeast of his hometown of Augusta, Ga., he didn't mind in the least that a gray-haired woman old enough to be his mother wanted to pin a yellow ribbon on him.

Bradford had left for the Gulf about five months earlier with Alpha Co., 2nd Medical Battalion, 2nd Marine Expeditionary Force. He'd traveled "up close to the Kuwait-Iraq border" before the fighting had ended in late February.

"I'm glad to be home," said Bradford, who eagerly anticipated a reunion with his wife and their two children. "It's great to have the support of all you folks here. We really appreciate your coming out and meeting us."

The war called another corpsman, Chris Moreno, far from his home in Baxter

Navy Corpsman Chris Moreno is a full-blooded Apache from Baxter Springs, Kansas. He went to war with a Marine Corps outfit.

Springs, Kansas. The Rand-McNally Road Atlas places Baxter Springs, a town of about 5,000 people, in the southeastern corner of Kansas, near the intersection of Routes 66 and 166.

Missouri lies just to the east, while Quapaw, Okla., lies just to the south. In fact, "if you go across the street (a dirt road delineates the Kansas-Oklahoma border south of Baxter Springs), you're in Oklahoma," Moreno said.

Standing about 5-foot-6, maybe 5-foot-7, the solidly built Moreno plopped into a chair near the Red Baron Lounge and discussed his role in the Gulf War with a reporter from the Bangor Daily News. A few friends kidded the 24-year-old corpsman about "talking to the press...tell the truth...tell 'im what kind of war heroes we are!"

Moreno, a full-blooded Apache, shipped for the Gulf on Christmas Eve 1990. "Wasn't exactly the way I'd planned to spend my Christmas, but what can you do?" he asked, attempting to stifle a grin. "We go where they send us. It's part of the job. Heck, we were preparing to leave about three weeks before that at Camp Lejeune." Since 1987, he'd been assigned with the so-called "8th & I" Marines in Washington, D.C. These leathernecks guard the White House, the Pentagon, even the Presidential helicopter. Duty in Washington wasn't too tough, Moreno said. In December 1990, the Navy transferred Moreno to Delta Co., 2nd Medical Battalion, the same battalion to which Bradford belonged. By New Year's Day, Moreno found himself learning to live with the sand in Saudi Arabia.

The 2nd Marine Expeditionary Force moved to the Saudi border with Kuwait and dug in across the berm from the defending Iraqis. Many Marines could sense the growing tension just before the air war started on Jan. 17, Moreno recalled. "When we heard the jets go overhead, and later on we could hear the explosions, we knew that it had begun. We almost felt like we were relieved, because it (the war) was finally under way," he said.

He described the 2nd Medical Battalion as a collection-and-clearing unit that accompanied the Marine infantry "all the way to Kuwait City."

During the 100-hour ground war, the battalion treated about 750 captured Iraqis and some 100 allied casualties, including some British soldiers. The Navy battalion initially treated the Allied wounded, then shifted to assist a field hospital that was treating POWs, Moreno said. "They were kind of busy when we got there. The Iraqis had a lot of wounded. We got more allied wounded after the ceasefire, especially from all the booby traps the Iraqis had left laying around."

Many Iraqis suffered from malnutrition or war wounds. One POW described how he'd been yanked off a street in a southern Iraq city and sent to Kuwait in a truck and without any equipment, Moreno stated. "Their condition was pathetic at times...some Iraqis were giving money to people to let them surrender."

He discovered that the Iraqi Republican Guards "were much better equipped than the regular grunts in the front lines. They (the Republican Guards) were like our Marines, but I can't put them up to our level. We're Marines. They never will be." The hungry Iraqi POWs "really liked MREs (Meals, Ready to Eat), which might be saying something for their diet in the weeks between the air war and the ground war," Moreno said.

"We ate MREs a lot, but I can't say that many people were crazy about them," he chuckled. Fortunately for the hungry Marines and Navy personnel assigned to the 2nd Medical Battalion, a nearby Marine field kitchen often served them hot meals.

"You know, it feels great to be on my way home," Moreno said. He grinned again as a Marine leaned over the vinyl-covered airport chair and whispered quietly in his ear.

Moreno laughed, and a broad smile spread across his face. "Yeah," he said, "I can't describe what it feels like, sitting here in this airport and hearing American being spoken again. I missed so much of America, the language, the food, the cars. I don't care if I see a desert or a camel again."

He wanted to talk about his life outside the Navy. Raised not far from an Apache reservation, Moreno proudly reflected on his Indian heritage. He took a pen in hand and wrote his Apache name, "Flihute Ouwa Tushita," in a notebook.

Then Moreno spoke his name in Apache and chuckled as the reporter tripped over the Indian words. "I wouldn't expect you to get the pronunciation right the first time," Moreno smiled. "In Apache, it means `Eagle Over Falling Water.' We look at the eagle as the mighty bird" and at falling water "as the falling or rushing wind. We attach great importance to our names," Moreno said.

The young Marine was planning a special homecoming. A far-away look slipped into his dark eyes as he said, "My girlfriend, that's Regina, I'm getting ready to ask her for her hand. I really missed her over there. She's a big reason why I'm so happy to be home."

Even as Moreno talked about the 2nd Medical Battalion, Hawaiian Airlines Flight 860 landed at BIA. The L-1011 brought home the soldiers of the Fort Bragg-based 5th Mobile Army Surgical Hospital, the outfit with which Fred Rice II and Rod Christoffer had served during the Gulf War.

Until airport personnel sorted them out a while later, the incoming soldiers and out-going Marines blended together in the terminal. A few soldiers even gathered to shake hands with the leathernecks, who soon reboarded their L-1011.

Staff Sgt. Marc Miller, an eight-year Army veteran, said that he came from Las Vegas, Nev. A respiratory therapist who'd been educated in the Army, he arrived in Saudi Arabia on Oct. 1, 1990. "The 5th MASH was in Dhahran when I got there," Miller said. On Dec. 12, 1990, the soldiers packed up their medical gear before driving to King Khalid Military City and re-establishing the hospital.

Miller recalled that on Valentine's Day, the 5th MASH moved to a staging area "six kilometers south of the Iraqi border, where we waited for the ground war to start," he said.

The medical personnel sensed the massive military buildup occurring around them, Miller stated. Jet aircraft and helicopters overflew their positions often, "sometimes almost all the time," he said. "We knew they were bombing the Iraqis, but there seemed to be more overflights than we'd expected."

The 5th MASH supported the 24th Infantry Division (Mechanized) during that outfit's blitz into Iraq. Unlike Fred Rice II, who went with the Forward Surgical Element when the 5th MASH divided, Miller accompanied the main hospital. "We usually stayed in the divisional support area," he said.

According to Miller, the 5th MASH reached a point "within 40 kilometers of the Euphrates River. There was some talk about going all the way to Baghdad, but when the president declared the ceasefire, we stopped where we were."

Col. Ken Steinway, commanding officer of the 5th MASH, said that the Army medical personnel treated about 80 Iraqi prisoners and some 11 Americans, including three soldiers who had died. He related the horrible results, from a medical officer's point-of-view, of an incident involving some Americans who were playing with a live grenade that finally exploded.

The 5th MASH treated more than 11,000 patients, Steinway said in confirming the figure provided by Fred Rice II. "We were the second hospital in-country, so we were busy from the moment we arrived," he said.

The hospital staff included 16 physicians, two general dentists, and an oral surgeon, as well as nurses and other medical specialists. "At times, our hospital was full," Steinway recalled. "We were averaging 40 to 45 in-patients a day in a 60-bed hospital.

"I'm proud of these men and women," the colonel stated. "We were working under less-than-pristine conditions in a very unfriendly atmosphere. These people are true professionals. Before we finished our work there, we convoyed the hospital 1,500 miles and set it up five times."

Asked about the legendary "Convoy From Hell," Steinway said, "It's true, every word of it. We swept around the Iraqi flank and well into their country. It was 36 hours of non-stop driving through storms, both rain- and dust storms, on roads that were only two lanes, under blackout conditions (no headlights)."

HAL Flight 860 also brought home Sgt. Vernon Brissette. Down East vernacular identified him as a "Maine boy" from Perham, a town with a population of less than 500 people located due west of Caribou. A Vietnam veteran who had graduated from Washburn District High School in 1969, Brissette worked for the Postal Service as a letter carrier in Presque Isle. He also served in the 1125th U.S. Army Hospital (Army Reserve) in Bangor, with an MOS of operating-room technician. The job kept him busy in the Gulf. The Army summoned Brissette to active duty on Jan. 8. He left for Saudi Arabia on Jan. 20 and arrived there a day later. Other reservists from the 1125th traveled to the Gulf, too, where the military in its infinite wisdom spread them among various units. Vernon Brissette joined the 5th MASH and accompanied that hospital on its wild advance into Iraq, where he helped treat some Iraqi prisoners.

Then word came that the 5th MASH was going home. Brissette drove with other soldiers to the airport in Saudi Arabia and flew out with Hawaiian Airlines. He assumed he'd fly straight to Fort Bragg, process out of the Army, and head home.

When the L-1011 landed to refuel in Athens, Greece, the flight crew told the soldiers that they'd be landing in Bangor. "I couldn't get off the plane to call!" Brissette recalled. "They wouldn't let us off the plane there, something to do with terrorist threats, supposedly."

When he landed at Shannon International Airport in Ireland, Brissette rushed to a telephone and called his wife, Jane. "It was late at night at home, but I had to talk to her," he said with a smile.

"You know how it is when you miss someone real bad," he explained. "All you want is to hear her voice again."

Brissette proudly talked about Jane and their three children, 9year-old Joshua, 8-year-old Elizabeth, and 3-year-old Cyrus. "I can't wait to see them again," he said.

Circumstances prevented a family reunion in Bangor. The four-hour flight time from Ireland roughly equated the drive from Perham, which cut too close the margin for Jane and the children to come to Bangor. "I felt kind of bad I was four hours, 200 miles from home, and I couldn't see my family," Brissette admitted. "It's a heckuva long drive, especially in the middle of the night with three young children. I should be home in a week or so. I'll see them then." Although his family could not meet him at BIA, the troop greeters sure did. When they discovered a Maine boy in their midst, the older women descended on Brissette, pinned yellow ribbons and other souvenirs to his uniform, and hugged him.

As the welcoming crowd swirled around him, Brissette thought back to his homecoming from Vietnam. "When we landed at San Francisco (International), there was no one there to greet us," he said. "We got off the plane, changed into civilian clothes, and headed home."

In 1991, "the whole plane just did a big cheer, with all sorts of shouting and clapping when we landed here (in Bangor). It felt good to hear the greeting when we got into the terminal. It was just incredible," Brissette said.

THE BEAR IN THE HELMET

George Nye once swore that never again would homecoming American troops receive the inadequate greeting that he endured while heading stateside from Vietnam. He'd turn out and meet the boys and girls in Bangor even if he were the only person there. If the weather tempted him otherwise, he never told anyone.

By mid-morning on Saturday, April 20, the brilliant sunshine and warming temperatures lured many Bangor-area residents outdoors, whether to watch the annual Kenduskeag Stream Canoe Race or to rake the lawns mauled by the previous winter - or just to be outdoors.

The smaller-than-usual crowd that gathered at BIA by 10:30 a.m. reflected the good weather. For the first time, troop flights competed with other interests for attention. With the novelty wearing thin, many people opted to pursue those other interests.

About 300 people still turned out to cheer the late-arriving Tiger Brigade, actually the 1st Brigade of the 2nd Armored Division, General Patton's old "Hell On Wheels" outfit from World War II.

The troop greeters included the students from the North Orrington School Fifth Grade Band. While not as well-balanced musically as other, older bands, the fifth-graders ardently played their music under their director's guidance. Adults standing near-by winced whenever the young musicians struck a sour note. Later, despite outspoken concern that the off-notes would embarrass the entire crowd, the soldiers indicated that they loved the music and the kids.

Many people arriving to meet United Airlines Flight 6464 learned that Hawaiian

Airlines Flight 838 planned to land about noon.

The UAL 747 touched down at 10:42 a.m. and taxied to the international terminal. The North Orrington School band launched into patriotic music, replete with squeaky clarinets and flat brass notes. People waiting for relatives on UAL Flight 6464 lined the lower ramp. A brunette wearing a white sweatshirt inscribed with the word "peace" stood by a plate-glass window and nervously fidgeted with a sign that read, "Stop here, Pfc. Braddy, Sgt. K. Nash." Next to the woman awaited other people, including a middle-aged man sporting a dark baseball cap that proclaimed, "Desert Storm, Persian Gulf." He, too, held a sign, one that told "Bernie Trott, Here's Your Family." The man's wife announced that they had come from Greenfield, Mass., to meet their son. She also wore a white sweatshirt, but hers read, "Operation Desert Storm: Support the Troops."

Then the soldiers poured down the ramp and into the terminal. The World War II vets who recognized the 2nd Armored's triangular shoulder patch cheered loudly.

Spec. Duane Elliott of Copperas Cove, Texas, had gone to the Gulf with the 1st Battalion, 3rd Field Artillery Regiment, 2nd Armored Division. According to Elliott, the 1st Battalion operated M-109 selfpropelled howitzers that fired 155 mm. shells.

The battalion, assigned to the media-mentioned Tiger Brigade that supported the 2nd Marine Division during its assault on Kuwait, "provided fire support with our 155s and with our MLRS's (Multiple Launch Rocket Systems) to prep the battlefield the day before the war started and on our way into Kuwait," Elliott said.

The artillerymen moved fast to keep up with the Tiger Brigade, he said. "We ended up just outside Kuwait City and stayed there for some time." Lt. Col. James Kerin, the battalion commander, pegged the stay near the Kuwaiti capital at 32 days.

On April 20, 1991, Norma Smart of the American Legion Auxiliary served as the colorguard for the soldiers of the 8th Battalion, 101st Aviation Regiment, 101st Airborne Division.

"We thought the day would never come that we'd get on the plane," Elliott grinned, "and now it's here. I've been gone for six months, two days, and I can't wait to get home. I missed the American way of life the most. Yeah, that's what I missed, especially a nice cold beer. I want to get home and take a few days off and relax." Elliott, who said that he worked in ammunition supply, reported that he'd be leaving the Army on Feb. 20, 1992. Serving in the military has been an education and an experience, he stressed, "and I wouldn't trade what I've done, but I'm a civilian at heart." Someone's family suddenly surrounded him on the ramp and cried as the young man hugged and kissed people he hadn't seen in months.

A Tiger Brigade member with a Maine connection was Sgt. 1st Class Gary Rumney of Kileen, Texas. Also a member of the 1st Battalion, 3rd Field Artillery Regiment, Rumney said that he'd been in the Army for 17 years.

Elements of the 1st Battalion started leaving for Saudi Arabia in early August 1990, Rumney said, but "we went over heavy in October." The artillerymen went to Dammam first and "from there to the middle of nowhere up towards the Kuwaiti border."

He described the art of "prepping the battlefield" as firing 155 mm. rounds into the Iraqi lines. Rumney worked as a field-artillery surveyor who accurately sited the firing positions "so the gun crews knew exactly where it was."

According to Rumney, the field-artillery surveyors used the hightech surveying system known as the Global Positioning System (GPS). A network of orbiting satellites that beam navigational information to earth, GPS provided American soldiers with the ability to determine their location in the desert to within an accuracy of 30 meters. "We used to do surveying the traditional way, transits and poles, the whole works," Rumney said. "GPS took some getting used to, but we proved that it worked."

Meanwhile, down-cast eyes and a deep sigh from a member of the Trott family indicated that Bernie Trott had not landed aboard this plane. There would be another time. His turn would come.

As Rumney spoke, Girl Scouts circulated in the terminal, seeking autographs from the 2nd Armored soldiers. Lt. Col. Kerin then stepped to the lectern, grabbed the microphone, and praised his soldiers for their hard work in the Gulf.

"We had better equipment and people," Kerin said, and the 2nd Armored troops "went up against an enemy that didn't have the will to fight."

Many people, especially the soldiers, loudly groaned and protested when Kerin announced that even as the 1st Battalion was flying to Texas, the 2nd Armored Division was being deactivated. The "Hell On Wheels," which had been activated in 1940, would no longer exist in a few weeks.

Fortunately, the 1st Battalion was being transferred to the 1st Cavalry Division, Kerin said. The crowd cheered at this announcement, of course, then waited expectantly as the lieutenant colonel awarded the gathered Post 84 Legionnaires a coin bearing the dual insignias of the 1st Battalion and the 2nd Armored Division.

As Kerin and an older Legionnaire shook hands, the entire terminal erupted into thunderous applause.

Working his way from the lectern, Kerin spotted a local newspaper reporter who was talking to Rumney. "Tell your readers that we couldn't have had a better welcome back to the United States," Kerin urged.

Referring to a question posed by the reporter, Kerin explained a remark he'd made at the lectern. Because of its outstanding history, the 2nd Armored had earned its members the right to wear their divisional patch over their hearts. "No other Army division has been permitted this honor," the lieutenant colonel said.

Sgt. 1st Class Rumney reaffirmed his commander's statement, then proudly commented that even when part of the 1st Cav, the 2nd Armored vets could wear the "Hell On Wheels" patch on their right shoulders. Rumney said that only one man from his outfit had been wounded in Operation Desert Storm. He recalled that the battalion had fired in support of the Tiger Brigade during the battle for Kuwait International Airport. Although a blow-by-blow description of that massive armor engagement had not been released by the Pentagon, initial press reports indicated that Marine armor had destroyed more than 100 Iraqi tanks while losing only a few tanks of their own.

The 1st Battalion had returned to Saudi Arabia about three weeks earlier and moved into the infamous Al Khubar Towers. The artillerymen "found out three days ago for sure that we were leaving the desert for good," Rumney said.

While stationed overseas, he'd missed the birthdays of his wife, Nam, and their 12-year-old son, Gary II, and also missed his wedding anniversary. Rumney had written his family "as often as you can out there in the desert," and he discovered that "AT&T did a pretty good job, providing phone service in the field."

During his tour in Saudi Arabia, Rumney established a correspondence with a Maine girl, 11-year-old Kimberly Wayman. "Aw, heck, I've got her address out in my baggage on the plane," he muttered. "I think she lives in a town that begins with the letter "P." Portland? Palmyra? Presque Isle? Pittsfield?

"Pittsfield sounds right," Rumney replied. "I got her letter through the `Any Soldier' mail. We wrote back and forth, and I enjoyed her letters. I just want to tell her, `Hi.'

"I can't wait to get back to Texas," Rumney said. "We'll get two days off, then we'll stand a battalion formation, and then we'll get two weeks off. Yeah, time off, that's what we need. And this reception, it made me feel good to be an American again. Like the colonel said, tell everyone `thanks' for me."

By now, the fifth graders from the North Orrington School had set down their instruments and gone after autographs. Two soldiers eyed the snare drums, silently reached an understanding, and stepped across the wire. As some band members drifted back and watched, the camouflage-clad percussionists set their helmets and teddy bears on the window sill, seized some drumsticks, and launched into a driving rhythm that echoed through the terminal.

More people surrounded the drummers and listened to their music. Among the soldiers watching was Pfc. Darius Peak of Macon, Ga. Assigned to Charlie Battery, he worked in communications (field telephones and radios).

"I was very surprised to ship out, because I never really thought we were going to go over to Saudi Arabia," Peaks said. "It was something that needed to be done. I'm glad we did it now and not later." As the 2nd Armored troopers gradually wandered back into the ramp and, with approval from the Red Cross volunteers, plundered the gift table, one soldier discovered a bubble pipe in the gift pack he'd selected. Dipping the pipe in its solution, he happily blew large bubbles that drifted across the entrance to the ramp.

Another soldier, a Sgt. Robertson, placed his desert-camouflaged kevlar helmet upside down on the newspaper-vending machine beside the duty-free shop. Intent on finding a few more goodies on the gift table, Robertson set a teddy bear upright in the helmet.

Until the sergeant returned, his teddy bear stood quietly in the helmet, the critter's fuzzy fur contrasting sharply with the militaristic image presented by the well-worn headgear. A helmet whose wearer had seen death and destruction in Kuwait, traversed sandy wastes far from Texas, and flown more than 16,000 miles round trip since October 1990, shared the same space with a fuzzy buff teddy bear manufactured in Korea.

The brown-eyed, beribboned teddy bear, nothing more than an inanimate object: What use did Sgt. Robertson have with the critter? Did he intend the bear for a young child at home? So many troops claimed the bears for their children, whom they listed by name. Was that the sergeant's intention, to take home to a lonely child a teddy bear to call its own?

In those initial moments when he reached the gift table and spotted the stacked bears, did Sgt. Robertson realize that he'd crossed the demarcation line between war and peace? Did he know, did he care, that the teddy bears epitomized the homecomings in Bangor?

Near the restrooms across the terminal, two other soldiers broke into a comedy routine that also symbolized the 1st Battalion's homecoming. They stood at the water fountain, where one soldier pressed the button. As the water squirted, the other soldier pointed at the spout and cried, "Look! It's water coming up! Isn't this fantastic?" Then he leaned into the tumbling water, sipped it, and exclaimed, "It's cold! It's not out of a bottle! It tastes great!" "Look! Look!" the uniformed comedians called to their comrades. "Real cold water out of a fountain! This is great!"

Many 2nd Armored soldiers remained in the terminal as HAL Flight 838 touched down at 11:58 a.m. Civilians who were tempted to stay for that flight or to skip out to the canoe races debated their decision. When they heard that the incoming L-1011 carried mostly military dependents, perhaps 200 people slipped out the doors before the plane unloaded its passengers.

As he left the domestic terminal, Staff Sgt. William Kuhn of Rochester, N.Y., also claimed a connection to Maine. "My wife's the former Ramona Blake of Camden," he announced, and she still had relatives living there.

"She's still got aunts and uncles living there, the Marstons and the Blakes. If this gets into the paper, say 'hello' to them for me, will you?" Kuhn asked. Among the veterans who met the 2nd Armored troopers that Saturday was Nye, the quiet, soft-spoken commander of John F. Kennedy Chapter No. 6, Disabled American Veterans. Nye had practically lived at BIA for three months, meeting most troop flights and warmly welcoming home every Gulf vet that he met. But Nye reserved a special place deep in his heart for the soldiers wearing the horsehead patch of the 1st Cavalry Division. That morning, he winced and muttered "geez, what a shame" when Kerin announced the 2nd Armored's demise. When Kerin mentioned that the lst Battalion would join the 1st Cav, however, Nye brightened and said he couldn't think of a more appropriate outfit.

After graduating from Bangor High School, Nye had joined the Army in 1958. Seven years later, he volunteered for duty in Vietnam with the 8th Engineer Battalion, 7th Cavalry Regiment, 1st Cavalry Division. Nye and the division's advance party arrived at An Khe in early July.

As demolitions team leader, Nye initially passed his time "blowing up trees mainly, clearing LZs (landing zones), widening LZs." By fall 1965, Nye had seen combat all along Highway 19 in Binh Dinh Province in the Central Highlands. By the time he came home, Nye had earned a Silver Star, three Bronze Stars, and six Purple Hearts. He retired from the Army on August 1, 1975, then worked 15 years as a service officer for the DAV. After learning in March 1991 that Gulf vets would land in Bangor, Nye decided to meet them. He listed his reasons for doing so.

"One, because I was a career soldier in the Army, and felt it was my duty. I'm still committed to the United States Army," he said. "The other reason is, I don't want these kids to go through what the Vietnam veterans did when they came home...(the) shame (and) degradation of having people turn their backs on them.

"And also, it's the right thing to do," he said.

Nye and other homeward-bound soldiers arrived at the Army facility in Oakland,

Calif., in June 1966. "Some guys from Berkeley spit on us," Nye recalled, "and an altercation broke out." Ignoring the disorderly students, the police arrested the soldiers and jailed them in San Francisco for the night.

"That's what it was like coming home," Nye said. "I think we owe our young men better than that, and our young ladies...who served so well over there."

Never again, he affirmed.

Shaking hands with the returning Gulf troops "makes me think back to people I've lost," Nye quietly said. "It's very rewarding, (but) it brings back memories." He was pleased that so many Gulf veterans were coming home alive. He hoped they would not have to fight again. Nye acknowledged the reluctance felt by many Vietnam vets about meeting the Gulf vets at BIA, yet he expressed little patience with those veterans who criticized the homecomings. Describing such critics as people who "are probably cynical every day of their lives," Nye pointed out that "Vietnam doesn't have anything to do with these kids (the Gulf vets)."

Later, after the last "official" troop flight landed on May 22, Nye would wonder if later-arriving Gulf vets would receive the same reception as did those landing in the spring. His doubts dissolved into sheer pleasure when he realized that certain people, the "regulars" among the troop greeters, would not let the troops come home unheralded.

"The positive thing of it is the people themselves who love coming out here," Nye said. "People wanted to get that `old flag' feeling back. Patriotism is a good feeling now. It's (the troop flights) a very positive thing, and I'm going to do it until it's over."

Nye stood on the ramp and shook hands with the outgoing tankers from the 2nd Armored Division. The soldiers cleared the terminal before the HAL passengers disembarked from their aircraft. Perhaps 100 people waited to greet them.

Since so many women and children accompanied the few soldiers and sailors who left the L-1011, the greeting seemed ineffective. Worried about their families, especially the young children, the few military personnel aboard the airliner displayed little interest in the greeting that awaited them.

In fact, the HAL crew that had ferried the L-1011 and its passengers to Bangor received as loud an ovation as did the deplaning military personnel.

Because the HAL passengers had to clear customs, they entered the terminal as families, three, four, maybe five people at a time. More than 30 minutes passed with fewer than 50 or 60 passengers offloaded, so most civilians still waiting in the terminal headed for the exits, too.

A few hundred people returned later that afternoon when a KC-135 Stratotanker belonging to the 101st Air Refueling Wing, Maine Air National Guard, returned home with more than a dozen guardsmen who had served in Saudi Arabia.

The Maine boys appreciated the welcome they received.

HOLY MAN

Chaplain, meet chaplain. Not Charlie, but the military equivalent of a Christian holy man. Long before United Airlines Flight 6465 landed at Bangor International Airport at 5:05 a.m. on Sunday, April 21, people parked their cars and pickups on Godfrey Boulevard and walked into the terminals. A few people, those later called the "regulars," knew that in stormy weather they could reach the entrance to the international terminal slightly faster than the double doors to the domestic terminal. This morning, a middle-aged and bespectacled woman from Lewiston lay claim to her place behind a stanchion. "It's my second weekend of catching flights," she said. "I think this is my twelfth or so." Why did she travel 100 miles one way to meet so many flights? "Well, the real reason is, I'm waiting for my son," she sheepishly grinned. "He's with the headquarters battalion of the 2nd Marines, the division, I think.

"But, all this, it's very infectious," the woman commented, waving her hand toward the people standing beside her. "What I want is someone to be here to meet my son if I can't. And I want to be here to meet someone else's son or daughter when they can't."

A few yards from the Lewiston woman stood a man from Hampden, the town just south of Bangor. He was a Korean War veteran who estimated that he was meeting his 22nd or 23rd flight.

"I've been passing out flags and Maine postcards," the man said. "So far, I've given the troops about 150 flags and 20 or more teddy bears. I have three boys in the military. Fortunately, none of them went to the Gulf, but other people's children did. My boys volunteered, but I guess they weren't needed. I'd like to have someone here to meet them, so I'm here to meet someone else," he concluded. Farther along the wire, a 13-year-old girl who attended the Hichborn Middle School in Howland, a town about 30 miles north of Bangor, held a Dunkin Donuts' box in her hands and patiently awaited the UAL jet. Attending her sixth troop flight that morning, she was hoping to meet a friend, Ron Ireland, of Howland, stationed with the Army at Fort Polk, La.

He had gone to the Gulf as a Blackhawk pilot in a medical-evacuation company, the girl said. "If he's on this flight, don't talk to him about the helicopter and six people that his company lost after the war. Some of them were his friends. He doesn't know it, but his mom's waiting for him in Louisiana. It's a big surprise," she said. Then she grinned, blushed, and patted the doughnut box. "He likes doughnuts, so I brought him some. We're pretty sure he's on this plane. I sure hope he is. Everyone's excited about him coming home," she said.

Nearby stood another middle-aged woman who lived in Bucksport, a town standing at the entrance to the Penobscot River. "I've been here several times, maybe 10 or 15 flights," she announced.

"It's the best emotional high I've ever had in my life," the woman said, explaining her persistence in meeting the troops. "It's free, and just to think that all our boys are coming home, oh, I think it's so wonderful."

She did not like "those humongous big crowds in the middle of the day, so we hit the middle-of-the-night flights. Five in the morning is still nighttime for many people," she said.

Unlike other people at the terminal this morning, the Bucksport woman waited for no one in particular. "I want to meet just the whole kit and caboodle," she chuckled. "I want to hug every one of them and tell them how glad I am that they're home."

Elsewhere along the wire stood Kathleen Trott and the Trott clan, a rollicking, joking, excited group that included relatives from Manchester, Conn., and Calais over in Washington County.

Kathleen and her husband said that their son, Bernie, had gone to Saudi Arabia on Oct. 17, 1990, with the 82nd Field Artillery Battalion, 1st Cavalry Division. He'd been recalled from an August 1990 leave.

Kathleen Trott pointed to the various relatives who had turned out to meet Bernie. Another son, her daughter, Bernie's grandmother, his cousins. "We've been here waiting for him since Friday. He's supposed to come home this weekend," Kathleen announced.

The Trott clan - or the Massachusetts connection, at least - had been staying at the Odlin Road Holiday Inn and had enjoyed their visit to Bangor, Kathleen said. "Yes, we were waiting for Bernie Saturday. I hope he's on this flight. We can wait for him only through today, because we've all got to return to work." By 5 a.m., perhaps 200 people lined the wire. Impatient for the day's events to begin, two or three women started singing "God Bless America." Other people added their voices and quietly clapped to the music. The police officers circulating in the crowd looked askance at each other, as if they could not believe their good luck at facing a non-boisterous crowd.

When the song ended, the troop greeters laughed and chatted with the police officers, who finally concurred that no terrorist threat existed in this crowd. People all along the wire launched into "It's a Grand Old Flag," and the police officers drifted to their assigned positions in the terminal or up the ramp. Fed up with the lack of official music, the restless crowd found an American flag to salute and sang the "Star-Spangled Banner." Several police officers turned toward the music and stood at attention. A Monarch airliner apparently landed about the same time as did UAL Flight 6465. The disembarking Europeans hit the top of the ramp simultaneously with the 400-odd soldiers aboard the 747.

Probably unaware that they had intruded on an American homecoming, the Europeans deigned to wait until the 1st Cav troops passed. Forming a solid phalanx along the wall facing the runway, the arriving civilians marched down the ramp side by side, shoulder to shoulder with the soldiers. By the time everyone entered the terminal, a human wall separated the troop greeters from their comrades in uniform.

The undeterred Americans thrust their hands between the startled Europeans and hugged the few soldiers who braved the avalanche of incoming tourists. Then, somewhere up the ramp, a smart tourist sensed the consternation rising audibly from the crowd. The man cut through the human wire near Gate 2 and steered the tourists behind him away from the chaos nearer the coffee shop.

After the last Europeans cleared the ramp, the troop greeters got down to business.

A relative standing near Kathleen Trott held aloft the sign that read, "Bernie Trott, Here's Your Family." Next to the woman, Bernie's ecstatic grandmother displayed an equally large sign that bade a warm "Welcome Home Bernie Trott and Dragon Company." The entire Trott clan cheered the arriving soldiers, then, with bated breath, strained to catch the first glimpse of their returning Gulf vet.

"There he is!" Kathleen Trott screamed. Desert fatigues flashed across the gap separating mother and son as Bernie Trott plunged into Kathleen's arms. The signs came down, and other relatives joined the reunion. Camera flashes winked and blinked, the sister from Connecticut cried joyful tears, and Bernie suddenly met the 5-month-old nephew whom he had never seen.

Even as the little boy expressed his displeasure at all the confusion, Bernie reached out and took his nephew in his arms. Perhaps the long journey to the desert had been worth the effort just for a moment like this.

Near the entrance to the coffee shop, Army Maj. Ray Dupere stood shaking hands with the 1st Cav troopers. His experienced eye scanned the uniform lapels for the telltale cross that indicated a chaplain. Dupere, the pastor of the Church of the Open Door in Hampden, was a member of the Maine Army National Guard, serving as the chaplain of the 262nd Engineering Battalion. He'd attended several troop flights and met a Marine chaplain and a chaplain from the 82nd Airborne Division.

This morning, he picked Capt. Marvin Luckie from all the soldiers packing the wire at BIA. The two men soon made their introductions. A Protestant chaplain assigned to the 1st Cav, Luckie had gone to war with the 1st Battalion, 82nd Field Artillery Regiment. Originally from Pensacola, Fla., he had been a minister since 1980.

Luckie explained that as a Protestant chaplain, he handled religious services for Baptists, Congregationalists, Lutherans, and members of the other Protestant denominations, including his own United Methodists. "I'm a Christian by faith, Methodist by practice," Luckie said with a grin. "The Christian's the important part, though." According to Luckie, the 1st Battalion (also known as the Dragon Battalion) had arrived in Dhahran, Saudi Arabia, on Oct. 6, 1990. Thirteen days later, the battalion left for Assembly Area Horse, an ad-hoc staging area about 75 miles west of the coastal city of Khafji. The 1st Cav artillerymen first saw action on Feb. 7, when the battalion fired Copperhead laser-guided artillery shells at an Iraqi border post.

When the ground invasion started on Feb. 23, the Dragon Battalion went with the 1st Cavalry Division into Iraq and "ended up 30 miles outside Basra," Luckie said. The battalion, which suffered no casualties during the war, returned to Saudi Arabia by mid-March and subsequently shifted its position to a town near Bahrain.

Serving as a wartime chaplain in Saudi Arabia afforded many challenges, Luckie said. Made conspicuous by the cross on his lapel, he refused to hide his Christian faith in the Moslem heartland.

Some news reports from the Gulf indicated that the military pressured many chaplains to conceal their insignia, particularly the Star of David worn by Jewish chaplains. "I had all my stuff sewn on. I was not a 'velcro' chaplain," Luckie said, referring to the habit adopted by some chaplains of velcro-fastening their crosses for quick removal when meeting any Moslems.

In fact, Luckie met no Moslems who took offense at the cross that he wore. Bedouin and their herds often wandered past the battalion's encampment. Luckie spoke to many tribesmen who apparently respected his position as the Americans' "holy man" or "religious man." A Bedouin named Issa Mohammed even gave the captain a prayer rug. Despite a few press accounts about chaplains not being permitted to conduct religious services in Saudi Arabia, Luckie experienced no difficulties. "Of course, we were way out in the desert where no one could see us," he said. "But, no one ever hindered our services." While in the Gulf, Luckie also served as a chaplain to the 312th Military Intelligence Battalion, another component of the 1st Cavalry Division. Since the 312th often scattered its members to various desert outposts, the captain relied on other chaplains to help with religious services and counseling.

This practice also applied to people with different religious beliefs within the 1st Battalion. A Catholic priest from the 115th Support Battalion came forward to say Catholic mass, Luckie said, and he personally escorted the unit's single Moslem to a mosque for prayer services.

The battalion also mustered three Jewish soldiers. Their presence in the desert "was kept under wraps, for obvious reasons," Luckie explained. "The Jews aren't popular people in the Moslem countries, so we didn't publicize their names and faith."

He would contact a rabbi to arrange a location and time for Jewish worship services and then would take the Jewish soldiers there. "I made sure there was a freedom of religion for anyone who had a bonafide faith," Luckie said. "By guaranteeing their freedom of religion, I guaranteed mine."

He talked about what were, to him, his three important responsibilities out in the desert. The first involved "visiting the troops wherever they were," even during combat.

Refusing to remain safely in the rear, Luckie visited the various batteries, even while their guns shelled the Iraqi Army. "I'm not the type of chaplain who's going to wait at the aid station. I would go forward to be with my troops," he said.

Did he fear for his life?

Yes, but Luckie placed that fear in God's hands. Explaining that he realized that he might die, a possibility that he shared with the other soldiers of the 1st Battalion, he claimed Psalm 138:7,8 as "my psalm for the whole war." In those verses, King David wrote, "Though I walk in the midst of trouble, you preserve my life; you stretch out your hand against the anger of my foes, with your right hand you save me. The Lord will fulfill his purpose for me; your love, O Lord, endures forever - do not abandon the works of your hands." (NIV)

"I went out knowing that God would take care of me," Luckie said. "I had an assurance of peace that the Lord was going to see me and my family through this."

The soldiers sensed his faith and confidence when he visited them in the field. Meeting a chaplain "right at the battery caused many of them to think about Christianity," Luckie said.

He counseled soldiers on matters ranging from "religious faith to any family problems at hand to the bottom line, life and death." The most frequently asked question during counseling sessions was, "How can I be a Christian and be a soldier?"

According to Luckie, the 1st Cav troopers exhibited "the American love of life, and they experienced some discomfort about shelling the Iraqis. "When we talked about this," the captain recalled, "I'd point out how much we valued life and freedom, that we weren't in Saudi Arabia to plunder, pillage, or take away anyone's freedom.

"We didn't come to the desert just to kill people," Luckie said. "We came to defend another people from an enemy who'd taken away their country."

Realizing that "we were fighting an enemy who didn't share any of our values, who crushed freedom in another, smaller country," helped the Fort Hood soldiers to know what they were fighting for, Luckie said.

The Americans "came to view this as a war against one man, Saddam Hussein. As the ground war started, I sensed almost a feeling of pity for the Iraqi soldiers, who didn't want to fight and had been abandoned by their government," he stated.

Luckie listed his third major responsibility as liturgical, from preaching to teaching the Bible to serving the sacraments. "We took communion out there in the desert, which wasn't that an unusual setting, considering where Jesus Christ lived," he said.

Throughout his six months in the Gulf, Luckie spoke to many soldiers about Jesus Christ. Reporting that he'd baptized 18 Americans, Luckie said that "I know of at least eight others who accepted the Lord."

As the boarding call sounded for his flight to Texas, the captain said he had missed his family while in the Gulf. He and his wife, Karen, had two sons: 8-year-old John and 4-year-old Michael. Luckie had called them from Saudi Arabia on April 20 and told them he was catching a ride home.

"I can't wait to see them," Luckie said before shaking hands with Maj. Dupere and bidding him a warm farewell.

Bernie Trott received a royal sendoff, too, of course. His family hugged him before he departed for Texas. "After eating breakfast somewhere in Bangor, we'll head home for Greenfield," Kathleen Trott said. "It's a long drive, but it's been worth it."

SOMEWHERE EAST OF DHAHRAN

Among the soldiers, airmen, sailors, and Marines who touched down at BIA after March 8, Air Force personnel displayed the greatest reluctance to tell the media where they'd served during the Gulf War.

Unlike the soldiers and Marines who literally didn't know where they were in the desert, and the sailors who lived and worked inside steel hulls, Air Force personnel usually remained at the same base, albeit somewhere in the countries rimming the Persian Gulf. For some reason, however, many airmen mentioned "top secret" and "ask the colonel about that" when asked their base location.

Unfortunately, the "colonel" often flew on the next plane, usually the airliner not met by the press.

The Middle East map published by the National Geographic Society in February 1991 marked air bases all over Saudi Arabia and the Gulf States with blue-silhouetted F-16s. If National Geographic can print where the air bases are, how come the Air Force can't talk about them? the troop greeters wondered.

Surprisingly, the National Geographic missed an air base. American Trans Air Flight 8248 apparently left that base sometime during April 20. The base didn't exist on any geopolitical map, and the Air Force wouldn't acknowledge its existence, but it was there, because Tech. Sgt. Ronnie Swanson spent seven months there.

Wherever "there" was.

The AMT L-1011 landed in Bangor at 6:05 a.m. on April 21. The Air Force personnel aboard the aircraft swamped the ramp, overran the volunteers at the gift table, and poured into the domestic terminal. An older, multistriped airman spotted a troop greeter wearing a T-shirt recently purchased at the Alamo. Noting the printed reference to Texas, the airman pointed and said, "Now, there's a smart man."

The uniformed men and women who flooded past the gift table commented time and again on the grass and trees they could see from the L-1011. Two airmen swung from the caval-cade, leaned against the window sill, and looked across the runway to the tall pines growing beyond the fence.

"I'm so glad to see big, tall trees - nothing like those stunt-ed things the camels would chew off over there," one airman said. "Camels?" a civilian inquired.

Air Force Technical Sergeant Ronnie Swanson of St. Louis, Mo., was sta-tioned with the 375th Services Squadron at an airbase not even located on most Middle East maps.

"Yeah, they're all over the place," the airman growled. "No better than rabbits back home, into everything, eating every-thing." "He's right," the other airman said. "Camels eat every-thing. They would get into the dumpsters and eat the card-board, and we'd have to clean up after them."

"We'd be sleeping at night," related his friend, a merry twinkle in his eye, "and one would get in your tent and kiss you on the lips, and you'd say, 'Not tonight, dear.'"

A while later, Tech. Sgt. Ronnie Swanson stood watching the pandemonium that encircled him. Assigned to the 375th Services Squadron at Scott Air Force Base in Illinois, Swanson hailed from St. Louis. Swanson said that he had left the United States on Sept. 2, 1990, and arrived at a final destination, Al-Ain in the United Arab Emirates, two days later.

Dispelling the lingering suspicion that all airmen were closemouthed, Swanson said that Al-Ain is "somewhere east of Dhahran, real close to Abu Dhabi, I guess." He described the airfield at AlAin as "a little asphalt airstrip about 13,000 feet long" that handled C-130 Hercules transports "doing in-theater deliveries." Knowing that the runway at BIA was only

73

11,000 feet long, making it one of the longest civilian strips on the East Coast, a troop greeter wondered who had constructed a 13,000-foot runway "somewhere east of Dhahran."

Yes, the runway was very long, Swanson confirmed, especially for an air base way out in the desert. "Our job was to take care of them (the C-130 crews) as far as housing and feeding. Whatever they needed, we provided," he said.

Diversity marked Swanson's assignment. While expected "to manage and maintain dormitory facilities" at Al-Ain, he knew that if tragedy dictated, he would be expected go after anyone who was killed in action.

"Our squadron had the unfortunate responsibility of being designated to retrieve the remains of Americans killed in action or in accidents," Swanson explained. "So far, we've been lucky." One member of the 375th was sent to Labrador a few years ago, however, to help recover the bodies of paratroopers killed there in a plane crash. "Any services squadron would have a similar responsibility," said Swanson. Detailing the hunt for the crewmen killed when a helicopter and an A-10 collided in West Germany, he commented, "It's part of our job. Because it is, we go in with the thought that this is someone's loved one."

Events reminded Swanson and his comrades that, although they were far removed from the Gulf War, danger awaited them even in the United Arab Emirates. The Americans stationed at Al-Ain initially "felt some concern about getting shot at," Swanson recalled. "Talk about terrorism was in the air."

The terrorist threat appeared greatest before the air war started on Jan. 17, Swanson said. After the local army set up a perimeter fence around Al-Ain, the Air Force's 436th and 443rd Security Police Squadrons set up a secondary defensive line based on this fence. "For a couple of weeks there, someone was coming out and testing the security system of the base to see if they could get through," Swanson said. A flare would occasionally trip and go off "without a camel in sight, so you figured there were two-legged intruders snooping around." As the weeks passed, more Americans poured into Al-Ain. The UAE army had to expand the perimeter fence "a few times because we kept growing," said Swanson. "By the time they were done, Al-Ain was very big."

Like many other airmen who'd landed in Bangor this Sunday, Swanson expressed his delight at seeing green grass and tall trees. Over there, somewhere in the UAE desert, "you could even count the individual blades of grass, it was that bad," he said.

The starry Arabian night was something else, however. "Out there,you can step outside and see all God's creation right over your head," Swanson explained. "The sight made you realize how really small you are compared to a sky full of stars.

"When you're so far from home," Swanson commented even as the PA system announced the boarding call, "you have a lot of time to think about life and things in general, about what's important to you. Seeing those stars like that really set me to thinking, to getting my priorities in life straight. But it's good to be home, and I wouldn't trade duty in the United States for any desert anywhere in the world," he said, smiling.

"Most of the airmen would have rather stayed home and let the deterrent do the job for us, but when the time came to go, we were glad to do our job," Swanson said.

As he shook hands and turned to leave, the tech sergeant said to the troop greeter, "Thank all your people for me. This reception kind of takes your breath away. You definitely caught us by surprise."

A few minutes after Ronnie Swanson vanished up the ramp, a young airman with eyeglasses walked along the wire, where he shook hands. Noticing how wet the man's hair appeared, a woman shouted, "Did you get your shower?" The airman grinned, waved to the woman, and yelled, "Yes, I did!" "He'd come in here looking for a shower, so I told him to go to the Hilton," the woman subsequently explained.

Later that day, the volunteer who had been talking with Swanson scoured his Middle East maps to find Al-Ain. He discovered that small map scales rendered the United Arab Emirates as only a colored blob on Oman's northern border. Many maps of the United States do the same thing to Rhode Island.

Then he flipped the National Geographic Society map to its nonmilitary side. Yep, there was a black dot called Al'Ayn, far east of Dhahran. The town nestled next to the Omani town of Al Buraymi, on the road from Abu Dhabi in the United Arab Emirates.

Ronnie Swanson had definitely lived and worked somewhere east of Dhahran.

WHEN MOM AND DAD GO OFF TO WAR

Joy.

Excitement.

Words cannot express how Anna Lacourse and her grandchildren, Michael and Jessica Timmer, felt about 9:30 p.m. on Sunday, April 21. As United Airlines Flight 6467 approached BIA that evening, about 100 people trailed into the terminals after catching "60 Minutes" or "America's Greatest Home Videos" on TV.

Tonight, the local country-western band known as "Desperado" performed for the gathering troop greeters. People standing a few yards apart had to shout to make themselves heard above the music.

A middle-aged woman with light gray hair and eyeglasses stood near the Gate 2 windows in the domestic terminal. Around her bounced a young boy - perhaps 9 or 10 - and an even younger, fairer-haired girl wearing a denim jumper and white knee-length socks. A striking resemblance between the children suggested familial ties.

Someone had propped a sign reading "Debbie Timmer, Welcome Home," near the three people. Pointing to the sign, a troop greeter asked the woman, "Is she related to you?"

"She's my daughter," replied Anne Lacourse.

"Is she coming in on this flight?" the man inquired. "I sure hope so. They do, too," Lacourse said, tilting her head toward the children. "They're her children."

As 5-year-old Jessica Timmer sprawled in an airport lounge chair and scribbled on some paper, her 9-year-old brother, Michael, fairly bounded from chair to window to chair to window, ad infinitum. Whenever the lights of a landing aircraft blinked across his vision, he asked his grandmother, "Is that my mommy's plane?"

His eyes registered their disappointment each time that Lacourse told him "no."

Twelve years earlier, Debbie Lacourse had enlisted in the Army. Later, she informed her mother, who lives in Buckfield more than 100 miles southwest of Bangor, that she intended to marry Ron Timmer, a soldier whom she'd met.

In summer 1990, Ron and Debbie Timmer found themselves assigned to the 1st Cavalry Division at Fort Hood, Texas. Life wasn't too bad, with son Michael entering the third grade and daughter Jessica starting kindergarten.

Home in Buckfield, Anne Lacourse often thought about the Timmers and wondered how big the grandchildren had grown since the last time she'd seen them.

Then Saddam Hussein muscled his way into Kuwait.

By mid-August 1990, "Debbie knew she was shipping out real soon, and there was a high probability that Ron would go, too, so we made arrangements for the children to come here," Lacourse recalled. "They came bag and baggage with some games and other stuff," she said, "and they left the dog and fish and the rabbit for a neighbor to care for."

Separated by a generation and by parents who'd gone to the Gulf, the children and their grandmother worked hard to adjust. They faced significant challenges.

Michael and Jessica shared a room, definitely a problem at their young ages. "They've adjusted well," Lacourse said. "It's a big enough room so they have their own space.

"The cold bothered them even in September. They don't get frosts around Fort Hood that early, if at all, for all I know. I hit up all my friends and relatives for whatever warm winter clothing they could spare, so I didn't have to buy much," Lacourse said. "They took skiing lessons and learned to ski. That's something they would not have the opportunity to do in Texas."

Even as the children struggled with many changes in their lives, their grandmother confronted important changes in her life. Education was never an issue. Transferring the school records from Texas to Maine presented no difficulties.

The children studied very hard at the Hartford Sumner Elementary School.

"Michael's on the honor roll. He's doing real well, as is Jessica," Lacourse reported. "I'm very proud of them."

Finding after-school child care for Michael and Jessica proved a headache, though. Lacourse worked full-time as a nurse at Elan One in Poland Spring. Unable to be there when the children arrived home from school, she arranged adequate care for them.

"The problem times were school vacations and if they (the children) got sick," Lacourse said. "I've been very lucky, as far as sickness goes."

Debbie Timmer, assigned to the 1st Cavalry Division, greets her children Michael and Jessica in Bangor on April 20, 1991. While Timmer and her soldier husband, Ron, served in the Gulf, their children stayed with her mother, Buckfield resident Anne Lacourse.

Lacourse made a big fuss of Christmas, with lots of presents under the tree. "I wanted it to be special for them, so I probably went overboard," she said.

Ron Timmer's parents arrived from Michigan after Christmas. They stayed a few days and cared for the children, who "really enjoyed a break in their routine," Lacourse said.

Her former husband and his wife helped after the holidays by taking the children home with them every other weekend. "It was great," Lacourse stated, "with the kids getting the chance to spend time with all their relatives from up north." Then came the announcement during the Jan. 16 evening news.

America had gone to war.

"The kids have missed their parents real bad," Lacourse said. Mom had called a few times, when she could find a working phone out there in the desert, and everyone had written letters back and forth. "The hardest time was when the war began, for them," Lacourse acknowledged as Michael leaned against her, then hugged her waist. Lacourse patted the boy's shoulders before he skipped to the windows. "Michael was certain his father wasn't coming home, because he drove a tank," Lacourse said. "Jessica is too young to fully comprehend the full story, but Michael was really worried.

"I think my daughter and son-in-law did a good job preparing them for what they had to do," she stated. "Two parents gone to war? Who would've thought it possible 25 years ago?" Ron Timmer had landed in Bangor after 8 p.m. on April 16. "He didn't call from the terminal, because we would not have arrived before his plane left," Lacourse said.

After Ron flew to Texas from Bangor, "he called them (Michael and Jessica) the next night," Lacourse said. "They were both thrilled to hear his voice and know that he was all right."

Debbie soon called her mother and said that she was leaving Saudi Arabia at 10 a.m. local time on April 21. The women figured when the UAL 747 would most likely arrive in Bangor, and Lacourse calculated her travel time from Buckfield.

Its beacon lights blinking in the darkness, UAL Flight 6467 landed in Bangor. "Is that my mommy's plane?" Michael asked, pointing out the window toward the conglomerated lights flashing past his vantage point.

"Yes, dear," his grandmother replied. The 9-year-old exploded into sheer joy, hopping from foot to foot and yelling as loudly as a 9 year-old boy could.

An airport official entered the terminal and invited anyone waiting for relatives on the United flight to move into the ramp. Escorted by other family members, Anne Lacourse and her grandchildren crossed the wire to stand by the duty-free shop.

Cheers erupted from the crowd as the first soldiers appeared at the top of the ramp. Lacourse, Michael, and Jessica edged slightly forward and craned their necks.

Then a young woman soldier with eyeglasses, collar-length dark hair, and tears in her eyes ran down the ramp and into the waiting arms of Michael and Jessica. Lacourse stood back for a few seconds before enveloping the soldier in her arms.

Debbie Timmer, mother and daughter, was home.

RED CROSS WORKER

Those Americans who were not there cannot imagine the disruption that occurred when 550,000 men and women shifted their lives from the States to a forsaken desert and an alien, often unsympathetic culture 8,000 miles from home. Within five short months, from mid-August 1990 to mid-January 1991, a population shift that approximated moving one out of every two Mainers to Saudi Arabia separated families, ended jobs, and called America's best far away to deal with a corrupt Middle Eastern despot with bloody hands.

The men and women who went to the Gulf experienced loneliness on a scale not seen since Vietnam. The older vets, the old hands, could relate to remote tours from the past, without families, but the young people born since Vietnam could not.

Unlike Korea, where a man or woman accumulated so many points and earned a trip home, or Vietnam, where the phrase "tour of duty" encompassed a year (13 months if you were a leatherneck), the Gulf was open-ended. Too many troops passing through Bangor remarked that they didn't know when they were going home. Not knowing the final date, or not "seeing the light at the end of the tunnel" - a well-bandied aphorism that justified "four more years" in Vietnam - kept the troops worried, tense, perhaps angry.

Imagine living in a hot, fly-ridden, dusty environment and never knowing when you can leave. The troops who compared duty in the Gulf to a temporary, official exile from the United States can be forgiven their complaints. The politicians who wanted the troops to remain indefinitely in the Gulf cannot. If the 525 members of Congress had decamped to Log Base Charlie, Hafr al-Batin, or Khafji with orders to remain in the desert until Ol' Saddam withdrew peaceably from Kuwait, how long before the soft-living, underworked representatives and senators would have been clamoring to come home?

As they whiled away the days and weeks in the desert, the troops often thought about home and their families - and the unknown Iraqi menace lurking to the north. The troops griped about the weather and the flies, wrote letters, and scrambled to reach out and touch someone at a desert telephone. All the while, they couldn't be sure what was happening at home. At best, they maintained a tenuous link with the States.

Working behind the scenes - and usually in the same cruddy conditions endured by the troops - people from the American Red Cross kept that link drawn tighter than the troops ever knew.

When UAL Flight 6467 landed in Bangor at 10:05 p.m. on April 21, the Red Cross volunteers staffing the gift table laughed, hugged, and chatted with the few hundred soldiers aboard the aircraft. Desert fatigues blended with desert fatigues as men and women from the 1st Cavalry Division mobbed the gift table, stuffed teddy bears into deep pockets, and swarmed into the coffee shop and Red Baron Lounge. As the band "Desperado" played country-western music to an appreciative crowd, Debbie Timmer and her family withdrew across the terminal to celebrate her return. A United Airlines 737 landed in Bangor on its regularly scheduled flight from Manchester, N.H. The passengers disembarked through Gate 2 and caught the Tail-End Charlies coming down the ramp from UAL Flight 6467. Those arriving civilians not involved in their own reunions cheered the straggling troops.

According to one soldier, most people on the UAL 747 belonged to the 15th Forward Support Battalion, which had arrived in Dhahran on Oct. 13, 1990. The mechanics and medics assigned to the battalion had supplied armored-vehicle parts and medical support for 1st Cavalry personnel during the advance into Iraq. More than the 1st Cav rode the UAL 747 home from the Gulf.

A sharp-eyed Red Cross volunteer detected an attractive brunette wearing a Red Cross tag where soldiers sewed their "U.S. Army" tags. A tag with the initials "A.R.C." pinned to the woman's left lapel and a metallic nametag introducing her as Gayle T. Koster was fastened to her left blouse pocket.

Recognizing Koster as one of their own, the Red Cross volunteers pulled her from the ranks of the celebrating troopers and during the 60 minutes that UAL Flight 6467 remained in Bangor, extended her a special welcome.

Koster, who lives some 30 miles from Fort Hood in Temple, Texas, had joined the Red Cross as a volunteer in 1982, when she and James Koster, her husband, were stationed in West Germany. He had since retired from the Army as a lieutenant colonel.

She became a national staff member of the Red Cross in 1984.

As smiling and happy soldiers swooped around her at the gift table and took teddy bears for their children, Koster talked about her role in the Gulf. "The Red Cross started alerting its staff about a possible overseas deployment last September," she said.

After her notification arrived by mail in late October 1990, Koster shipped for Saudi Arabia within a few weeks and landed at Dhahran on Nov. 14, 1990. The Red Cross then sent her "out to the middle of the desert" to work with the 1st Cavalry Division.

The Red Cross staffers provided a vital link between the troops in the Gulf and their families back home. Even as Americans deployed across the Saudi desert, their loved ones in the States endured other hardships. People got sick, suffered accidental injuries, or died. The military services relayed this information and requests for emergency leave through its communications centers, including those set up in the desert. From there, the Red Cross did its duty.

Koster worked with the military communications center to notify service members of emergency messages. The center's main function was to distribute such messages to the appropriate officials, usually a unit's commanding officer or first sergeant. These people delivered the messages to the respective soldiers. Once in a while, a chaplain acted as the intermediary.

When she arrived in the desert, Koster lived in a Bedouin tent at first. "We worked in an Army tent that was the communications center, so we set up small Bedouin tents around this so we'd be available for night duty. Most Red Cross stations had 24-hour coverage," said the assistant station manager.

Messages arrived singly or in clumps. Early morning would be the hardest hit, because of the time change. "After supper in Texas meant the wee hours of the morning in Saudi," Koster recalled.

"We never knew a message's contents until it arrived, of course. I think a death was the most difficult information to relay, since I didn't know how close the relationship was (between the soldier and the family member)," she said.

No matter when a message arrived, a Red Cross staffer relayed it to the appropriate unit. With the 1st Cav "scattered across the desert, sometimes we took a while tracking down the right outfit," Koster stated.

"One night, late at night, I went from tent to tent, calling a first sergeant by name. Honestly, I don't know what those young soldiers thought, hearing an American woman outside their tents at such a late hour!" she laughed. The Red Cross handled outgoing messages, too. Once the proper authorities decided whether or not to grant emergency leave, "we would pass this information along to the military communication center," she said.

Like the soldiers, Koster often thought about her family. Unlike most soldiers, however, her thoughts needn't stray far, for a daughter, Karrie Koster, had joined the Red Cross just to help during the Gulf Crisis. Assigned to the 1st Armored Division, Karrie wound up near the Iraqi border when the ground war started.

Besides living with the soldiers and sharing their food, Koster also wore desert fatigues bearing her name and Red Cross tags. During her tenure with the 1st Cav, she sported a kevlar helmet and web gear, items that "I wondered if I would ever really need," she said. "They got bulky at times."

Koster subsequently transferred to the Air Force, but her heart remained with the 1st Cav troopers. She rejoined them on the morning of April 21, after a flight out on an Air Force C-141 Starlifter was cancelled. Pleased to be among the men and women wearing the 1st Cavalry's horsehead shield, Koster noted that "the most pleasant aspect of my life over there was the gratitude shown by the soldiers.

"They were ecstatic to learn that I was a civilian, a person who didn't belong to the military hierarchy. They'd look us up and just want to talk about their thoughts, their hopes and fears, stuff that you can't discuss with an officer or sometimes with each other," she said. "They were super. I couldn't have asked for a better bunch of soldiers, especially in a place like the Saudi desert."

Politely excusing himself, a young soldier squeezed between Koster and the gift table and reached for a teddy bear. Koster smiled and quietly reported that "I love these boys and girls. It's great to come home with them."

After thanking the Red Cross volunteers for their hospitality, a physically tired, but emotionally refreshed Koster departed the terminal. Many 1st Cav troopers lingered behind her to listen to music from "Desperado." Later, as the soldiers left to catch their plane, the Red Cross volunteers filled plastic bags with goodies and begged the cavalrymen to take all they wanted. As they had in Saudi Arabia, the soldiers knew they could trust the Red Cross to be there.

Six months later, long after Bangor's powers-that-be decreed the troop flights officially ended, the Red Cross was still there, meeting and greeting the last troops coming home from the Gulf.

SGT. PERRY'S SUMNER HIGH SCHOOL BAND

If there's a character in every crowd, the Bangor crowd got its character on Tuesday, April 23.

About 350 people gathered at the airport that morning to meet a flight headed for Wright-Patterson Air Force Base in Dayton, Ohio. Mike Stott, the local representative for American Trans Air, rolled into the international terminal to ensure that Flight 8276's stopover in Bangor went routinely. Behind Stott arrived a dedicated Tom Dean, who sheepishly admitted that he had missed AMT Flight 7799 real early on Monday. "I guess I missed the signal from the alarm clock," Dean said.

The country-western music provided by "Desperado" some 36 hours ago had given way to a jazz presentation by the Sumner Memorial High School Band. After enduring an hour-long bouncing and jouncing ride in a school bus from Sullivan, a coastal town east of Ellsworth, the young musicians carted their instruments into the domestic terminal, unpacked the music and the brass and the woodwinds, and listened to last-minute instructions from Director Jan Dodge.

Beginning some time before AMT Flight 8276 touched down at 10:45 a.m., the Sumner band entertained the thickening crowd with a mixed repertoire that included jazz numbers.

Soldiers from several units soon filled the ramp and poured into the terminal. World War vets who belonged to the VFW shook hands with the incoming troops and welcomed them to Bangor. As flags waved overhead, women with children no older than the younger soldiers bouncing along the wire eagerly extended their arms and warmly hugged the surprised desert warriors.

The band played on.

More soldiers swarmed into the terminal, where people gradually shifted their clapping to accompany the music. Some soldiers openly wept as they listened to Dodge and her musicians. Others, attracted by the well-practiced jazz, drifted across the wire and gathered by the band. Then, laughing and waving to the noisy crowd, a mustached soldier rounded the corner and announced, "I'm the vet you can't forget!"

He and a comrade leaned across the wire, tried to catch Dodge's attention, and admonished the Sumner High band to play louder. Then the unforgettable vet shouted, "Give me a beat!," and waltzed into a responsive throng now lining the wire.

Sgt. Emerson Perry worked the voters in true political fashion, swinging young Nicora Long into his arms and urging her to smile for the camera. Returning the giggly Nicora to her dad's attention, the sergeant plucked other youngsters from the crowd and hugged them. He even engaged 3-year-old Brett Duffany in a spirited conversation for a few minutes.

Spec. Greg Aebker of Lima, Ohio, watched Sgt. Perry vanish into the crowd. Assigned to the 79th Quartermaster Co., an Army Reserve unit from Marion, Ohio, Aebker said that he'd been activated on Sept. 12, 1990. He arrived at Dhahran on Oct. 24, 1990.

Aebker had been planning to start classes at Ohio State University, but "this whole mess changed all that, so my education's been set back a whole year," he said.

Aebker had volunteered for the Gulf by transferring to the 79th from an engineer outfit. "You could say I'm patriotic, I guess," he said. "I'd planned to join the regular Army anyway. This way, I got there faster, but I plan to return to OSU right now."

The 79th Quartermaster Co., a storage-and-distribution unit, primarily handled water supplies. The Army attached smaller water-purification outfits to the 79th, which operated with 32 rubberized bags capable of holding 50,000 gallons apiece. These bags were connected with rubberized hoses, not steel or copper, Aebker stressed.

With water such a vital commodity in the desert, the 79th moved four times as Allied troops moved closer to the front. "We lived in tents the whole time we were over there," Aebker said. "We did stay in a barracks our last night in-country. Was kind of nice to have a real roof over our heads."

The 79th ultimately set up a "bag farm" near Rafah, a town on the Tapline Road well northwest of Hafr al Batin. By now, Allied forces were moving westward to initiate the epic flanking maneuver that saw them drive as far as the Euphrates River.

The 79th obtained water from Saudi irrigation systems. The purification units attached to the quartermaster company used a process called "reverse osmosis" to remove any salt from the water. According to Aebker, no salt was present in the water wells away from the Gulf coast.

"Our water went to the 18th Airborne Corps and the French," Aebker said. "We were shipping, oh, on average, about 200,000 gallons a day. That sounds like a lot, but, boy, you needed a lot of water in the desert."

When the Allies launched their wide-ranging flank attack against the Iraqis on Feb. 23, one platoon from the 79th traveled far into Iraq and established a bag farm about 100 miles north of Rafah. A slightly surprised Aebker invaded Iraq as a truck driver for the 24th Infantry Division (Mechanized). While hauling rockets for a Multiple Launch Rocket System, he traveled about 200 miles to wind up outside Basra.

Aebker later returned to Rafah. He passed the Iraqi bag farm set up by the 79th Quartermaster Co. and soon learned that this facility received its water from the Rafah bag farm.

Six months spent in the desert thoroughly educated Aebker about the alien culture. The Saudis often tried to buy wood from the Americans. "Floor boards, pallets, packing crates, you name it, we were offered something for it," Aebker recalled. "One man even tried to trade his teen-age daughter for wood, it's so rare over there. "Driving was a bigger danger than anything else," he said. "Out on their highways, even in their towns, the

Saudis would signal one way and go the opposite way. They won't dim their bright lights at night, and all the time, if they're in a hurry, they'll drive off into the desert to go past a convoy on the highway.

"It was nothing to see wrecked cars and pickups lining the roadsides. The Saudis, they'd have an accident and just push everything off into the sand," he said. "By the time we got to Rafah, we were ready to open a chapter of MAAD, Mothers Against Arab Drivers." As Aebker spoke, Sgt. Perry spotted his band and beelined for it. While he was stationed in Saudi Arabia, Aebker received an "Any Soldier" letter from an OSU co-ed named Angela. Through their correspondence, he found that "she really picked up my spirits there. She is an artist. She sent me some examples of her work. I'm eagerly looking forward to meeting her." Angela wouldn't meet him at WrightPatterson Air Force Base, but Aebker anticipated that one or more of his four brothers would.

More people had surrounded the Sumner Memorial High School Band. For almost

an hour, the student musicians had played extremely well for the crowd. Suddenly, the entertainment turned on them.

Led by Sgt. Emerson Perry, a few soldiers infiltrated the percussion section and exploded into action. With a soldier slipping behind the snare drums and pounding out a driving beat, Sgt. Perry, an older

Army Sergeant Emerson Perry of Flint, Mich., plays drums borrowed from the Sumner Memorial High School band.

woman who stepped from the crowd, and a third soldier launched into a wild, joyous dance. Bouncing between the drums, the cymbals, a nearby kiosk, and some metal chairs, the three dancers twisted, shouted, and laughed as other soldiers and civilians clapped their approval. Breathing slightly hard and begging her age, the woman hugged her companions, laughed when Sgt. Perry whispered in her ear, and stepped into the crowd. A fourth soldier dropped the kettledrum harness over his shoulders and attempted to tap out a beat as the sergeant grinned and joked with the student musicians.

Then, after the soldier removed the kettledrum harness, Sgt. Perry picked it up, slid it across his shoulders, and pounded hard while Dodge summoned her charges to another performance.

As the student musicians played their music, their sergeant tried to maintain the beat, but he gradually fell into a rhythm of his own making. The soldiers who packed the available space between the band and the terminal windows laughed and told Sgt. Perry to keep playing.

Up front, Jan Dodge simultaneously and enthusiastically directed the band and worked her trombone. Momentum built as the crowd, excited as much by Sgt. Perry's joie de vivre as the band's excellent performance, applauded, and cheered louder. Responding to the emotions rising around her, Dodge kept the musicians seated and playing several songs in a row.

A Maine Air National Guard "Maineacs" baseball cap in hand, Sgt. Perry material-ized beside Dodge. Consummate performer that she was, the unflappable band director moved her flashing slide to avoid the sergeant, who waved and called to the student musicians. Hard, long hours of drill paid off at this moment: Although smiles peaked from lips pressed against saxophone reeds and trumpet mouthpieces, no one stopped playing as Sgt. Perry attempted to direct the band.

The song finally ended, and Dodge lowered her trombone. When she talked to the young musicians about their next number, the sergeant complimented them on their efforts. He laughed, tugged the baseball cap over his close-cropped hair, and tried again to direct the band when Dodge led it into its next song. Far in the background, the PA system summoned the soldiers back to their aircraft. Sgt. Perry ignored the warning from his comrades and lingered near Dodge, who barely suppressed a smile, too.

But all good music must end sometime, and even Sgt. Perry's Sumner High School Band tired after playing so long and so well. Cheering broke out as the sergeant bade his band good-bye and vanished into the crowd. Dodge thanked the students for their hard work and excused them from their seats.

The band defected en masse to the already mobbed wire, where the students shouted farewells to the departing soldiers. A student drummer remained at his post and provided a driving cadence much appreciated by the younger soldiers. The senior sergeants and officers shook their heads at this unexpected transition from the comfortable jazz. As the last soldiers passed along the wire, Sgt. Perry coalesced a final time near his band. He walked a few yards into the ramp, then turned and waved to the Sumner musicians.

The members of Sgt. Perry's Sumner High School Band cheered their would-be director from the terminal.

MIDNIGHT FLIGHT TO COLORADO

A brilliant half moon glistened in the clear night sky as a few troop greeters straggled into the BIA domestic terminal about 11:30 p.m. on April 23. These people represented the hard-core "regulars," the men and women who would meet the troops anywhere, anytime. Tired from the week's already exhausting schedule (nine flights since Sunday), the Maine residents still rousted themselves to meet the tenth flight, a United Airlines 747 on its way to Colorado Springs.

The 100 people who gathered at BIA that night included Lynne and Ted Dziok from Hadley, Mass. Their daughter, Army Capt. Linda Paroline, had shipped for Saudi Arabia on Jan. 3 and spent the war with the 10th Mobile Army Surgical Hospital.

Well before noon on April 23, Linda's husband called his in-laws from Colorado Springs and told them that their daughter was en route home aboard UAL Flight 6470. "She's supposed to be landing in Bangor," he said.

Lynne Dziok called Westover Air Force Base in nearby Chicopee to confirm the 747's arrival time in Bangor. The Dzioks piled into their car about 4 p.m., headed east on the Mass Pike, and took the circuitous I-495 farther eastward past Lowell, Lawrence, and Haverhill. Then they caught I-95 for the northbound run through New Hampshire. "We got here into Bangor about 10:30 p.m.," Lynne said. "It's a long drive, but it's worth it."

The terminal clock slowly ticked towards midnight as more people entered the ter-minal. The Dzioks chatted with several women who had learned about Linda's impend-ing arrival. A few diehards formed their line along the wire, but most troop greeters

83

struggled to stay awake and alert.

Then the clock's long hand crossed the witching hour, and a VFWer standing on the ramp welcomed everyone to Wednesday.

UAL Flight 6470 slipped from the darkness at 12:30 a.m. A ragged cheer erupted from the dozen people watching at the terminal windows.

Within 20 minutes, the soldiers belonging to the 10th MASH, the 183rd Maintenance Co., and the 43rd Combat Support Group (Headquarters) exited their airliner and poured into the terminal. Civilians cheered the troops, who included many women.

Lynne and Ted Dziok stood anxiously by the duty-free shop, shook hands with the passing soldiers, and peered up the ramp for a sign of Linda. Other women soldiers, some of them crying in unspeakable joy, thanked the Dzioks for their welcome.

As the minutes passed, doubt arose among the people who were monitoring the Dzioks. Had Linda actually been on this plane? Other people had traveled long distances to Bangor, only to learn that a relative had missed the flight from Saudi Arabia or been aboard a plane that had bypassed BIA.

Up the ramp, seven or eight soldiers stopped and blocked the passage so two comrades could kneel and photograph the crowd. Some cameras flashed in their direction, too. The soldiers laughed and waved. The incoming flow of soldiers gradually slowed to a trickle, primarily the Tail-End Charlies who'd stopped and used the phones in the international terminal. Their faces displaying their anxiety, Lynne and Ted edged farther into the ramp.

"There she is!" Lynne suddenly cried, pointing toward a bespectacled captain who exploded down the ramp and into her parents' arms. A tired, but ecstatic Linda Paroline had arrived to a warm greeting in Maine.

But the cat had been let out of the bag, she later confessed. "I called my husband from the (international terminal)," Linda laughed. "Honestly, I didn't expect anyone to be here for me, but he asked me if I'd seen my parents, so when I hung up, I was watching for them as I came in here."

Two or three nurses who had finished shaking hands with the crowd stopped and chatted about their Gulf assignments. The 10th MASH left Colorado Springs aboard a civilian airliner on Jan. 3 and touched down at King Fahd International Airport near Riyadh a day later. Initially, the 10st MASH transferred to Cement City, set up operations in a concrete plant, and later shifted to Log Base Charlie, a desert outpost "about 190 kilometers west of the Gulf coast," a nurse said.

"We supported the 24th Infantry (Division)," a companion stated. "I think it was the day after the war started, `H + 24' they called it. We crossed the border in a convoy about three kilometers west of Rafah. We chased the war, but we couldn't catch up. Things were moving so fast, we didn't even set up the hospital. We treated no American casualties."

The 10th MASH remained in Iraq a week before returning to Saudi Arabia. Later, the medical personnel assembled at King Fadh International Airport for the flight home to Colorado Springs. The nurses vividly recalled the Scud attacks that started after Jan. 17. "We went through 17 Scud attacks," the taller nurse recalled. "They were blowing them up right over our heads." "We saw Scuds coming in over Riyadh and Dhahran," her companion confirmed. "It was frightening, I'll tell you. Oh, we're so pleased to be going home. It's the end of a nightmare."

Sgt. 1st Class John Spearman had gone to war by catching a ride to Colorado from Alabama. A Green Beret medic from the Special Operations Group at Fort Rucker, Ala., he'd been working with a clinical hyperbolic program sponsored by the United States Surgeon General's office. "The program's the only one of its kind in the Army," he said.

According to Spearman, "the medical profession has learned that patients with certain medical conditions, like a vascular insufficiency, can be treated in a chamber like those used to help divers to decompress.

"In this chamber, we literally bombard the body with oxygen under pressure," he explained. "This way, the cells get much more oxygen than they normally would, if the patient were left in normal atmospheric pressure. With proper treatment in a decompression chamber, you probably should call it that, because the public understands what it is, we can treat patients suffering from burns, gas gangrene, and other medical conditions." As the Gulf Crisis extended into the late fall, Spearman volunteered for duty in Saudi Arabia. The Army assigned him to the 10th MASH, so he reported to Fort Carson on Dec. 10, 1990. A counterterrorist specialist, he said this was his "third or fourth war." When the 10th MASH arrived in Saudi Arabia, Spearman served as the unit's security NCO, responsible for creating perimeter defenses. "While we were in Cement City, there were many nights when I would be floating around the perimeter, and we'd see someone flirting with the wire," he noted. "Word had reached us that Americans were targets of Palestinian terrorists from Al Fatah," Spearman said. "We never actually got into a shootout with anyone, but there were a lot of people interested in whether or not our security was good."

Spearman looked forward to returning home by Friday, April 26. "I have two daughters, two beautiful girls, and I can't wait to see them again," he said, his features softening at the thought. "One daughter is 13, the other will turn 6 on May 11. I'll be home in time for her birthday." Although he was separated from his wife, he hoped for reconciliation, saying "I missed them all."

Once his life settled into a peacetime routine, Spearman planned to complete his studies for a master's degree in education. He already had an associate's degree in engineering and bachelor's degrees in nursing and law.

"Yes, I'm a busy man," he laughed, explaining that in the eyes of the Army, he was an RN. "In the real world, or at least what most civilians call it, I'm an LPN and a national-and state-registered EMT. I will go for my RN boards in Alabama in July. I've been doing medical work now for 15 years. If I don't know it now, I never will." Once he returned to Alabama, Spearman anticipated resuming part-time weekend jobs. Two weekends a month, he serves as a deputy sheriff with the Dale County (Alabama) Sheriff's Department. The county, which encompasses most of Fort Rucker, has its county seat in Ozark, Ala. Spearman lives just to the west in Enterprise, a town located in Coffee County.

About 1:20 a.m., an airport employee announced the boarding call for UAL Flight 6470. A few people asked Spearman to autograph notebooks or T-shirts. Wielding an indelible marker with gusto, he graciously thanked the civilians for their reception. "I can't believe all this has happened tonight," Spearman said, watching the civilians hug the departing soldiers. "It's a much different greeting than I got coming home from Southeast Asia.

"You know, I can't tell you what this greeting means to me. Like I said earlier, this was my third or fourth war. They're all different, yet all the same. Someone always gets hurt. I lost good friends in Southeast Asia and in Panama, too," he said. "Tell everyone `thank you' for me." As the soldiers raided the gift table and shook hands with the veterans aligned on the ramp, Linda Paroline hugged her parents and said good-bye. Lynne and Ted Dziok stood watching and waving while their daughter vanished up the ramp and into the security-screening area. A big smile on her face, Linda turned and waved once or twice. "This has been such a pleasure," Ted said. "The trouble is, we have to head back home tonight, because we've got to be at work in the morning."

By 1:35 a.m., the big red-and-white UAL 747 taxied past the terminal windows and disappeared into the darkness. A few minutes later, the aircraft thundered down the runway and lifted off, its flashing lights announcing the departure of the midnight flight to Colorado.

DEXTER NIGHT

Many troops who passed through Bangor never realized where they were, except somewhere in Maine. As Richard Shaw, the assistant editorial page editor at the Bangor Daily News, subsequently wrote, one happy soldier extended a warm "thank you from the bottom of my heart to the people of Bangkok." Another time, Shaw noted, some Marines offered multiple thank yous to "the wonderful people of the city of Bam-Bam."

Shaw also captured in print perhaps the greatest misconception the troops experienced about Bangor, population 33,000. Many times, particularly during March and April when the welcoming crowds remained so large, troops looked across the sea of adoring faces and cried, "Gee, it's great to see the whole town turned out to greet us!" In a way, though, the soldiers who deplaned at BIA about 8 p.m. on April 24 did find "the whole town turned out to greet us." Right analogy, but the wrong community, for on this Wednesday night, many people living in Dexter decamped to Bangor to greet the troops. Dexter is a town of about 3,000 people located in the hills an hour's drive northwest of Bangor. Home to Dexter Shoe and a few other manufacturers, the town marks the western boundary of Penobscot County. The campaign to turn April 24 into "Dexter Night" at BIA began when the school administration agreed to send the combined junior high and high-school bands to play for the troops. About 70 youngsters and their band director traveled to BIA, unfolded some chairs, expanded the metal stands, and unlimbered their instruments. By 7:15 p.m., trilling flutes, squeaky clarinets, and brassy trumpets competed for attention as the musicians tuned their instruments.

The people who witnessed this logistical display could not doubt the band's origination. Most musicians wore red T-shirts emblazoned with white "Dexter Band" logos, while other youngsters - apparently the seventh- and eighth-graders - sported white T-shirts or blouses, some bearing a printed red "Dexter." A few musicians wore sweaters, although the atmosphere inside the terminal felt quite warm.

Many parents had accompanied the Dexter band. "I hurried home from work, cooked supper real fast, and hurried down here," one woman said.

The L-1011 that the crowd awaited belonged to American Trans Air, which had tagged the plane as Flight 8306. On its way to England Air Force Base near Alexandria, La., the jet was scheduled to land at 7:45 p.m.

The combined Dexter bands finished tuning their instruments, then launched into a long performance that a spectator later described as "played well, with great enthusiasm." The director varied the repertoire, which the young musicians handled with distinction.

About 7:45 p.m., the AMT L-1011 rolled down the runway from left-to-right, and people watching from the terminal windows cheered their approval. Some too-curious musicians, especially those playing clarinets or flutes, stood up and looked out the windows. Despite the distraction, the students hardly missed a beat.

BIA representative Gary Leighton stepped to the microphone to announce the L-

1011's arrival. "The aircraft missed its first cutoff from the runway, so it will take a few extra minutes to reach the international terminal," Leighton told the crowd.

He then asked his audience, which was later estimated at 400 people, "How many of you are here for the first time?" Countless hands, perhaps half the crowd's, shot into the air. When Leighton asked how many people came from Dexter, the hands barely wavered and probably increased in number.

Beside the duty-free shop, an anxious Ralph Field paced back and forth, occasionally looking up the ramp or into the terminal. The Milford man doggedly met every troop flight that might be carrying his wife, Deborah Field. A reservist with the 1125th U.S. Army Hospital in Bangor, Deborah had been called to active duty about three months ago, according to Ralph. "I talked to her last Saturday, and she expected to leave Saudi Arabia at any time," Field said, crossing his fingers. "I just hope she's aboard this plane!"

A few minutes later, a BIA employee escorted the incoming troops through the double-glass doors at the top of the ramp. Some veterans standing in the receiving line cheered, but their voices echoed hollowly down the ramp. Caught off-guard by the soldiers' sudden appearance, or distracted by something happening in the domestic terminal, the waiting crowd hesitated.

The Dexter musicians did, too, but students were half-rising from their seats to glimpse the soldiers. For many students, tonight marked their first and only troop flight. They could be excused for wanting to watch the troops.

Then the crowd awoke, and thunderous cheering and applause rolled up the ramp. Satisfied that they'd witnessed history, the Dexter students settled into their chairs, took their director's cue, and provided the necessary mood music for the occasion.

The soldiers, who belonged to either the 15th Evacuation Hospital or the 1083rd Transportation Co., a National Guard unit, waved to the civilians, shook hands, and accepted the proffered hugs. Ralph Field welcomed the troops, of course, but kept his attention focused on the ramp.

Deborah Field didn't arrive on AMT Flight 8306.

Another Maine soldier did, though. Joyful cries announced when a soldier named Roger Roy, a Lewiston Army Reservist, met his wife and young child on the ramp. Clutching a large American flag and a metallic balloon stencilled "Welcome Back" in his right hand, Roy lifted his wide-eyed son with his left hand and held the boy close. As the family cleared the lectern, Roy kissed his son on his right cheek. The Louisiana-bound soldiers encountered more than the usual T-shirt- or sweater-clad civilians that night. As the Dexter band performed, an older man wearing full Indian regalia edged to the wire and shook hands with the soldiers. The man's costume seemed authentic, except for the long, trailing headdress, a clothing style never affected by Maine Indians. As the last soldiers passed along the wire, the crowd dissolved and mingled with the troops already inside the terminal. Aware they might not catch another troop flight, Dexter-area youngsters sought autographs and collected some souvenirs. Their parents chatted with the soldiers and welcomed them to Maine. Maj. Douglas Hale, a surgeon assigned to the 15th Evac Hospital at Fort Polk, La., said that he hailed from Buffalo, N.Y. The 15th Evac Hospital left for Saudi Arabia on Jan. 8, landed in Dhahran, and arrived at Log Base Charlie on Jan. 20.

Log Base Charlie was the same outpost at which the 10th MASH had been stationed before the ground war started. "According to the maps - as accurate as they were - we were about 60 kilometers east of Rafah and about five miles from the Iraqi border," Hale said.

The 15th Evac, approximately twice the size of a combat support hospital, contained about 400 beds. By comparison, a MASH would have 100 to 150 hospital beds, Hale pointed out, while a CSH would field about 200 beds. From almost the moment they arrived in the Gulf, the personnel assigned to the 15th Evac Hospital put their equipment and training to good use.

Initially, the Americans treated non-combat injuries (automobile accidents, self-inflicted gunshot wounds, etc.) and the typical medical ailments like hernias and appendectomies that could be found in any modern stateside hospital, Hale said. "Just because people are living way out in the desert, that doesn't protect them from injuries or sickness," he said. As the 18th Airborne Corps gathered strength in the desert outposts stretching eastward to Log Base Victor, the 15th Evac went on a wartime footing. The hospital supported the corps during its invasion by staying at Log Base Charlie and treating the casualties that "they evacked back to us from the forward aid stations and the MASHs and CSHs," Hale stated.

The patients initially arriving at Log Base Charlie included some Allied soldiers and many Iraqi prisoners-of-war. The coalition wounded suffered from combat wounds, most of which were minor in nature, Hale recalled.

The Iraqi POWs presented a different story, however. Hale estimated that the 15th Evac Hospital saw about 150 Iraqi soldiers, most of whom suffered from shrapnel wounds. "Our biggest push was Iraqi prisoners during the war," he said.

"They seemed to be reasonably healthy and not malnourished," Hale said, but many wounded Iraqis "hadn't seen their medical teams for a while.

"I'd attribute this to an organizational mess, to a breakdown in Iraqi communications and medical evacuation," he commented. "With all the bombing, and the Iraqis dug in so deep, apparently they believed it was unsafe to travel for help. I guess their medical teams weren't exactly beating a path to the wounded, either."

About two weeks after the war ended, the Shiites rebelled in the towns along the lower Euphrates River. The Iraqi army, primarily the remnants of the Republican Guards, swiftly and brutally crushed the rebellion.

Hale vividly remembers the aftermath.

"As the Republican Guards moved into the southern (Iraqi) cities and retook control, Iraqi physicians started sending their hospital patients to the Americans," he said, "because they knew the Republican Guards would kill them.

"From what we heard and saw," Hale said, "those stories that got out about the Guards killing patients in their hospital beds were true. Once word got out (among the Shiites) what the Guards were doing, the Iraqi doctors emptied the hospitals as fast as they could. I will tell you right here and right now, it happened, people being gunned down in the hospitals and on the streets."

The 15th Evac Hospital treated many children suffering from gunshot wounds or shrapnel. In time, children comprised the majority of refugees seen by the American medical personnel. "Some children came in DOA. They'd been shot at close range, you could tell from the powder burns," Hale related memories that angered him.

"The ones (children) who came to us healthy enough to be operated on survived, and are doing reasonably well," he said.

"The refugees were coming in dirty, a mother would be coming in covered with blood from her child...a mother standing there, holding her dead child, looking at you as if you could restore life. I can't adequately describe the scenes," Hale said, lowering his voice. The 15th Evac Hospital treated refugees suffering from more mundane medical ailments, too. Hale remembered that just like American parents at home, the parents of Iraqi children on whom he operated "were very, very grateful, and for that fact, that attitude applied to the wounded Iraqi EPWs (enemy prisoners-of-war)." The refugees treated by the 15th Evac Hospital were later flown by helicopters or C-130 Hercules to a refugee hospital at King Khalid Military City in Saudi Arabia. The hospital shut down on April 7 and returned to Dhahran, where "we packed our bags and went home," Hale said.

He eagerly anticipated a long-awaited reunion with his wife, Antonia, and their 18-month-old daughter, Julia, and 4-1/2-month old son, Douglas Jr., who'd been born just before Hale flew to the Gulf. "I missed them real bad," the major said.

The Dexter band, which had entertained its combined audience for a half hour, suddenly launched into "Rock Around the Clock," a well received arrangement that drew a few soldiers and civilians to dance. The band director then invited the soldiers to join the musicians in playing their instruments. Two or three soldiers accepted the invitation.

Soldiers and civilians alike expressed their disappointment when the first boarding call sounded about 10 minutes later. Pausing along the way to shake hands and accept a final hug or two, soldiers gradually filtered from the terminal. Dexter children grabbed last-minute autographs while their parents snapped color photos to remember the occasion.

As the last soldiers rounded the corner into the ramp, Col. Kevin Kiley returned to the lectern and seized the microphone with his left hand. BIA employee Shawn Frederick stood at the colonel's elbow while Kiley, the commanding officer of the 15th Evac Hospital, spoke on behalf of his troops.

Kiley thanked everyone still in the terminal for the welcome they had extended his command. His voice slightly choking, the colonel bid Bangor farewell and vanished up the ramp to catch his flight.

The Dexter musicians cheered as Kiley exited the domestic terminal. They'd always remember April 24 as "Dexter Night," when they'd made a few hundred soldiers feel proud about being Americans.

SCENES FROM THE TABLE

For the "regulars" among the BIA troop greeters, the pace of life slowed in late April as the number of Gulf-launched aircraft touching down in Bangor dwindled. During the seven days stretching from April 25 to May 1, only eight troop flights landed at BIA, compared to the 20 flights that landed during the previous seven days.

On April 25, in fact, no troop flight put into Bangor. The momentary disruption worried many people, who wondered if they'd meet more returning troops.

They needn't have worried, but should have enjoyed their weeklong vacation. After May 1, the troop flights resumed with a vengeance. Of course, no one could predict the resumption as United Airlines Flight 6474 approached BIA about 10 p.m. on April 26.

This week, the Greater Bangor Chamber of Commerce supplied volunteers for the gift table, and one would assume the responsibility for finding enough people to staff the table during a particular shift. That task proved effortless while the public still considered the troop flights a novelty. As interest in greeting the troops waned after mid-April, however, phone calls and personal requests located far fewer people willing to work at the gift table.

Since March 8, the BIA staff had let the Chamber of Commerce and Red Cross volunteers use the closet located beside Gate 2 in the domestic terminal. Until late May, this closet usually remained packed with donated sodas, brownies, cookies, fudge, fruit, magazines, post cards, books, Red Cross gift packs, and assorted souvenirs.

Before each troop flight, volunteers filled the table with food and souvenirs, then sent someone to retrieve two or three cartons of teddy bears from the boiler room in the international terminal. Although Russ Berrie & Co. Inc. had donated 25,000 teddy bears for the troops in early April, initial estimates indicated that if every incoming troop received a bear, the Ursus Berries would be gone within a few weeks.

The decision was made to pass out only 50 teddy bears per flight. So, as volunteers unpacked teddy bears that night, only 50 bears graced the gift table. "I wish we could spread out more," a disgruntled woman muttered.

She understood why. When an airliner deposited homesick troops at BIA, 50 bears didn't go far. Discontented troop greeters growled when too many troops left Bangor bearless. The "regulars" among the troop greeters didn't approve, and quietly voiced their anger.

About a half hour before UAL Flight 6474 landed, members of the American Legion Auxiliary from the post in Madison assisted the volunteers by stuffing informational flyers into the newspapers that the troops would receive. The women later joined the official reception line on the ramp.

Realizing that two people could not adequately staff the table, one volunteer walked slowly along the wire. He sought familiar faces belonging to people who'd met other troop flights. A request for assistance was well-received by Mildred Bowden, who despite an arm in a sling, agreed to pass out American flags.

Shortly before UAL Flight 6474 landed at 10:15 p.m., BIA representative Richard Myrshall finished addressing the crowd, estimated at 250 people, then left the lectern and walked past Ralph Field. "Are you still here looking for your wife?" a compatriot asked. "She told me it could be any flight this week," Field replied, "and that's the hard part."

"Driving you crazy?"

"Yes." It was hard coming down with two children at home, Field acknowledged. "It's hard, because if she doesn't get off the plane, it's a let-down."

Adorned in their plumed bicornes and vivid capes, the Knights of Columbus impressively augmented the official receiving line. Legionnaires and VFWers lined the ramp, too.

At last, Marilyn May stepped from the crowd to help with the gift table. Like Bowden, she came to meet many troop flights.

According to Richard Myrshall, tonight's flight was flying to McChord Air Force Base in Tacoma, Wash. The plane apparently carried a few people with Maine connections.

Dale Hanington and his wife, Jean, had driven from Benton to meet their son, Aaron, who was assigned to the 497th Transportation Co. out of Fort Lewis, Wash. "We sure hope he's aboard this flight!" Hanington exclaimed. Believing her son to be coming home aboard UAL Flight 6474, a woman had driven from Connecticut to meet the plane. She edged into the ramp and clutched her hands tight to her chest. As soldiers swung the corner leading to the double-glass doors, the woman stepped furtively into the ramp, stood on tiptoe, and studied the faces advancing along the official receiving line.

Then a young soldier, the vanguard, burst down the ramp and into his mother's arms. As other soldiers flooded past them, the Connecticut woman cried her delight. Her son finally steered her to a quieter location.

Other reunions took place that night. Dwarfed by their desert fatigue-clad soldier, two women tightly hugged the happy youth. Again, tears freely flowed, and nobody minded.

Ralph Field and the Haningtons closely examined the incoming soldiers. Deborah? Aaron? Disappointment etching his face, Ralph watched the incoming soldiers dwindle to a dribble. Realizing that his Deborah would not land in Bangor tonight, he stalwartly stood on the ramp and shook hands with the arriving troops.

But Aaron Hanington burst from the uniformed ranks and enveloped his parents in his arms. Dale and Jean cried for joy, too, ecstatic that their boy had returned safely from the war. They quickly moved away to a private reunion.

According to the soldiers passing the gift table, UAL Flight 6474 carried the 497th Transportation Co., the 542nd Maintenance Co., "one emergency leave," and the 543rd Supply Co., among other units.

As the soldiers flooded the ramp, the Chamber of Commerce volunteers maintained their position, shaking hands and telling the troops "welcome home" or "welcome back." The soldiers kept coming and coming and coming, patiently standing in line when movement slowed along the wire.

One soldier who walked past the table wore jungle fatigues. "Yes, I'm a little out of place with this group!" he laughed. Some soldiers commented favorably about the Maine hospitality. A few even promised to return for a visit. Come in the summer or fall, the Chamber volunteers suggested.

As the soldiers continued pouring into the terminal, a film crew from United Airlines circulated in the crowd while pursuing material for a promotional film. One moment, a cameraman emerged at wireside to capture a hug, a handshake, maybe a kiss. A few minutes later, a soldier found a microphone thrust beneath his chin and heard a voice ask his opinion of all these shenanigans in Bangor. Other times, the film crew simply shot long footage of people welcoming the troops home.

Then Whitney Houston's "One Moment in Time" soared from the tape player that provided tonight's music. People cheered and applauded the incoming soldiers, especially a woman soldier who chose that moment to turn the corner from the ramp. Behind her came another woman soldier with tears trickling down her cheeks.

By now, the Tail-End Charlies wandered into the terminal. Unfortunately, the soldiers who'd beat them down the ramp had already attacked the teddy bears. Noticing the big gap left by the missing Ursus Berries, a volunteer broke into the remaining carton of bears. Bruce Springsteen broke into "Born in the USA" as the Knights of Columbus accompanied the remaining Tail-End Charlies into the terminal, looking almost like warriors from another period in history, with their hats and cloaks. The UAL film crew continued shooting while two local politicos, Bangor City Manager Ed Barrett and a city councilor, Marshall Frankel, wandered through the celebrating mob. People packed the place, blocking the entrances to the coffee shop, the Red Baron Lounge, and Mr. Paperback, sitting or standing on chairs (the best efforts never discouraged the youngsters from treating the airport chairs as their private trampolines or observation posts), or leaning against walls and kiosks. The woman who had driven through the evening from outside Danbury, Conn., sought out airport officials when she arrived at BIA. "Can you call the airliner and ask them to let my son off first?" she asked.

"You bet," the BIA employees apparently responded. A brief transmission bumped the woman's son to the head of the line and a joyful reunion with his mom.

Shortly after 11 p.m., a few soldiers slid into the ramp, raided the gift table, and headed for their aircraft. The ladies from Madison converged on the table as a handsome young Pfc. stopped to pick and choose among the goodies. Like grandmothers at a church social, the auxiliary legionnaires hovered near the soldier as he chose what he wanted. Then a gray-haired, bespectacled woman who remembered the horrors of World

War II slapped open a plastic shopping bag that the Gulf veteran could use to carry his loot.

The women remained at the table as more soldiers left the terminal. Word suddenly reached the Chamber volunteers that some soldiers, maybe nine in all, had stayed on the 747 to guard left-behind gear or to catch some sleep.

Realizing their opportunity, the ladies from Madison deployed to the airliner with gift-packed shopping bags in hand. Customs officials immediately cleared the ad hoc "welcoming committee" to enter the 747 and give the merchandise to the soldiers.

More soldiers stopped at the gift table, reconnoitered the goodies, and usually opted for homemade fudge and chocolate-chip cookies not seen since late summer 1990. Mildred Bowden and Marilyn May did yeomen's duty, steering the outgoing soldiers to the table, loading them with American flags and newspapers, and bidding them a friend-ly farewell.

"You got no more teddy bears?" a woman soldier asked.

"All gone," a troop greeter replied.

"All gone?" the soldier responded, disappointment evident in her voice. Comrades echoed her request, and the greeter wondered if the haphazard bear distribution might cause problems on the flight. But word filtered back to Bangor a week or two later that, no, there were no hard feelings because some soldiers got teddy bears while others did not.

Richard Myrshall issued the first boarding call. Soldiers flocked into the ramp, where the Chamber of Commerce volunteers urged them to take all they wanted from the gift table. As the clock ticked toward 11:30 p.m., the volunteers started telling the outgoing soldiers to "take the table if you want! If you take it, we don't have to pack it away!"

Dale and Jean Hanington held onto Aaron as they entered the ramp. Words passed quietly between parents and son, then with a last hug, a happy Aaron Hanington depart-ed the airport. His mom and dad stood there a long time looking up the ramp. When the last soldiers cleared the ramp, the Chamber of Commerce volunteers discovered that the gift table had been stripped clean.

UNDER A FOOL MOON

The half moon that greeted Linda Paroline after midnight on April 23 gradually brightened into the full moon that transformed a Georgia soldier at Bangor International Airport five days later.

As the soldier, a companion, and the Cable Guy discovered, a full moon does strange things in Maine.

Going into the last weekend of April, the announced flight schedule for Saturday listed only American Trans Air Flight 8329, inbound for Philadelphia from the Gulf. The aircraft "might or might not stop in Bangor," AMT representative Mike Stott said, predicting the jet's ETA as 6:45 a.m.

Although Stott knew his airline well, yet even he did not expect the switcheroo that American Trans Air pulled that Saturday morning. Flight 8329 flew directly to Philadelphia, giving the troop greeters an opportunity to enjoy a leisurely breakfast.

Another L-1011, AMT Flight 8330, dropped onto the BIA tarmac at 6:45 a.m. Saturday. Airport personnel learned about the plane's arrival only a short while before it flared over the runway. While en route to Philadelphia and Andrews Air Force Base, Washington, D.C., the L-1011 made an emergency stop in Maine. Only a few people greeted the military personnel aboard the aircraft.

"That happens sometimes," Stott later explained. "There are occasions when I don't know until the last minute that a plane's making a pit stop here."

By Sunday afternoon, word reached the radio stations that United Airlines Flight 6475 would land in Bangor that evening. People hearing the radio announcements weighed their plans for the evening. As would happen too often beyond late April, TV shows and social engagements and early bedtimes won the argument. With 150 troop flights already inked on the board at the passenger-service desk, what was one more flight in late April? Perhaps 75 to 100 people headed for BIA that night. That number included an excited and determined Ralph Field. He showed up on the ramp about 10 p.m. "I really think she's on this flight," Ralph exclaimed, referring to his wife, Deborah. "She called me about nine yesterday morning and said the bus was coming to take them

to the airport. Oh, man, I hope this is the plane!" So certain was her family that Deborah Field would come home tonight, her parents accompanied Ralph to the terminal. Clifford and Constance Pennell lived in East Holden, perhaps eight miles east of Bangor. "We believe Deborah's coming home at last," they said. UAL Flight 6475, with a final

Bangor resident Tom Dean taped incoming troop flights and sent a copy to the military commander of each aircraft.

destination of Fort Stewart, Ga., touched down at the predicted time, 10:51 p.m. A few people peered into the darkness from the terminal windows to see when the 747 would taxi past the terminal. The airliner "went 'round the other way," to coin a Maine expression, taxiing to the north end of the international terminal. As the Legionnaires and VFWers formed the reception line on the ramp, Dottie Thibodeau took her place as the official flagbearer for tonight's flight. She patiently waited for 10 to 15 minutes. Bob Jones, the Cablevision technical manager, had arrived about 10:30 p.m. While walking into the domestic terminal tonight, had he noticed the full moon shining high overhead? With Halloween still six months away, Jones never anticipated the adventure that awaited him at the place belonging to novelist Stephen King, the master of horror.

Jones was filming on the ramp when Thibodeau stepped toward the double-glass doors. Motion rippled along the reception line as veterans hitched their belts higher and adjusted their hats. Then, walking in single file, soldiers exited the security corridor, swung to the right, and encountered an American homecoming.

The people waiting in the domestic terminal applauded and cheered when they spotted the incoming soldiers. Men and women wearing desert fatigues predominated at first, but jungle fatigues soon intermingled with the sandstone variant.

Ralph Field and the Pennells joined the Red Cross volunteers in greeting the soldiers

93

from the Deep South, but Deborah Field would not come home tonight.

A passing officer identified the units aboard the UAL 747 as the 127th Medical Group from Alabama, the 345th Combat Support Hospital and the 495th Transportation Co. from Florida, and the 624th Quartermaster Co. from Mississippi. "Yeah, we're all Rebels, but we're all glad to see you Yankees!" the officer said, laughing.

Sheila Dean sat in her wheelchair near the gift table and shook hands with the soldiers. Like Jones, she could not foresee the fate awaiting her tonight. For a woman who enjoyed seeing men in uniform, Dean would find herself surrounded by more uniforms than she could imagine. She enjoyed every minute of it. The relatively small, but enthusiastic crowd kept cheering as more soldiers entered the terminal. Someone pointed out the well dressed people, several men and women, standing along the wire and applauding the soldiers. The elegantly clad people - one man wore a tuxedo - had come directly to BIA from a wedding reception. "No, the bride and groom are not here!" chuckled the tux man. After a while, the last soldiers reached the terminal. The crowd quickly dissolved as its members scattered to talk with the troops. Master Sgt. Mike Milne belonged to the 345th Combat Support Hospital, an Army Reserve outfit based at the Jacksonville Naval Air Station in Florida. A financial planner and consultant in civilian life, Milne served as the 345th's field first sergeant while in the Gulf.

The Pentagon activated the 345th Combat Support Hospital on Dec. 11, 1990, and sent the Army Reservists to Fort Stewart, Ga., for a few weeks. "We left for Saudi Arabia on Jan. 12," Milne recalled. The 345th landed at Dhahran on Jan. 14. Some time later, the unit moved north to Log Base Alpha, located "somewhere in the desert about 30 miles south of Hafr al-Batin," the master sergeant said. "Wherever we were, you can bet there was nothing there but sand and camels."

Milne remembers his first days in Dhahran as relatively, but deceptively quiet. In-country only a few days, the Florida reservists still sensed the tension around them. Despite the threats of war after the Iraqis refused to blink in Geneva, Dhahran seemed at peace. That changed real fast.

About midnight on Jan. 16, as the Florida reservists attempted to sleep, bomb- and missile-laden Air Force F-15 Eagles launched from the air base at Dhahran. Journalists noted the unusual activity and passed the word to New York and Washington.

So many jets departing Dhahran at this late hour meant that America and her Allies were going to war.

Far to the northwest of Dhahran, somewhere along the Saudi-Iraqi border, special hunter-killer helicopter teams swept into Iraqi airspace and attacked Iraqi radar sites. The assault blew holes in Saddam Hussein's early warning system.

Catapulted from carrier decks in the Persian Gulf, Navy jets flew toward targets in southern Iraq. Allied aircraft, particularly Royal Air Force Toronados and Armee de l'Air Jaguars, raced from their desert bases to bomb Iraqi air bases and missile installations.

Before 3 a.m. on Jan. 17, an Air Force F-117A Stealth fighterbomber fired a laser-guided weapon that shattered an Iraqi communications center in downtown Baghdad. As the Iraqi antiaircraft defenses awoke and sprayed the night sky over Baghdad with colorful, but very dangerous tracer and standard rounds and surface-to-air missiles - a deadly combination called "Triple A" by Allied air crews - the world awoke to war.

So did the men and women assigned to the 345th CSH. "They started the air war on my birthday, Jan. 17," Milne said. "We heard the jets going out, and later the sirens started going off" to warn Dhahran about the first Scud attack against the city. The noise and the explosions "frightened many people, but we came through the Scud attack A-okay," he said.

When word came that they were moving to Log Base Alpha, the reservists thought that any place would be safer than Scud City, Milne said. The 345th CSH's personnel thought that way until they encountered the so-called "kamikaze camel jockeys," the local drivers whose exploits entered American military legend.

"Saudi drivers are incredibly bad," Milne opined. "While we were on the move north from Dhahran, one of our trucks was hit by a Saudi driver. There was another accident just two weeks before we left, involving a truck and a Nissan 200SX."

That accident happened to Lt. Col. Danny Neil, the executive officer of the 345th CSH. "I was riding in a 5-ton truck," he recalled. "We were traveling down this two-lane highway out in the desert, way out there, and this crazy Saudi driver pulled out to pass everything in sight.

"They'll do that without signaling and without thinking, I guess. The wheels of a semi caught his front end - he was in a Nissan 200SX - and spun him around," Neil said. "The truck I was in drove right over the back of his car and sort of crushed it. You ever seen a 200SX go into a guard rail at 80 miles an hour? That's what it looked like.

"The Saudi driver got a severe head injury. Lord, he's lucky that he wasn't killed," Neil stated. "I would swear that the Saudi drivers were more dangerous to us as a hospital unit than the Iraqis were."

Mike Milne reported that from Hafr al-Batin, the 345th CSH followed the 3rd Armored Division. "They went through the Iraqi defenses like a hot knife through butter. It was incredible," he said.

The 345th never set up its hospital, a factor that possibly added to the complaints that some soldiers voiced, Milne said. Dissatisfied with living conditions in the desert and worried about their families back home, a few reservists had discussed getting out of the Army after they returned to the States.

"Those of us older hands who'd been through a war before talked a lot to the younger soldiers," said Milne, who'd been to Vietnam with the Navy and later transferred to the Army Reserve.

"I knew from experience what the young people were feeling," Milne said. "But there are big differences between Vietnam and the Gulf. The outpouring of support from the American public really boosted our morale over there (in Saudi Arabia).

"And coming home to this (the troop greeting), well, emotionally it's a real high," the master sergeant continued. "The war and this, it's the most exciting thing we've done in a while. This is so much different than Vietnam. Unless you were there, you didn't hear much about it, how the Vietnam vets were treated as they were coming home. There's a big contrast."

While anxious to return home to his wife, Dianne, and their son and daughter in Ocala, Milne recalled a few lighter moments from duty in the desert. "The camels were big and ugly and short-tempered. We didn't mess with them," Milne said. "They'd go where they wanted, even into our defenses. We started calling them `Iraqi minesweepers.'" As Mike Milne spoke, Bob Jones, a.k.a. the Cable Guy, fell into the clutches of two soldiers who wanted to see the home of Stephen King, Bangor's own Master of Horror.

Jones said later that he'd mentioned Stephen King to the man and woman, who immediately "kidnapped" him and hustled him out the terminal door to his two-door hatchback. With his camcorder rolling, Jones taped a true confession from the soldiers as to why they were hijacking him and his car to 47 West Broadway.

"I'm an English major," the wide-eyed male soldier said. "My only dream is to be exactly like Stephen King when I am his age." Everyone who watched Cablevision's

Channel 35 the next night saw what happened next. Jones never protested as everyone piled into his car and headed across the airport to Hammond Street. For someone who had been "kidnapped" in Bangor, the Cable Guy showed no fear on camera, and his fans later wondered just who had kidnapped whom.

Jones pulled his car to a stop beside the wrought-iron fence surrounding the King estate. Playing to the eerie atmosphere created by the full moon, he announced their arrival and said, "It's pitch black to boot."

Like a novitiate priest approaching St. Peter's Basilica in Rome, the male soldier reverently stepped toward Stephen King's fence. Shadows vanished when Jones switched on the camcorder's light. There, about midnight and under a full moon, he filmed a transformation seldom seen in central Maine.

Gone was the cocky fighting soldier who'd slogged into Iraq. Present was a Stephen King disciple, who dared ask, "I wonder where Stephen King is right now?"

Kneeling beside the gate, the newly transformed horror fan raised his hands in supplication toward an imaginary master. The Georgia man clasped a notepad tightly between his uplifted fingers as he intoned, "If he were here, I would do this. 'Stephen King, teach me. Teach me, Stephen King.'" The disciple's hands shook as he said, "The number 11 is prevalent here."

The woman soldier cracked up laughing.

So did Bob Jones.

Then, after he stood, the awestruck Stephen King proselyte dared to reach toward the gargoyle guarding the gate. When his fingers contacted the holy relic, the horror devotee shivered for a moment.

A moment later, the uniformed acolyte transformed into the happy, joking soldier he'd been perhaps 10 minutes earlier. Everyone posed for photos outside the wrought-iron gate. The soldiers "released" an excited Jones so he could return them to the airport. During the "hijacking," Lt. Col. Danny Neil kept an eye on his soldiers in the domestic terminal while chatting about the war.

In civilian life, Neil purchased fuel for Delta Airlines' operations on the West Coast. Based in Atlanta, he'd been to Bangor three times for meetings with the former airport manager, Peter D'Errico. As an officer, Neil had reported for active duty three days earlier than the other soldiers in the 345th CSH. During the ground war, the unit was reconfigured into a MASH and wound up traveling in a convoy with the 159th MASH."

When the convoy finally stopped in Kuwait, the 159th MASH set up its hospital, but the 345th CSH did not. "Like everybody else in the 345th, I'm very pleased that we didn't have to treat American casualties," Neil stated. "Being in a combat hospital, I can tell you that we were quite happy that there were so few Americans hurt during the war." The Florida reservists remained in Kuwait only four days before returning to a position about 12 miles east of (Al) Qaysumah, Neil said. They stayed there about seven weeks.

Across the terminal, another Army officer stepped to the lectern and announced that UAL Flight 6475 would delay two hours in leaving Bangor. The soldiers cheered this proclamation, then moaned when the officer added "the bad news is, the bar closes at midnight."

Neil smiled as he overheard some enlisted personnel grouse about the midnight closure. "It's hard to put in words the feeling I have about being home," he commented. "There's no place like here, in the United States. We're so glad to be gone from the Gulf." He remembered one night when the soldiers had clocked a sandstorm's wind at 55 knots. And beyond the misery caused by the blowing sand, "in the last eight to 10 days, the temperatures were getting real hot, 100 degrees plus," he noted.

The lieutenant colonel mentioned that the Georgia-bound soldiers would deplane in Savannah and take a bus to Fort Stewart, where their families would meet them.

"I've been told that we'll all be issued a pass through Wednesday, then we'll need about a week or so to process out of the Army," he said.

Two other officers from the 345th CSH joined the conversation. Capt. Donna Casey, a full-time AGR (active Guard-Reserve or military technician), was the hospital's S-3, or operations officer. She enjoyed a special insight into Saudi culture; her parents had lived in Jiddah for two years.

"My parents did an `in-country' briefing on life in Saudi for the 345th some days before we left," Casey recalled. "They tried to give us an idea as to what the cultural mores were, those do's and don't's that Westerners needed to know."

Despite the personal briefing, "I wasn't prepared for the `touchie-feelies,' especially from Saudi men who were overly attentive to blonds," the captain said.

Even when the Florida reservists were doing their physical training, "Saudi men would show up and perhaps take photos of us women," Casey stated. "Yes, it was embarrassing at times, because we're not used to such behavior in the United States. Actually, other than their affinity for blond women, they're (the Saudis) very gracious people."

Mail really boosted morale in the desert, and Casey was especially grateful for letters from schoolchildren. "We'd read them through. A lot of the kids were very knowledgeable about what was going on," she said.

Capt. Marc Hardesty, a tall, dark-haired man who commanded a company in the 345th CSH, worked as an assistant state attorney in Jacksonville. When he changed his civilian attire for jungle fatigues, he did not leave his legal background at home, however.

Many legal questions arose when the Army mobilized the 345th, the captain said. The soldiers hustled to write their wills and establish powers of attorney. The hospital "has many single parents, especially single mothers, who faced questions about legal guardianship of their children.

"I couldn't act as a full-time lawyer, but I helped the troops as best I could," Hardesty stated. "I really would just give spot advice on what people should do."

He discovered that American men could mingle easily with the Saudis, at least Saudi men. Islamic laws forbade any fraternization between Saudi women and any men outside their families. Invited to a Saudi wedding, "I never saw the bride," Hardesty said, "since the men and women were kept separated. We had a good time, and I must say, it was a bit unusual. Camel was the main course. The camel's carcass was chopped up, and we had to pull chunks of meat off it. It definitely wasn't your Western steer basted over an open fire."

By 12:20 p.m., tired civilians and soldiers started dropping into the airport chairs, and the hubbub gradually diminished. Word filtered down that the general who commanded the assorted units on the UAL 747 wanted to meet them at Fort Stewart. The airliner must linger in BIA until everybody, including the general and the returning soldiers, could simultaneously arrive at Fort Stewart. Some troop greeters later wondered if this story were apocryphal. What general would ask his tired, homesick soldiers to wait past midnight in Maine so he could meet them at sunrise in Georgia? Later that night, BIA employee Marianne Mitchell called a blond woman soldier to the lectern. Civilians and soldiers gathered round and sang "Happy Birthday" to the embarrassed, but happy soldier. Mitchell issued the first boarding call about 20 minutes later. As the soldiers hugged their greeters and exited the terminal, the Cable Guy filmed the departures. Jones, toting his camcorder, wandered through the terminal and finally wound up outside the restrooms, where a laughing soldier informed Cablevision subscribers that he was going to use the bathroom "one more time just to hear the toilet flush, because I haven't heard that in six months."

An unarmed "kidnapping" to Stephen King's house, a religious experience on West Broadway, soldiers cheering a midnight delay in the middle of Maine, and now a young soldier admitting that he missed the sound of a flushing toilet.

A full moon does strange things in Maine.

OPERATION MAY DAY

The images contrasted sharply.

The already disintegrating Soviet Union celebrated May Day 1991 with a military parade through Red Square. Tanks, APCs, and rockets, interspersed with goose-stepping troops, rumbled and thudded past a reviewing stand containing the nation's leaders. Meanwhile, the people whom those leaders could not feed or house grudgingly formed an unappreciative audience.

Beginning two days earlier, Bangor celebrated May Day 1991 with a hearty "welcome home" and May baskets for its returning military. While en route to Pope Air Force Base in North Carolina on April 29, United Airlines Flight 6478 landed at BIA about 4:10 p.m. Knowledgeable troop greeters recognized Pope as the jetport for the 82nd Airborne Division at nearby Fort Bragg. Could the UAL 747 be hauling paratroopers, always a favorite among the Bangor crowd?

Perhaps 100 people turned out that Monday afternoon to meet the incoming soldiers. Several May basket-laden women and children circulated in the terminal, nervously checked the troopless ramp, and chatted with one another.

Robin Ashe and Carole Bassi, both residents of Bangor, belonged to the Patawa Club, a women's service organization. Other club members and their children had accompanied Ashe and Bassi to BIA today. Myriad May baskets clutched in their hands, the Patawas had planned a special, though premature May Day for the troops aboard UAL Flight 6478.

"We wanted to do something for the troops," Ashe said. "Most of us have been to troop flights out here, but not as a group. We wanted to do something to show our appreciation for what the troops have done, so we aimed for May baskets and created 'Operation May Day.'" About 20 women had made up 400 baskets, Bassi said, and all 45 members of the Patawa Club had donated candy to fill the baskets. As a tape deck blared mood music in the domestic terminal, the
soldiers on UAL Flight 6478 rounded the corner from the security corridor. Affecting that rolling, cocky gait common to uniformed men and women who know they're the best, the red-bereted troopers shook hands with the Legionnaires on the ramp.

Spotting the characteristic red berets, the crowd roared its approval. No one knew that few paratroopers would pass through BIA in the future.

The Patawas and their May basket-toting children scattered along the wire and soon overwhelmed the smiling, joking paratroopers with goodies. A woman and at least two children offered May baskets to Lt. Col. Shack Robinson of the 44th Medical Brigade. Just yards away, Bangor teenager Kristi Titcomb extended a May basket to Spec. Loretta Aiken of the 815th Personnel Services Co. Ashe and Bassi circulated among the soldiers, too, finally catching Spec. Joseph Keller and Spec. Stacey Manigo and giving them candyladen baskets. A few minutes after the last soldiers cleared the ramp, someone discovered that today was Sgt. Carlton Solomon's 34th birthday. Hurriedly locating a cupcake, a civilian placed a candle in it and lit the wick with a match. As people sang him "Happy Birthday," an embarrassed, but obviously delighted Solomon laughed and held his cake up where his buddies could see the burning candle. Once Solomon blew out the candle, he made short work of his cake. 2nd Lt. Herman Miller, who commanded the supply and service platoon of the 600th Quartermaster Co., hailed from Little Rock, Ark. Commissioned in May 1989 through Army ROTC at Northeastern Oklahoma University, he said that his platoon had left Fort Bragg in December 1990.

Miller described his platoon as parachute riggers, able to slingload supplies from helicopters or to attach chutes to supplies being dropped from aircraft. In the Gulf, the platoon specialized in slingload missions, particularly those flown by the big, twin-rotored CH47 Chinooks ferrying supplies to the 101st Airborne Division and the 24th Infantry Division (Mechanized). The supplies included fuel, water, ammunition, and, on one occasion, two engines.

Assigned to Log Base Charlie near Rafah, Miller and the 62 people in his platoon were never fired on by the Iraqis, although the soldiers entered Iraq at different times, he said.

At one point, Miller sent about one-third of the platoon on a recovery mission deep into Iraq to a site near the Euphrates River. The soldiers returned with parachutes and extraction systems left behind during a previous supply run to the 101st Airborne Division.

They returned to Dammam on April 15 and arrived in Dhahran about midnight on April 28, Miller said. Most of his platoon left for home in mid-April, leaving Miller and their remaining 26 comrades to follow on UAL Flight 6478.

His troops couldn't wait to land in North Carolina, Miller said. "I've been married six years," he explained his own anticipation, "and we've got a daughter who's 7 months old. Since I left, she's got teeth now, and she's gained 15 pounds." On his way into the domestic terminal, the young lieutenant had liberated a teddy bear from the gift table. "The bear's for my little girl," he smiled. "Oh, I really missed my family. April 3rd was our wedding anniversary, and I celebrated my birthday last December 8th over in the Gulf. I just want to go home."

Of the four platoons assigned to the 600th Quartermaster Co., only Miller's had gone to Saudi Arabia before the war. Another platoon would replace his in the Gulf.

As Patawas scouted the terminal for any soldiers lacking May baskets, Richard Myrshall walked to the lectern and announced the first boarding call. Paratroopers and civilians blended as the soldiers departed the terminal through a ragged semblance of a wire. Deafened by the sustained applause that echoed from the walls, a little girl clamped her hands to her ears as she dodged the outgoing paratroopers. Noticing the quiet sanctuary provided by the soldiers still clinging to the phones, the child edged closer to the wall and examined the crowd for a friendly face.

With the 747's departure apparently delayed by the extended farewell, Richard Myrshall waded into the throng and asked the civilians to move behind the stanchions.

When Myrshall issued the final boarding call at 5:24 p.m., a few stragglers dallied in the lounge or at the phones. Lt. Col. Shack Robinson swept the terminal clean by 5:28 p.m., but as he turned into the ramp, several Red Cross volunteers grabbed him.

Offered a large, homebaked oatmeal cookie, Robinson paused by the gift table and chatted with Delores Rush, Elaine Gustafson, and Paulette Dillingham. He nibbled the cookie, took a big bite, and thanked the women for their courtesy and the good food. Then, with some Patawas waving good-bye, Robinson vanished up the ramp.

EARLY MORNING CHAOS

An alarm summoned the troop greeter from a deep sleep at 2 a.m. on April 30. His reflexes slowed by his befuddled mind, he instinctively dressed in the Tuesday darkness and trundled outdoors to his Chevette.

Across Bangor and the surrounding towns, other people reacted in similar fashion at this ungodly hour. Some people - delivery drivers and McDonald's employees included - headed for work. Others, notably older men and women, headed for Bangor International Airport.

More troop flights.

The posted schedule called for United Airlines Flight 6476 to put into BIA at 2:50 a.m. before flying to Charleston Air Base, S.C. American Trans Air Flight 8347 planned to touch down at 3:13 a.m. while en route to Davis-Monthan Air Force Base in Ohio.

Two for the price of one. Not a bad deal, but infinitely more palatable during daylight hours, the troop greeter thought as he swung onto Union Street and drove through the blinking yellow lights. UAL Flight 6476 flashed past the domestic terminal at 2:32 a.m.

"What do you mean, it's already on the ground?" a surprised Gary Leighton questioned a greeter standing at the windows. The man pointed to the runway and shrugged his shoulders.

"There's no one here!" Leighton exclaimed.

He was right, as usual. Perhaps 20 people awaited the troop flight. Leighton looked at them, they looked at him, and then everyone moved, fast.

People hustled to the phones and called their buddies. "The plane's on the ground!" a woman hollered into a phone. "Are you coming?"

The few Legionnaires sipping coffee in the coffee shop hurriedly downed their java, grabbed their jackets, and bolted for the ramp. A quick-thinking Leighton passed them going the other way. He carried a table and a record player scrounged from the bowels of the international terminal. "Here, someone set it up," Leighton told a half dozen troop greeters. "The American Trans Air jet is right behind the United Airlines jet. I gotta go!"

He even left a record selection.

Two young Bangor residents, Jeff Dunn and Dana Leathers Jr. - or "DJ" to his friends - flipped open the legs of the table and set it against the wall by the duty-free shop. Excited by the possibility of helping with the music, Jeff and DJ pawed through the records. Their eyes expressed what their tongues diplomatically refused to say.

An Andre Kostelanetz album...another album titled "Now Hear This" by the Royal Netherlands Navy..."Anita Bryant: The Battle Hymn of the Republic"..."The Best of Kate Smith"...the records must've been left over from the days when BIA was Dow Air Force Base.

"Play the patriotic stuff," a volunteer suggested.

Dunn and Leathers gamely deciphered the record player's antiquated controls and powered into the "Navy Hymn" and other songs. Leathers finally decided it wasn't going to work. He bolted for a phone and contacted radio station WKIT-FM. "We've got a troop flight at BIA! Play some modern stuff!" he begged the deejay. "We can pipe it through the radio in the record player." At 2:45 a.m., the crowd still numbered only 20 people. Tom Dean and George Poulin ran down the ramp and unlimbered their gear. "We thought we had another five minutes!" a bleary-eyed Dean announced to the Red Cross volunteers.

A few minutes later, Valerie Bellomy and her daughters dragged a tape deck into the terminal. In the confusion, the tape deck did not reach Dunn and Leathers until the soldiers aboard UAL Flight 6476 entered the ramp.

American Trans Air Flight 8347 landed at 2:50 a.m.

Within two or three minutes, the UAL soldiers reached the ramp. Gary Leighton beat them into the domestic terminal as they slowed to shake hands with the outnumbered Legionnaires and VFWers.

Their ranks bolstered by late-arriving troop greeters, the civilians forming a makeshift wire applauded and cheered, making noise far greater than a crowd twice the size usually made. The two young volunteers finally solved the tape deck's mechanics, pulled the plug on Kate Smith and the Royal Netherlands Navy, and jacked the volume on Lee Greenwood's "God Bless the USA."

The incoming soldiers, who represented a melange of units, invariably swarmed to the phones or the restrooms. Some soldiers straggled into the Red Baron Lounge. Perhaps five or six civilians stepped away from the wire to pursue autographs.

At 3:03 a.m., a woman soldier leaned from the lounge entrance. A partially swiggled beer clutched in her hand, she shouted to an unidentified comrade, "Walter! It's cold! And it tastes wonderful!" Soldiers stampeded into the lounge.

Staff Sgt. Eric Miles and Spec. Scott Floro belonged to the 475th MASH from Frankfort, Ky. "We got in-country (into Saudi Arabia) Jan. 9th," Floro said. "We went to Dammam first, then they sent us up to Log Base Alpha."

The 475th MASH entered Iraq three times after the ground war began, Miles said. "The last time we went up there, we set up the hospital and stayed a few weeks."

Floro, who said that he lived in Lexington, Ky., proclaimed a strong desire to return home and resume his civilian life. "The experience has been good, but I'll admit that when I joined the 475th, I never thought I'd go to war," he stated.

At 3:10 a.m., soldiers from AMT Flight 8347 poured into the ramp. Their air crew, the AMT flight attendants and flight officers who'd flown them safely into Bangor, intermingled with them as the soldiers overwhelmed the official reception line and flooded the gift table. The 161 soldiers aboard the AMT L-1011 belonged to the 403rd Combat Support Hospital, an Army Reserve unit located in Phoenix, Ariz. The desert fatigues that the troops wore camouflaged them well as they blended with the soldiers from the UAL 747.

Maj. Joe Kentz, the personnel officer for the 403rd CSH, need not have gone to war. He belonged to another Army Reserve component, the 6251st Augmentation Hospital in Tucson, which did not go to the Gulf. Gainfully employed as a safety professional for Tucson Electric Power in Phoenix, Kentz volunteered for duty with the 403rd CSH. "I've been in the reserves for 22 years, so I thought it was my duty," he said. Kentz talked with Kathleen Cashin, an AMT flight attendant who'd accompanied the 403rd CSH into Bangor. "I've been working the troop flights since last November," Cashin commented. "I took them over in the fall and winter, and now I'm bringing them back. Their mood is some different now than last December."

According to Kentz, the 403rd CSH left Travis Air Force Base in California on Jan. 4 and landed in Dhahran on Jan. 6. "What a way to spend my birthday, getting introduced to the desert!" the major said. The CentCom staff finally sent the Arizona reservists traveling to a desert base just 10 miles below the Iraqi border, Kentz said. The base was not far from Hafr al-Batin.

"Along with the 128th Combat Support Hospital out of Germany, we were the most forward CSHs until the ground war started. We were so close to the border, we could see the bomb flashes from the nightly B-52 strikes," he recalled, "and we could feel the concussions ever so slightly in our tents." The 403rd and the 128th CSHs moved into the desert base 13 days before the Allies struck Kuwait and Iraq. The soldiers set up a hospital equipped with tents that featured padded floors, heat, and air conditioning.

When the ground war started, the casualties rolled into the desert base. "We took care of 27 percent of the casualties for the 7th Corps, including the 1st Infantry Division, the 3rd Armored, and some 1st Cav," Kentz stated.

The allied casualties seen at the base totaled about 50 soldiers, several of whom suffered serious wounds. Wounded Iraqi prisoners also came into the base. Their ranks included some Republican Guards, whom Kentz described as "trained soldiers, but the other guys, the regular grunts, were just thrown into the front line."

At another time, Kentz flew over the Iraqi border and the intricate defensive system that the Iraqis had created: minefields, berms, bunkers, wire. "It didn't work; our kids rolled right over them. Our kids did a helluva job in my estimation," he said. "That includes the kids working in the hospital. Hey, the conditions were less than stateside sanitary. Everyone worked hard. We didn't lose a patient in the hospital."

Word finally came to tear down the hospital and return to a rear staging area. "A day, maybe a day-and-a-half into doing this, three people were brought in who'd collected cluster bombs as souvenirs," Kentz said. "Within 30 minutes, we were up and running and operating on the American kids."

With its last patients out of danger, the 403rd CSH packed up its gear and returned to Saudi Arabia for seven weeks. The Arizona reservists finally boarded AMT Flight 8347 in King Khalid Military City at 5 p.m. local time on April 28. Since he was the senior officer aboard the L-1011, Kentz was named the aircraft commander, charged with carrying the passenger manifest and making sure that everybody reboarded the plane after each stop.

The airliner refueled in Sigonella, Sicily, and at Shannon International Airport in Ireland, then flew to Bangor, the last stop before home.

Kathleen Cashin had anticipated the homecoming awaiting the soldiers at BIA. Tired from the long overwater flight, Kentz heard only that "we were supposed to spend an hour-and-a-half on the ground in Bangor. I never expected anything like this. The support from you guys back home here was terribly important to the troops in the field."

Cashin, too, mentioned the "outstanding support the American people have shown our troops over there in the Gulf. We can't thank you enough for what the people of Bangor have done."

She and Kentz laughed and talked for a few minutes. After posing for photos, they moved off into the crowded terminal, where soldiers from both troop flights compared their war experiences and regaled a tired, but alert civilian contingent with hair-raising tales about Republican Guards, camels, and minefields.

Cashin later wrote the following letter to the Bangor Daily News: "I am a flight attendant for American Trans Air. Our flights with returning soldiers all stopped at the Bangor airport. All of us, crew members and soldiers, were overwhelmed with the reception the townspeople gave the returning troops.

"When the soldiers reboarded the aircraft in Bangor, some were speechless, some had tears in their eyes. All were very touched by the outpouring of love and support.

"When this conflict began, I volunteered to work the flights bringing them to war. It was a heart-wrenching job to watch young men and women walk off into the desert, and not know how many you'd be bringing home. It was gratifying to work on the flights with returning soldiers. The townspeople of Bangor made a real difference to these men and women."

THROUGH A PARENT'S EYES

While a culture apart, American and Iraqi parents share something in common: love for their children.

When United Airlines Flight 6476 touched down at BIA at 2:32 a.m. on April 30, the 747 carried soldiers from several outfits, including the 372nd Military Police Battalion of the Washington, D.C., Army National Guard. 1st Lt. Ernest Hobley served as the battalion chaplain. The UAL jet also ferried home soldiers belonging to the 475th Mobile Army Surgical Hospital of the Kentucky Army National Guard. Michael Cadrette, a 1975 graduate of Richmond (Maine) High School, went to war as the chaplain for the 475th MASH.

Two men, two chaplains, one black, one white: Hobley and Cadrette never met during their duty in the Gulf, yet they encountered a harsh brutality only briefly mentioned in the American press - Iraqi troops slaughtering helpless, unarmed children.

Before the Gulf War, Hobley had been the associate pastor of the Meridien Hills Baptist Church in Washington, D.C. "I was apparently destined to be a minister," he commented. "I was baptized when I was 12, and the pastor who baptized me predicted that one day I'd become a preacher."

The 372nd Military Police Battalion got to Saudi Arabia on Feb. 8, just two weeks before the Allied invaded Iraq and Kuwait. Part of the 14th Brigade, 7th Corps, the battalion traveled into Iraq during the war.

Service in the Gulf War challenged military chaplains. First Lieutenant Mike Cadrette (left) of Wilmore, Ky., brought solace not only to American soldiers, but to Iraqi parents whose children had been savaged by the Republican Guards. First Lieutenant Ernest Hobley (right) of the Washington, D.C., Army National Guard, also dealt with the horrors of war.

In May 1990, Michael Cadrette had graduated with his M.Div. from Asbury Theological Seminary in Wilmore, Ky. While attending the seminary, he served as the part-time pastor of the Community Missionary Church in Wilmore. By late spring 1990, the 100-member congregation "could finally afford to hire me full time," Cadrette said. "I was looking forward to that, but the war sort of intervened."

He left Wilmore in May for training as an Army chaplain. "I knew all the theological issues, but being a chaplain in the military requires additional training," explained the eight-year Army veteran. The 475th MASH followed the 1st Cavalry Division into Iraq, did an about-face and returned to Saudi Arabia, then "boomeranged right back to Iraq. We were told to set up our tents and equipment," said Cadrette. "We hadn't set up the hospital the first time we went into Iraq, but we did the second time." The hospital subsequently treated more than 300 patients, including Americans and Iraqi prisoners-of-war and Shiite refugees.

The Shiites fled a failed rebellion in the lower Euphrates Valley, where the local populace rose against the regime of Saddam Hussein in cities like Basra and An Nasiriyah. The Shiites enjoyed the upper hand for several weeks following the ceasefire. Then, confident that the Allies would not interrupt, the surviving Republican Guard ruthlessly put down the uprising.

Frightened, exhausted, and often wounded refugees fled into Iran or into Allied lines in southern Iraq. The exodus flooded the Allied hospitals with people suffering from various diseases, malnutrition, and wounds.

Ernest Hobley and Michael Cadrette will never forget the cruelty that Saddam Hussein's soldiers inflicted on their own people. In the weeks after the Gulf War ended, the two chaplains saw its aftermath through the eyes of Iraqi parents who found their families caught between warring factions - and who saw their children pay the price. Hobley talked about "getting some new insights into human nature" during his two years as a National Guard chaplain, especially in the issues shared by all humanity (i.e., life and death). "What I saw in Washington never really prepared me for what I witnessed in the Gulf, however," he said.

"There's a level of violence in Washington that affects everyone, families everywhere, but it's on a much smaller scale than what Saddam Hussein did to his people," Hobley noted. "And yet I learned that for the innocents, the kids and their moms and dads, issues were all the same in Iraq or Washington. The kids who get hurt never knew why or what hit them, and their parents just wanted them to be okay." The 372nd Military Police Battalion processed many Iraqi prisoners-of-war and assisted "many, many refugees," Hobley recalled. Though he was a Christian minister, Hobley visited the prisoners, whom he described as "decent Moslems who were very respectful toward religion. In fact, I believe that Moslems are more respectful of religion than most secular Americans are. To my surprise, I was very well received, even though I wore a cross and not a crescent (the Moslem symbol) on my uniform."

Despite the language barrier, Iraqi refugees welcomed his visits to Allied military hospitals, where the medical personnel struggled to save adults and children "who'd been shot, bombed, shelled, you name it," the lieutenant said. He found it "a very trying thing to sit in a hospital and see a 4-year-old girl with blown-up legs and blown-up arms and see in her face the horror that I could see in the face of my own child.

"It's something your eyes don't want to see," Hobley explained. "I've seen the same hurt and the same fear in the eyes of Iraqi parents as I have in the eyes of parents in Washington.

Hobley spoke with many refugees who, either through broken English or a translator, indicated that they "wanted freedom, more democracy, not another dictatorship. They'd put their lives on the line for freedom. They'd lost the fight in Iraq, but they tried. "America was holding up the light of freedom to the Iraqi refugees," Hobley said. "They'd reach American lines, and their reaction was incredible. I imagine that's what it's been like for people fleeing communism or other forms of organized, sanctioned terror." Cadrette encountered the refugees at the 475th MASH's camp. "The biggest shock to everyone's system was seeing so many Iraqi kids who had been hurt," he said, the memory flickering in his eyes. The lieutenant explained the obvious differences between wounds caused by shrapnel and mines. Pausing for a moment, Cadrette shook his head and stated, "These kids and their families weren't hurt by Allied action. We saw them long after the ceasefire took effect. "The Shiites rebelled," he said, "and (Saddam) Hussein sent his surviving Republican Guards to deal with them. They couldn't fight us, but they were real good on unarmed civilians.

"Hussein would just park (his tanks and artillery) around a town and obliterate it. The Iraqis brought their casualties to us. We saw what Hussein did to his people," Cadrette affirmed.

"How do you ask an Iraqi dad and mom who're watching their child die that you'd like to pray for them, but you pray to Jesus Christ, not Mohammed? Will a prayer to Jesus suffice for a Moslem? I didn't ask; I just went ahead and prayed," the chaplain said. "Jesus hears the prayers said to him in every language."

Unlike Hobley, Cadrette encountered some opposition to wearing a chaplain's cross in the desert. He described the Saudis "as more uptight about Christian ministers than the Iraqis were. I believe it's because the Saudis were more fundamentalist."

Not all the resistance came from the Saudis, however. A few times during trips to headquarters, Cadrette listened dumbfounded as superior officers asked him to remove his cross. "The general's policy was, do not wear the cross when you're in the built-up areas," Cadrette said. "Don't want to affront Saudi sensibilities, that sort of thing. I did-n't appreciate it a bit." Serving God in Saudi Arabia presented challenges not found back home. "I really enjoyed preaching in the desert, even though my pulpit sure didn't face pews or a well-dressed congregation like I did back home," Cadrette said.

Along with the Bible studies that he conducted, Cadrette enjoyed "praying with peo-ple, especially when they'd get lonely." With mail being a problem, particularly with the 475th MASH moving across the desert, phone calls home made a big difference for the soldiers. "That's probably one of the most important things that AT&T did for us, was the phone system that they installed, even in the middle of the desert," he said. In one week, Cadrette made 22 special phone runs, collecting soldiers and taking them to where the phones were. While in Iraq, Hobley baptized several soldiers in an open trailer lined with plastic and filled with water from a water buffalo (an Army vehicle). "It was unbe-lievable how God's Spirit was moving in Iraq, among the American troops," he said.

Hobley discovered that in wartime, a chaplain's role becomes very important. "The soldiers look for a chaplain," he said. "They depend on the chaplain."

The Gulf troopers were aware of the debate in Washington about Operation Desert Storm, and they asked questions about why they were there.

The soldiers looked directly up the chain of command to the Oval Office in the White House. "Asking `what right did he (George Bush) have to activate me?' was a question softened by realizing that Mr. Bush knew what it was like to be in combat for real," Hobley stated. Such knowledge was a key to morale, Hobley said. "He (President Bush) wasn't another stuffed shirt, another guy in a suit who didn't know anything about combat."

Because of his combat experience as a naval aviator in World War II, "the president could easily relate to the soldiers," the lieutenant said. "He was genuine, and they felt that. At this particular time in history, when America needed a George Bush, God pro-vided one. In 1991, George Bush was God's man on the scene."

MIXING BEARS AND BASKETS

At 2 a.m. on Wednesday, May 1, American Trans Air confirmed that its Flight 8399, an L-1011 bound for Fort Campbell in Kentucky, would land in Bangor about 5:20

a.m. A BIA employee updated the troop-arrival tape, and by 4:45 a.m., the first troop greeters began trickling into the domestic terminal.

The Red Cross volunteers staffing the gift table that May Day encountered an unusual problem: a lack of food for the troops. By late April, the flow of donated baked goods slowed, occasionally requiring the volunteers to ration the cookies, brownies, and fudge.

The Greater Bangor Chamber of Commerce had appealed for more edible goodies in an article published in the May 1 newspaper, but a request read at 6 a.m. could not deliver cookies to a flight landing at 5:20 a.m.

Faced with a virtually empty table, the Red Cross volunteers wondered what to do. "Fill it with bears," a woman suggested.

A bureaucrat might have responded by scheduling a meeting to discuss the proposal to exceed the allotted two boxes of bears per flight. But the Red Cross volunteers, like the other regulars among the troop greeters, weren't bureaucrats, and they weren't afraid to throw the two-box-per-flight restriction to the four winds. Today, the soldiers would get all the Ursus Berries that they wanted.

About the time that two or three women invaded the boiler room in the international terminal and lugged carton after carton of bears to the gift table, reinforcements rode over the hill - or in this case, up the escalator.

The reinforcements may not have been the 1st Cavalry, yet they arrived in the nick of time. Valerie Bellomy, her two daughters, and a niece hauled 260 colorful May baskets into the ramp just minutes before the AMT L-1011 landed.

Bellomy introduced her daughters, Andria and Mary Jane Eaton, and her niece, Tracie Bradford, and said that they all lived in Hampden. The younger women helped Bellomy make the May baskets and filled them with candy donated by the Downeast Pharmacy. "The baskets are intended for the troops," Bellomy announced. "Some people from the VFW post in Hampden are going to help us pass them out."

A blue-and-white AMT L-1011 touched down in a dismal light drizzle at 5:19 a.m. As a few cheers echoed up the ramp, Bellomy's three helpers placed the finishing touches on the display of May baskets. Then the women divvied up their responsibilities, but stayed on the ramp. If they'd joined the crowd along the wire, they'd have boosted its size by 15 percent.

A Balair DC-10 backed away from Gate 5 as AMT Flight 8399 taxied toward the international terminal. By the time the L-1011 rolled to a stop at the gate, the Hampden VFWers had joined the reception line on the ramp.

The veterans quickly made room for Matt Poulin, a young man with a mission. Wearing a University of Maine sweatshirt, he displayed a large white poster to which he had affixed a blown-up color print of his brother, Sgt. Marc Poulin. In the photo, a properly attired soldier knelt somewhere in the Saudi sands and proudly butted an M-16 against his left leg. In big letters above the photo, Matt had printed, "Welcome Home, Sgt. Poulin."

Poulin talked about the snarled communications that had prevented his family from being present when the AMT L-1011 landed. Until the airport changed the troop-arrival tape after 2 a.m., the plane was scheduled to land about 7:30 a.m. Poulin's family, who lived in Waterville, had planned to arrive about breakfast time to meet Marc, who was supposed to be aboard the L-1011.

Poulin awoke early that morning, dialed the airport, and listened in disbelief as the tape-recorded message announced a 5:20 a.m. arrival for AMT Flight 8399. Since he lived not far from BIA, a very surprised Poulin could meet the L-1011 on time. His family could not, though. Bangor was about an hour from Waterville on I-95, once the

Poulins could reach the highway. Phones rang in Waterville before sunrise that Wednesday, and sleepy people rushed to dress and hit the road.

Soldiers began unloading from the AMT L-1011 at 5:35 a.m. Holding his sign in his left hand, Poulin shook hands with 101st Airborne paratroopers. He scanned the approaching faces and hoped that Marc would suddenly appear on the ramp. He didn't. By 6 a.m., a visibly disappointed Matt Poulin lingered to greet the Tail-End Charlies, but he knew that his brother would not come home today...and he could not inform his family before they arrived in Bangor.

Another Maine boy did walk from the AMT L-1011 that morning. Beside the duty-free shop stood Hugh Michaud Sr., who'd driven to Bangor from Mattawamkeag with his wife, Betty, and their daughter, Lori. They'd pulled into the airport in time to welcome home Spec. Hugh Michaud Jr., a 1988 graduate of Mattanawcook Academy who'd gone to war as a light-wheeled vehicle mechanic with the 101st Airborne Division. "We almost missed him," Hugh Michaud Sr. said as he hugged his son. "I was contacted by the Army at Fort Campbell, and they told me that his plane would land there at 11:10 a.m. today, but that was only the promised time.

"I've been watching the schedule in the paper every day, and I've been calling the airport," the senior Michaud said. "Geez, I am glad I called them about 3 this morning. We thought the plane was going to get here later, and we'd have missed Hugh if I hadn't called."

As the Michauds slipped into the coffee shop for an off-the-beaten-path reunion, the soldiers from AMT Flight 8399 cleared the phones in the international terminal and straggled down the ramp. A startled Red Cross volunteer wondered aloud how many passengers the L-1011 had carried.

"About 250," someone replied.

Those passengers included Spec. Gwendolyn Remington of Goldsboro, N.C., who had joined the Army in August 1988 and had flown to Saudi Arabia with Alpha Co., 311th Military Intelligence Battalion, in September 1990. "Sure was a quick two years," she laughed.

Citing confidentiality, Remington described the battalion's primary mission as "keeping the 101st abreast of what everyone was doing around it, not only the enemy, but the friendlies, too."

The 311th gathered intelligence by various methods, often by conferring with infantry patrols or interrogating Iraqi prisoners. Other sources such as electronic or airborne surveillance also provided intelligence needed by the staff of the 101st Airborne Division.

"You can keep that desert," Remington said. "As far as being home in the United States, I wish I could kiss the ground. It looks a little cool out there, but I wouldn't mind."

Besides the 311th Military Intelligence Battalion, other outfits aboard the L-1011 included components of the 101st Aviation Brigade and HHC, 101st Airborne Division.

American Trans Air wasted no time in turning around Flight 8399. The first boarding call came at 6:05 a.m., and homesick paratroopers poured from the terminal. They swept around the corner into the ramp and crashed into the Immovable Eight, the four Red Cross volunteers and Bellomy and her relatives.

The eight women refused the paratroopers passage until they took a teddy bear, a May basket, maybe both. Young soldiers stuffed bears into deep pants' pockets, where the critters hibernated all the way to Kentucky. Officers and senior noncoms who remembered Vietnam graciously accepted plastic-sealed May baskets from a little girl clad in a sailor's suit.

Hampden VFWers passed out May baskets, too, sometimes handing a soldier a basket while slapping him on the back and thanking him for a job well done. Bears and baskets alike quickly vanished, with the Immovable Eight insisting that any soldier with more than one child "take an extra basket (or bear) or two."

The soldiers did, stripping both tables clean of teddy bears and May baskets before clearing the ramp at 6:20 a.m.

LAURIE LITTLE COMES HOME

During late January 1991, Iraqi forces briefly captured Khafji, a Saudi town on the Gulf Coast. Allied troops, primarily Saudi and Qatari armor and infantry backed by Marine Corps artillery, ejected the Iraqis within two days.

Its attention focused on the Battle of Khafji, the media initially overlooked a report that two American soldiers had vanished while driving a supply truck on the Tapline Road. A patrol later found the truck stuck in the sand not far from Khafji.

Someone, probably an Iraqi patrol, had stripped the truck of its cargo and occupants. When a subsequent report described the soldiers as a man and a woman belonging to a transportation company, the news electrified a United States not yet comfortable with sending its women to war. The information terrified a Maine woman whose daughter drove an Army truck in Saudi Arabia.

A thick fog, similar to the fog that diverted two American Trans Air jets to Boston on April 18, blotted the sun as troop greeters assembled at BIA about 6:30 a.m. on May 2. "Deja vu," a woman muttered to a passing reporter. "It's foggy, and American Trans Air's got another flight coming in. I bet it won't land."

AMT Flight 8403, confirmed to land at 6:55 a.m., carried soldiers on their way to Fort Bliss in El Paso, Texas.

As people wandered into the terminal and asked if the L-1011 had been diverted, they compared notes on the fog. Bangor residents felt chagrined: Nope, no fog downriver in Hampden or Orrington, no fog on the outskirts of Brewer. Nope, the only fog around is right here at the airport.

Troop greeters gathered by the terminal windows and peered into the fog as AMT Flight 8403 landed on schedule. As the plane taxied behind the Delta and United airliners parked at their respective gates, people pressed their noses to the terminal windows and waved to the unsuspecting troops.

Unsuspecting? Not quite. Sgt. Laurie Little taxied to a reunion with her family. Sgt. James Delzeit taxied to a greeting with a woman whom he'd never met.

Among the people clustered near Gate 2 stood a nervous Judy Little, a Cooper resident who'd traveled more than 90 miles to meet her daughter, Sgt. Little. "There's a good group of relatives with me," Judy announced, then added "and one friend" after a young woman whispered in her ear.

About 20 people raised their hands when asked to identify themselves as Littles, relatives, or friend. Grandparents, at least one sister, and a niece, 4-year-old Tiffany Crowe, who had not seen her aunt in three years. They were all here, encouraging each other as the L-1011 taxied past the windows and clutching posters adorned with oversized yellow ribbons and a message welcoming home the 233rd Transportation Co.

According to her mom, Laurie Little had graduated from Woodland High School in 1985 and had joined the Army under its delayed-enlistment program. A truck driver by military profession, she had shipped to the Gulf in October 1990 with the 233rd Transportation Co. out of Fort Bliss, the unit to which the two Americans captured near Khafji belonged.

"When I heard about it, I cried and was up and was watching the TV all the time," Judy recalled. "I couldn't help wonder, is my baby okay? Was she captured? Is she all right? I was scared to death for a day or two there. It's a horrible feeling, not knowing, wondering who it is, wondering if Laurie's all right."

When the Army identified the two missing soldiers as Specialists David Lockett and Melissa Rathbun-Nealy. Judy Little relaxed, but felt bad for their families, "because I knew what they were going through. The news had been good for us, not for them."

Iraq later announced that it held the soldiers and released them after the ceasefire. Lockett and Rathbun-Nealy flew home with other American prisoners-of-war and rejoined their families. This morning at BIA, Suzanne Pineau of Millinocket awaited Sgt. James Delzeit, a good friend of her Army son, Sgt. Todd Pineau. Assigned to the 233rd Transportation Co.

When Army trooper Laurie Little (center) landed in Bangor on May 2, 1991, she was greeted by her grandparents, Helena and Perley Tucker (left), her mother, Judy Little, and a niece and sister, Tiffany and Terri Lynn Crowe. Their reunion epitomized many at BIA from march 1991 to early 1992.

as a squad leader, Pineau left for Saudi Arabia last October, Suzanne said. He was supposed to be aboard this flight, she confirmed, but at the last minute, had given up his seat for another soldier. "He said he'd catch the next available flight out. I hope he does; I haven't seen him in two years," Suzanne said.

James Delzeit, an assistant squad leader in the 233rd, came from Oakley, Kansas. "Todd frequently mentions him in his letters," Suzanne said, "and I've been in contact with his wife. If Todd couldn't be on this plane, I'm happy that I can meet a friend of his."

AMT Flight 8403 soon disgorged its passengers, who eagerly flooded the ramp and swept along the wire. Laurie Little trailed the vanguard, and the Little clan recognized her as she reached the gift table. Tears flowed when the blond-haired soldier hugged her mother. Suzanne Pineau carefully scanned the name tags moving past her. A hand bolting ceilingward, she wildly signaled a tall, mustached soldier who stepped from line and hugged the Millinocket woman. "I picked him out by his name," Suzanne said, "but I think he'd stand out in any crowd. His wife told me how tall he was!"

Delzeit bade Suzanne a warm "hello" from Todd, who regretted not catching the flight. "He's doing real well, and he wants you to know that he's a-okay," Delzeit said. After standing in the ramp a while, he and Suzanne moved into the terminal to talk about the war and the young man they shared in common.

Sgt. William Fields of Akron, Ohio, had been in the Army almost seven years. He'd served the 233rd for almost three years as a heavy wheeled-vehicle mechanic. "If it's got tires, I can fix it," Fields said.

The 233rd Transportation Co. went to war with 22 M-911 HETTS, or Heavy Equipment Transportation Trucks. "The HETT is a full-size tractor-trailer rig," Fields explained. "We had 22 coming over...we lost two due to repairs or whatever, so we're bringing 20 back. The other two are in pieces."

Other equipment operated by the transportation company included three five-ton trucks and a massive wrecker that towed disabled tanks or armored vehicles. The equipment traveled by sea to Dammam, the same place where the 233rd's personnel landed after shipping for the Gulf on Oct. 16, 1990.

"Dammam seemed to be a place where everyone from that side of the country (Saudi Arabia) was disembarking," Fields commented. "Our vehicles went there. We sent an advance team to pick everything up." The 233rd Transportation Co. moved to Cement City, then later "to another place right beside it," Fields said. "Even over there in the desert, we learned that it's hard to find a place where you can maneuver the HETT. It's a big rig.

"Our main objective was to haul tanks from one place to another," Fields said. "M-1s, M-1A1s, Bradleys, M-113s, and whatever else they needed moved. We would move a battalion's armor (tanks and Bradleys) and come back for everything else."

The 233rd gravitated northwest along the Tapline Road to the infamous Log Base Charlie. "Being it was only a 100-hour war, I went to Rafah up close to the border, but I never got the chance to cross," the sergeant recalled.

After the war ended, the company moved from Log Base Charlie to TTC (Tactical Transportation Consolidation) North, a staging area 80 miles south of the logistics base. From there, the 233rd hauled many armored vehicles to Dammam and Dhahran. "Tanks, APCs, and artillery, we were bringing back Iraqi equipment along with American tanks and gear," Field explained.

1st Lt. Scott Sadler, acting CO of the 62nd Transportation Co. the other outfit aboard AMT Flight 8403 - described the captured gear as "the biggest assortment of intact tanks, artillery, APCs, and junk I've ever seen. Iraq was getting its equipment from all over. We saw stuff from China, France, the Soviet Union, Czechoslovakia, and other East Bloc countries. It was incredible."

"As the time got closer for us to leave, things seemed to keep us from going," Sgt. Fields said. "We were notified that we were leaving a few times, but nothing would be confirmed until the last minute. We just wanted to go home."

The sergeant's eyes softened as he talked about his wife, Joyce, and their two children, 18-month-old Christie and 6-year-old Bill Jr. "He's 5. No, wait, he's 6," Fields said, shaking his head. "Heck, he had a birthday while I was gone. Hey, it was a long six-and-a-half months."

Fields talked a few minutes about Lockett and Rathbun-Nealy. The sergeant expressed his delight upon learning that his comrades had survived their captivity and had gone home ahead of the company.

As an airport employee announced the first boarding call for the AMT flight, Laurie Little hugged her relatives and slowly backed into the ramp. There she encountered Capt. Elizabeth Dunlop, the CO of the 233rd Transportation Co.

Laurie brought Dunlop back into the terminal and introduced her to the Little clan. "Thank you for taking care of my daughter," Judy Little told Dunlop, who beamed and praised Laurie as an outstanding trooper.

James Delzeit said good-bye to Suzanne Pineau and departed for his plane. "Just meeting him makes me feel a lot closer to my son," Suzanne commented as she waved to Delzeit. "Kind of a a small world, isn't it, that Todd would go to war in Saudi Arabia, and his friend would come home through Bangor?"

Laurie Little, Capt. Dunlop, and some other soldiers comprised the last contingent to enter the ramp. They turned and waved to the crowd, and Laurie flashed another smile for her family. Judy Little stood watching the ramp for some time after Laurie vanished from sight.

CARNATIONS AND A WARM EMBRACE ON A WILD FRIDAY NIGHT

A driving spring wind blew sheeted rain along Godfrey Boulevard as American Trans Air Flight 8520 approached Bangor at suppertime on Friday, May 3. Motorists jockeyed for parking places near the terminals. Venturing into the gusty squalls that blanketed eastern Maine, people popped open umbrellas or drew jackets over their heads before bolting for the terminal doors.

After stopping at the passenger-service desk, AMT rep Mike Stott ventured down the ramp and peeked into the terminal. "Well, look at the size of the crowd!" he exclaimed, surprised that about 300 people had already arrived at BIA by 6 p.m.

The people kept coming. Children played on the escalator as their elders walked upstairs to find a packed waiting area. Near the windows in the domestic terminal, the country-western band "Desperado" finetuned its guitars and electronics and played chords for the crowd. The crowd kept growing, eventually swelling to an estimated 500 people. Excitement stirred the air. Did Bangor-area residents sense the special evening awaiting them? Did the fact that American Trans Air and World Airways planned to land troop flights about four hours apart play a role in attracting the largest crowd in a few weeks? Mike Stott thought so. "Hey, two for the price of one," he said. While en route from the Persian Gulf to Altus Air Force Base in Altus, Okla., AMT Flight 8520 planned to land at 6:38 p.m. "She's only 20 minutes or so out," Stott said. World Airways Flight A18522, headed for Forbes Field in Kansas, was scheduled to land at 10:11 p.m.

The crowd roared its approval when the AMT L-1011 touched down at 6:42 p.m. About 10 minutes earlier, when a Caledonia L-1011 had landed through the gray overcast, some people listening to Desperado had noticed the aircraft and cheered. Thinking the plane was his, Stott rushed back to the windows and glimpsed the Caledonia jet before it vanished along the runway. "Wrong plane! Wrong plane!" he informed the people nearest him.

Scottie Bell stepped to the lectern this wild Friday night. She welcomed everyone to the airport, explained the welcoming procedure, and inquired as to how many people were catching their first troop flight.

Dozens of hands shot into the air.

Rumors about a possible third troop flight circulated among the regulars standing near the gift table. Someone pointed out Valeree Foss and her daughters, Tavi and Stefanie. "Her husband's coming home tonight," someone whispered.

Valeree confirmed that her husband, Stephen, was en route to Bangor "even as we speak, I think." He flew on a commuter airline, however, not with AMT or WOA. An

111

Army Reservist assigned to the 1125th U.S. Army Hospital in Bangor, he'd gone to the Gulf. "We came early to catch his commuter flight, so we thought we'd meet the troops on this plane, too," Valeree said. "We weren't there to greet Steve when he got home, because he didn't come into Bangor, but we can be here for these other troops." Forming on both sides of the stanchioned wire that ran down the ramp, the Legionnaires and VFWers cheered as the first soldiers cleared the double-glass doors in the international terminal. The AMT L-1011 carried 243 passengers, Mike Stott had said. The astonished veterans of past wars disappeared in a moving, rolling sea of desert fatigues as all the AMT passengers apparently disembarked together. Desperado launched into "God Bless the USA," a song that set the crowd to clapping in rhythm. People stood on tiptoe or on chairs to glimpse the incoming soldiers. As the first trooper reached the bottom of the ramp, the crowd went delirious, vibrating the walls with thunderous applause and cheers.

The soldiers went absolutely nuts, too.

Hands reached across the wire to touch troops who hadn't seen an American woman in decent civilian clothes since early winter. Women soldiers openly cried tears that trickled down their cheeks to spot their blouses. Men soldiers grinned, laughed, and accepted hugs from any woman willing to rub a little desert dust on her clothing. People packing the wire between the coffee shop and the weather kiosk started chanting "USA! USA!" A soldier locked his hands together and raised them high overhead in a Rocky-style victory signal. Civilians and soldiers alike laughed and cried as the last troopers entered the terminal.

Civilians greet the soldiers arriving at BIA aboard American Trans Air Flight 8520 on May 3, 1991.

Then the crowd dissolved as the soldiers sought the phones and the beer. Undaunted children swarmed after the troops to seek autographs and souvenirs.

AMT Flight 8520 brought home the members of the 345th Transportation Co. and the 745th Military Police Co. (Guard). The latter unit belonged to the Oklahoma Army National Guard. Spec. Jack Dragoo, who sought some refreshments in the coffee shop, belonged to the 745th. The outfit, which was activated on Dec. 6, 1990, was based in Oklahoma City, Dragoo said. The troops "spent three days going to the armory. We were coming home at night then." The following Saturday (Dec. 8), the National Guardsmen went to Fort Sill, stayed there a month, then left for Saudi Arabia. The 745th Military Police Co. (Guard) arrived at Dhahran on Jan. 12 and remained there about two weeks, long enough for the soldiers to experience war at a distance. "The first Scud intercepted by a Patriot blew up off to the south," Dragoo recalled. "You could see it out the window."

He lived in the Khubar Towers, the seven- and eight-story apartment buildings built by the Saudi government for the Bedouins. "They refused to live in 'em," the specialist said, "probably because they didn't like being so far above the ground."

Late in January, the Oklahoma Guardsmen moved north to help construct a prisoner-of-war camp near Al Sarrar. The camp was named the 403rd POW Camp in honor of the Army Reserve's 403rd Military Police Co. (POW Camp), the Kansas-based outfit responsible for running the facility.

"When we first got there, it was just sand," Dragoo commented. "I couldn't envision a POW camp there."

As part of the 800th Military Police Brigade, the 745th Military Police Co. (Guard) and the 146th Military Police Co. assisted personnel from the 403rd Military Police Co. (POW Camp) in erecting 30 prisoner "cages." Concertina wire surrounded each cage, and a sand berm formed by a bulldozer surrounded each section of 10 cages, effectively creating three camps within the camp.

The Americans erected 30 tents in one (cage), and 25 (tents) in another until every cage was complete, Dragoo said. These tents, initially unoccupied, would later shelter captured Iraqi soldiers. Its designation as a POW camp permitted the facility to hold prisoners two weeks or longer. With the massive surrenders during the ground war, however, so many POWS poured into the camp that it was designated a holding area, where the Iraqis could be held overnight. "For a while there, they were truckin' them all day, so we had to keep 'em movin' through," Dragoo said.

Each arriving prisoner-of-war removed his clothing before taking a shower. The camp guards burned the clothing and deloused the Iraqis with a harmless chemical spray. Many prisoners had not taken a shower in weeks.

The Americans issued the Iraqis new clothing and boots "definitely better than what they'd shed," Dragoo noted. Then the guards assigned the prisoners to their respective cages.

The military police experienced few problems in feeding the hungry Iraqis, "who were grateful for anything we'd give them. They would receive good food," Dragoo said. "When hot food wasn't available, we would feed them MREs, which they seemed to like. I guess after going hungry so long, any food tasted good to them."

Specialist Jack Dragoo of the 745th Military Police Co. (Guard), Oklahoma Army National Guard, helped run a prisoner-of-war camp in Saudi Arabia.

The 403rd POW Camp handled about 33,000 POWs before shutting down in late March. After the last large group of Iraqis left, 200 of them stayed behind to tear down the cages, Dragoo said.

A bulldozer buried the concertina in the sand, and "the latrines and the showers were all given to the Saudis," he remembered. "Nothing was coming back this way. Even with all the sanitary precautions we took, we couldn't take the wire or even the tents back home." The 745th Military Police Co. (Guard) had returned to the Khubar Towers about three weeks ago, Dragoo said. When the company finally reached the airport to catch their flight home, "there wasn't enough room on the plane, so nine of our people volunteered to stay behind. They'll probably catch the next flight out."

As the airport's PA system summoned the soldiers to their L-1011, the civilians quietly hugged the outgoing soldiers. "Have a safe flight home!" people told the happy Sooners.

A few soldiers lingered to sign autographs or coax the last beer from a bottle. A tall, handsome soldier too young to remember Pleiku, Khe Sanh, or Hue started across the terminal toward the ramp. "Hurry, or you'll miss your flight!" a woman called to him.

The soldier turned toward her, placed his hands on his hips, and shouted, "I'm an American! I can hitchhike home!"

AMT Flight 8520 left behind one passenger. Bill Novichuk, a ground-operations supervisor for American Trans Air, had spent the last month coordinating troop movements from the Gulf aboard AMT aircraft.

American Trans Air "has been taking back, oh, 200-230 troops per plane, one to four planes a day out of Dhahran mostly, with some from Riyadh," Novichuk said.

The airline belonged to the Civil Reserve Air Fleet (CRAF), primarily an organization that provides additional airlift capabilities for the American military. From August 1990 to summer 1991, the government drafted such civilian airlines as AMT, United, Pan Am, World, and Hawaiian Airlines to commit aircraft to ferrying troops to Saudi Arabia or the United States. American Trans Air had committed seven L-1011s to the operation, Novichuk stated.

His work in Saudi Arabia focused on taking care of ground operations for the aircraft. "You know — fuel, food catering, cleaning. It was imperative that we ensured each plane's correct weight before it took off, especially in that 100-degree weather," he explained. Although the American military "has been very helpful in loading the aircraft and distributing the weight, we don't always leave when we want," Novichuk said. "We just juggle the schedule to accommodate the military. A plane might leave on time, or it might wait a day. "There are a lot of troops moving from the Gulf right now. In one day on the ramp, I saw Pan Am; American West was through with a 747; American Airlines had a 747 there," he recalled. "The word is out to get them home as soon as possible."

His month's tour completed, Novichuk had hitched a ride home with AMT Flight 8520. The L-1011 changed crews in Sicily and Ireland. The crew that boarded at Shannon International Airport would remain with the aircraft as far as Altus Air Force Base, where another crew would board the plane for the final leg of its journey to Davis-Monthan Air Force Base in Tucson, Ariz. There the L-1011 would drop off people from the 348th Transportation Co. of the Arizona Army National Guard. As American Trans Air Flight 8520 taxied past the domestic terminal and vanished into the darkness, troop greeters stood at the large glass windows and waved to the departing soldiers. Then people drifted away to kill time until World Airways Flight A18522 arrived.

The terminal eerily emptied. Where 500 people had packed the place 90 minutes earlier, perhaps 50 to 100 people lingered, preferring to sit and read a book or chat with a friend.

Other people went home in the rain-soaked darkness, but promised to return by 10 p.m. Desperado left its instruments and speakers in place, but the musicians disappeared for a while, too.

Everett Steele wandered through the terminal about 8:25 p.m. and spread the word: "We've got another troop flight coming in downstairs." A commuter flight was bringing home two Maine soldiers, he said, "so we're planning a greeting for them."

Downstairs, Ralph Field stood beside Gate 3, the entrance used by passengers aboard the twin-engined prop jobs linking Bangor with Presque Isle, Portland, and points south. Field held a metallic helium balloon and a dozen paper-wrapped carnations. "Yeah, she's coming home tonight!" he exclaimed. Not exactly a troop flight, but it would do. Field introduced his children, Monica and Joshua, who anxiously awaited their mother's return.

Deborah Field had landed in New York "four or five days ago," Field explained. "She called to let us know that she was okay and would be coming home as soon as she processed out of the Army." Deborah had hopped a USAir jet to Logan International Airport in Boston, then caught Northwest Airlink Flight 3732 for the final ride home. Field expected his wife to arrive about 9 p.m. "This foul weather makes me nervous," he admitted. "It's not a good night for flying."

Valeree Foss and her daughters stood beyond the Fields. "Yes," Valeree confirmed with a big smile, "Steve is coming home on this plane. He got back to the States just a few days ago."

More people drifted downstairs and swelled the crowd waiting near Gate 3. Everett Steele quietly told the Fields and the Fosses, "Since your soldiers couldn't receive an official greeting upstairs, we decided to bring the reception to them down here."

As the crowd gathered, members of Girl Scout Troop 331 from Glenburn stood near the luggage carousel and sang. Legionnaires and other volunteers joined the crowd. Robert Jones drifted downstairs to videotape the landing. He briefly interviewed Debbie Langley, Stephen Fosses' sister-in-law, before turning the camera toward Gate 3.

A few people wandered upstairs to watch for the commuter flight. Rain streaked the windows, which already reflected the terminal's interior lights, so visibility toward the runway "sure isn't good," one woman commented as she pressed her face against the glass.

Then some blinking lights set too close together for a large airliner rolled along the runway. "Is that it?" people asked.

As the twin-engined, propeller-driven plane swung toward the terminal, a color pattern finally coalesced on the fuselage. "Yep! It's

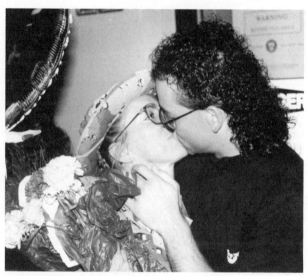

Months after she went to war, Ralph Field kisses his wife, Army Reservist Deborah Field.

Northwest Airlink!" a man exclaimed. People stampeded downstairs and relayed the news to the waiting crowd. The Fields faced Gate 3, as did Valeree Foss and her daughters, who held a ribbon-decorated, green posterboard sign that proclaimed in dark letters, "SSG. S. Foss, Welcome Home! 1st Engr. Bn./1125th U.S. Army: Love, the Girls!"

Ralph Field peered through the double doors that formed Gate 3. Detecting movement near the parked Northwest Airlink aircraft, Ralph straightened his shoulders and waited.

Deborah Field burst through the entrance and into her husband's arms. She and Ralph held tight for a long time and then burst into joyful conversation as Monica and Joshua joined them.

Steve Foss plowed through the double doors and beelined for Valeree and their daughters. People cheered the poignant reunions even as the other passengers from the commuter flight entered the domestic terminal. "Aw, just for the heck of it, let's cheer them, too!" someone exclaimed, so onlookers cheered the arriving civilians. Ralph Field gave Deborah the dozen carnations, then swept her into a warm embrace captured forever on Kodak film and videotape. Smiling and laughing, the Fields chatted quietly.

Steve Foss paused a moment to autograph a child's T-shirt, hugged his daughters again, and momentarily vanished, apparently to find his luggage. Everett Steele edged from the noisy crowd and hugged Deborah Field just before Bob Jones told her, "Sgt. Field, on behalf of all of us, as representatives of your home town, welcome home!" "Thanks," Deborah replied, grinning at the unexpected reception. "It's so great to be here. I can't believe all the people!"

Carl Lindh pinned a yellow ribbon on Field, who then turned to speak to her husband. Ralph suddenly held out his hand, uncurled his fingers, and displayed a small black box balanced on his palm. Deborah's eyes widened as the sergeant gingerly opened the box to find a ring "that I've been saving for you," Ralph quietly explained. He slid the ring onto his wife's finger. The Fields embraced, holding a long kiss that drew a "wooo" from an observing Girl Scout.

After all those days and nights spent greeting other soldiers, a dedicated Ralph Field had finally welcomed his soldier home.

When she reported for active duty with the 1125th U.S. Army Hospital on Jan. 29, 1991, Deborah Field had anticipated working at a hospital in the Bay State. Eighteen days later, to paraphrase Judy Garland's famous line in the "Wizard of Oz," she realized that "gosh, Toto, I don't think we're in Massachusetts anymore."

When the reservists from the Bangor-based 1125th U.S. Army Hospital reported to Fort Devens, Mass., on Feb. 1, no one envisioned what awaited them. "We were all supposed to go into a hospital in Massachusetts, so I thought I wouldn't be too far from home," Field recalled.

In its infinite wisdom, the Pentagon decided otherwise.

"Then the Army said they needed `super medics' (combat medics); I was the only female that was a 91-Bravo (the Army's designation for a combat medic), so they said I was on my way to Saudi Arabia," she said. She received a day's notice before shipping from Fort Devens. After bidding her family farewell, Field traveled to Fort Jackson in Columbia, S.C.. On Feb. 16, just one week before the Allies invaded Iraq, she left Shaw Air Force Base en route to a Saudi Arabian odyssey.

About the time that Field left for the Persian Gulf, the military dispersed many other soldiers from the 1125th. Vernon Brissette joined the 5th MASH for its epic "Convoy From Hell," and Staff Sgt. Stephen Foss ultimately invaded Iraq with a medical unit. Other personnel scattered across the globe, filling vacancies left by wartime deployments.

Field finally received orders dispatching her to the Headquarters and Headquarters Co. (HHC), 1st Infantry Division, the outfit known as the "Big Red One."

"When I found out it was an infantry outfit, I was sure some surprised," she said.

When Field arrived at her duty station in late February, she was told that the unit had several combat medics already, "but they said they could always use the help if we got casualties. I heard some talk about expecting 60 percent casualties. "I thought I could finally open my bags," Field commented, "but they said we were jumping tomorrow. Not `jumping' like the paratroopers, but moving out for Iraq. That news made me think.

"We went to a position just in range of their (Iraqi) artillery the first day, with seven or eight other companies waiting nearby in the desert," she remembered. "The next day, we crossed the berm at a place where D-TAC (Division Tactical) left a sign that said `Welcome to Iraq, courtesy of the Big Red One.

"Everybody was really excited. We couldn't wait to go into Iraq. It was almost like an adrenaline rush, the excitement was so strong," she said.

Her unit stayed just inside the berm one night and then went on a three- or four-day road trip, backtracking once to shelter for the night with some engineers from the 82nd Airborne Division.

"The Air Force had just finished bombing the area, which had not been swept for explosives," Field explained. "It was too dark out. They said we shouldn't go through."

The 82nd Airborne engineers accompanied the Big Red One troopers into Kuwait. The convoy rolled into the hell-on-earth created by the burning Kuwaiti oilfields. Deborah Field described the horror as "total destruction, lots of dead bodies everywhere, burned-up bodies..." The combat medics treated captured Iraqis in Kuwait. "They didn't have shoes. Saddam Hussein didn't want them to leave, so they weren't permitted shoes, an Iraqi colonel told me," Field said. "We checked their feet real close because of that.

"Their diets were really terrible. They didn't have any food for the last four or five days," she said. "They didn't even have water for two or three days."

Conditions had deteriorated badly among the Iraqi soldiers defending Kuwait. "The Americans found some Iraqi officers with six or seven bullet holes in them, after being shot by their own people. I talked to some EPWs who said they shot their officer in order to surrender," Field said.

The American medics visited local refugee camps and helped set up tents at an airstrip. The Allies and the Iraqis used the tents during the ceasefire negotiations. Afterward, refugees occupied the tents in considerable numbers. The medics called on these refugees, too. "That was really tough, seeing little kids die because of Saddam and his stupidness," Field reflected. "I had a hard time finding some 24-gauge IVs for little babies. We tried to save a lot of them. We gave the refugees whatever food we could, yet they would chase the trucks to grab even more food from the soldiers."

On March 15, 1991, Field called Maine for the first time from the desert. "It was wonderful. I had to call my mother and tell her to contact Ralph," she commented. "He went to my parents' house and waited for my call. It was just so incredible. It was like, `I'm alive, I'm here, I'm not where I was supposed to be, but I'm here.'" Later, the Army broadcast a need for some women medics at Hubner, a staging area about 30 miles out-side KKMC in Saudi Arabia. "My hand went right up," Field remembered. "I said it was fine, because it was one step closer to home." On April 22, the Army informed Field that she'd be leaving, but this was cancelled after she had called Ralph and told him she was coming home. The next day, her departure was cancelled again.

"This went on until April 28, when I finally left for Rome," she said. "We stopped at JFK in New York. I missed Bangor. We flew right over it."

She landed at Shaw Air Force Base on April 29 and rode in a military bus to Fort Jackson, where she and Stephen Foss processed out of the Army together. With accrued leave, Field would officially depart the Army on May 12, nine days after she returned home. "While I was in South Carolina, other people were flying in and saying, `Oh, my goodness, we flew into this place called Bangor, and there were thousands of people there to greet us.' I was really disappointed that we didn't land in Bangor," she said.

On May 3, the two Maine medics flew via USAir to Boston and connected with a Northwest Airlink flight to BIA. Their plane turned up late "somewhere along the way, and it hadn't arrived, and the terminal called another flight," Field stated. "It wasn't our plane, but we wanted to go home."

Other passengers with reserved seats on that flight volunteered their seats. A young lady said, ```I'll wait for the next one.' We thanked them and got aboard in such a hurry, we even left our bags behind. We said, 'Heck, there's nothing we want in those bags, we just want to go home!'" Field explained.

The Northwest Airlink flight on which she had intended to fly put into Bangor just five minutes after Deborah Field landed. She grabbed her baggage before leaving the airport. "I couldn't believe how many people were there to meet us," she said.

"I'm finally starting to relax. I want to thank everybody. Sometimes when I drive down the street, I get depressed about being over there," she stated later. "Then I see the ribbons and flags, and I feel so much better. I think I'll put the memories about the oilfields and the refugees behind me in time." By 9:30 p.m. that Friday, the Fields and Fosses had cleared the airport, and the troop greeters had floated back upstairs. By then, the crowd waiting for World Airways Flight A18522 numbered about 200 people. Many troop greeters who went home after AMT Flight 8520 departed for Oklahoma returned to the airport.

Then Santa Claus blew in.

No one noticed whether Old Saint Nick landed his sleigh and eight reindeer on the runway or maneuvered them to a tricky touchdown atop the domestic terminal, but, suddenly, there stood the red-coated Jolly Old Elf.

As the crowd swelled to more than 300 people, Santa Claus pulled a magic act and produced a Christmas tree decorated with a large yellow star. Then he summoned his helpers - members of Girl Scout Troop 38 from Dexter - to gather around the tree, which he placed between the lectern and the entrance to the coffee shop.

While Santa decorated the terminal, four Massachusetts residents anxiously awaited Flight A18522's arrival. Rita Laurence of Marlboro, Massachusetts, introduced her husband, Ernest; a daughter, Sonya Laurence; and a nephew, 5-year-old Jeremiah Franczyk.

They'd traveled to Bangor to meet the Laurences' older daughter, Spec. Elizabeth Meyer. Since joining the Army in 1988, Elizabeth had been assigned to the 701st Support Battalion, 1st Infantry Division, at Fort Riley in Kansas. There she met and fell in love with Patrick Meyer, an investigator for the military police.

After learning that she would ship for the Persian Gulf, Elizabeth married Patrick in October 1990. They enjoyed a brief honeymoon before she bid him good-bye on Dec. 18, 1990, a date engraved along with Elizabeth's name on the bracelet that her mother wore.

Through phone calls to Patrick, the Laurences learned that Elizabeth should land in Bangor on May 3. "We promised her that we would try to meet her, wherever and whenever she returned," Rita said. "Up here in Maine was fantastic; it's practically next door. We left last night about 11 o'clock and got here about 4 in the morning." Another family awaited WOA Flight A18522, too. A Scarborough woman had cut short her workday, picked up her two school-aged children, and driven almost three hours north on the interstate to catch the plane.

The woman explained that although divorced from her husband, she wanted their children to meet him as he came home from the war. "He's supposed to be on this plane," she said as her son and daughter stood beside her and watched the noisy crowd.

The crowd numbered about 350 people when Gary Leighton announced tonight's flight as "Christmas in May." After introducing the Dexter Scouts, he explained that the girls would pass out Christmas-related bookmarks and would sing "Jingle Bells" and "Joy to the World" with the band Desperado. Ragged cheering heralded the WOA DC-10's arrival at 9:45 p.m. Leighton then invited everyone expecting a relative on the incoming flight to cross the wire and wait beside the duty-free shop. People cheered as the Laurences and the Scarborough family passed along the wire and took their positions at the ramp entrance.

Within 10 minutes, soldiers strolled into the ramp to a rousing welcome from the Legionnaires and VFWers. Cheers echoed up the ramp, and the crowd started clapping in rhythm with Desperado's music. Rita Laurence clutched a large bouquet of flowers in her hand as she examined the faces approaching her on the ramp. Soldiers flooded past her. Then, with a joyful cry escaping her lips, Rita bolted into the ramp to hug a dark-haired woman soldier who wore eyeglasses. Mother and daughter clung together a long time. Ernest and his family moved toward them. Spotting her family, Elizabeth extended them a hand across her mother's shoulder and drew them into the reunion.

The Scarborough family watched as the last soldiers entered the ramp. Realization slowly dawned for the bitterly disappointed children, who cried their frustration as their mother coaxed them to wait until the ramp cleared. Their father had not come home aboard this plane.

As soldiers poured into the terminal, Leighton invited people to extend the troops "a Bangor welcome." Taking their cue, 350 civilians hooted and hollered...

...and the Christmas party began.

Raising his voice above the din, Leighton again introduced Santa Claus and the Dexter Girl Scouts and told the startled soldiers that "we wanted to help you celebrate the Christmas and the holidays that you missed." He deferred to Desperado, which launched into a country western version of "Joy to the World" and a wild "Jingle Bells" that clinched the party.

Even as the Girl Scouts sang the Christmas carols, soldiers and civilians swirled into impromptu dancing near the band. Someone gave two women soldiers red, white, and blue "Uncle Sam" hats, which they promptly donned to the crowd's delight.

Pfc. Nancy Culbert hailed from San Diego, Calif., while her friend, Spec. Paula Scheuneman, came from Oklahoma City. Assigned to the 201st Forward Support Battalion, they'd shipped for Saudi Arabia on Jan. 7.

"Oh, it's great to be coming home," Scheuneman said, and Culbert nodded in agreement.

"And this party you're throwing for us: It's fantastic!" Culbert exclaimed, shouting to make herself heard. "Say `thank you' to everyone in Bangor for us!"

Phil McCombs, a reporter from the Washington Post, interviewed people a few yards away. This week - tonight - marked the high tide for the national press coverage at BIA. A day earlier, Mary Tabor of the New York Times had covered the flight bringing Laurie Little home. Crews from the four major networks had shot footage in Bangor. A Vietnam vet, McCombs caught the May 3 flights and interviewed local notables who expressed opinions pro and con on greeting the troops. McCombs wrote an article subsequently published in the Post on May 12. The article erased some damage caused by an earlier, inflammatory rage published by Post columnist Colman McCarthy that vilified Americans who cheered the successful conclusion of the Gulf War. McCarthy had referred to the "vast crowds rabid to be pleased to the tips of their hokey yellow ribbons."

McCarthy wrote that "the sentimentalizing of the Iraq massacre has begun...Some citizens in Bangor, Maine, have lives so devoid of meaning or stimulation that they have been breaking the boredom by hieing out to the airport to cheer and hug troops passing through on a refueling stop.

"It's hyped as New England bedrock patriotism," he wrote, "except it's no more than a citizenry displaying a willingness to be snowed by the Bush-Schwarzkopf line that this was a valorous war overseen by the Good Lord himself." Needless to say, the column had irritated many troop greeters. The wild party in the terminal swirled into a hurricane, its eye whirling around a tanned young soldier who held a tiny baby tight to his chest. Oblivious to the chaos sweeping past him, the soldier quietly kissed the little pink-clad girl time and again.

Sound asleep, 10-week-old Meagan Alley of Bangor sucked a pacifier as she cuddled

in the arms of Sgt. Robert Toth, who was stationed at Fort Riley with the 437th Armor Battalion. Toth spotted Meagan in the BIA crowd and asked her mother, Billey Alley, if he could hold her.

Sporting a green Dysart's Truckstop baseball cap, Toth kissed the sleeping Meagan on her forehead. "I miss my own daughters," he said before the tears welled into his eyes. "The oldest girl is 4. Her birthday was last month. My youngest is 2. Good Lord, how I miss them."

The Christmas party maintained its frenetic pace. After the Girl Scouts sang three additional carols with horribly off-key accompaniment from the troops, the band resumed its country-western repertoire. Within seconds, soldiers and civilians again hopped onto the dance floor and boogied into the night.

Later, when WOA Flight A18522 finally taxied from its gate, many soldiers slowly unwound by comparing notes about their Christmas in May. Yellow ribbons, plastic flags, and lollipops comprised their material gifts, but this night, the soldiers took with them an intangible gift: a nation's love and a lifetime's memories.

As a wild party enveloped BIA on May 3, 1991, Sergeant Robert Toth quietly rocked 10-week-old Meagan Allen of Bangor. Tears rimmed Toth's eyes as he held Allen for several minutes. Assigned to the 1st Infantry Division, Toth had left his two young daughters stateside.

THOUGHTS FROM THE IVORY TOWER

As the troop flights unwound through BIA, letters poured into the Bangor Daily News. Men and women who'd landed to tumultuous greetings in Bangor dashed off thank-you notes while flying to a final destination or after arriving home in North Carolina, Texas, California, and elsewhere. Parents and spouses who heard all the good talk about Bangor also penned letters to the BDN, the only memento with an address that the troops usually took from the Queen City.

The responsibility for opening the envelopes and reading the correspondence fell to Dick Shaw, the newspaper's editorial page assistant. His job placed him in the "Ivory Tower," the bastion of editorial thought found in most daily newspapers.

When American Trans Air Flight 7254 landed in Bangor on March 8, Shaw didn't pay the plane's arrival much attention. While the chaos spread through the domestic terminal early that morning, he sorted the mail and started reading the day's incoming letters. By midmorning, however, he had heard from an excited Marc Blanchette, the BDN photographer assigned to cover AMT Flight 7254, that something unusual was happening at the airport.

Highly respected as a local historian, Shaw listened as rumors buzzed in the newsroom. Was something of historical interest occurring just a few miles from the office? He had to find out.

After battling the traffic on Godfrey Boulevard, Shaw finally found a place to stand in the domestic terminal. Hundreds of similarly curious people jostled for elbow room. Like Shaw, they wondered what all the morning's excitement entailed. "The terminal was packed. It's all sort of blurred now. I just remember lots of people coming down the ramp, the confusion, the noise," Shaw said.

A quiet man who seldom displays his emotions, Shaw sensed the undercurrent rippling through BIA. Like other people who had ventured to the airport on a lark or a whim, he could not pinpoint the exact moment that his cool, calm demeanor melted. Sometime during that

Richard "Dick' Shaw, editorial page assistant at the Bangor Daily News, greets an Air Force technical sergeant in October 1991. A noted local historian, Shaw quickly recognized the national historic significance of the troop flights.

troop flight, Shaw passed from detached professional journalist to emotionally involved participant.

"I had no interest in going out there before then," Shaw said. He had little interest in things military, not having joined the military or hung around people who wore jungle or desert fatigues. During that emotionally charged morning, however, things just clicked. That particular flight proved "something to be happy about," Shaw recalled. He found the excitement "so infectious, almost like a rush of adrenaline, something that I can't describe. I just had to keep going back. It was almost like a disease, only a happy disease that I didn't mind catching."

Shaw returned to the airport that Saturday and Sunday and 130-140 times afterwards. He became a fixture on the wire, typically standing across from the lower ramp entrance with Joy and Aubrey Brown, neighbors from Howard Street in Bangor. Their vantage point granted them a clear view as far as the passenger-service desk and a great location for shaking hands with troops rounding the corner into the terminal. By late April, the people welcoming home the troops coalesced into two groups: occasional visitors and the "regulars," the tightknit, unofficial assemblage that tapped Shaw as a member.

People developed friendships that lasted after the flights ended. Bangor-area residents who wouldn't usually associate with each other grew very close, and by summer, when someone referred to "Dick," the other troop greeters could place a face with the name.

That meant a lot to the soft-spoken man from the Ivory Tower. "I never was in the Scouts or a group with a tremendous sense of camaraderie," Shaw explained. "For the first time in my life, I felt that. You were part of a team, doing something that made me feel like I was participating in an event that would make a big difference in someone's life. "I liked the core group of people I was with," he said. "It was like a fraternity of people with a common objective. I've never felt anything like that in Bangor before."

The troop flights baptized Shaw in military ways, from the look-alike uniforms to the polite conversations that he enjoyed with the troops. He described the experience as "an education, being able to talk to war veterans. It was like being an eyewitness to history. "I just couldn't stop going, not so much for any interest in the military, but because of the people and the excitement," Shaw said. "I think each flight was almost like Christmas morning, waiting for the big door to open to see what Santa Claus had left. Being in the middle of 200 Marines who were all shaking my hand was just incredible.

"Whenever I travel, I always watch people. This was a tremendous opportunity, watching the interaction between complete strangers. It was like a big movie to me, an overwhelmingly positive experience." Every troop greeter remembers a particular flight, perhaps two, that stand out from the rest. Shaw's memory lingers long on Hawaiian Airlines Flight 7840, an L-1011 that broke down in Bangor on April 8 while en route to Fort Campbell, Ky.

The plane carried Green Berets from the 5th Special Forces Group. That morning, more than 100 Green Berets stood in the domestic terminal and sang "The Ballad of the Green Berets." "I think I could've cried at that moment, they were singing so loud and proud," Dick remembered.

He met a Special Forces trooper "who had a savage look about him. He'd been in the thick of it, and he had come back to Saudi Arabia or wherever still covered with the dirt he'd dragged off the battlefield in Iraq." The Green Beret had wound up at a press function where Defense Secretary Richard Cheney was. "Because he was still in his desert dirt, he was shunted out of the picture, and they replaced him with some guys in clean uniforms. He didn't like that," Shaw said.

The trooper told Shaw that he still had a ringing in his ear because a missile had landed too close. "Just to look at him, I knew he wasn't kidding me. In fact, I was really surprised at how quiet and human the Green Berets were. They weren't the John Wayne types, all braggadocio. Yet this soldier, he had such a hard stare, it was almost like he didn't see me," Shaw recalled.

That night, a Green Beret gave Shaw a Special Forces' medallion, a memento that he will always cherish.

"This entire experience has changed my life in some ways. I am more comfortable in large groups of people now. I'm just a sentimental person. I was moved by this awesome human drama," Shaw said.

A WARTIME ROMANCE

A marriage proposal by Scud light?
Not quite, but close enough.

After enjoying the weekend off, troop greeters returned to Bangor International Airport after lunch on Monday, May 6, to cheer for the Patriot missile crews landing aboard United Airlines Flight A18590. A quick check with passenger service indicated that the plane's destination was Fort Bliss in El Paso, Texas.

The Boeing 747 touched down at 2:50 p.m. and taxied to the international terminal. About 50 people awaited the flight, along the Searsport High School Band.

The soldiers who unloaded from UAL Flight A18590 belonged to various units, including the 3rd Battalion (Patriot), 43rd Air Defense Artillery, and the 978th Military Police Co.

The schedule called for other troop flights that Monday, which no one could predict would mark the next-to-last heavy surge of aircraft moving from the Gulf. For the next 16 days, planes would land almost around the clock in a blitz reminiscent of mid-March.

By 9:15 p.m. that Monday, perhaps 75 people lined the wire in the domestic terminal at BIA. According to the posted schedule, Hawaiian Airlines Flight 866 should land within five minutes while on its way to Cherry Point Marine Corps Air Station in North Carolina.

Hank Trumble Sr. and Susanne Trumble of Danville came to Bangor that Monday night. They lived on the outskirts of Auburn, a city of about 23,000 people located 100 miles southwest of Bangor, and seldom traveled this far north. Their son, Tony, and 2-year-old granddaughter, Jasmine, accompanied them on their late spring journey. Susanne talked about Hank Trumble Jr., the son who'd shipped from Camp Lejeune on Dec. 10, 1990. A corporal with the 2nd Truck Co., Hank Jr. had already been bumped from three homeward-bound flights. The first time, he'd willingly surrendered his seat to a Marine whose pregnant wife "apparently was due at any time," Susanne Trumble said. The second and third times, "I don't think Hank wanted to give up his seat," she commented.

Since December, Trumble had talked to his parents three or four times by phone. His letters averaged two a month, his mother said. "I treasured every one of them," she confirmed. "He's been too far away."

A 1982 graduate of Lewiston High School, Trumble called his family on April 28 and told them about his inability to get out of Saudi Arabia, Susanne Trumble said. He'd also spoken to his wife, Sue, who lived at Camp Lejeune.

"We have a Sue Jr., a Sue Sr., a Hank Jr., and a Hank Sr. It gets confusing," Trumble's mother laughed.

Since few bands now appeared for the troop receptions, volunteers lugged a York Newave sound system into the terminal and set it up at the corner to the ramp. Someone slipped a tape into the sound system and jacked up the volume. "Coming to America" blared for all to hear. A light, but warm drizzle fell outside the terminal as 9:20 p.m. passed into history. As more troop greeters entered the terminal and swelled the crowd to about 100 people, two teen-age girls practiced their troop-hugging with pleasantly surprised Legionnaires standing in the ramp.

The sound system blared "My Baby's American-Made."

"Where's the plane?" a woman muttered. Moments later, a falcon-eyed man standing near the windows shouted the arrival of Flight 866. People cheered, then jostled for positions on the wire. The L-1011 touched down at 9:27 p.m., just seven minutes late. While the Legionnaires and their VFW allies formed a line on either side of the ramp, Gary Leighton addressed the crowd. He mentioned that after United Airlines Flight A18590 landed that afternoon, the police discovered a woman and her children who were "harassing the soldiers for souvenirs."

The woman was escorted from the terminal, Leighton said, "and this will happen to anyone we catch asking for souvenirs tonight." The crowd cheered.

Leighton also urged families waiting for Marine relatives to come and stand by the duty-free shop. Someone unclipped the wire where the Trumbles stood and coaxed them to take Leighton's offer. They moved across the ramp to stand anxiously by the plate-glass windows.

Then the Marines appeared at the top of the ramp.

Valerie Bellomy flipped "Okie from Muskogee" into the sound system. Civilians applauded, hollered, and waved their hands in the air. Their mouths agape, dumbfounded Marines momentarily stood still, then happily plunged down the ramp behind two women flagbearers from American Legion Post No. 84.

The Trumbles anxiously studied the young faces moving past them. Where was Hank Jr.?

The ramp became crowded as Marines formed a line along the wire and exchanged greetings with their civilian fans. The two flagbearers took one look at the traffic jam, marched back into the ramp, and grabbed a mess of Marines. "Come with us, and you'll get to the phones faster," the flagbearers said.

Perhaps attracted by the thoughts of the beer that another Marine kept shouting was waiting for them, some Marines took the flagbearers at their word and squeezed around the corner of the ramp. Their exodus made little difference, however, as more Marines jammed the ramp. After working her way only a short distance along the wire, a woman Marine captain with close-cropped brown hair spread her arms and hugged a short, much older woman with gray hair. As the Marine wept on the civilian's shoulder, "God Bless the USA" reverberated off the walls.

By now, the last Marines had filed into the ramp. So disappointed that Hank Jr. had not made this flight, the Trumbles quietly slipped into the crowd. Their turn would come another time.

As Marines chug-a-lugged beers around him, Pfc. Ethan Jackson of Somerset, N.J., stopped and talked about his war. Assigned to a 2nd Marine Division artillery battalion that fired 8-inch howitzers (a cannon known as the M-110A2), Jackson had left the United States on Dec. 17, 1990. His battalion invaded Kuwait on Feb. 23, 1991. Suffering no casualties, the battalion withdrew from Kuwait on March 16, 1991. A long stop in Jubail, Saudi Arabia, saw the Marines cleaning the cannons, trucks, and other equipment and loading it aboard ships. Jackson said that his job involved surveying the sites where his battery would unlimber its howitzers. After checking for terrorists and snipers, Jackson and his comrades helped position the guns "exactly where we wanted them to be. We had to know right where we were so we could accurately fire at the Iraqis," he said.

Jackson and six Marines formed the rear party of their battalion when they landed in Bangor. "Yes, someone has to be last guy out," he said, "but I wish it hadn't taken so long." The main body of his battalion had exited the gulf on April 16. As the Marines and assorted Navy corpsmen turned the terminal into a fiesta, the Marine captain who'd earlier hugged the older civilian wearily plopped into a lounge chair. Although tired by the long flight from Saudi Arabia, Capt. Leslie Janzen graciously granted an interview.

"Reality had not sunk in when we landed here," Janzen admitted. "I don't recall when I've been so tired. It's so hot in the desert now, and the sand blows all the time. I'm glad to be home."

She warmed to the reception, however. Then, as she shook hands with the civilians who were packed two or three deep along the wire, Janzen realized that "the first friendly face I saw reminded me of my mother. That's when I cried on her shoulder. We were perfect strangers, but, my God, she looked so much like my mother."

Until her assignment in the Gulf, Janzen served as the executive officer of the Marine Corps Detachment at Fort Lee, Va. The 45 Marines assigned to the detachment supported "the 120 or so (Marine) students attending the Army schools at any one time," she said. Janzen left for the Gulf on Jan. 22, 1991. She spent most of the war at the airfield in Jubail, where "I couldn't seem to keep a job," she said with a smile. "They kept shifting me from one job to another, although mainly I was the maintenance management officer for the 3rd Marine Air Wing." The wing flew various aircraft, including F-18 Hornets, OV-10 Broncos, helicopters, and AV-8B Harriers.

As the maintenance management officer, Janzen supervised maintenance for equipment worth about $4 million.

She said that duty at Jubail, which "at least was a place you could find on the map," proved little different from an assignment at a desert post. "The only difference between us and the Marines going up to the border was that we knew where we were." The women Marines lived in tents with concrete floor pads. Janzen praised the Navy Construction Battalions (Seebees) for pouring the slabs and erecting the tents "nice and tight, which helped a lot to keep the sand out."

The Marines ate in a mess hall with a small galley equipped with propane stoves. "Under the circumstances, flies and sand and all, it (the food) was very good," Janzen said. One night, Janzen slept through a Scud attack. No one activated the alarm to warn her about the incoming Scud, she said. "I was so tired, I don't know if I'd even have awakened if the alarm had sounded."

Janzen even slept through the resulting explosion when a Patriot missile intercepted the Iraqi Scud.

Later, after the Allies liberated Kuwait, she traveled there for a day, "looking for equipment left in the breach. It's horrible; it's just awful, the oil fires in Kuwait. The smell of it, a stench is what you could call it. We in America aren't aware of how fortunate we are."

While stationed in Jubail, Janzen met Capt. Bob Wilson, a Marine from Camp Lejeune. The two fell in love during what Janzen described as a "wartime romance. It's pretty classic in some ways — (two) people thrown together in a dangerous environment where you might not be alive tomorrow."

Their subsequent courtship followed an unorthodox route, at least by the standards of peacetime America. "We haven't been able to date in a normal sense of the word," Janzen explained.

She and Wilson would often walk around their camp and talk. "The topic would get serious because of the war setting," She said. "You tend to drop all the trivialities of life when there are Scuds and Patriots blowing up overhead."

Although there were no chaperones, there was also no privacy. As she sat in the domestic terminal and watched the chaotic mixture of Marines and civilians, Janzen waved her hand toward the intermingled Americans and said, "Our dating at Jubail was like sitting and talking here, with everyone all around you. They can see everything you are doing."

The war's end in late February eased some tension at Jubail. "At least we weren't worrying about Scud attacks any more," Janzen said. Her relationship with Wilson grew each day as they tried to see each other whenever their work schedules permitted. One day in mid-April, Janzen obtained a copy of the Marine promotion list. Noticing Wilson's name on it, she called him and said, "Congratulations."

"What for?" he asked. "You've been selected for promotion to major," Janzen replied. "Great! Let's get married!" he responded.

Janzen smiled warmly at the memory. She and Wilson planned to marry that summer at her parents' home in Dutch Harbor, Alaska. Then they would hold another wedding ceremony that fall for their friends at Camp Lejeune.

When Gary Leighton issued the first boarding call for Flight 866, Janzen grabbed her gear, shook hands, and vanished up the ramp. Other Marines quickly exited the terminal, too, as the strains of the "Marine Hymn" struggled to be heard over the cheering.

Rain fell hard by 10:40 p.m., when the last Marines left the domestic terminal. Leighton paused at the lectern, leaned toward the microphone and thanked the crowd "for making this a memorable evening for these Marines."

REGGIE AND LANCE

Reggie joined the homecoming act on May 7.

Beneath a sky that alternated clouds and patchy sunshine, perhaps 35 people gathered at Bangor International Airport that Tuesday morning to meet United Airlines Flight A18065. The airport staff indicated that the 747 carried 297 passengers to Louisville, Ky. As the slowly swelling crowd milled at the lower ramp entrance, a few people edged to the terminal windows and waited for the United Airlines jet to land. Security personnel politely told the half dozen onlookers to step back from the corridor left open for passengers boarding a United Airlines flight to Portland and points south. Once the last passenger answered the final boarding call, a Bangor police officer waved the onlookers back to the windows.

Here the men and women discovered a birdwatcher's paradise. During the years past, swallows had built their mud-daub nests beneath the stairwell leading to the old observation deck atop the domestic terminal.

This morning, the swallows staged an air show for the people at the windows. Chasing the insects that a departing Delta Airlines 727 had stirred with its engine exhausts, the swallows swooped, swirled, dived, looped, and plummeted in the air space between the two gate extensions attached to the domestic terminal.

Flight A18065 touched down at 7:45 a.m., 11 minutes ahead of schedule. At first, only those people nearest the windows cheered. A moment later, other people recognized the BIA signal for "the plane's down" and added their voices to the din.

More people had joined the homecoming crowd by now. Several people who'd waved goodbye to friends or relatives boarding the UAL 737 remained to cheer the arriving troops. This practice continued in one form or another well into May: See off the in-laws and then celebrate by welcoming home more troops who'd survived the Gulf War. Suddenly, about a dozen people shifted position to a point nearer the entrance to Gate 4. From here, they could see up the ramp to the doorway through which the incoming troops must pass. Someone from Maine must be coming home aboard Flight A18065. Then...movement underfoot opposite the side entrance to the duty-free shop. A short dog passed between two women and walked along the wire to join an elderly woman standing among the people clustered by Gate 2. She bent slightly and spoke quietly to the dog.

A dog loose at BIA? In a state where most restaurants and supermarkets strategically post "No Pets Allowed" signs at their doors, a dog walking the carpet at an international airport must be breaking the law. The dog walked right past a police officer, who never batted an eyelash.

Perhaps the mutt's low-slung stature helped the canine evade the all-seeing eyes of the Bangor police. Built with the frame of a Welsh corgi, but sporting the black top coat and white shoulder stripe of a beagle or basset, the pooch moved with a grace that belied its years. The people gathered near Gate 2 spread their ranks back along the wire. Two girls lifted the poles bearing a sign that read "Lt. Lance Gilman." "Lift the poles higher," urged an older woman. Even as the girls obeyed, the corgi-beagle circulated at their feet.

Three generations of his family had come to BIA to welcome home 2nd Lt. Lance Gilman, a 1984 Bangor High School graduate assigned to Charlie Co., 19th Engineer Battalion, Fort Knox, Ky. The pooch belonged to a grandmother who'd never considered leaving the dog at home.

Lt. Gilman had left for Saudi Arabia in late December 1990. His battalion marched into Kuwait during the land war. Gilman came safely through that 100-hour conflict. An after-the-fact phone call to his parents' home in China had confirmed that hope.

A brother, Navy Lt. Commander Thane Gilman, spent the war aboard the USS San Diego in the Mediterranean Sea.

About 8 a.m., soldiers finally poured down the ramp and into the terminal. Two sharp eyes somewhere in his clustered family separated Lance Gilman from the other desert fatigues and pointed him out to the other relatives. Joy and relief flooded the faces that had worried a little too long about their son, grandson, or nephew.

A warm smile brightening his face,

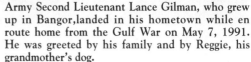

Army Second Lieutenant Lance Gilman, who grew up in Bangor, landed in his hometown while en route home from the Gulf War on May 7, 1991. He was greeted by his family and by Reggie, his grandmother's dog.

Gilman swept into his family's arms and tried to talk to everyone at once. He laughed, exchanged a comment or two with older relatives, then excused himself to follow his comrades along the wire to shake hands with the waiting crowd. Then Gilman looked down and saw the corgi-beagle waiting patiently at his feet. The lieutenant knelt, grasped Reggie, and swung the dog into his arms. Cradling the animal like he would a baby, Gilman momentarily rocked the corgi-beagle from side to side and grinned all the while.

"His name's Reggie!" Gilman explained as the crowd cheered. "He's my grandmother's dog! We've known each other for 11 years or so, I think!"

Apparently glad to sniff home an old friend, Reggie still registered in his dark eyes the shock he felt while held tight in Gilman's arms. "What's happening to me?" the canine eyes asked.

Gilman cradled Reggie a moment longer before speaking quietly to the corgi-beagle and setting him down on the carpet. As family members pulled Gilman out of line for a more private homecoming, Reggie dutifully tagged along, sniffing the delicious and exotic aromas of the desert that still clung to the lieutenant's uniform.

127

By now, soldiers flooded the wire. Some soldiers stopped to grab teddy bears and other goodies at the greeting table. Warned by official greeters that the bears would not last forever, other soldiers, too, also paused to claim a furry critter for a wife, sweetheart, or child. Forward momentum slowed in the terminal.

Sgt. Donald Lagesse bypassed the logjam and walked into the terminal. Noticing a police officer, a member of the press, and an airport employee standing near the lectern, the soldier asked, "Is Stephen King here today? I'd heard that he met some flights here in Bangor."

Sgt. Lagesse could not conceal his disappointment when informed that King was not in the crowd.

Spec. Robert Collins, a medic with the 19th Engineer Battalion, stopped and talked briefly about his war. He said that the 19th, an element of the 194th Armor Brigade, had "shipped out the day the war started." The battalion lost four men killed.

Lagesse, who's from Kankakee, Ill., was a team leader with Alpha Co., 19th Engineer Battalion. He folded his arms across his chest and looked out the windows at the woods several hundred yards away across the runway. "It is so nice to see the trees and grass," he said. "You can't imagine what it's like in a world without green in it. I'm so glad to be home."

Lagesse said that the 19th Engineer Battalion had landed in Bangor while flying to the Gulf in January. "We learned the air war had started before we landed," he recalled. "Boy, that made us think real hard about what we were getting into. The attitude was, `Heck, they're shootin' already. This is really serious.'"

The Kentucky engineers helped build a main supply route (MSR) before moving up to the Iraqi border by mid-February. "We went straight up through Iraq" with the 1st Armored Division, Lagesse said.

Far across the terminal, Lance Gilman stood talking with all his relatives. Probably bored with a conversation that didn't center on food or cats, Reggie had wandered off seeking canine excitement. He walked past Lagesse that moment and headed toward the Mr. Paperback Gift Store. Right at Reggie's heels followed an older NCO. He bent over and quietly said, "Here, doggie, doggie."

Lagesse's features softened as he spoke about the men the 19th had lost. Referring to the havoc wreaked among Iraqi armor by allied air power, the sergeant confirmed, "If it weren't for the Navy and the Air Force, we would've lost a lot more guys."

The 19th had pulled out of Iraq by the end of March, Lagesse said. Returning to Saudi Arabia, the battalion cleaned its gear and awaited the order to ship home.

Their departure, which took the engineers out of King Khalid Military City, came none too soon for Lagesse. He and his wife had three children, two sons and a daughter. The youngest boy had turned one on April 29. Lagesse "celebrated" his birthday in the desert on Jan. 28. His wife observed her birthday without him on March 27.

"We have a lot of making up to do when I get back," Lagesse said. "We're planning a big birthday bash, as well as Valentine's, Easter, and whatever else I've missed."

Reggie appeared from the direction of the gift store. He headed toward Gilman's reunion, then paused as he trotted past the stairs and escalator. An interesting odor apparently caught the corgi-beagle's attention, and he plopped down the stairs as fast as his short legs would take him. The first boarding call soon recalled Gilman and Lagesse to the UAL 747. After hugging his son a final time, T.A. Gilman turned to his family and asked, "Where's Reggie?"

"Chasing something downstairs," someone replied.

NORTH DAKOTA WELCOMES YOU

The day that Gilman and Reggie met at Bangor, the weather turned sunny and gradually descended into a calm, clear, warm spring evening. In Maine, such weather rarely occurs so early in May. The crowd that arrived at Bangor International Airport about suppertime could be excused if it numbered little more than 70 people. Warm temperatures and abundant sunshine caused many troop greeters to linger in their yards that Tuesday evening.

Yet, even as American Trans Air Flight 8580 approached BIA that afternoon, people from as far away as the Midwest gathered to greet the arriving troops.

George and Jean Olson of Litchville, N.D., stood by the terminal windows. Holding a white posterboard sign that read "North Dakota Welcomes You," they patiently awaited the AMT L-1011, scheduled to land at 5:57 p.m.

Volks Field (an Air National Guard base) in Wisconsin was the final destination for the AMT jet. "The reason we're meeting this plane is that many of these boys are going home through Wisconsin," George Olson said. "We thought that somebody from home might be aboard." "I feel almost like I'm meeting someone I know," Jean Olson said. "I really hope there are some North Dakota boys on the plane."

The Olsons were visiting their daughter who lived in Hermon, just a few miles from the airport. Arriving on April 30, they intended to stay until May 16 and enjoy their first springtime visit to Maine. Waiting for the AMT jet reminded Olson of his time away at war. During World War II, he served with the Army in the Pacific Theater of Operations. "I trained as an infantryman, but they worked me as a tank driver," he said. The Olsons had raised four daughters and two sons on the Litchville farm where Olson had been born. They proudly mentioned that five children had graduated from the University of North Dakota and a son had graduated from a junior college.

Specialist Norman Stone of Sturgis, S.D., went to war with the 730th Medical Co., South Dakota Army National Guard.

The Gulf War had called some components of the North Dakota Army National Guard away from home, the Olsons said. The government activated an engineer battalion based in Cando, a city near Litchville. Many men and women had been gone several months, George said. At 6:08 p.m., the AMT L-1011 gently dropped from the sky to the cheers from the waiting crowd. As the airliner's wheels touched the runway, bleached gray smoke swirled from the sudden contact between concrete and rubber.

The borrowed sound system played various songs as the AMT L-1011 taxied past the terminal. People pressed their faces to the windows and waved at the jet. Later, the soldiers would comment on how they felt when they saw the crowd waiting for them. The Olsons inched their way closer to the ramp while the L-1011 passengers suffered through a rudimentary inspection by Customs. "I really enjoy this," Jean Olson said, a smile brightening her eyes. "It's almost like witnessing a rebirth."

The soldiers marched down the ramp to sustained cheers and applause from the crowd. Troop greeters quickly discovered that among the units aboard the plane were two Army Reserve transportation companies from Ohio: the 656th out of Springfield, and the 705th from Dayton. Also aboard were soldiers from the 452nd General Supply Co., an Army Reserve unit from Winthrop, Minn.

The Olsons didn't meet any North Dakota soldiers that night, but they opened their hearts to the 62 troops belonging to the 730th Medical Co., an Army National Guard unit based in Vermillion, S.D. Spec. Norman Stone, a tall young man from Sturgis, S.D., grinned broadly when he discovered that the Olsons lived "not that far from home." After chatting with them for a few minutes, he stood near the ramp entrance and described what his company had done "over there in the desert."

The Pentagon activated the 730th on Nov. 21, 1990. The South Dakota soldiers left the United States on Jan. 15, 1991. "We were over the top of Cairo when the bombing started on the 16th," Stone said. "They turned us around in mid-air and took us into Rhine Main (Air Base in Germany)." The 730th finally arrived at King Fahd International Airport in Saudi Arabia on Jan. 19, 1991. The company supported the 1st Cavalry Division during February. "We spent 55 of the 100 hours (of the ground war) traveling in our trucks," Stone said.

His platoon subsequently spent a week in Iraq, returned to Saudi Arabia for two weeks, then drove back to Iraq for 24 days. In those last three-and-a-half weeks, the platoon supported the 2nd Armored Cavalry Regiment and the 1st Infantry Division. The South Dakota soldiers treated Iraqi refugees, Stone stated. He expressed his sympathy for the civilians who'd stepped on mines or who'd been shot by Saddam Hussein's security forces. Other refugees, especially the children, suffered from malnutrition and dehydration.

The 730th encountered the refugees about 20 miles southeast of An Nasariyah, an Iraqi city on the Euphrates River. "To be honest, I don't know exactly what happened to the refugees we treated," Stone said. "We believe they were moved to camps further south."

He planned to leave the Army within a week and return to his job as an athletic trainer with the Sioux Falls Sky Force of the Continental Basketball Association. "Yeah, it's great to be home," he grinned. "Thanks for everything you've done for us here. We appreciate it."

A troop greeter suddenly appeared out of the noisy, but friendly crowd with Capt. Scott Kranz in tow. Introducing himself as the commander of the 452nd General Supply Co., Kranz said that his unit had been activated on Nov. 19, 1990.

"We spent Thanksgiving at the Reserve Center," Kranz said. An advance party flew to the Gulf on Jan. 4, 1991. The main body of the 452nd arrived in Saudi Arabia on Jan. 22. The Minnesota soldiers served with the 13th Supply and Service Battalion, 2nd COSCOM (Combat Support Command).

Kranz, a correctional officer at the federal penitentiary in Rochester, Minn., asked a Bangor Daily News reporter if he could write a letter to the paper. "Sure," the reporter replied. "Let me give you the address."

"No, no," Kranz shook his head. Reaching deep into a pocket on his desert fatigues, he produced a little black notebook and a pen. Writing as fast as he could, Kranz dashed off a letter, tore it from the notebook, and told the reporter, "Here, give this to your editor. I can't really tell you how much you're being here (at the airport) has meant to us. Tell all the people of Bangor that we thank them." Later, after the Midwesterners reboarded their L-1011 and departed Bangor, the reporter read Kranz's letter.

"I would like to thank your small town for the friendship and appreciation that made every member of my unit and the other units feel proud of this country," Kranz had written. "My unit is 452 General Supply Co. from Winthrop and Worthington, Minn. We began serving on Jan. 22. Thank you for your support. You have something to be proud of."

The newspaper published Kranz's letter, as it would many similar letters that it would receive from other military personnel who had been welcomed home by the enthusiastic crowds at BIA.

A THIRTY-HOUR DAY

Sgt. David Melochik, who during the troop flights often commanded an airport-security detail for the Bangor Police Department, stood by Gate 2 in the BIA domestic terminal during late morning on Wednesday, May 8.

From this vantage point, Melochik monitored the escalator and the stairs leading from the first floor. His viewpoint encompassed Gate 1 and its security-screening apparatus, the entrance to the skywalk, an excellent sweep up the ramp to the passenger-service desk, and United Airlines' Gate 2.

If any trouble started on this level, Melochik would know as soon as it began.

Of course, with the terminal nearly empty, Melochik found his job much easier today than during March and early April. About 50 people had gradually filtered into the terminal to meet a Sun Country flight on its way to McChord Air Force Base in Tacoma, Wash.

Six weeks earlier, people would have packed the terminal wall-to-wall, especially for a mid-day flight. Melochik remembered times when "you couldn't breathe in here, it was so crammed. I really don't know how we pulled it off, and I'm really glad that nothing happened." The sergeant referred to a constant fear rarely mentioned in public in Bangor. Time and again, Melochik and some Vietnam veterans among the troop greeters quietly discussed the potential for terrorism.

With soldiers and civilians pressed together within the confining terminal, someone armed with a hand grenade or a semiautomatic pistol would have faced, in a fighter pilot's words, "a target-rich environment." There wouldn't have been many ways to stop a terrorist, either. Although BIA officials immediately enacted the appropriate security measures ordered by the FAA in January 1991, the Maine public apparently did not comprehend the terrorist threat. Counting the daring Confederate attack that had captured the "Cushing" in Portland Harbor during the Civil War, Maine had not experienced a hostile foreign army on its soil since the 1860s. Except for two Nazi saboteurs who had landed at Hancock Point during World War II, no known enemies bent on causing problems during wartime had touched Maine soil in almost 50 years.

Unlike the Israelis or Lebanese, Maine residents did not consider terrorism a fact of life. This mental lapse applies to most Americans living outside high crime zones.

In Bangor, this attitude revealed itself in a tendency to park as close to the terminals as possible, even by the front entrance if necessary. When concrete barriers blocked many available parking spaces along Godfrey Boulevard, people expressed their shock at being denied a Maine birthright, the ability to park wherever they wanted.

Oh, many civilians said they understood the security precautions, of course. Can't have those Iraqis parking a bomb-laden Chevy next to the terminal and blowing it to pieces, people agreed during lunchtime conversations. Can't let a suicide jock drive his bomb-laden Ford into the terminal, either, Bangor-area residents concurred.

The possibility that a terrorist might make his actions more personal seldom entered the conversation, except between people who knew the powerful political statement that a detonated grenade could deliver.

Gaining access to the troops posed no problems for a terrorist or Iraqi sympathizer. During the cold weather from March 8 to mid-April, a terrorist clad in a warm overcoat, blue jeans, and sneakers - standard Maine issue for non-dressy occasions - would probably blend well with the myriad civilians who came to BIA. After mid-April, jeans and a T-shirt would suffice as appropriate camouflage clothing.

The potential for terrorism extended beyond an armed attack. What if someone concealed a bomb among the coats piled on the vinyl chairs or slipped a carefully camouflaged bomb into the teddy bears and other gifts intended for the troops?

What if someone left poisoned cookies at the gift table? The possibility caused nervous laughter among some Red Cross and Chamber volunteers. If a troop had sickened and died after eating a cookie from Bangor...well, the thought dismayed many people.

Melochik and the other Bangor police officers who provided security for BIA during those heady weeks from March 8 to late May knew about these potential threats, as well as the possibility of others: a rooftop sniper who wielded a high-powered rifle with incendiary bullets; a bomb-carrying terrorist posing as a reporter to enter a plane filled with soldiers; a terrorist armed with a shoulder-fired SAM, waiting in the trees beneath the approach path to the airport. These scenarios - some admittedly wilder than something in a John le Carre spy novel - sounded outrageous to the civilians who overheard them played out verbally during quiet conversations.

Weeks after Dave Melochik saw the May 8 noontime troop flight safely on its way, an ostensibly adoring woman approached Rajiv Gandhi, the Indian prime minister. Using a hidden bomb, the woman blew apart the heir to the Gandhi political fortunes and disrupted national politics on the subcontinent.

A similar scenario could have worked in Bangor, only the dead and wounded would be American.

Despite the terrorist threat, many troop greeters believed a political demonstration more dangerous to the American homecomings. Just days before the Gulf War started, a professor or two from the University of Maine organized an antiwar demonstration that drew 300 people to downtown Bangor.

The demonstration did not sit well with commuters who found their routes blocked or with families whose loved ones had departed for war with the Reserves or the National Guard. On Sunday, Feb. 3, about 2,500 people marched two miles from Brewer into Bangor to demonstrate their support for the troops. That demonstration overwhelmed the antiwar sentiment splashed across the local media in January.

But the "regulars" among the troop greeters anticipated a political demonstration sometime during the troop flights. One scenario saw sign-carrying demonstrators hassling the civilians arriving to meet a flight. Another scenario pictured anti-war activists sneaking incognito into the airport and suddenly confronting the thoroughly surprised troops aboard a particular flight. How might troop greeters react to such a demonstration?

"If demonstrators limited their activities to the sidewalk outside the terminal, well, I'd leave them alone," a Vietnam vet replied. "But, let 'em come inside, and it's war."

"A knuckle sandwich," another vet said.

"We'd make plenty of arrests on both sides if things ever got out of hand," David

Melochik responded. A terrorist act or a political demonstration never occurred at BIA during the troop flights. In mid-January 1992, however, persons unknown made a political statement that went unreported by the press. According to a source at BIA, someone entered the domestic terminal early on Jan. 17, 1992, and graphically protested the Gulf War in the side stairwell leading to the second floor. A few hours later, a BIA employee found partially melted dolls in the stairwell. Signs referring to the first anniversary of the war and references to "baby killers" reportedly had been left behind, too. Airport staff quickly cleansed the stairwell, and no reports about the incident reached the public.

That incident lay in the future, however, as Sgt. Melochik watched the people arriving at BIA just before noon on May 8. Nothing should happen here today.

Touching down beneath a partly cloudy sky, the Sun Country airliner taxied past the domestic terminal at 12:04 p.m. People spaced out a row deep along the wire and await-ed the troops, who weren't long in leaving their aircraft.

Soldiers, soldiers, and more sol-diers poured down the ramp, where a few veterans greeted them. Traffic backed up beside the gift table, and some soldiers liberated Ursus Berries, cookies, and other goodies before their comrades got to them.

According to an Army officer, the Sun Country jet carried several units. The 2186th Maintenance Co. was headed for Camp Withycombe in Oregon, and the 651st Water Purification Co. was returning to Kali-spell, Mont.

Spec. Josie Ortivez belonged to the 159th Combat Support Group of Helena, Mont. The Pentagon had activated the Army Reserve unit on Dec. 14, 1990, requiring Ortivez to leave her job at Albertson's Sundries in Boise, Idaho.

When she was called to active duty with the 159th Combat Support Group, Army Reserve, Specialist Josie Ortivez of Nampa, Idaho, left her three young sons in her mother's care and went off to war.

Ortivez, a single mother who lived in Nampa, Idaho, arranged with her mother to take care of her three sons, ages 7, 6, and 3. The middle boy had his birthday on March 17, Ortivez said. After taking a teddy bear for each son, she said, "I think I'm going to make it home for Mother's Day. That would make it real special."

Ortivez spent two weeks in Iraq with the 159th. "Our mission over there, in Saudi Arabia and afterwards, was to support the 1st Infantry Division with food and water and other supplies," she said. Spec. Craig DiCarlo hailed from Missoula, Mont. Another member of the 159th Combat Support Group, he'd been studying health and physical education at the University of Montana at Missoula when the Army called him to active duty.

According to DiCarlo, the 159th CSG left for the Persian Gulf on Jan. 1 and arrived in Dhahran two days later. The reservists then headed north to a point about 60 kilome-ters east of Hafr al-Batin. "We were supporting the 1st Infantry Division by providing them with food, water, fuel, and transportation. We pretty much did that throughout the whole war," DiCarlo said.

The Army attached subordinate units, particularly transportation companies, to the 159th CSG. One transportation company hauled fully laden fuel tankers north to the 1st Infantry Division.

Some soldiers from the 159th CSG traveled into Kuwait and Iraq, DiCarlo recalled. He went north for four days. "I was almost in the port of Basra. We could see the ships in the port. They didn't seem to be in great shape," he recalled.

"Everywhere up to where we were was a mess, blown-up tanks, APCs, lots of unexploded ammunition, truckloads of it. Those people (Iraqi soldiers) were leaving fast, and they were dropping anything too heavy to carry," DiCarlo said.

His convoy passed through a refugee camp located just inside Kuwait near the Iraq border. "There were tons of hungry kids and families there," DiCarlo remembered. "The kids would make gestures like they were really hungry. Our first time through, all we had with us was a big box of M&Ms. We tossed 'em out to the kids. I don't know if they had ever seen M&Ms, but they knew real quick they could eat 'em. "The next day, I went back with two other soldiers and a Humvee and dumped out cases of MREs and Mott's Applesauce. Hey, those Iraqi kids knew what that was. They saw the containers and cried, `Applesauce! Applesauce!'" DiCarlo said.

"The refugees were taking anything they could get (to eat)," he stated. Laden with food, the reservists made two round trips to the refugee camp. One time, a male Iraqi unexpectedly boarded the Humvee from the rear and made off with a case of MREs.

"Heck, he didn't have to do that," DiCarlo said. "We were going to give them the MREs anyways. I guess he was somebody's father and was trying to get his family some food."

The Americans ate many MREs when they first arrived in the Gulf. "I didn't like them too well, but as time progressed, I stopped eating them, because we were able to cook our own food, and we learned how to alter the MREs to make them tastier," DiCarlo said.

"We were eating Saudi Arabian snacks, too. Let's see, there was their version of cheese puffs, (Hostess) Twinkies, chips, stuff like that," he recounted. "And fresh fruit like apples and oranges."

At their base deep in the Saudi desert, the reservists witnessed the air war against Iraq. "The first night of the air war, we could see flashes of light in the distance," DiCarlo said.

"There were streaks of light that we thought were Patriots going up after Scuds. It was awesome to watch, almost like fireworks, but we knew it was serious business," he said.

At other times, "we saw a lot of B-52s flying over...even fighters refueling right overhead all the time, the sky was so clear most days," DiCarlo stated. "It's kind of a spectacular sight to see something like that."

The soldiers saw A-10 Warthogs fly over occasionally and waggle their wings. "That was a reassuring feeling. Helicopters, we saw them quite often, too, buzzing back and forth. There were aircraft everywhere," he said.

Before the 159th CSG retired to Desert Sands, a rest area for the 7th Corps (II COSCOM), DiCarlo and other soldiers retrieved some captured Iraqi helmets and gas masks for souvenirs. Later, their outfit shifted to King Khalid Military City.

"Our date for leaving changed several times, from May 3rd to the 2nd, then back to May 5th, the 6th, and finally, the 8th," the young DiCarlo commented. "We took off at 3 a.m. Saudi time," leaving from KKMC for the long flight to the United States.

"I'd been up since 2 a.m. the day before that. Today's still the 8th, isn't it? Let's see, it's about one-thirty here, which makes it ten-thirty back home, and we've still got a six-hour flight ahead of us," DiCarlo calculated. "That means we'll get home about nine-thirty your time, if what they said about the delay is true.

"Geez, that'll mean that we left Saudi Arabia on the 8th and got home on the 8th. We'll probably have a 30-hour day!" he exclaimed.

THE TENNESSEE VOLUNTEERS

Shortly after 11 p.m. on Wednesday, May 8, a beat-up Chevy rolled beneath the blinking traffic light on Godfrey Boulevard and sped into the paved loop around the Hilton. Searching for a parking space nearest the brightly lit terminals, the driver negotiated the course once and settled for a spot less than 100 hundred yards from the skywalk. If he parked farther away, he'd consider it too long a walk. Other cars approached the terminals in the next half hour. People repeated the loop du jour, reconnoitering the Hertz slots and the lot supposedly reserved for airport employees. As the drivers chose their spots, the vehicles soon backed around the bend from the international terminal.

The clock indicated 11:30 p.m. Philip and Kristen Bailey of Brewer entered the domestic terminal with Carol Harrison, Kristen's mother. Harrison had come from Dayton, Ohio, to visit her family. Just by chance, her sojourn in Maine coincided with the possible arrival, direct from the Gulf, of her nephew, Bruce Workman.

A resident of Arthurdale, W. Va., Workman had gone to Saudi Arabia with the Army Reserve. His mother, Kay, was a sister-in-law to Carol Harrison. Kay had called her two nights earlier and informed her that Workman might pass through Bangor this week. Since he was traveling to Fort Campbell, Ky., could the United flight scheduled to land at BIA in another 20 minutes be his?

Carol Harrison and the Baileys sure hoped so. United Airlines had warned BIA that Flight 8616, en route to Fort Campbell from somewhere in Saudi Arabia, would land at 11:56 p.m.

The red-and-white 747 touched down a minute early.

Perhaps 50 people - the standard number by now - patiently waited while the huge airliner taxied to the international terminal. Minutes later, soldiers rounded the corner from the security corridor, slowed when they saw the Legionnaires and VFWers waiting for them, then took the greeting in stride.

Although escorted by a flagbearer from the American Legion, these arriving soldiers brought their own colorguard. As the soldiers moved along the ramp, people standing near the gift table noticed a trooper proudly carrying a large maroon flag emblazoned with white stars surrounded by a white circle.

"That's the Tennessee state flag," someone whispered.

Spec. Jack Warren held his state flag high as he walked into Bangor at 12:15 a.m., Thursday, May 9. Until he left Maine about an hour later, Warren and the flag proved inseparable.

He belonged to the 776th Maintenance Co., Tennessee Army National Guard. The outfit was based in Elizabethton, Tenn. Unfortunately for Carol Harrison and the Baileys, all the 230 passengers on the 747 came from the 776th Maintenance Co. Bruce Workman was not aboard the aircraft.

As the Tennessee Guardsmen worked their way to the pay phones and the lounge, soft Southern accents soon dominated conversations in the domestic terminal. A smiling

Tennessee Volunteer introduced a father and-son team, Sgt. 1st Class Stanley Barnett and Spec. Terry Barnett. The elder Barnett, who'd spent 28-and-a-half years in the military, said that he served the 776th as its maintenance-platoon sergeant. His son had belonged to the Army Guard for four-and-one-half years. He was a construction equipment operator.

Called to active duty on Sept. 12, 1990, the 776th arrived in Dhahran on Oct. 26, 1990. "We went to a place called Bastogne and stayed there until March 2," Stanley Barnett recalled. Then the 776th entered Kuwait to participate in Task Force Freedom, the humanitarian effort aimed at restoring basic services in Kuwait City.

A crew from the maintenance company had already supported the Tiger Brigade during its assault on the Iraqi army.

After he arrived in Kuwait City, Stanley Barnett took a work crew to the American Embassy, where "we put the gates back up and basically made sure the place was secure," he said. The Tennesseans helped get some Kuwaiti police cars running until they got some new cars. "What they had left for cars were in real bad shape," he said. Terry Barnett helped deliver portable generators to various parts of the city. "They really needed electricity in places like hospitals and police stations, so they used the portable generators until they got their generating plants repaired," Terry said. "We lifted approximately 20 generators.

"It was a mess in Kuwait City. The Kuwaitis had a habit of firing their guns in the air to celebrate. That made us nervous, because the bullets had to come down sometime," he said.

Barnett remembered that in one neighborhood, "this KuwaitiAmerican who was studying at Purdue (University) invited us home for a regular meal. Hey, it was great: chicken and rice, hamburgers, onion rings. I really appreciated it. The man had two wives, a Kuwaiti and an American. "I guess that after the Iraqis invaded Kuwait, he sent his American wife home to keep her safe," Barnett said.

While Barnett was stationed in Kuwait, his father occasionally traveled the infamous "Highway to Hell" from Camp Bastogne. "There were a lot of accidents on that road," the elder Barnett said. Different assignments usually kept the Barnetts apart during the war, but father and son often tracked each other's whereabouts via a company grapevine. Stanley Barnett said that he "came back out of Kuwait April 4" and returned to Camp Victory in Saudi Arabia.

Terry Barnett remained with the 776th Maintenance Co.'s rear party in Kuwait until mid-April, when those Tennesseans, too, departed for Camp Victory. The Barnetts, who were were reunited there, looked forward to returning to their families.

By 12:45 a.m., Spec. Warren convinced two companions, Staff Sgt. James Andrews and Chief Warrant Officer Robert Davis, to participate in the photo ops afforded by the Tennessee state flag. The impromptu colorguard posed throughout the terminal, even on the ramp, patiently smiling for civilians who wanted to capture the moment on film. Staff Sgt. Andrews, who had spent 22 years in the military, came from Valley Forge, a small town located southeast of Elizabethton in eastern Tennessee. He belonged to the tank support platoon, the recovery team that operated two massive wreckers called "88 tanks."

Sometime after they arrived in Saudi Arabia, Andrews and the recovery team were detached to the 502nd Armor Brigade from Fort Hood, Texas. "We were just assigned to them, it was only for five days or so," he said. "We were lucky. As far as workwise, we had no tanks blown up that we had to retrieve."

The recovery team attached two five-ton tractors to trailers and "used these to haul supplies one way and prisoners another," Andrews said. "We'd just load them into the (open-top) trailers and haul 'em south with no guard watching over them. They were so tickled to give up, they were no danger to us. I've seen thousands of them (the captured Iraqis). They weren't any problem.

"I think about 90 percent of them didn't have their boots on," he said. "It was a funny thing. The Iraqis said it was against their religion to die with their boots on. I thought that was strange." During the last six weeks that the 776th Maintenance Co. was stationed in Kuwait, Andrews and seven other soldiers worked for the embassy, retrieving workable equipment that they had captured.

"We brought in D-30 artillery pieces, antiaircraft weapons of all kinds, and tanks. There were tanks everywhere. We counted two T-72s, 16 T-62s, and the rest were T-55s," Andrews recalled.

"In the yard at Camp No outside of Kuwait City, when I left, there were 300 pieces of Iraqi equipment, including 36 tanks. There was a lot of stuff there," he said.

After the Gulf War ended, the American public heard little about captured Iraqi hardware. TV crews filmed Army engineers dropping explosives into badly damaged Iraqi tanks and then hustling for cover before the vehicles blew up and burned. The Pentagon downplayed the disposition of intact equipment, however. The captured T-72s that Staff Sgt. Andrews saw at Camp No might have arrived at Savannah, Ga., on April 24, when the charter vessel "Stena Sea Rider" sailed into port after a long voyage from the Persian Gulf. The ship carried 73 captured Iraqi military vehicles, including some T-72s. The rumor mill later placed the Iraqi armor at Fort Stewart or at Fort Hood, maybe even transported under tarps all the way to Fort Irwin, Calif. Other troops who returned from the Gulf in the months after the 776th Maintenance Co. headed home reported that the United States sent back enough captured Iraqi armor to outfit an armored brigade. Unfortunately, no one could verify the whereabouts of a few top-of the line Soviet fighters allegedly captured at an Iraqi air base in the Euphrates River Valley.

Andrews said that during the Gulf War, "I was never fired on by the Iraqis, but the Allied artillery would fire over our heads. Funny thing was, we usually couldn't hear the artillery because of the roar of the oil fires." Andrews left Kuwait on April 28 and went to Dhahran. His outfit departed Saudi Arabia at 3:15 p.m. Saudi time on May 8.

"I lost a case of beer on that. Me and another guy bet when we'd leave, and I lost," he waxed philosophical. "But, we didn't mind going home. The day we left - geez, was it only yesterday? - the temperature was 104 degrees (Fahrenheit). That's too hot for me, I will tell you."

At 1:15 a.m., word reached the terminal "to start loading United Airlines Flight 8616." When they heard the announcement, the Tennessee Volunteers poured into the ramp, where they ravaged the gift table before departing the terminal.

Spec. Jack Warren lingered a while to chat with some civilians. The Tennessee state flag draped over his left shoulder, Warren spoke about his home and again politely posed for photographs.

He confirmed a suspicion voiced by some troop greeters. They had noticed how many older soldiers there were in the 776th Maintenance Co. "I think the average age in our company's 37 years," Warren commented. "Many are Vietnam vets."

Long after the final boarding call sounded, Warren talked to the Maine residents. Finally, as someone wildly signaled from atop the ramp, Warren bid his hosts "farewell." Lifting the flag slightly higher, he vanished from the ramp at 1:25 a.m.

Hawaiian Airlines Flight 870 landed five minutes later.

As the Tennessee Volunteers mingled with civilians inside the BIA domestic terminal, John and Janet Foley of New Gloucester arrived after a long drive north on Interstate 95. Finding a parking space some distance from the terminals, they entered the airport in time to witness the 776th Maintenance Co. leaving for Fort Campbell.

The Foleys came to meet their son, Corp. John Alan Foley, who had shipped for the Persian Gulf with the 410th Quartermaster Detachment of Gainesville, Fla., in December 1990. A student at the University of Florida at Gainesville, John Alan was an Army Reservist who had served four years in the Marines.

Like so many other young men and women who'd joined the Guard and Reserves during the 1980s, he had never imagined that he would go off to war. "Being a Marine made him philosophical about it, I think," John Foley said about his son.

The Foleys had last seen John Alan at Fort Stewart, Ga., last Thanksgiving Day. It was hard saying good-bye to him, knowing where he was going and what he might have to do, Janet remembered. "Not that he belongs to a combat unit," she quickly explained. "From what he's told me, the 410th Quartermaster Detachment is a water-purification unit, and it wasn't supposed to get close to any fighting."

Other people had traveled with the Foleys to meet John Alan. Two cousins who lived in Gray, Sally Foley Harvey and Amy Foley Wilbur, stood on either side of their aunt and uncle, as did some friends of the family. Janet held a sign on which someone had printed, "Welcome Home Alan of the 410th."

Foley had called from Shannon Airport in Ireland, saying that he was on Hawaiian Airlines Flight 870, and that he was supposed to land in Bangor, Janet Foley said. "He thought he would come back on a military flight, but we're not complaining. I think this is great, being able to see him again!" John Foley said that his son hoped to be out of uniform by May 13, when he was supposed to start school in Florida. At 1:30 a.m., the winking and blinking lights belonging to HAL Flight 870 swept along the BIA runway. Someone standing at the terminal windows shouted, "It's down!", and the 50 people awaiting the aircraft's arrival cheered.

Though their older relatives appeared unruffled, the younger Foleys bobbed with anticipation as the citrus-colored L-1011 taxied to the international terminal. The excitement visibly increased when an airport employee announced the landing to "all shops and government agencies."

Then some soldiers marched onto the ramp.

"Do you see him?" Janet Foley asked her nieces.

"No, not yet!" Amy Foley Wilbur exclaimed. "Oh, they all look so much alike in their uniforms!"

The first soldiers past the gift table said that the L-1011 carried home personnel from the 312th Evacuation Hospital and the 377th Combat Support Hospital. "Hey, we're going to Pope Air Force Base in North Carolina!" a soldier reported. "These guys over there, they're headed for Hunter (Army Air Field in Savannah)."

Joyous cries echoed up the ramp as John Alan Foley met his family and hugged everyone within reach. The terminal clock - an apt description for the worn-out time-piece - registered 1:45 a.m.

The soldiers beamed their approval as they shook hands with the cheering crowd. Older women among the troop greeters hauled soldiers into their arms and hugged them. Taking the cue, a few enterprising young men dared to hug some women soldiers, none of whom declined an invitation. "I can't believe this!" one soldier quietly said after stepping outside to watch the homecoming. He dabbed at an eye, then raised a camera and squeezed off several frames to capture the occasion. Then a man wearing a flight suit passed along the wire. An older woman bent close to the man and, peering through her bifocals, read the patches on his chest. "An Air Force guy!" she exclaimed, drawing additional attention to the slightly embarrassed aviator. As a few other women converged on Capt. Bill Heslin, the woman asked, "What are you doing with all these soldiers?"

"Hitching a ride home!" Heslin replied.

He explained that he'd gone to the Gulf with the 16th Special Operations Squadron, 1st Special Operations Wing, out of Hurlburt Field in the Florida panhandle. "I'm a navigator on the (AC-130H) Spectre gunship," the young captain said.

Hailing from Manchester, N.H., Heslin had joined the Air Force and earned his commission through Officers Training School after graduating from Plymouth State College. When his outfit deployed to Saudi Arabia in September 1990, he was still training in the gunship. Heslin finally joined the 16th Special Operations Squadron in the Gulf in late January. The squadron participated in the Battle of Khafji.

"Seven days after I checked out (in the plane), I was over there in Saudi Arabia," Heslin said.

And now, like the other military personnel aboard the flight, he was eager to be reunited with his family — a wife and 3-year-old daughter. "It's been an incredible time for us, for all of us, and I can't wait to see them again," he said.

YES, WE HAVE NO BANANAS

Two more troop flights came into Bangor before noon on May 9. Yet another two flights touched down at BIA before 5 p.m.

Six in one day. The strain showed.

American Trans Air Flight 8624 landed at 5:10 a.m. and disgorged several units, including components of the 142nd Field Artillery Regiment, a National Guard outfit. Many troop greeters who'd met the two flights either side of midnight, May 8, struggled to remain awake for the AMT L-1011.

When the aircraft left for Altus Air Force Base in Oklahoma about 6:30 a.m., the exhausted troop greeters finally collapsed. During the night, a few people curled up in the airport lounge chairs and slept, while other greeters hurried home for short naps or snoozed in their cars parked on Godfrey Boulevard.

With dawn announcing another day, however, and the posted flight schedule calling for a United Airlines flight about 11 a.m., civilians who had not slept in more than 24 hours could not maintain such a hectic pace. Weary men and women straggled from the domestic terminal and went home to sleep for a few hours.

Not everyone responded to the alarm clocks that started clanging about 10 a.m., but some people staggered back to the airport with less than four hours' sleep. When the UAL 747 landed at 10:55 a.m., the 1st Infantry Division soldiers that it ferried to Forbes Field in Topeka, Kansas, received the red-carpet treatment.

Before leaving the airport at noon, troop greeters confirmed the ETAs for AMT Flight 8628 and Hawaiian Airlines Flight 872. "Looks good for four-thirty or so," a woman said on her way out the door. "Maybe I can get some more sleep."

A light southwesterly breeze rippled the flags outside the McDonald's on Union Street as troop greeters drove to BIA late that afternoon. The sun beamed from a brilliant blue sky on this perfect day in May.

A camera crew from ABC-TV was testing lighting conditions inside the ramp as more than 100 people wandered into the terminals to meet the incoming troop flights. The TV crew hoped to obtain good footage in the next few hours.

AMT Flight 8628, scheduled to land at 4:12 p.m., would refuel before flying to Charleston Air Force Base in South Carolina. Right behind that L-1011 came HAL Flight 872, another L-1011 bringing Marines home to Cherry Point Marine Corps Air Station in North Carolina. That plane should land at 4:41 p.m.

At 4:16 p.m., Gary Leighton stepped to the lectern and briefed a rowdy crowd. "You know the rules," he reminded them. "Just observe the do's and don't's, if you'd be so kind."

He pointed out the camera crew, which briefly acknowledged cheers from the crowd, and then announced that AMT Flight 8628 had just landed. "They'll be a few minutes taxiing to the terminal," he said. Moments later, an L-1011 gracefully eased from the sky and landed at BIA.

Air Force Lt. Col. Brian Finnan, stationed at Malmstrom AFB in Montana, praised the young men and women who went to war with him.

The plane rumbled eastward on the taxiway, spotted the "follow-me" truck, and swung onto the ramp across from the domestic terminal. As people waved, cheered, and took photos, the tape deck serving as the day's music source blared "God Bless the USA."

About 10 minutes after the AMT L-1011 vanished beyond Gate 2, a BIA employee stepped through the doors leading to the security corridor and swung left onto the ramp. The Legionnaire flagbearer fell into step behind the airport employee and escorted the first troops down the ramp.

By now, the restless crowd stood two rows deep along the wire. A woman spotted green flight suits approaching on the ramp. She nudged a companion and hissed, "Army or Air Force or what?"

"Air Force, I think," her friend replied.

Air Force they were, more than 200 pilots, navigators, and other Air Force personnel returning from the Gulf War. The TV crew filmed the incoming air crews for a few minutes, then shifted position down the ramp to a site adjacent Gate 2. As the Air Force personnel continued flooding into the terminal, the film crew ultimately went with the flow, abandoning their static vantage point to go mobile along the wire and into the crowd.

Lt. Col. Brian Finnan said that the AMT L-1011 carried many personnel assigned to the 1707th Air Refueling Squadron (Provisional). Activated just for Operation Desert Storm, the 1707th was composed of crews from the 301st Air Refueling Wing at Malmstrom Air Force Base, Mont., and the 384th Bomb Wing at McConnell Air Force Base, Kansas.

"We had crews from Griffiss Air Force Base (in New York), Loring Air Force Base for a while, and Robbins Air Force Base in Georgia," he said.

Finnan, who had been stationed at Malmstrom Air Force Base, left for the Gulf in March. "Our people were in place from the beginning of November 'til now. Col. Wax and his folks (from another refueling squadron), some of those folks had been over there since August of last year," he said.

Although he could not reveal the base from which the 1707th Air Refueling Wing flew its missions, Finnan did say that the mission included air-refueling support for B-

52s, as well as all of the Air Force fighter aircraft and some Navy aircraft.

"Our aircraft total on the ramp varied anywhere from 10 up to 15. Our squadron was composed of active-duty Air Force," Finnan said. "However, there were other units there as well that were composed of Reserve and National Guard."

"From here, we're going to Charleston Air Force Base, South Carolina, where we'll drop off about 40 or so of these people (destined for East Coast assignments). After Charleston, we're going to Malmstrom Air Force Base in Montana to drop off the rest of the folks," Finnan said.

Until June 1990, Lt. Col. Finnan had commanded the 91st Air Refueling Squadron at Malmstrom Air Force Base. He'd since been transferred to an assignment as the wing assistant deputy commander for operations. During his 19-and-a-half years in the Air Force, Finnan had accumulated about 4,000 hours in the KC-135 Stratotanker. The wings mounted over his name on his flight suit indicated his status as a command pilot. Despite nearing the 20-year eligibility date for retirement, he said that he would "probably not (retire) for another six or seven years, and after that, I don't know."

While press reports often depicted flying conditions in the Gulf as atrocious, particularly during dust storms, Finnan said "the weather generally was pretty good" and did not affect operations for the 1707th Air Refueling Squadron (Provisional).

"We flew throughout the whole period, from the beginning of the air war as it's come to be known," the lieutenant colonel said, adding that "we flew about 3,000 sorties. As you might imagine, the air space was pretty congested at times.

"Depending on the type of airplane that we were refueling," Finnan stated, referring to Allied fighters, "we would do anywhere from four to six (planes), because they were flying very heavy.

"We call it `dirty,' meaning that they were loaded with bombs or missiles, and consequently, they used a lot of gas. We were capable of offloading up to 100,000 pounds each flight," he said. A gallon of fuel weighs about six-and-one-half pounds.

Refueling missions initially took place below the Kuwaiti border, but after the first part of April, the planes flew a little farther north. Although aircraft from the 1707th never deployed into Saudi Arabia, "there were tanker aircraft in-country," Finnan said.

Many such KC-135s came from Air National Guard refueling outfits, including the 101st Air Refueling Squadron, Maine Air National Guard. Bangor-based tankers and crews rotated through Jiddah on the Red Sea. The Air Force personnel assigned to the 1707th ARS (P) returned safely from the war, with no significant mishaps, he reported. Finnan praised the squadron members. "They did exactly what the U.S. public paid them to do, they did it well, they did it safely, and I'm proud to be associated with them," the lieutenant colonel stated.

A woman spotted the lieutenant colonel's undecorated flight suit and pinned a ribbon on it. "Thank you, ma'am!" Finnan exclaimed. "It's really neat what the people of Bangor are doing for all the guys."

After HAL Flight 872 touched down at 4:40 p.m. Gary Leighton inspected the ramp and terminal a final time to ensure a clear passage for the incoming Marines. The ABC-TV camera crew returned to its original position beside Gate 2 and awaited the Marines.

They weren't long in coming. Smiling and waving as they entered the ramp, fatigue-clad leathernecks rolled into the terminal like a local football team returning victorious from the championship game. The adoring civilians served as cheerleaders, and Gary Leighton emceed the rally from his position at the microphone.

Marines swept into the domestic terminal and good-naturedly shook hands with their Air Force counterparts. Marines and aviators laughed together and shared Desert

Storm jokes. A soccer ball bounced down the ramp and past the gift table. Heads whirled as a mustachioed Marine expertly regained the soccer ball with his booted feet and worked it back and forth as he entered the domestic terminal. Civilians and military cheered the soccer-playing leatherneck, later identified as Staff Sgt. Tom Scalavino, a Marine Corps Reservist from North Providence, R.I.

Despite the din in the terminal, Gary Leighton caught everyone's attention. "We want to say, `Welcome home, Marines!'" he spoke into his microphone.

The crowd cheered.

Turning to the Marines, Leighton told them, "We have some of your military friends here from the Air Force who provided you a lot of support over there. They're here to say `welcome home!'"

The crowd went nuts again, to be joined this time by Marines who shook their fists in the air and grunted the gut-wrenching "oo, oo, oo" that civilian tongues couldn't duplicate.

As the opening bars of the national anthem emanated from the tape deck, military personnel standing at attention near the table started singing the familiar words. Civilians added their voices to the refrain. By the time the music ended, everyone appeared to be singing. Then the terminal echoed to the thunderous cheers and applause offered by grateful Americans, both in and out of uniform. Air Force Capt. John Bryk escaped the chaos within the terminal by seeking refuge at the gift table. Noticing some shiny red apples set out for the troops, he asked the Chamber of Commerce volunteers, "Do you have any bananas?"

Disappointed that they could not comply with Bryk's request, the volunteers informed him that "Yes, we have no bananas. But we do have apples grown here in Maine."

"We haven't seen a banana in months," Bryk said, explaining his desire for the fruit. "If you could put bananas on the table, you'd have a riot on your hands."

Assigned to the 301st Air Refueling Wing at Malmstrom Air Force Base, Bryk said he had deployed to the Gulf on the 12th of January. "I was on station on the 14th of January, just in time for the festivities," he said.

Although he did not fly in the Gulf, Bryk worked with the 301st Air Refueling Wing and with the 1640th Tactical Airlift Wing, which flew C-130s out of Pope Air Force Base in North Carolina.

Asked why the wartime banana supply proved so insufficient, Bryk laughed and replied, "We were at the very end of the supply line of the civilized earth, and sometimes we think we may just have been beyond the civilized side. That could have had a lot to do with it." On the flight home, the troops had everything to eat but bananas, he said. "For some reason, that's just the thing I think I need. I'm just dying for one. It's been on my mind right behind pizza (and) beer." He'd already taken care of the beer. The pizza would come later that night with his family. He anticipated landing at Malmstrom "about 1:25 in the morning, Mountain Time" and looked forward to a reunion with his wife and two children: 7-year-old Heather and 5-year-old John.

An eight-year Air Force veteran who'd earned his ROTC commission at the Baptist College of Charleston in South Carolina, Bryk said he had missed his birthday, "missed my little girl's birthday, my wife's had a birthday, and our anniversary, so the only one I saw was my little boy's fifth birthday back in November."

Bryk highly praised the AMT flight crews who brought the military home from the Gulf. "The flight crews were outstanding. They couldn't have done more to welcome us," he said. "They made us feel like they were glad to be taking us home. They told us what we'd been missing, put movies on for us, set things up, got addresses for us if they had 'em. We had a good thing."

When the L-1011 crossed from Canadian air space into the United States, "there was quite a cheer," he said. "It's great to be home, especially with this welcome. You people couldn't have done more to make us feel good, and even with all the things we've seen and heard coming home, we were just never prepared for this. It brought tears to everybody's eyes."

Air Force Capt. Steve Smolen sported an American flag from a pocket on his flight suit as he edged into the ramp. A member of the 91st Air Refueling Squadron from Malmstrom Air Force Base, he had graduated from the Air Force Academy in 1984 before attending flight school. Smolen came from Butler, N.J., "45 minutes out of the tube from New York, (the Lincoln Tunnel)." A KC-135 Stratotanker pilot, he had about 2,100 flight hours and in the last three months had logged 330 hours.

"Flying like we did throughout the war, the efficiency level was the highest I'd ever seen," he said.

Smolen deployed to the Gulf on Valentine's Day, about 10 days before the ceasefire. "I flew 13 combat-support missions, and the rest were CAP (Combat Air Patrol), giving fuel to the fighters...that provided the CAP for the soldiers on the ground." He helped refuel various fighters, including Navy and Marine aircraft.

His wife awaited him in Montana. "You want to hear something interesting?" Smolen asked. "She's a (KC-135) pilot as well" who "was in Oman with me. She roomed two tents down from me," had been there for a month, and had flown a tanker back.

After Gary Leighton announced their first boarding call, the Air Force personnel gradually disengaged from their Bangor reception and headed into the ramp. As she passed the gift table, an Air Force woman encountered a Marine walking the other way. "Welcome home," she said with a big smile.

"Thanks," he replied.

At 5:45 p.m., Leighton returned to his microphone to announce a boarding call for HAL Flight 872. "Please, have your green boarding cards ready," he said, "and we thank you for what you did, and it's been our pleasure to have you with us for a brief time."

The crowd went wild again.

The opening notes to "Born in the USA" resounded in the terminal as Lance Corp. Gus Grivas of Matawan, N.J., worked his way into the ramp. He'd belonged to the H and S (Headquarters and Supply) Co., 6th Motor Transport Battalion, a Marine Corps Reserve unit that would send other components through Bangor in the next few weeks. According to Grivas, H and S Co. was based in Red Bank, N.J. The outfit "was called up almost almost six months ago."

While stationed in Saudi Arabia, the unit ran the Baghdad Express, a supply line. "It went everywhere, like to Jiddah," Grivas said. "We delivered everything, from water to tools to ammunition, everything.

"On the way back, we brought POWs," he said. "I remember this one time, they went out, there was only about 40 of us, and there were about 2,000 POWS. They were very cooperative. They were half starved. They'd had bombs dropped on them for 30 days and were ready to surrender. They were totally unarmed."

The Marines hauled the prisoners from southern Iraq to POW camps in Saudi Arabia. Later, the Saudi government boarded the POWS on aircraft and flew them elsewhere in the country.

Although he was a mechanic, Grivas was pressed into service as a driver. "They had us doing everything; everyone was driving," he commented.

The Saudi roads "aren't very good. They're dusty, with pot holes, and a lot of 'em are unpaved. And Saudi drivers, they drive like maniacs. I'm from New York originally, from Brooklyn, and they (the Saudis) drive worse than New York cab drivers," Grivas observed. "They don't care. They cut tanks off."

Unlike many other outfits that passed through BIA, the 6th Motor Transport Battalion lost a man in the Gulf. "One corporal from Providence was involved in an accident. He was fixing a truck, and something happened," Grivas recalled.

This visit marked the first to Maine for Grivas, and he noticed differences between the desert and the north woods. "It's very green around here. It's been five months in the desert, and you see greenery, you appreciate it," he said.

"It's hot there, even during the winter," he said. At night, temperatures might hit 85 or 90 degrees. At the port where Grivas was stationed, the temperature was 15 to 20 degrees cooler because of the ocean breezes.

The Marines saw camels in the desert. "Every once in a while, one would stray out on the road. I didn't hit one, but I've seen 'em laying on the side of the road," Grivas said. "They're just like a deer, only bigger. And they spit at you."

Grivas had worked as a diesel mechanic for Cummings Diesel Engine Co. in Newark, N.J. He anticipated returning to his job as soon as possible.

"When I joined the Reserves, I didn't really think I would go anywhere. But I've gone to Southwest Asia, been involved in a war, got more than I thought would happen. I'm a third-generation Marine," he proudly stated. "I'd do it all over again."

He shook hands with the civilians standing around him and vaulted up the ramp. Moments later, the soccer ball bounced past the gift table in the opposite direction as Staff Sgt. Scalavino headed for his plane.

He grabbed the soccer ball and flipped it into his arms. "I found this lying around in the middle of the desert," Scalavino announced. "I've taken it with me since then, and everywhere I go, I get people to autograph it." He rolled the Wilson soccer ball on its axis to reveal numerous signatures, including some from Bangor troop greeters. Then he posed for a photo with a Chamber volunteer, dropped the ball onto the carpet, and worked it back and forth with his feet as he departed the airport.

A CLOSE CALL FOR THE ARKANSAS RAZORBACKS

Aircraft operators worry when more than the tires meet the road, especially when an aircraft's carrying a few hundred passengers home from their country's latest war.

Sunlight streamed above the clouds as people wandered into Bangor International Airport about 5 a.m. on Saturday, May 11. The telephone line to the airport had been jammed since 3 a.m. with calls inquiring about Hawaiian Airlines Flight 874.

According to the pre-recorded message that most people heard, the HAL L-1011 would land at 5:46 a.m. while en route to Fort Campbell in Kentucky. Perhaps 100 people gathered to meet the plane.

"There it is!" a woman exclaimed while pointing toward the Dedham Hills. A quick glance at the terminal clock showed that the airliner would touch down at 5:32 a.m., 12 minutes early.

Paul Tower, George Nye, and a newspaper reporter stood adjacent to Gate 2 and watched the approaching aircraft. As the L-1011 swept into view, the three men edged toward the windows. "Something's wrong," one man observed. "His tail's too low!"

"His nose is way too high!" another exclaimed.

Its fuselage sharply tilted above its horizontal axis, the L-1011 eased over Hammond Street and staggered toward the runway. Anyone experienced at aircraft-watching would realize how much higher than usual the L-1011's nose had been raised.

A raised nose meant a lowered tail.

"Good Lord, he'll hit!" an observer exclaimed.

"Maybe not," another replied.

Excessive smoke swirled and roiled as the L-1011 lowered its rubber tires onto the pavement. Some unsuspecting troop greeters cheered and applauded, while others sighed in relief.

Any concern about the smoky landing momentarily dissipated as the three men positioned themselves to meet the incoming troops. Stepping to a microphone, Gary Leighton announced that the coffee shop and the Red Baron Lounge were temporarily closed and that May 11 would be Fairfield Day to honor the people living in Fairfield, a Kennebec River town about 50 miles southwest of Bangor. Then Leighton introduced Jennifer Marr, a 17-year-old student at Messalonskee High School.

The well-dressed Marr wore a tiara in her hair and a body-hugging sash that proclaimed her as Junior America City Queen, an honor she'd earned while representing Fairfield. Along with Marr, many other residents from Fairfield, Oakland, and surrounding communities had driven to BIA early this morning to welcome home more American soldiers. And soldiers they were, more than 200 Razorbacks belonging to the 2nd Battalion, 142nd Field Artillery Regiment, Arkansas Army National Guard. As the artillerymen poured through the double-glass doors next to the passenger-service desk, they and the crowd launched themselves into a wild party.

Soldiers marched into the domestic terminal as passengers boarded the United Airlines flight to Manchester and Chicago. Some passengers lingered to cheer. Their flight attendants waited long past their

Soldiers bound for Fort Campbell, Ky., unload their gear and walk to the BIA international terminal after Hawaiian Airlines Flight 874 experienced a hard landing in Bangor on May 11, 1991.

normal boarding time to applaud the arm-waving, V-flashing Arkansas Razorbacks.

Capt. Dallas Harmon grinned hugely as he greeted civilians along the wire. Soon after clearing the last troop greeters, he slipped into the just-opened coffee shop, poured himself a huge cup of coffee, and then re-entered the terminal to watch his friends celebrate a safe homecoming.

According to Harmon, the Pentagon had activated the 2nd Battalion on Nov. 21, 1990, and sent it to Fort Sill in Oklahoma to process into the Army. On Jan. 19, the Razorbacks departed Altus Air Force Base in Oklahoma for the war in the Gulf.

"We'd have gone earlier," Harmon commented in his pleasant southern accent, "but we were waiting for our equipment to get over there. The Army didn't want us sittin' around with nothing to shoot!"

The guardsmen landed at King Fahd International Airport on Jan. 21. "Our advance party was already there in Dhahran when the air war started," Harmon said. "They knew what it was like. For most of us, we'd never been to war." Two weeks later, the 2nd Battalion shifted northward toward the Iraq border. Harmon, the outfit's fire-direction officer, said the the troops were initially assigned to the 7th Corps, then further detached to the 1st Infantry Division. A soldier stepped to the microphone, cleared his throat to stifle his nervousness, and gave thanks to God for bringing all the Razorbacks home safely. Soldiers and civilians cheered and applauded. Harmon said that the battalion was equipped with 12 M-110A2 howitzers, 8-inch self-propelled cannons that could travel anywhere in the Saudi desert. The guns fired very heavy shells. "Each projectile is about a 200-pound bullet," the captain explained. The 2nd Battalion started firing days before the (ground) invasion, he said. "We went on artillery raids on enemy artillery positions, to engage his deep-fire assets and draw them out where we had a good opportunity to swat them.

"We were using radar to track any incoming fire. Another brigade would cover us in case the Iraqis shot back. This is called counterbattery fire, where you're shootin' back right down the other guy's trajectory," Harmon stated.

"On the day of the first (artillery) raid, we fired and tried to pull back as fast as we could, but we received some return fire. The day of the second raid, we had to remain in place after we fired at the Iraqis. We didn't get any return fire," he said.

According to Harmon, the 2nd Battalion belonged to the 1st Infantry Division through Feb. 23, but "that evening, we were farmed out to the 1st UK (the Royal Army's 1st Armored Division), the Desert Rats. I met some British interrogators the first day of the war. "We were hauling butt, trying to keep up with the armor and the infantry," Harmon recalled. "We took about 500 prisoners. They were poppin' up everywhere. We were on the move into Iraq, then we turned due east toward Kuwait City, but we didn't make it to Kuwait before the war ended." A young boy, perhaps 5 or 6 years old, approached Harmon to ask for his autograph. The captain smiled, took the proffered felt-tip marker, and signed the folder that the boy carried.

"It was something else over there, going to war like that," Harmon commented. He sipped his coffee and sighed. "We didn't lose anyone killed, but some guys were seriously wounded by mines.

"After the ceasefire, we immediately road-marched to northern Kuwait. We sat in Kuwait for a long time, then we pulled back into the middle of Iraq and sat there for a solid month," he said. "I did get to Kuwait City."

Setting aside his coffee cup, Harmon folded his arms across his chest and peered at the floor. Then he described a graphic memory. "It was wild, it was incredible," he said. "You wouldn't believe the carnage. TV wouldn't do it justice. You'd have to see it, it was so unreal. Dead Iraqis, blown-up tanks and APCs. I never want to see anything like that again."

Harmon expected his wife, Marietta, to meet him at Fort Sill. "I can't wait 'til I'm home. I'm still in disbelief, in fact. Here I am, back in the good old U.S. of A.," he said, grinning.

A sergeant from the 2nd Battalion asked the two-man band providing the morning's patriotic music to play the hymn "Amazing Grace." Rick Aiken and Bill Trowell performed the first verse as many Arkansas soldiers stood to attention and sang: "Amazing grace, how sweet the sound, that saved a wretch like me.

I once was lost, but now I am found, was blind, but now I see."

Voices carried the words in baritones and deep Southern basses. Afterwards, the SFC wiped tears from his eyes as he explained, "We sung that hymn at all our chapel services in Saudi Arabia. I wanted to sing it again on American soil."

Besides the Arkansas Razorbacks, HAL Flight 874 carried home the 1st Battalion, 623rd Field Artillery Regiment, Kentucky Army National Guard. An enlisted man said that the 1st Battalion, also equipped with the M-110A2 eight-inch howitzer, had been activated in December 1990 and had left for Saudi Arabia on Feb. 10.

Attached to the 18th Airborne Corps, the Kentucky unit "went as far as Basra. We fired at different times along the way," the trooper said.

An officer stepped to the lectern and tested the microphone. He announced that the L-1011 had been damaged while landing. "We won't be going on to Kentucky and Oklahoma aboard this plane," the officer told the disappointed soldiers. "We want you to return to your seats in the plane, and then we will disembark by units, store our weapons in the belly of the plane, and return to the terminal."

The soldiers reluctantly departed the terminal and headed for the L-1011. Just like Sgt. Robert Toth from a May 3rd flight, one soldier walked along the wire while wearing a Dysart's Truck Stop cap. Civilians who were not aware of the L-1011's rough landing started questioning airport officials about the incident. One BIA employee speculated that the HAL pilot "apparently came in a bit too high and dragged his tail."

"There's a tail skid on the back of the plane," Rick Aiken, who also worked in BIA operations, later explained. "It has something like a shock absorber on it, and the skid sort of acts like a sensor, telling the pilot when his tail's close to the ground.

"I watched him (the L-1011) come in, and it was a normal type of landing," Aiken said. "The plane's nose was in a normal position. I think the plane probably touched a little too hard, and the skid was probably jolted too hard.

"That would read out in the cockpit, and it's one of those things you've got to look at," he stated. "The skid must be operational, or the plane can't fly passengers."

A few days later, the Bangor Daily News ran an article about the damaged L-1011. The story downplayed the rough landing and quoted a soldier who'd noticed nothing unusual when the plane touched down. Yet at least three soldiers had said that morning that they'd felt the plane hit real hard. An old-timer, a Vietnam veteran who had flown home back then on another civilian airliner, said "I thought something wasn't right."

To this day, some people believe that the Arkansas Razorbacks had a close call - probably the closest experienced by any troop flight passing through Bangor.

ACRONYMS

Fairfield residents fulfilled their promise to make May 11 their day by returning en masse to Bangor International Airport that evening to meet United Airlines Flight 649.

Exchanging her conservative dress for a debutante's gown, Jennifer Marr joined her friends and neighbors in the BIA domestic terminal about 5 p.m. People kept pouring into the airport. Within a half hour, more than 500 Maine residents packed the wire, while musicians from Lawrence High School unfolded some wire stands and plopped into chairs by the expansive windows.

Gary Leighton did a doubletake as he rounded the corner from the ramp and spotted the 500 people waiting for the UAL jet. Straightening his tie, Leighton introduced himself to the crowd. "How many of you are meeting your first troop flight?" he inquired. Between 50 and 60 hands shot up from the crowd. Most members of the band raised their hands, too.

Leighton then familiarized the crowd with welcoming procedures and mentioned that UAL Flight 649 was headed for Forbes Field in Topeka. "I assume that means the 1st Infantry Division," he said. "When do you expect the troops to disembark?" he was asked. "ASAP (as soon as possible)," Leighton responded. "Their ETA (estimated time of arrival) is in 10 minutes or so."

ASAP. ETA.

Acronym night, when the letters of the alphabet would drop incoherently into conversations with the military passengers deplaning from UAL Flight 649. After flying all day from its POD in SWA, the UAL 747 had a 1746 ETA at BIA, back in the good old USA.

People cheered and applauded as the UAL relief crew passed along the wire before the 747 rumbled from the sky at 5:46 p.m. The flight attendants - most of them middle-aged women - waited patiently on the ramp beside the duty-free shop. They wanted to meet the men and women whom they'd be flying to Kansas.

When the big red-and-white 747 touched down outside the terminal, people erupted into loud cheers and applause. More people slipped into the ramp and stood behind the UAL relief crew. At one point, about 15 people who claimed they were meeting relatives, crowded the ramp. The 747 taxied to the international terminal. Some minutes later, three soldiers stepped through the doors leading to the security corridor. Confronted by the American Legion flagbearer, the startled men paused and gazed down the ramp. Wild cheering and applause resounded from the domestic terminal. Consternation registered on more desert-tanned faces as additional soldiers exited the corridor. What's going on here? read the question written on so many tired eyebrows.

Then a soldier broke the logjam by following the flagbearer into the ramp.

A sound wave washed over and under the soldiers as they cautiously advanced toward the domestic terminal. The older soldiers, possibly many Vietnam vets among them, appeared stunned by the enthusiastic greeting they received. The younger soldiers listened in shock while the band played "My Country, 'Tis of Thee."

The first troops turned the corner into the terminal, and in typical fashion, the 500 civilians waiting for them went bonkers. Yet the soldiers failed to respond, as if an invisible emotional barrier separated them from reality.

Somewhere between the fortieth and fiftieth soldier to march into the terminal, someone finally grasped what was happening. Excitement rippled along the long fatigue line backing into the ramp. A soldier hollered, "Hoo-rah!," and all heaven broke loose.

As they swung into the terminal, more soldiers started waving the little American flags given them by Les Stevens and other Chamber of Commerce volunteers. The Lawrence band broke into a patriotic repertoire as soldiers shouted for joy.

Sound rolled and bounded from wall to floor to wall to ceiling as 500 Maine residents cheered, applauded, yelled, cried, screamed (perfected by teen-age girls), talked, yelled, or sang.

"Hoorah! Hoorah!" another soldier roared at the crowd. A big grin on his face, the man plunged into the women packed along the wire and hugged everybody standing between Gate 2 and the coffee shop.

The UAL relief crew finally departed the terminal, but not until a flight attendant invited a soldier to "come out and meet me on the plane sometime, big boy." He laughed uproariously and told her he'd be right out after making a phone call.

Everyone waiting for a relative on the ramp had left disappointed. Had someone crossed their signals?

The 747 carried soldiers belonging to the 12th Chemical Co., two components (C and D Co.'s) of the 2nd Battalion, 16th Infantry Regiment, and D Battery of the 25th Field Artillery Battalion. Tom Dean scribbled the outfits as the 12CHEMCO, C/2-16, D/2-16, and D/25FA.

More acronyms!

Spec. Ed Weatherald, who hailed from Cincinnati, was assigned to E/2-16, an acronym translated as Echo Co., 2nd Battalion, 16th Infantry Regiment.

Weatherald and E/2-16 had shipped for Saudi Arabia on Jan. 8, almost four weeks after the company's advance party left the United States. "We landed close to Dhahran and stayed there a while," Weatherald said. "We headed for the border about three weeks after getting over there."

He described his MOS as 11-H, driving an M-901 ITV (improved tow vehicle). "We got to the Iraqi border on Feb. 19 or Feb. 20, just

a few days before the war started for us," Weatherald said. "You talk about a strange feeling. Three weeks in-country and, bingo, we're off to war.

"We crossed the border into Iraq at 6:15 a.m. on the 24th, maybe a few hours after the invasion kicked off," he stated. "We took on a little bit of their artillery at first, but there wasn't much to come our way. The Air Force was way ahead of us, taking out artillery, armor, and infantry concentrations."

The soldiers assigned to E/2-16 fired their TOW missiles at Iraqi bunkers and vehicles. "When we fired our first set," Weatherald said, "we got some return fire, but very little.

"The TOWs were very accurate, usually hitting their targets. They probably made a difference. We didn't have any casualties, and we believe our ability to hit our targets kept down the return fire," Weatherald stated. The curly-haired, mustachioed specialist said, "I'm definitely glad to be home. I can't wait to see my three kids. They live with their mom in Cincinnati. We're divorced, but we keep in touch." Weatherald anticipated that friends would meet him in Kansas, but "my big party will start when I get to Indianapolis." The 32-year-old soldier explained that he'd graduated from Columbus North High School in Columbus, Ind., where his parents and relatives still lived. Employed as an ironworker in Florida, Weatherald had enlisted in the Army for four years in September 1989. "I figure on returning to Florida when my hitch is up. They're holding my job for me," he said, "and I'll retain my seniority. I think I'll probably go back and attend night school too. I'd like to work as an inspector at construction sites."

Weatherald beamed when asked about his three children: Brant, 12; Christina, 9; and Vonda, 7, whom he'd last seen in December 1990. "I got mail from them, and I wrote them real often, of course. I called them as much as I could," Weatherald said. "Oh, man, I missed them so bad, you don't know how much. We're gonna have a big party, and I intend to visit all three of their classes. Their classmates sent me letters," he said. "It's just great to be back," Weatherald quietly said. "It's so hard to describe the feeling as you step off the plane or descend through the clouds and realize it's American soil."

Throughout the terminal, autograph-seekers mobbed the weary soldiers. 1st Lt. Mimi Collins, who commanded the decontamination platoon belonging to the 12th Chemical Co., 1st Infantry Division, discovered that many young girls especially wanted autographs from women soldiers. Collins said that the 12th Chemical Co., a combat-support unit with give platoons, had arrived in the Gulf on Jan. 14. She explained that the recon(naissance) platoon did NBC (Nuclear, Biological, and Chemical) recon "to make exactly sure where the chemical agent is. With all that talk about Iraqi biological or chemical weapons, we were really concerned that they'd use something against us." Another platoon, the smoke platoon, could mask the movements of Allied soldiers by laying down a smoke screen from M-1059 smoke generators. These devices used fog oil, Collins said, and "can lay it on pretty thick."

The 12th Chemical Co. deployed three decon(tamination) platoons, including the lieutenant's command. "My job during the war," she explained, "was to set up a decon site if anything happened at or below the breach."

The platoon had three M-12s, large water-filled tanks mounted on 5-ton trucks. By adding a decontaminant agent to the water, the soldiers could wash chemical agents off trucks and other large vehicles with high-pressure hoses. If a soldier contaminated his MOP gear, "we'd have him exchange it for clean gear," Collins said. "There was always the chance that you could get an (NBC) agent on your skin. To counteract this, most soldiers usually had decon units on them."

The 12th Chemical Co. accompanied the 1st Infantry Division into Iraq and past the blazing Kuwaiti oilfields. After the war, the company redeployed to Iraq and ultimately Saudi Arabia, where the tired soldiers stayed in the Khubar Towers for a short time.

"We're glad to be coming home," said Collins, who considered Norfolk, Va., to be her hometown. "There's nothing like being away for a while to appreciate what you've got."

About 7 p.m., Gary Leighton returned to the terminal to announce the first boarding call for UAL Flight 649. "Time to go home," Leighton told the Big Red One troopers, who needed little coaxing to leave for Kansas.

Soldiers filed from the terminal as the Lawrence High School band played "America the Beautiful." Soldiers and civilians shook hands or exchanged hugs. When Leighton issued the final boarding call at 7:07 p.m., only a few soldiers remained in the domestic terminal. "American Trans Air wants your plane airborne by 7:30 p.m.," the softspoken Leighton told the stragglers, "so they require your presence on board right now." He then announced the flight schedules for Sunday and Monday.

As Ed Weatherald, Mimi Collins, and the other soldiers reboarded United Airline Flight 649 that Saturday evening, one of the civilians standing two or three rows deep along the wire was Aaron Hanington, the young soldier from Benton who'd landed in Bangor on Friday, April 26. Now, 15 days later, here he was, clad in comfortable civilian clothes, watching the greeting extended the soldiers from UAL Flight 649.

Hanington explained that he was home on leave. He and his parents had driven from Benton to meet a relative landing on a Delta flight. A delay pushed that plane's arrival into the time frame bordering UAL Flight 649's. Hanington couldn't help but watch as civilians mobbed the troops. "It sure seems different, seeing everything from this point-of-view," he said. He'd set his eyes on the military a few years earlier. In fact, Hanington had joined the 1135th Transportation Co., Maine Army National Guard, before graduating from Waterville High School in 1989. Part-time employment didn't appeal to him, however, so he went on active duty, a decision that took him to Fort Lewis, Wash., and an assignment with the 497th Transportation Co. of the 80th Ordnance Battalion.

When the Gulf Crisis erupted, the Army desperately needed transportation companies in Saudi Arabia, so Hanington and the 497th shipped for Dhahran on Oct. 11, 1990. When the Fort Lewis soldiers got to the Gulf, "we had no responsibility at first," he said. "I guess there were transport outfits galore, so we waited for a battalion to pick us up."

The Army finally assigned the 497th to the 189th Maintenance Battalion, which was attached to the 82nd Airborne Division. The 497th's trucks arrived about a week to 10 days after the company did. As soon as the trucks checked out as mechanically sound, Hanington and his fellow truckers hit the road.

And travel they did.

During their first four months bouncing and jouncing on the Saudi highway system, "we were on the road, delivering everything from medical supplies to ammo," he said. The ordnance alone ranged from M-16 rounds to howitzer shells. Though he could not remember every item he hauled, "if the Army wanted it shipped, we took it," he said. Hanington learned that driving in Saudi Arabia differed tremendously from driving in Maine. "Basically, their roads were not all that bad, until the convoys hit them...and tore them all apart," he said. Most Saudi roads were two lanes wide and paved with asphalt, although Hanington did recall finding two freeways with four lanes in either direction.

He drove primarily on two military supply routes (MSRs), Audi and Dodge. The Allies usually named their MSRs after automobiles. MSR Audi, for example, dashed from Dhahran to An Nu'ayriyah, from where MSR Dodge bolted across the desert to Hafr al-Batin. Both roads comprised the beginning stages of the Tapline Road, the highway that witnessed massive Allied traffic during January and early February.

According to Hanington, MSRs Audi and Dodge led "to the Iraqi border and back again, but we didn't cross the border before the ground war, of course."

Other MSRs included Toyota, which handled traffic moving from Riyadh to Dhahran; Mercedes, running from An' Nu'ayriyah south through Uray'irah to Al Hufuf; and Sultan, the non-automotive designee linking Hafr al-Batin, King Khalid Military City, Al Artawiyah and, ultimately, Riyadh.

The Saudi highways swiftly deteriorated after the Army initiated largescale convoys near the end of October or the beginning of November, Hanington said. "They just basically crumbled apart under the weight and the traffic."

As if road conditions weren't a major problem, the American drivers encountered the Middle East's equivalent of Japanese kamikaze pilots: Saudi drivers.

The Benton native imaginatively described how "a Saudi would pass you on the left, on the right, or straight down the middle with a semi coming at him. They'd whip out into the desert on the side of the road, send the sand flying everywhere, and cut in front of you with inches to spare."

Wrecks dotted the MSRs, but "we never saw a Saudi tow truck coming after them, like we would back home," Hanington said. "When they had an accident, they'd leave the car or truck right there. We saw abandoned wrecks all the time. I don't know if they ever come back for them."

The 497th went into Iraq for two weeks and took some hostile fire before the ground war ended. The transport soldiers left Saudi Arabia on April 28 and returned to Fort Lewis 23-1/2 hours earlier the same day. "We were flying back into time," Hanington joked.

UAL Flight 6474 brought the soldiers into Bangor. Not expecting a reception like he and his comrades received, Hanington noted that "it was beyond explanation...with perfect strangers saying 'hello' to everybody."

His comrades talked about their Maine homecoming even as they reboarded their aircraft. "They were very touched by it," Aaron stated. "Most of them didn't want to get back on the plane because of the reception."

THE DAY OF THE GENERALS

American Trans Air Flight 8657, a gleaming blue-and-white L-1011, swept westward with the sun that Sunday. Arcing across New Brunswick after its long overwater journey from Saudi Arabia and Shannon International Airport in Ireland, the airliner entered American airspace somewhere near Houlton.

When the AMT pilot announced the border crossing, his passengers roared their approval.

Canadian air-traffic controllers gradually passed the aircraft to their American counterparts at BIA, the L-1011's first destination in the United States. Radar registered the incoming plane as a blip that steadily closed the distance to Bangor.

The rising sun glistened on the L-1011's fuselage as the aircraft flew high over Maine. Far below the white clouds, people woke to tend their farms or head for work at places that never shut down. A glance out the window before breakfast confirmed their morning as sunny and warm. A glance at the wall calendar confirmed the day as Mother's Day 1991.

At BIA, however, May 12 would be forever known as the Day of the Generals.

After midnight Saturday, a passenger-service employee had updated the message tape to announce that AMT Flight 8657 had been confirmed for 5:56 a.m., with a final destination of Atlanta, Ga. The many people who dialed the airport before dawn included mothers and grandmothers intent on spending Mother's Day with their families.

Before they did, though, the women had someone else's children or parents to meet.

About 50 people had gathered in the BIA domestic terminal by 5:46 a.m., when Sheila Dean and two other women quietly began singing the national anthem near Mr. Paperback. A friend wandered past and asked Dean, "What's happening?"

"We're practicing," she machinegunned between "rockets" and "red glare."

"For what?"

"Just practicing," Dean replied, smiling secretively.

The friend shook his head and walked away.

AMT Flight 8657 touched down at BIA at 5:50 a.m. Richard Myrshall came into the domestic terminal and announced the plane's arrival. He also told the crowd that the L-1011 carried three generals among its military passengers.

George Nye stirred when he heard that pronouncement. "Sounds like someone's staff," he noted. "Wonder who it can be?"

"Lots of brass, lots of brass," Tom Dean said as he walked along the wire to take his station on the ramp.

Apparently desperate for good music, the women operating the tape deck that morning resorted to a tape by Mitch Miller, a musician unknown to anyone under age 25. As soldiers entered the ramp to a rousing welcome from Legionnaires and Red Cross volunteers, a few teenagers in the crowd listened to the "ancient" music and gave it their thumbs down.

Officers - many, many officers - formed the vanguard as soldiers poured into the ramp. Lt. Gen. John J. Yeosock led the way, a smile brightening his countenance as he graciously acknowledged the cheers and applause from the crowd.

Col. Mike Flynn strolled into the terminal and reported that the L-1011 carried the staff of the 3rd U.S. Army, U.S. Army Central Command, which was headed for Fort McPherson near Atlanta. Startled upon hearing this information, George Nye wondered "why they would put all that brass in one plane. One crash, and you've wiped out everybody." Col. Flynn said he had joined the 3rd U.S. Army staff as its intelligence officer last January, just in time "to get ready for the (ground) offensive. Our staff took all the available intelligence we could glean and pushed it forward so the combat commanders could make the right decisions in the field.

"I can't discuss all our intelligence sources, of course," Flynn said, "but aerial reconnaissance does come to mind. There were other sources like electronic listening, but that's highly classified. I can tell you that whatever we had for an intelligence-gathering capability, it was very, very good."

He recalled a time during the ground offensive "when a division, I think it was the 1st or 3rd Armored Division, looked at some overlays and saw where the Republican Guards were. Our tank crews could hang back out of the Iraqis' range and pick off their tanks. "Really great soldiers on the American side, great training, and terrific equipment made the difference in this war," Flynn said. "In all my 28 years in the Army, these are the best soldiers I have ever seen — even better than the platoon I commanded when I was with the 82nd Airborne Division in 1963."

According to the colonel, the main headquarters of the 3rd U.S. Army was located in Riyadh, but many officers often traveled in the field. Flynn went to King Khalid Military City. On the second day of the ground war, he found himself tearing through southern Iraq with rapidly advancing American forces. He described "passing through an area where American armor took on Iraqi tanks at a range of about 2,500 meters, which was outside their (the Iraqis') range.

"I saw a T-72, their top tank, that had its turret reversed over its engine," Flynn said. "The first American shell hit the right side of the turret, passed through the tank commander and his cupola, and spun the turret around 180 degrees. The second shot entered the turret and detonated the ammunition. The Iraqis never knew what hit them. They were expecting us to come from another direction."

Lt. Gen. Yeosock, who commanded the 3rd U.S. Army and all the Army units in the Gulf, proved a center of attention as he puffed a cigar and signed autographs. "I tell you, I've been gone a long time," he said, "and it feels real good to be coming back."

Lieutenant General John J. Yeosock, commander of the Third Army and of all Army troops in the Persian Gulf, received a warm welcome when he landed in Bangor on Mother's Day 1991.

Yeosock had flown to Saudi Arabia with Defense Secretary Richard Cheney on Aug. 4, 1990, just two days after Iraqi troops had occupied Kuwait. Yeosock and Cheney arrived on Aug. 6, about the time that President George Bush decided to commit American ground troops to defend the Saudi kingdom.

The general remained in Riyadh while Cheney flew home after consultations with Saudi officials. Though Yeosock established his headquarters in the Saudi capital, he kept a forward mobile headquarters that took him to places like Dhahran and Kuwait. As the American military buildup intensified, the 3rd U.S. Army staff guided the influx of Army units to their respective posts. According to Flynn, troops poured into Saudi Arabia by the tens of thousands.

"It was an incredibly quick buildup," said Yeosock, his gravelly voice delivering his thoughts in clear, concise sentences. When his cigar went out, he relit it and puffed a few times.

"I'd never seen anything like it, not even in Vietnam. Our people were the best damned troops we could field to take on a tough assignment. I'm proud of every one of them," he said.

Civilians surrounded Yeosock and repeatedly asked him to pose for photos. He obliged every request, then usually wrote a short personal message on a T-shirt or in a notebook.

As Yeosock watched Maine residents bombard his men and women with souvenirs and love, his eyes gradually misted. He chewed his cigar as he autographed another T-shirt. Civilians and soldiers swirled around him. Unable to contain his emotions, Yeosock reflected on the joyous homecoming the soldiers on AMT Flight 8657 had received.

"Listen, I tell you, I was absolutely overwhelmed by this welcome you've given us," the general said, punching the air with his cigar. "I've seen a lot of things in my lifetime, but this is absolutely incredible. If it hadn't been for the support of the American people, we wouldn't have done so well as we did. Your support made all the difference for us," he told the civilians standing around him. "I thank you for it."

Brig. Gen. James W. Munroe, the deputy chief of staff for logistics for the 3rd U.S. Army, also flew into Bangor that morning with Yeosock and a third general. Like their boss, Munroe and his unidentified companion found themselves surrounded by admirers.

"A far cry from Vietnam," Munroe later commented.

Another high-ranking officer said that the American military personnel remaining in Saudi Arabia and Kuwait included 85,000 soldiers, 12,000 Marines, and about 13,000 Air Force personnel.

"They're coming out as fast as possible. A brigade of 3,000 soldiers will remain in Kuwait as a presence, a deterrent, if you will. We don't want Saddam thinking that just because we've pulled out, he can get away with anything," the officer said.

Of course, Saddam Hussein did flex his weakened muscles later in 1991, but swiftly deployed combat aircraft and support personnel convinced him to back down from his opposition to United Nations' nuclear inspections.

The soldiers from AMT Flight 8657 remained in Bangor less than an hour on the Day of the Generals - not a long time, but sufficient for two soldiers to celebrate their birthdays. Many civilians gladly sang "Happy Birthday" and wished the soldiers well.

By 6:45 a.m., the last soldiers headed up the ramp toward the AMT L-1011. Civilians would not let Yeosock depart until he signed every last autograph. Then, again thanking his hosts for their hospitality, the general waved good-bye and joined his staff for the final leg of their journey to Fort McPherson.

Neither Yeosock nor the troop greeters realized that they'd meet again on another Day of the Generals.

FEEDING LOUISIANA

Bound for England Air Force Base in Alexandria, Louisiana, United Airlines Flight 6496 had landed at Bangor International Airport about 4 p.m. on Sunday, May 12. The 747 carried 325 passengers.

More than 150 people listened patiently as Richard Myrshall explained the welcoming procedure. The crowd swelled as more people entered the domestic terminal. With Mother's Day festivities winding down, the airport became the place to be that Sunday afternoon. When several soldiers rounded the corner from the security corridor about 4:15 p.m., the crowd exploded into sustained cheers and applause. Ignoring the noise echoing up the ramp, the soldiers vanished downstairs to use either the phones or the rest rooms.

No more soldiers appeared on the ramp.

When the crowd finally realized the soldiers weren't headed their way, the din gradually diminished, and someone pulled the plug on Lee Greenwood's "God Bless the USA." A woman behind the passenger-service desk explained that the troops would not be deplaning. Their commander had cited a problem with paperwork.

Then, at 4:22 p.m., cheers erupted in the domestic terminal as the UAL relief crew made its way across the carpet and into the ramp. A representative from the Greater Bangor Chamber of Commerce stopped the flight captain and spoke quietly with him.

"The commander has decided to let them off the plane after all," the Chamber rep told the UAL pilot. "Hallelujah," Tom Dean said as he retrieved his parked camcorder. "Let's get this show on the road."

At 4:25 p.m., the UAL pilot disappeared into security screening, leaving his flight attendants to chat with attentive Legionnaires. A World War II vet beamed as he joked with a pretty brunette born when Vietnam was winding down.

Counting heads in the domestic terminal, one troop greeter pegged the crowd at 200 people plus, with the numbers increasing by the minute. He also sensed a growing restlessness, a tense undercurrent that demanded, "We want our troops, and we want 'em now!"

"Something had better happen here," one man said to Dean, "or we'll have a riot on our hands. I wonder if they'd storm the plane? Wouldn't put it past them," Dean replied.

A UAL flight attendant joined the two men. They talked about the delayed re-entry for the passengers aboard the 747 and its effect on their time in Bangor.

"If they're not allowed off the plane, well, we just might claim fatigue," the flight attendant commented.

"Yeah," another attendant said. "The crew that's on the plane right now can't fly it any further. They're at the end of their hours. And if we're too tired to fly, the plane sits right here." "FAA regs," her friend explained.

"Can you do that?" a troop greeter inquired.

The women looked him eye-to-eye and winked. "Those boys are getting off here," one flight attendant responded.

At 4:28 p.m., the UAL flight captain returned to the ramp and informed his crew that "the delay's got something to do with the paperwork."

At 4:31 p.m., soldiers finally appeared atop the ramp, and an almost mutinous crowd broke into wild applause and cheering. UAL flight attendants cheered and applauded, too, as someone restored the power to "God Bless the USA."

At 4:32 p.m., the vanguard reached the wire, and the civilians now standing three rows deep went bananas.

As soldiers flooded the wire, the tape deck switched to Neil Sadaka's "America" before thundering into Bruce Springsteen's "Born in the USA." As Springsteen hollered "I was born in the USA," emotions kept bottled up so long by the soldiers burst into joyous whooping and shouting across the terminal.

Hands reached from the crowd to clasp young men and women, older men, fathers, grandfathers, aunts, and uncles, the personnel belonging to the 527th Engineer Battalion from Camp Beauregard, La., or the 82nd Chemical Co. out of Fort Polk, La. The latter outfit was from the regular Army; the 527th was a component of the Louisiana Army

National Guard.

Civilians hugged soldiers who cried on their shoulders. A woman soldier sobbed as she worked her way along the wire. No one shushed her tears, which she shed from pure joy. The grandmothers she met in the crowd understood her tears, of course. They'd done the same when their men came home from Kasserine, Anzio, Tarawa, the Frozen Chosin, Pleiku, and the Iron Triangle.

A male soldier grinned and waved a V with his fingers as he came along the wire with an orange balloon in tow.

The wild celebration soon spread throughout the terminal, as the Louisiana soldiers completed their phone calls or connected with the cold beers in the Red Baron Lounge. Autograph-seekers soon zeroed on the troops who had finished their initial obligations on American soil.

Staff Sgt. Jerry Ashmore, a member of the 527th Engineer Battalion, Louisiana Army National Guard, was an oil driller in the Gulf of Mexico in civilian life.

Staff Sgt. Jerry Ashmore, a member of the 527th Engineer Battalion, hailed from Ball, Louisiana. A driller on an offshore oil rig owned by the Atlantic-Pacific Marine Corp. Ashmore said that he was a Vietnam vet who'd returned home through Fort Lewis, Washington.

"We didn't get nothing," he said. "I'm glad to see (that) America's back on its feet again. This welcome here, it makes up for some of what we never got."

Ashmore said that the Army had activated the 527th Engineer Battalion on Dec. 6, 1990. "We were stationed at Fort Polk to learn demolition training," he stated. "We're combat heavy engineers, more used to building things, not blowin' them up."

According to Ashmore, "all we did was close up the berm and maintain the MSRs" while supporting the 7th Corps. The 527th lost no personnel, and only a few Louisiana soldiers suffered injuries in equipment accidents.

Sgt. Ted Mays, another member of the 527th from Tioga, Louisiana, joined Ashmore near the terminal windows. Mays laughed and joked with two UAL flight attendants, Francine Gerardi and Elizabeth Smentkowski of California.

Ashmore said that he'd traveled "a mile or two into Iraq, just to see what it looked like from the other side (of the berm)." According to Ashmore, the berm was "located on the Saudi side, about 100 yards from the border."

He anticipated a warm reunion with his wife, Mary, and their two children: Rusty, 17, and Katherine Ann, 10. "Mary's from New England, you know," the sergeant said, "Grand Isle, Vermont. I'll tell her all about the friendly people here in Maine."

Ashmore joined the conversation with Gerardi and Smentkowski, who kidded him about something that had happened on the plane. Explaining that they had flown soldiers home from Vietnam, the flight attendants compared notes about Vietnam and the Gulf with the two Louisiana Army Guardsmen.

Then a tearful Mays locked his arm around his friend, Ashmore. He looked at the sergeant before saying, "We're two Vietnam vets who've waited 25 years to march home and have someone say, `Welcome home.'" Gerardi and Smentkowski hugged Mays, then enveloped Ashmore in their arms. "I was really moved by all this," Mays said, sweeping his hand across the terminal. "You probably don't know what it's like, comin' home to such a wonderful greeting."

By 5:10 p.m., soldiers started filtering into the ramp. While his companions gleaned the gift table, a sergeant observed that the delay in departing the aircraft was not appreciated.

"They couldn't get us off the plane," he said. "They didn't have the right papers, the Army didn't. All this way from Saudi, and they weren't gonna let us off. I'm sure glad they did. You tell everyone I said that."

The initial boarding call stampeded the Louisiana-bound soldiers into the ramp. Gerardi and Smentkowski, who had brought the soldiers into Bangor, waved good-bye and hugged particular troops whom they remembered from the trans-Atlantic flight.

The Louisiana soldiers endured another false start before departing BIA. Someone let Whitney Houston sing her eternal version of the "Star-Spangled Banner." Ashmore, Mays, and their companions stood at attention while Houston warbled through her music. When the notes finally died, the soldiers cheered and applauded - and poured into the ramp for the long flight home.

Most people who met UAL Flight 6496 didn't leave the airport when the plane departed Bangor. Only 90 minutes separated the UAL plane's takeoff and the arrival of Hawaiian Airlines Flight 876, another aircraft also en route to England Air Force Base, Louisiana.

Coincidental?

No.

People who'd watched HAL Flight 874's brush with the runway a day earlier stood near the terminal windows as Flight 876 flared into its final approach. "They couldn't get it wrong two days in a row - could they?" a woman asked.

"Just watch," her husband growled.

The L-1011 lumbered into view with its wheels locked down. "Attitude looks good," a veteran Air Guard pilot observed.

When the L-1011 gracefully touched its wheels on the runway, the air pressure within the terminal changed as 30 or 40 people collectively released their bated breaths at 6:45 p.m.

Richard Myrshall rounded the corner into the terminal and gave a masterful, succinct rendition of the welcoming procedure. The 150 people facing him across the wire cheered his words, although they'd heard them a dozen times.

By 6:55 p.m., the crowd numbered about 200 people. They strained to glimpse any activity far up the ramp. Would the troops delay this time in leaving their plane? No. Desert fatigues suddenly swarmed onto the ramp, overran the delighted welcoming party, and cascaded into the domestic terminal. Loud applause and cheering lifted from the crowd as the soldiers entered the terminal and swung along the wire.

"Patch looks familiar," Tom Dean observed as the uniformed crush swept him along. "Hey!" a civilian called to the soldiers. "Are you guys part of the 527th Engineer Battalion?" "Sure am!" a sergeant replied, grinning beneath his sunglasses. The Louisiana Guardsmen patiently awaited their turn to meet the civilians who packed the wire, tilting the stanchions at odd angles. Comments like "thank you, ma'am" and "it's sure great to be back" resounded across the terminal as the soldiers lingered in the line until it ended near Mr. Paperback.

Those soldiers who cleared the wire bounded toward the phones or the lounge, however. A Pfc. or a corporal - the metal tags proved illegible from outside the lounge - twisted the cap off a beer and signaled his friends still greeting people on the wire.

"Come 'n get it!" the trooper summoned his comrades. Excusing their sudden departure from the line, they obliged his request. "Have one on me!" a Bangor man laughed. "Great! I'll send you the bill!" a Louisiana soldier responded. Sgt. 1st Class Norman Norris came from West Monroe, La. A food-service sergeant with the 527th Engineer Battalion, he said his unit "left Louisiana on 8 February and arrived over there (in the Gulf) on 8 February. Not bad, eh?

"My mission there was to oversee the feeding of about 400 people. Now, there are about 700 people in the battalion," Norris explained, "but we've got two field messes.

"We carry all of our equipment with us, including the stoves and cooking utensils, right down to the spoons, pots, and pans. All this stuff, it was shipped by boat from out of Houston before we left and got there after we did."

When the 527th Engineer Battalion arrived in Dammam, a civilian contractor fed the Louisiana soldiers. The battalion remained in Dammam eight to 10 days, Norris said, "before we started heading out in increments, groups being sent here and there.

"Wherever our guys went, we had to feed 'em," he said. "We were serving them two hot meals a day, breakfast and dinner, and MREs for lunch. Now, those MREs, they weren't so popular."

All his Army training never really prepared Norris and his staff for cooking in the Saudi desert. "Our biggest problem we had was the wind. And, oh, yeah, the flies were terrible bad.

"The blowing sand was a problem, too," Norris concluded. "It would get into everything. We ended up with a lot of dust storms, and it would be hard to breathe. We'd do our best to keep the sand out of the food, but, sometimes everything tasted like the beach."

Norris seldom cooked under a permanent roof. "We would put up tents, and you could drive a wood stake a few inches into the sand, and you would hit rock. Hey, we got imaginative, because we're engineers. The guys took metal fence posts and cut them into 3-foot lengths. Then they'd drive them into the rock with sledgehammers." The American logistics network kept the guardsmen amply supplied with food, ammunition, water, and other necessary materials. Despite their assignment deep in the desert, the soldiers ate well.

For breakfast, "oh, we'd serve scrambled eggs, homemade biscuits - if you know what you're doing, you can make biscuits anywhere - or pancakes, cereal, all topped off with fruit juice, coffee, or tea," Norris mentally read the menu. "And then there was SOS," the soldier's age-old designation for chipped beef on toast.

According to Norris, getting fresh fruit in the desert could be a problem at times. "The few times I would get bananas, they'd be ruined," he said.

"I'd reach times in my personal life, where I'd kill for a head of lettuce," Norris groused. "It made you appreciate the things you took for comfort back home. I don't believe I'll ever walk by a produce aisle in a supermarket again without stoppin' and inhalin' the fragrance of fresh fruits and vegetables."

Dinner "got to be the biggie meal for the troops," he said. "We were serving a lot of chili mac, quite a bit of chicken. Toward the end, we were cutting a good gravy steak, and we had ground beef. We had hardly any fish at all. While we were in the desert, we had grilled steak once," Norris commented. Easter Sunday, March 30, called for a special meal. "Some guys dug barbecue pits in the sand and said they were going to have one real homestyle meal before they left the desert," Norris said.

"We served barbecued chicken, yellow cake with chocolate frosting, potato salad, shrimp cocktail, baked potatoes, the works," Norris recalled. "It was great, stuffing the guys with everything like we'd have back home. The guys, they'd complain about the food, of course, but grunts always complain about everything and anything. I think we lived real comfortable. We sure had some creature comforts that people in past wars didn't have," he observed.

Sgt. Samuel Duskin, another member of the 527th Engineer Battalion, stepped behind the lectern. He announced that he wanted to sing "Always and Forever" on American soil. Asking the crowd's patience, Duskin launched into the song a cappella.

As Duskin moved into the music, the crowd gradually fell silent. Richard Myrshall watched from his vantage point beside the American flag while Duskin tightly closed his eyes and sang a song difficult to perform even with accompaniment.

When Duskin reached his finale, the crowd erupted into sustained applause and cheers. A comrade, Spec. Edward Wempe of Knoxville, Louisiana, said, "He's been wanting to sing that song for a long time." A few minutes later, the national anthem lifted from the sound system. Across the terminal, soldiers already attentive to Duskin's singing drew themselves to attention and faced the flag. Beside the coffee shop, a bespectacled Spec. Bordelon riveted his eyes and his salute toward the flag. A yard or two away, a Spec. Stone clasped his right hand to his heart as he, too, listened to Francis Scott Key's immortal words.

Then the boarding call sounded for HAL Flight 876. Bidding farewell to the troop greeters, the Louisiana Army Guardsmen emptied the domestic terminal and practically stripped the gift table clean before vanishing into the ramp. A Lt. Thomas reappeared in the terminal and conducted a search-and-locate mission for any malingerers in the Red Baron Lounge. After flushing a few soldiers from the lounge, the lieutenant scoured the men's room and the remaining airport shops. "Well, I guess they're all aboard the plane," Thomas told troop greeters as he shook hands along the wire.

THE BOOT TRADE

By late afternoon on Monday, May 13, the days were already dwindling to the last "official" troop flight to pass through Bangor International Airport. When the public learned that American Trans Air Flight 8683, which was destined for Lawson Army Airfield at Fort Benning in Columbus, Ga., would land at 6:45 p.m., countless people believed the flights would last forever. Tonight's was just one more flight of many to come, they figured.

Not so. By 6:32 p.m., about 70 people stood along the wire at BIA. Ruth Stearns, a Hampden resident, had recently returned from Florida. She had seen nothing about the troop flights in the Sunshine State media. Her Maine friends had informed her about the homecomings, so she decided to meet the passengers on AMT Flight 8683. "This has brought back memories of when I met my husband in World War II. He came into Boston, and I went down to meet him alone," Stearns commented, sensing the excitement around her. "It's just like I'm meeting my children again!"

An Air Belgium jet touched down at 6:45 p.m. Five minutes later, another jet settled onto the tarmac. "Trans Air!" a woman yelled into the terminal. People gathered at the windows to cheer and wave as the L-1011 came into view. The crowd had more than doubled its size by the time the L-1011 parked at the international terminal. Ignoring the cheers emanating from the windows, 12 to 15 people dropped quarters into the pay

TVs and watched an ABC-News broadcast featuring the footage shot in Bangor the previous week.

Every time the troop greeters recognized a face, they cheered. A quizzical Gary Leighton checked the noise source before stepping to his microphone to introduce himself to the crowd and ask where they were from.

The spontaneous response indicated that a busload of people from the Sherman-Island Falls axis had traveled to Bangor tonight. Leighton announced that AMT Flight 8683 carried 199 soldiers. He asked the crowd to extend the troops "a Bangor welcome". The civilians roared their approval.

Soldiers appeared way up the ramp, where Carl and Kathleen Lindh and Legionnaires from Post 84 shook hands and quietly bid the troops "welcome home, welcome home." As the soldiers descended the ramp, however, the noise intensified before reaching painful levels in the domestic terminal.

When they rounded the corner from the ramp, some soldiers opted for the Red Baron Lounge and bugged from the line along the wire. A few comrades watched their friends vanish into the lounge and joined them, but most soldiers remained in line to shake hands.

AMT Flight 8683 ferried home several units, including the 1206th and 1209th Quartermaster Detachments, the 71st Ordnance Detachment, the 386th Adjutant General HHD (an Army Reserve outfit from Mississippi), and the 114th Military Police Co., Mississippi Army National Guard.

Sgt. 1st Class Earl Dorris belonged to the 114th Military Police Co., which was based where he lived in Clinton, Miss. "We reported for duty last September, after the 114th was activated on the 12th," Dorris said.

The Mississippi Guardsmen left for Saudi Arabia on Nov. 10, 1990, spent a month in Dhahran, then shifted to Riyadh. Dorris out lined the company's missions as fourfold: performing routine law-and-order functions; providing security for Central Command; patrolling the MSRs; and patrolling Eskan Village, a combined Army-Air Force facility near Riyadh.

"We had detachments all over Saudi Arabia," Dorris stated. As the operations sergeant, he helped plan and prioritize missions that were assigned to various platoons.

"I can't say we ever really got involved in the war," Dorris commented. "The only thing we basically had in our area was three weeks of Scud attacks. The excitement wore thin after a while, and I think everyone felt safe with the Patriots around.

"After the war ended, the rumors in Saudi Arabia were rampant as to who's leaving and when. We got a tentative date in early April as to a two-or-three-week time frame when we might leave. Our missions were ending, so we knew we'd be leaving," he said.

Another SFC, overhearing Dorris' remarks that many desert troops were dressed in jungle fatigues, stamped his feet on the carpet. "A lot of us went over there wearing our jungle boots," the Guardsman said.

"Well, they're great for hot, humid climates, where you want the sweat to drain from your feet, but over in Saudi, the holes designed to let the water out let the sand in," the Mississippian explained. "I was lookin' to switch, I'll tell you," he said. "I ran into a British staff sergeant who took one look at my boots and offered me a fair trade: his for mine. No questions asked, just off and on with the boots. I think I got the better part of the deal, unless the Brit was headed for Malaysia or something."

Gary Leighton issued the first boarding call for AMT Flight 8683 at 7:35 p.m., about 40 minutes after the plane had landed. Apparently subdued by their long flight from the Gulf, the Southern soldiers never switched into the party mode, a fact noted, but not begrudged by their Yankee hosts.

After all, there would be plenty of other times to party at BIA, people reasoned. Guess again.

FLYING THE FRIENDLY SKIES OF UNITED

When United Airlines Flight 6496 landed in Bangor with the 527th Engineer Battalion on May 12, UAL flight attendants Francine Gerardi and Elizabeth Smentkowski anticipated a two-day layover in the Queen City.

They'd earned their brief respite from the joyous task of flying home with America's best.

In another time and half a world away, however, that task proved far different. "You see," the two women explained, "the Persian Gulf is not our first war. It's our second."

Smentkowski, a demure woman with a sharp wit and a ready smile, had joined United as a flight attendant on May 4, 1966, just as the Vietnam War kicked into high gear. Francine Gerardi, a brunette with an effervescent personality, signed on with UAL the following September.

During the Vietnam War, the Pentagon chartered several flag carriers to haul troops and supplies across the Pacific. When homewardbound troops reached the West Coast - usually at Seattle, San Francisco, or Los Angeles - regularly scheduled flights usually ferried them to an airport closer to home. Sometimes, though, an airliner flew a full complement of troops across the United States from the West Coast.

After completing their training, Smentkowski and Gerardi reported to their initial assignments. Friends since they met in the late 1960s, the two women, as well as many Americans, could not envision a time when Vietnam would end.

United Airlines flight attendants Elizabeth Smentkowski (left) and Francine Gerardi compared the differences between bringing home the troops from the Gulf War and soldiers from Vietnam 25 years earlier.

When Smentkowski and Gerardi joined United, troops were already coming home from Southeast Asia, but not to the receptions that the Gulf veterans would receive 25 years later. "I was working out of Seattle, where I flew all-nighters to New York, bringing the boys home to the East Coast," Gerardi said. "Oh, it was so sad at times, 'cause sometimes we'd be carrying boys who'd been hurt real bad." Smentkowski reflected on her friend's words and recalled flying on similar routes, occasionally with some soldiers still in bandages. She remembered "the pain you'd see in their eyes, not all of them, but enough of them to make you realize they'd been through a hell." The years slipped away as the two women thought about the homeward-bound vets from the late 1960s and early 1970s. The young men who curled up and slept on airliner seats "seemed so older, so different, so matured, perhaps hardened, even while they snored deeply," Smentkowski related.

Except for their families, few people ever turned out to welcome home the soldiers whom she brought home safely from the West Coast. "The contrast between now and then, just from that point-of-view, is amazing," Gerardi said.

"When we're bringing troops home from the Gulf, we can touch them as they sleep," she observed. "You know, tuck a pillow under a young man's head, and he might smile in his sleep, but not wake up. Almost like a mother would do for her child, and that's what so many of the troops seem like our own children."

"Oh, we couldn't do that with the boys coming back from Vietnam," Smentkowski confirmed.

"Oh, no, we couldn't," Gerardi agreed. "If we touched them while they were sleeping, they'd jump out of their seats. You'd think you were sneaking up on them or something."

"That's the difference we noticed between the Gulf and Vietnam," Smentkowski said. Maybe the greatest differences lie in how the wars were fought and the troops were perceived by the American public, she added, comparing the Iraqi mass surrenders to the situation in Vietnam, where "people of all ages, even the kids, attacked Americans. "And, of course, few people cheered the troops as they returned home," she said. "Can you imagine being booed after spending a year fighting a war?" By 1991, Gerardi and Smentkowski were flying out of Los Angeles to Pacific Rim destinations like Sydney, Tokyo, and Seoul. They bid their monthly flight schedules and try to fly together.

Under the contract signed between UAL and the flight attendants' union, flight schedules are awarded based on job seniority. With 25 years behind them, Gerardi and Smentkowski usually obtain the routes they desire. When her daughter was younger, Gerardi tried to avoid the longer, more grueling routes. She and her husband, a UAL pilot, tried to organize their schedules so that a parent was always home. The two women had believed all their wars long behind them when Iraq invaded Kuwait on Aug. 2, 1990. By year's end, UAL was ferrying thousands of troops across the Atlantic Ocean to Europe and the Gulf. Gerardi and Smentkowski continued flying their Pacific routes. During the weeks before the air war started, they sensed a growing tension all along the international flight corridors. "Everyone was tense, there was such a feeling in the air," Gerardi recalled. "I wouldn't call it explosive, just a case of the nerves. It didn't matter where we flew, everyone's eyes were on the Middle East." The women were at home in Los Angeles when the air war started. Smentkowski described her relief when the FAA immediately implemented tightened security measures at all airports serviced by airlines. "The passengers were pleased to see that even the attendants were being checked by security people," she said.

For weeks after the air war began, "the planes flew almost empty, since people were frightened about traveling," Gerardi noted. "Travel fell right off. We could see the results in the practically empty cabins."

Then the war ended in February, and United started bringing home troops by the thousands. Gerardi and Smentkowski bid the flights together, flew into Saudi Arabia, and made their first landing in Bangor on April 2 aboard UAL Flight 6434. The 747 brought home soldiers from the 82nd Airborne Division.

Getting the soldiers out of the Gulf presented a challenge. They had to clear U.S. Customs in Saudi Arabia, which could take up to 24 hours, with the baggage being checked and cleared, Gerardi said. The troops waited patiently, yet strong emotions welled up inside them by the time they reached their seats in the 747.

As the airplane's wheels rose from the Saudi runway, the soldiers vented their feelings. "The first time we took off from the desert, I thought we were going to crash, the noise from the cheering (in the cabin) was so intense," Smentkowski laughed. "Oh, they were so happy to be going home!"

Standard operating procedure called for one flight crew to take the 747 to its next destination, often Brussels in Belgium, and another crew to ferry the aircraft and its human cargo across the Atlantic Ocean. Soldiers had to remain on the plane in Brussels, Gerardi said, but the delay didn't matter. "Every time you lift off, there's a big round of applause," she said. "They're that much closer to home."

Bangor afforded the paratroopers their first opportunity to leave their plane in 14-18 hours. As UAL Flight 6434 approached Bangor from Brussels on April 2, the flight attendants told the troops about the reception awaiting them in Maine.

During the flight from Belgium, "some soldiers wanted to sleep. All that others wanted to do was follow you around and talk," Smentkowski said. When the pilot announced the 747's entrance into American airspace near Houlton, "they (the troops) hooted and hollered," she recalled. "They even cheered when they landed in Bangor."

The two women invariably described their tired, homesick passengers as well-behaved, friendly, and well-mannered. "They're such gentlemen," Gerardi smiled. "They're sweethearts."

Smentkowski mentioned one flight from the Gulf, when she estimated that between the various airports to which they ferried troops between Saudi Arabia, Europe, and the United States, their crew handled "1,700 young men, and I didn't hear a single cuss word.

"It's hard to put into words the wide spectrum of emotions that you feel," she said. "They (the soldiers) tell you so much. The public isn't aware of how much some of the soldiers, especially younger soldiers, have been traumatized even by a short war." "The emotions, I find it very hard to say 'good-bye,' because I have spent seven, eight, or nine hours with the troops," Gerardi observed. "We bring them so far, and then we have to let them go. It's hard, very hard."

The troop receptions that greeted the soldiers and the UAL flight crews in Bangor "have been something else," Smentkowski said. "I don't know what it is, I can't put my finger on it, but it's like an emotional release for these young people who've been locked into the desert without knowing what would happen to them.

"The front-line soldiers tell us they felt a flood of relief when the jets flew over (on Jan. 17)," she explained. "They were afraid they'd just sit two years on the border with nothing to do.

"But the welcomes in Bangor made a big difference. Even the Vietnam vets among the troops feel so good (that) they're finally getting this acknowledgement," Elizabeth Smentkowski said.

Bringing troops home from two wars has helped both women comprehend what their fathers endured during military service in World War II. Gerardi and Smentkowski felt a kinship with later wars, too; they knew cousins who fought in Korea and friends who fought in Vietnam. During their first stop in Bangor, the UAL flight attendants met Helen Schacht, a Hampden resident who, with her husband, owned a local hardware store. A close friendship developed with Schacht and her family, who took Gerardi and Smentkowski to visit Bar Harbor, Acadia National Park, and other scenic Maine sites.

During their May layover, Gerardi and Smentkowski again visited Helen Schacht. About 8:30 a.m. on Tuesday, May 14, with UAL Flight 6497 scheduled to land within two hours, Schacht met her friends at the Main Street Holiday Inn in Bangor and accompanied them to an interview at the Bangor Daily News. At the time - and like Lt. Gen. John J. Yeosock from the Day of the Generals - Gerardi and Smentkowski did not know when they would return to Maine. No matter when their paths might converge at Helen Schacht's door again - as they would when Yeosock, too, revisited a city where he'd enjoyed such a warm welcome - the two women realized that they'd shared a special experience at BIA.

"This has been the greatest experience of my life," Gerardi said, dabbing a tear from her eye. "The warmth that's been shown these boys and girls. I can't describe how they feel, but I know it's meant the world to us."

"I wouldn't have traded it for anything," echoed Smentkowski. "I can't thank the people of Maine enough for what they've done for the troops. You've made them proud to be Americans again, proud to stand on their own two feet and not to apologize for who they are and what they've done.

"I just wish it could've been like this during Vietnam," she commented. "It wasn't, of course, but I'm so happy that it is now. Nothing else matters but getting the troops home. It's good that they're coming this way, and not headed for war."

BUT FOR THIRTY MINUTES

No one present at BIA that Tuesday morning will ever forget what happened.

Their interview at the Bangor Daily News required Francine Gerardi and Elizabeth Smentkowski to awaken earlier than their crewmates. According to the posted schedule, United Airlines Flight 6497, which was en route to Altus Air Force Base in Oklahoma, should land in Bangor about 11:30 a.m. on Tuesday, May 14.

That left sufficient time for the other members of the UAL relief crew to catch additional zzz's at the Main Street Holiday Inn. As long as the entire crew arrived at the airport about an hour before UAL Flight 6497 arrived, there'd be no problem.

The phones rang early that morning in the UAL rooms at the Holiday Inn. "Guess what?" a UAL rep asked the sleepy flight personnel who answered the incessant chirping. "Flight 6497's putting in at 10 a.m.!" A mad scramble ensued, Gerardi and Smentkowski said later. "We were already dressed, but the call caught everyone unprepared. We don't know why the plane's so early."

The advanced ETA surprised other people, too, that Tuesday. Only a hundred civilians would meet the UAL jet when it landed at 10 a.m. Many other troop greeters would arrive shortly before the plane left at 11:45 a.m.

The huge 747, its red-and-white fuselage gleaming in the brilliant sunshine, rumbled into view about 9:58 a.m. Foreign-flag carriers jammed every gate at the international terminal.

UAL Flight 6497 landed at 10 a.m., swung off the runway, and taxied toward the terminals. Its nose pointed toward the southeast, the plane rolled gracefully along the tarmac and halted beside the blast wall across from the international terminal.

"Holy cow! They're making them walk in!" a troop greeter exploded. People rushed to the windows in the domestic terminal to glimpse the motionless 747. Gate 2 partially blocked their view of what was perhaps the most unusual homecoming at BIA.

As BIA ground personnel rolled portable ramps into position, UAL employees popped the forward-and-aft starboard hatches on the plane. Moments later, Sgt. James Valentine and Staff Sgt. Glenn Coonts, the designated flagbearers for the 1st Battalion, 142nd Field Artillery Brigade, Arkansas Army National Guard, stepped through the forward hatch and unfurled an American flag and a red flag fringed with gold tassel.

The flagbearers bounded down the portable ramp, snapped to attention shoulder-to-shoulder, and let the flags momentarily wave in the light northwesterly breeze. Other soldiers crowded the ramp.

Then Valentine and Coonts took turns holding the flags while each soldier knelt and lovingly kissed American soil.

"I haven't seen anybody do that yet," a veteran greeter said. "Too icy and cold out there in March 'n April," his companion responded.

Each flagbearer clasped the appropriate standard in his hands and stood either side of the portable ramp, the American flag nearest the aircraft's nose, the battalion flag nearest the wings. Other soldiers who'd patiently stood on the ramp during the impromptu welcoming ceremony thundered down the steps and passed between the banners carried from Saudi Arabia to Maine...

...but not before the next guardsman in line behind Valentine and Coonts also knelt, pressed his lips to the tarmac, and stood to his feet. He then thrust his arms above his head.

Cheers echoed up the ramp from the domestic terminal.

Soldiers poured from the starboard hatches like ants flooded from a noxious anthill. Singly, in their two's and three's, or in clumps, the soldiers unerringly beelined for the appropriate door leading to the international terminal. About three minutes after Valentine and Coonts touched the pavement, their comrades appeared on the ramp.

A United Airlines 747 carrying Arkansas Army National Guardsmen landed early in BIA on May 14, 1991, so the passengers had to walk to the international terminal.

The crowd waiting for them lost all semblance of civility.

In a performance paralleling the May 11 landing of their friends in the 2nd Battalion, 142nd Field Artillery Regiment, the Razorbacks moved slowly and politely along the wire. Soft Southern accents fell gently on Yankee ears as the soldiers exchanged greetings and shook hands with Maine residents.

Gary Leighton leaned into his microphone and said, "On behalf of Bangor and the State of Maine, welcome home, troops!" The Guardsmen, still overwhelmed by their greeting, paid little attention to Leighton's salutation. The civilians went bonkers, of course. They didn't need a cue card to know when to cheer.

According to Staff Sgt. Jerry Wright, a husky, jovial guardsman from Rogers, Ark., UAL Flight 6497 carried the 1st Battalion and the headquarters of the 142nd Field Artillery Brigade. The 1st Battalion hailed from Harrison, Ark.; the brigade headquarters came from Fayetteville, a city in northwestern Arkansas.

He'd shipped to war as a cook this time around. "Last time I was off to war, I was a crew chief on a Marine Corps helicopter (a model known as a UH-34D) in Vietnam. Guess you could call me an early bird. I went over there in August, 1963, and came back 13 months later," Wright explained.

Wright said that when the Gulf War started, his unit was assigned to the British and later to the 1st Infantry Division.

"We crossed the berm with the Brits," Wright said. "Before it all started, we moved up, shot a `prep,' and went across the berm at the Neutral Zone and into Iraq. Then we turned into Kuwait.

"By the fourth day of the war, we got to where about 120 of the oil wells were burning near a four-lane highway in Kuwait," he said.

The 1st Battalion subsequently returned to Iraq through an area that was littered with the wreckage of Iraqi equipment. "It was just miles 'n miles of burned-out stuff, tanks, personnel carriers. What a mess: just a bunch of destroyed litter," Wright recalled.

As it advanced into Iraq and Kuwait, the battalion would receive orders from divisional staff and "stop and shoot. The second day, we pulled into a position and stopped because a sandstorm was coming in.

"I could see movement about a mile away. It was kind of hazy, maybe dusty, but we could see they were a group of Iraqis coming toward us. Every few minutes, someone would join them.

"The brigade had a bag of about 200 prisoners that one day. There was another time in the desert, about 50 of our guys rounded up about 100 Iraqis out of bunkers," he remembered.

During and after the Gulf War, military analysts like Newsweek's David Hackworth - a decorated Vietnam combat veteran turned journalist who wrote excellent reports from the front in the Gulf - strongly doubted the National Guard's combat ability, especially in ground combat. Their opinions often turned on the armored brigade from Georgia that never left Fort Irwin in California until the war ended.

Perhaps the analysts should have talked with the Razorbacks from the 142nd Field Artillery Brigade. The outfit, equipped with M-110A2 howitzers, did its job exceptionally well. "We heard afterwards that apparently we took out all but six of 126 artillery pieces the Iraqis had moved up near the border," said Wright. "Guess we did that during the 'prep.' We were really pouring it on them."

He recalled sleeping in a 2-1/2-ton truck "when we fired the 'prep.' Suddenly some MLRS's (Multiple Launch Rocket Systems) and 8inchers (howitzers) started going off. It was just like waking up in daylight."

Wright, who kept a journal during his Gulf travels, recalled "I stopped to talk to some Brits. Some of the Scottish boys were kind of hard to understand," he chuckled. "Hey, they probably couldn't understand us that well, either. I don't think many of them have ever been to Arkansas. But, they did a superb job. Everybody did."

As Wright spoke, Carl Lindh spotted him standing near the terminal windows. "Are you a Vietnam vet?" Lindh asked Wright, who nodded his reply.

"Welcome back, from all us Vietnam vets," Lindh said, pinning a yellow ribbon to Wright's left blouse pocket. The Arkansas soldier chatted quietly with Lindh, then shook hands and wished him well.

Gary Leighton leaned into his microphone and asked, "Is there a Lois Bourquin in the terminal? If she is, will she please report to me?"

The clock indicated 10:55 a.m.

"Back home in Arkansas, I'm a surveyor," Wright said. "You know, I can't wait to get back to my family." He worked his fingers underneath his olive-drab T-shirt and hauled out a chain to which he'd attached a photograph of his two young grandsons. He studied the photograph before tucking it securely under his T-shirt. "I'm looking forward to getting back to those two, and I'm really excited about spending some time with my wife. She's going to meet me in Lawton (Oklahoma)," he said. When not working or exercising, the guardsmen filled their time as best they could. "When you get over there, and you've got a lot of time on your hands, you read anything you can get your hands on," Wright explained.

"Westerns were popular, and so was 'Any Soldier' mail. I wrote back a little girl from Illinois or Indiana, and we got to writing regularly," he said.

The Arkansas soldiers left Saudi Arabia through King Fahd International Airport and ultimately put into BIA. "We didn't expect anything like this," he commented while watching his friends enjoy the Maine welcome. "Tell everybody we appreciate it.

"That's a welcome sight, anything green," he noted, pointing to the pine trees and grass far across the runway. "Reminds me of home. Everything's green in Arkansas this time of year."

Across the terminal from where Wright stood, people gathered as Lt. Col. Gary Meeks, commander of the 1st Battalion, told Tech Sgt. Stanley Brown to "raise your right hand and repeat after me." In an impromptu ceremony, Meeks swore Brown into another enlistment in the National Guard.

Brown came from East Eddington, a town upriver from Bangor, and belonged to the Maine Air National Guard. Faced with an impending reenlistment, he'd wanted the job done by someone who'd fought in the Gulf.

Brown got his wish in Lt. Col. Meeks.

Gary Leighton still insisted on speaking to the celebrating crowd this morning. A petite, fortyish woman clad in a white turtleneck and faded jeans stood beside the lectern as Leighton inquired, "Is there a Charles Bourquin here? Your mother would like to see you."

From somewhere near Mr. Paperback, a young, bespectacled soldier streaked across the terminal, vaulted the wire, and threw himself into Lois Bourquin's arms.

The clock read 11:05 a.m.

Charles and his mom laughed and cried and hugged until Lois ran a finger across her cheek and exclaimed, "You've got my mascara running!" Her son held her at arm's length while grinning from ear to ear. Then he hugged her tightly.

When his airliner delayed 30 minutes in leaving BIA on May 14, 1991, Staff Sgt. Charles Bourquin of Arkansas enjoyed a long-awaited reunion with his mother, Lois Bourquin.

According to Lois, "The UAL people called me at 2 this morning. They said his plane was coming into Bangor about 11:30, so I left my home (in Nashua, N.H.) about 6. I've been on the road since then.

"It was really important that I catch his flight," she said. "We haven't seen each other in two years, and here he'd gone off to war, and I couldn't see him to say good-bye! But this is wonderful!"

Since he'd landed at BIA, Charles had repeatedly asked Leighton to page Lois. By 11 a.m., "Yeah, I started thinking she wasn't going to make it," he said. "I was getting pretty disappointed."

Lois Bourquin had arrived to discover that in the sea of military uniforms, every face looked alike. She found Gary Leighton and asked him to page her son.

The rest, as they say, was history.

As the Bourquins slipped away for a quiet reunion, the flagbearers of the 1st

Battalion unfurled their standards in the terminal. A delighted crowd gathered to photograph Valentine and Coonts, and Lt. Col. Meeks joined his soldiers for a moment.

Francine Gerardi and Elizabeth Smentkowski, preparing to leave the terminal with the other members of their crew, said the plane's takeoff had been delayed half an hour. They awaited the flight crew that had not met the plane's early arrival.

Lois Bourquin would have arrived five minutes late if UAL Flight 6497 hadn't been delayed for a half hour.

When Gary Leighton announced the first boarding call about 11:20 a.m., the Arkansas soldiers displayed their reluctance to leave Bangor. Somewhere near the coffee shop, Guardsmen started lustily chanting "Soo-eee! Soo-eee! Soo-eee!"

"That's the hog call for the University of Arkansas Razorbacks!" a delighted Rebel explained to the appreciative Maine Yankees.

As the soldiers slowly worked their way toward the ramp, Lt. Col. Meeks grabbed Leighton's microphone with his right hand. "We've had a helluva greeting here!" he announced before warmly thanking the Maine residents for their hospitality.

This time, the soldiers went wild.

All too soon, Charles and Lois Bourquin walked across the terminal and stood near the entrance to the ramp. Disinclined to let her son go, Lois soon escorted him a short distance into the ramp, where they said their final farewells.

The Arkansas Razorbacks took their time leaving BIA that Tuesday morning. Three soldiers lingered deep within the lounge, until a multistriped sergeant chased them from cover. As they emerged from their place of concealment, two soldiers burst for the restroom. Their companion ran into Mr. Paperback to make a final purchase.

The brawny Razorback sergeant pursued his recalcitrant troopers, until the last man from the 1st Battalion, 142nd Field Artillery Brigade, vanished up the ramp.

A SCHWARTZ! A SCHWARTZ! MY KINGDOM FOR A SCHWARTZ!

Schoolkids comprised the crowd when Hawaiian Airlines Flight 884 landed at BIA at 11:28 a.m. on Wednesday, May 15.

Along Godfrey Boulevard, school buses were parked wherever adequate roadside space existed. Large black letters painted on each bus indicated that people - probably schoolchildren - from Winterport, Ellsworth, Springfield, Milbridge, and the Mount Desert Island Workshop had traveled to Bangor today to meet HAL Flight 884, which was bound for St. Louis.

More than 350 people - mostly youngsters and teachers and chaperones - packed the wire and cheered as the HAL L-1011 eased onto the BIA runway. The plane rolled smoothly to the international terminal. The passengers immediately disembarked to a raucous homecoming.

Jungle-fatigued troops poured like a rain-swollen river on to the ramp. The kids, especially the pubescent girls lined four, five rows deep alongside Gate 2, screamed in delight, their best rock-concert cheers redlining the decibel Richter scale.

When the soldiers swept into the terminal, the schoolkids redoubled their verbal bedlam. Hands bounded upward as soldiers who'd seen Saudi Arabia exchanged "high fives" with kids who'd never traveled outside the United States or Canada.

The troops, most of them from the 3175th Military Police Co., an Army National

Guard outfit from Warrenton, Mo., responded warmly to their welcome. Soldiers knelt to chat with little kids or took a moment to autograph a T-shirt thrust across the wire. Adults shook hands with the Missouri soldiers. Maine grandmothers, of course, got their hugs and embraces.

Troop greeter Brian Swartz pointed his camera into the ramp to focused on a bespectacled soldier approaching the gift table. The name tag on the lieutenant's shirt read "Schwartz." When Swartz recognized the name, he bounded after 2nd Lt. Ken Schwartz.

When Swartz caught up with Schwartz, he introduced himself as "a Schwartz without the `ch.'" The lieutenant grinned.

A resident of St. Louis, Ken Schwartz said that he commanded the 1st Platoon, 3175th Military Police Co. "We've got two armories, one in Warrenton, and the other in St. Clair (Missouri)," he reported. "I work out of the Warrenton Armory."

According to Schwartz, the Pentagon mobilized the 3175th on Jan. 17 and told the guardsmen to report to their armories. Once they had processed into the Army, the military policemen traveled to Fort Leonard Wood, Mo., and ultimately flew to Germany.

"We left for Europe on February 4th," Schwartz said. "We went into Ramstein, and from there, they dispersed us all over Europe. For the most part, we were augmenting existing security forces. Geez, we had detachments all over, Germany and Belgium and the Netherlands.

"We did everything from rail security to terrorist counteraction, even typical law-enforcement duty on American military bases. Another function was providing security for school buses and schoolyards. We'd been told that American kids were particularly vulnerable targets for terrorists, so we were there to prevent that.

"The Army needed us in Europe because so many regular MP companies had shipped for the Gulf. In the Netherlands, we probably beefed up the available security forces 200 percent," Schwartz said. "Everyone was looking at Saudi Arabia, but the potential for trouble existed in Western Europe, too."

Schwartz, who had earned his Army commission through ROTC at the University of Missouri at Columbia, anticipated attending the Thomas Cooley Law School in Lansing, Mich., in January 1992. Commissioned in May 1989, he'd immediately joined the 3175th MP Co.

Maine residents, particularly the schoolchildren who had swarmed into BIA this sunny Wednesday, continuously sought Schwartz's autograph. He momentarily excused himself to get a beer in the Red Baron Lounge, then stepped into the terminal and spoke a while longer.

"I read an article somewhere in Stars 'n Stripes a few weeks ago about the troop receptions in Bangor, but I never thought I'd experience one," the lieutenant said. "This is kind of exciting. I've never been through anything like this."

A dark-haired woman asked Schwartz if he'd like a Maine gift. She presented him a big pine cone decorated with a yellow ribbon.

Seeking soldiers on whom to pin yellow ribbons, Dottie Heath wandered past the pair of S(ch)wartzs standing outside the coffee shop. She espied Schwartz's undecorated uniform, whipped out a "Welcome to Bangor" ribbon, and affixed it to the lieutenant's right pocket flap.

Then Heath noticed the name tag. She peered through her eyeglasses at Schwartz, at Swartz, and at Schwartz again. "Well, well," Heath commented before shaking hands with the lieutenant. "Everyone in Maine this friendly?" Schwartz asked Swartz.

"All the people here in the airport are," Swartz responded to the question from Schwartz.

A few minutes later, a boarding call summoned Ken Schwartz to his aircraft. Schwartz and Swartz bid each other adieu.

Ken Schwartz would land in St. Louis later this afternoon. Swartz would return to BIA for another troop flight within 30 hours. The men with similar last names would never meet again, but Swartz would meet another Schwartz before the troop flights ended.

If there were any Schwartzs on the next two flights that he met, Swartz never knew. He did encounter the large welcoming party waiting for Lance Corp. Rick Broschard, however.

Broschard hailed from Somers Point, N.J., but he had family in Maine. About 20 people traveled to Bangor International Airport to meet him on Thursday, May 16. "One way or the other, we're all related to him," Old Town resident Elaine Vermette proclaimed as she waited on the ramp that evening for Hawaiian Airlines Flight 882.

The security detachment from the Bangor Police Department figured that 300 people packed the wire three rows deep that night. Thanks to a twist of fate, people would enjoy two flights for the price of one, since American Trans Air Flight 159 should land right behind the airliner from Hawaii.

And just two hours behind the HAL and AMT jets flew another troop flight, United Airlines Flight 6499.

Elaine Vermette, an aunt to Rick Broschard, introduced the young man's grandmother, Marie Mitchell, another aunt, cousins galore, and "more relatives than I can count!" she grinned. "We're from the Penobscot Nation on Indian Island (in Old Town)," Vermette said.

"Are you sure he's on this flight?" a woman asked her.

"This one, or the later flight going to North Carolina," responded Vermette. "He called from Saudi Arabia a few days ago and said he would be leaving at 4 in the morning our time today."

Both HAL Flight 882 and UAL Flight 6499 listed their final destinations as Cherry Point Marine Corps Air Station, N.C.. AMT Flight 159 was flying to Omaha, Neb.

"Naw, there aren't any Marine bases in Nebraska," the woman told Vermette.

Minutes before HAL Flight 882's scheduled 7 p.m. arrival, 25 people - all of whom claimed to be awaiting relatives - packed the ramp opposite the gift table. Gary Leighton walked down the ramp, studied the wall-to-wall humanity, and moved out the aunts, uncles, cousins, and "other people who aren't married to or parent to anyone on these flights."

Then he entered the domestic terminal and explained the greeting procedure to a friendly crowd.

HAL Flight 882 touched down at 7:05 p.m. Elaine Vermette anxiously waited for the Marines to deplane. They did so within 10 minutes. The crowd enthusiastically welcomed them home to the United States.

Rick Broschard was not on the L-1011. "Well, maybe the next one," Vermette commented.

Then a bespectacled Marine burst down the ramp and into his family's arms. Corp. Hank Trumble Jr. had come home aboard the airliner, even if Rick Broschard had not. Finally, after all the waiting, Trumble was back in Maine.

AMT Flight 159 landed at 7:18 p.m. Leighton announced the plane's arrival as the L-1011 taxied to Gate 6. He urged the Marines "to help us greet your fellow troops," a phrase that hinted at soldiers.

And soldiers they were, 159 men and women belonging to the 222nd Transportation

Co. from Tucson, Ariz., and the 2222nd Transportation Co. from Sierra Vista, Ariz.

Capt. Debra Clark, who blinked back tears of joy as she stepped from line beside the gift table. "I'm with the 222nd TransCo!" Clark shouted above the din caused by 300 civilians, 196 Marines, and 159 soldiers staging an early July Fourth celebration inside the terminal. "The 2222nd's the `Four Deuces!' They're another outfit, but we are all from Arizona, and that's where we're all headed!" she said.

Clark introduced herself as "a Flannery from Fort Fairfield," a town in far northern Maine. "I'm an Air Force brat," she laughed. "I grew up in Limestone. My grandmother, Phyllis Flannery, still lives there (Fort Fairfield)."

When the women staffing the gift table learned that Clark hailed from The County, they offered her cookies and other fresh-baked pastries. "Oh, no! Thank you just the same!" Clark said, declining the offer. "They stuffed us on the plane. I can't eat anything else!"

Marines and soldiers swirled around the gift table, so the captain stepped aside and talked briefly about the war. "We were called up on Nov. 17," she said, "and we left for Saudi Arabia on Jan. 17, exactly two months later. We were delayed a couple of days because of the air war. It was like every plane headed for the Gulf was held up along the way."

The 222nd Transportation Co. provided petroleum to 7th Corps' units, especially the 1st and 3rd Armored Divisions, even while they engaged the Republican Guards, Clark said. "We were hauling diesel fuel for the tanks and a little jet A for the helicopters."

More Marines appeared by the gift table. Gunnery Sgt. Paul Muncy of Ohio belonged to the 2nd Light Armored Infantry Battalion, 2nd Marine Division. The battalion was equipped with the Light Armored Vehicle (LAV), an eight-wheeled armored vehicle that "swims, but it does not make beach landings," the sergeant stressed.

Worn out by the long flight from the Gulf, Muncy said that most personnel assigned to the 2nd Battalion had shipped overseas in December 1990. He'd joined the outfit two months later, in sufficient time to participate in the ground war.

"We played a role in the fighting," Muncy recalled. "C Company that's Charlie Company in the Marines - they were among the first to cross the border, and they did it before the actual invasion.

"Three days before we actually invaded Kuwait and Iraq, Charlie Company crossed into Kuwait and actively probed the Iraqi defenses," he said. "The Iraqis thought the war had actually started three days before it did. When the full invasion hit them, they were shocked."

Muncy succinctly described an operation that effectively masked the 2nd Marine Division's westward movement along the Saudi-Kuwaiti border. Divisional staff assigned a probing mission to the 2nd Light Armored Infantry Battalion, which was commanded by Lt. Col. Keith Holcomb.

On Thursday, Feb. 21, Holcomb took the battalion and its 159 vehicles cruising along the border. The Marines probed the sand berm, where they attracted attention from Iraqi defenses. While exchanging fire with Iraqi armor and artillery, the fast-moving Marines radioed for air strikes against enemy positions, bumped into other Iraqi defenders, and captured a few prisoners.

During the next two days, the 2nd Light Armored Infantry Battalion probed deeper into Kuwait while moving southeast along the berm. The Marines charted the Iraqi defenses they encountered. Whenever an Iraqi artillery tube opened fire, the leathernecks would summon counterbattery fire or Marine aviation to silence the opposition.

By the time the battalion completed its diversion on Feb. 23, the Marines had suffered some casualties while fooling the Iraqis into believing the assault would fall where it did not. The Marines got little chance to rest, however, before the ground war started. According to Muncy, the 2nd Battalion invaded Kuwait late night on Feb. 23 and finally stopped at Kuwait International Airport. The Marines gradually filtered into Saudi Arabia, with the last contingent coming out of the desert at the tail end of April.

"You know, I'm glad to be going home, but it feels strange to be back in the States, to see green instead of brown," he observed. "We did see palm trees over there, plus grass in the built-up and irrigated areas. I even saw some greenhouses, but I'm not sure what they had growing in them. Vegetables, maybe."

Muncy, a diesel mechanic, confirmed that the 2nd Battalion took some casualties during the fighting. "I can't say as I'll miss that place," he stated. "If I'm ordered to go back, I go back. Otherwise, I didn't leave anything there."

Throughout the terminal, children darted from Marine to soldier and back to leatherneck while pursuing autographs and souvenirs. People who'd never met - even by "Any Soldier" mail - laughed and talked like old friends. Hank Trumble enjoyed his own crowd, of course, as jubilant relatives filled his brief tenure in Bangor with hugs and kisses and small talk that fell pleasantly on the young Marine's ears.

Gary Leighton broadcasted the boarding call for HAL Flight 882, but few people heard him. He finally cleared his throat into the microphone and authoritatively informed the Marines that "it's time to go home!"

The leathernecks thundered into the ramp. Red Cross volunteers hawked newspapers to the grateful Marines. "Gawd, a paper that's not three weeks old!" a grizzled sergeant hooted.

"Hey, I can read the news that happened today!" another leatherneck exclaimed.

Lt. Col. Fred Phelps and Sgt. Major Bill Hubbard lingered behind their departing Marines. Phelps commanded Marine Aviation Logistics Squadron 29 (MALS-29) from New River Marine Corps Air Station, S.C.

"We're not all on this plane," Phelps said. "Seventy people are two days behind us. Some of us have been gone since last August, although I arrived in Jubail, where we were stationed, on Jan. 5th."

According to Sgt. Major Hubbard, MALS-29 "was all over the place in Saudi Arabia. We even had people aboard the SS Wright," a Marine Corps' ship. "The people of Bangor have done a wonderful thing here," Phelps commented while watching the civilians cheer his departing Marines. "We're among the last ones out, and we were afraid people had forgotten about us."

"Here? In Bangor?" a Red Cross volunteered responded, raising her eyebrows. "Impossible!"

Soon after Phelps and Hubbard left the ramp, Gary Leighton reluctantly announced the boarding call for AMT Flight 159. Soldiers slowly abandoned their positions in the terminal and retreated toward the gift table.

His hands laden with teddy bears, a newspaper, and other goodies, a Sgt. Gonzales stopped to chat with George and Leatrice Higgins, two Bangor residents. Higgins, a reticent man with a razor-sharp wit, had fought across North Africa during World War II. He respected the people who'd fought America's latest campaign on foreign sands.

Higgins shook hands with Sgt. Gonzales, who quietly said, "Thank you so much for this. This is my second time around," Gonzales explained. "I was in Vietnam, and it wasn't pretty coming home back then. You can't imagine...Geez, I was afraid we'd be forgotten again."

"Not around here, you won't be," Higgins told him.

"This is really appreciated, how much, you'll never know," Gonzales said.

Reaching for his free hand, Leatrice Higgins squeezed it before intoning, "God bless you, sergeant."

Gonzales departed BIA a happy man.

Soldiers kept pouring into the ramp. They overran the gift table and looted whatever they could find — papers, suckers, chocolate chip cookies, whoopie pies, sodas. Red Cross volunteers gave the troops plastic bags and helped stuff them with additional teddy bears (someone broke open an extra case that night) and assorted merchandise. By 8:15 p.m., the last soldiers vanished up the ramp. In the domestic terminal, civilians hurriedly reformed the wire. "What a deal," a man said. "We got to see two flights at one time, and now there's another one inbound!"

A SAILOR'S TEARS

A Navy captain cried when he passed through BIA on May 16. United Airlines Flight 6499, bound for Cherry Point Marine Corps Air Station with 280 passengers fresh from the Gulf, landed at 8:40 p.m., only minutes after American Trans Air Flight 159 departed for Omaha. As the 747 taxied toward Gate 6, Elaine Vermette and her family edged into the ramp. This time, Gary Leighton didn't chase relatives into the terminal. Though the two earlier flights had produced a few reunions, many people still waited for family members on UAL Flight 6499. More than 300 people packed the wire that night.

People started applauding and cheering minutes before the Marines disembarked through Gate 6. Leighton attempted to read the procedural rules, but comments like "we've heard this already!" and "send us Marines!" dissuaded him from pressing the issue too far.

Rick Broschard's relatives enfiladed the replenished gift table. At their forefront stood two stylishly dressed young women - cousins from Indian Island - who held aloft a sign that proclaimed in large letters, "Lc. Cpl. Richard Broschard, Welcome Home!" Then the Marines appeared atop the ramp. Elaine Vermette and her family cheered.

Marines flooded the ramp. Its reunion now guaranteed, one family whirled away into the domestic terminal. Rick Broschard's relatives watched both the ramp and their sign-bearing vanguard. When one cousin clapped a hand over her mouth, the cry went out, "He's here!"

A red-headed lance corporal bobbed into view on the ramp stuffed with Marines, and about 20 people - including little children mounted atop their parents' shoulders - overwhelmed the young leatherneck. Rick Broschard had arrived to a joyous homecoming.

According to Staff Sgt. Gary Huff from Texarkana, Texas, the UAL 747 carried Marines and sailors from the 8th Motor Transport Battalion and the 2nd Medical Battalion.

Huff, a Marine Corps Reservist, said that he belonged to the 6th Motor Transport Battalion, a reserve component with its headquarters in Red Bank, N.J., and armories in Texarkana; New Haven, Conn.; Providence, R.I.; and Orlando, Fla. The battalion was attached to the 8th Motor Transport Battalion during the war.

Huff was assigned to Charlie Co., which left Texas on Dec. 3 and arrived in North Carolina on Dec. 6. "We stayed there until the 15th, when we flew out to Saudi Arabia," he said. "We landed in Jubail on December 17th, and from there, we were everywhere."

The battalion transported fuel, water, food, ammunition, and Marines, with everything headed north toward the Saudi border with Kuwait and Iraq. "During the ground war, we were providing support for anyone who was asking for it," Huff said. "The trucks ran around the clock. Convoys sometimes traveled 24 hours or longer.

"On February 23, we were about 15 miles from the front line," he recalled, "pushing material from the supply points to the front. One group of my Marines was real close to a Humvee that was hit, I think by triple-A (antiaircraft fire).

"The Humvee was blown up, and two Marines were killed. Our drivers were scrambling for cover, but none of them were hurt," the sergeant said.

He confirmed the information provided by Gus Grivas on May 9 that a Marine from Rhode Island had been accidentally killed in the Gulf. "We were fortunate in that our casualties were much fewer than we were led to expect," Huff said.

A production worker at an International Paper Co. mill in Texarkana, Huff said he and his wife would celebrate their 20th anniversary on July 3, 1991. He had been in touch with his three children while stationed in the Gulf. "I can't wait to get home and see them," Huff said.

Gary Leighton introduced 10-year-old Danielle Brayall of Bangor. "She wants to sing for us tonight," Leighton told the crowd while Danielle apprehensively eyed her audience.

After performing "Last Night I had the Strangest Dream," Danielle tackled "God Bless America." As her soprano voice lifted phrases like "stand beside her and guide her through the night with the light from above," other voices gradually joined the musical tribute to the United States.

Civilians, sailors, and Marines stood to attention and struggled with the words they'd learned as children. Eddie "Spoons" Michaud, a dedicated entertainer is his own right, stood slightly behind a muscular sailor who struggled to dam his tears.

Navy Capt. Kenneth Noel, who was returning to the Naval Hospital in Jacksonville, Fla., choked back the tears as Danielle launched into the closing refrain of "God Bless America." An anesthesiologist assigned to the 2nd Medical Battalion in the Gulf, Noel had patched up the wounded in Vietnam. He'd anticipated a similar experience in Saudi Arabia, but it hadn't happened.

"All I can say, thank God our casualties were so few," Noel said later. "The Marines lost more people to traffic accidents than to combat.

"You don't know how prepared we were for the worst," he said. "I figured it would be Vietnam all over again, with so many young men shot to pieces. There were combat casualties over in the Gulf, of course, but nothing like the volume we'd expected."

After four months in the desert, Noel wanted to see his wife and three children ASAP. The oldest child, a son, was attending an infantry school at Camp Lejeune in North Carolina. "He's a machinegunner," the captain said. "We'll get together as soon as we can, but I should see everyone else when I get home."

The crowd cheered as Danielle finished singing. A passionate Noel stepped to the lectern and tightly hugged Danielle, who blushed from the attention that she received. How'd it feel to be going home? Tom Dean asked the captain.

"I think you can tell," Noel weakly smiled as he choked back his tears. The beige phone mounted on the wall by the lectern rang at 9:48 p.m. Leighton grabbed the receiver, paused to stick a finger in his opposite ear, listened, nodded, and set the receiver on its cradle.

"That's it?" a troop greeter plaintively asked Leighton while he stepped to the lectern.

"Yes, it is," Leighton replied over his shoulder.

He announced the first boarding call for UAL Flight 6499. Sailors and Marines slowly headed for the exit through a friendly gauntlet of laughing, well-wishing civilians. The record player belted "Anchors, A-Weigh" before tearing into the "Marine Hymn."

Kenneth Noel lingered to chat with Danielle Brayall and some other people, thanking them for their support. His tears had dried by the time he waved farewell from the ramp and departed for his plane.

LISTEN TO THE RHYTHM OF THE FALLING RAIN

Schoolchildren from Ellsworth crowded the wire by Gate 2 as American Trans Air Flight 8750 landed at 11:57 a.m. on Friday, May 17. En route to Forbes Field in Topeka, Kansas, the L-1011 carried 200 military passengers.

According to a teacher doubling as a chaperone, two yellow school buses had ferried more than 60 sixth graders from the Bryant E. Moore School in Ellsworth to meet the troops coming into Bangor on this extremely warm, muggy day that threatened a monsoon. Other students had come from Millinocket, a paper-mill town located about 70 miles north of Bangor.

The crowd numbered about 200 people.

As she eagerly awaited the incoming troops, a petite blond named Jamie Phillips confirmed that she came from Ellsworth. She'd been to a Saturday troop flight and "got a whole sweatshirtful of autographs from all the troops I met."

To her right stood a friend, Suzanne Shaw, a brunette with brown eyes that sparkled as she laughed with her companions. "I haven't been to a troop flight, Shaw announced. "I've watched on the TV, on local and national news, where the soldiers have been welcomed in Bangor. I think a lot of them will come in and be surprised at being greeted like this." Both girls confirmed their plans to cheer. "We're gonna make noise!" Phillips exclaimed.

"I want to get names and autographs, too, so I wore this T-shirt and brought some notepaper for the soldiers to write on," said Shaw.

Audrey Ryan, another Ellsworth student, said she had sent a Garfield card to an "Any Soldier" address in the Persian Gulf. "A Marine named Charles got my card, and he sent me a 'thank you' note. He was real nice about it," she said.

"I've been here before. It's really exciting to meet the troops," Ryan giggled. "Oh, I've got a whole shirtfull and a couple pages of autographs."

While the Ellsworth sixth-graders laughed and talked, a blue-and-white AMT L-1011 flared into its final approach to BIA. Grayish smoke swirled as the plane's tires touched the runway pavement. "Does that happen all the time?" a young girl asked.

"Gosh, I hope not," a comrade replied.

Two older women - cousins, actually - stood on the ramp. Gretchen Mangin of Winthrop and Rosemary Rowe of Vassalboro said they hoped to meet another cousin, Frank Tabbutt, who might be on the AMT jet.

"Frank turned 41 just yesterday," Mangin said. "His immediate family is living in Laurel Beach, S.C. He's got relatives down in the Augusta area, though. His wife called us last Tuesday and told us he'd be leaving Saudi Arabia on his birthday."

"We figured out he'd be in Bangor between 9 and 11 this morning, if he comes home through Bangor," Rowe said. "He told his wife it would be foolish for us to sit up here and wait, but we decided we'd come. We haven't seen him for two years."

About 12:10 p.m., troops appeared atop the ramp. The Ellsworth kids went into patriotic hysterics, shouting and screaming like collegiate cheerleaders pumped up for homecoming. The teenagers unabashedly vented their feelings for their Desert Storm heroes. Other kids waved tiny American flags. Phillips wielded two, hers and Shaw's, who was busy photographing the arriving troops with a tiny camera.

As they rolled down the ramp, the soldiers - and Air Force personnel sprinkled among them - acknowledged the ear-shattering cheers by grinning, waving their hands, or turning their thumbs up.

The kids loved it.

The Ellsworth students and their friends could not realize the turning point their generation marked that Friday, that month, that long spring. Twenty years earlier, children from another generation had marched with their parents in antiwar demonstrations throughout the United States. Returning war veterans were people to be scorned.

But the generational clock had ticked into 1991, when youngsters who knew not Vietnam and the hatred heaped on war-weary troops were learning what the baby boomers had not: You might hate war, any war - which all soldiers do, if the truth be told - but you have no right to hate those placing themselves in harm's way.

Louis Cortez of the 403rd Military Police Co. (POW Camp) helped guard Iraqi prisoners of war.

Unless you're willing to go where the bullets whisper your name, you have no right to criticize those who do. If you sleep soundly in your clean bed each night while other Americans swat sand fleas and dodge Scuds in Saudi Arabia or, a long time ago, battled malaria and ambushes in Vietnam, who are you to vilify them?

But on this overcast Friday, the kids didn't care about philosophy. Their natural exuberance carried their riotous cheers deep into the ramp, where war-weary veterans wondered at the noise. One generation touched two other generations that afternoon. As soldiers poured into the terminal, Mangin and Rowe anxiously scanned the sun-tanned faces for their cousin. They quickly realized that Frank Tabbutt had not come home aboard AMT Flight 8750. Maybe, just maybe, he would be aboard a Hawaiian Airlines jet scheduled to land at 1:30 p.m.

After Marianne Mitchell officially welcomed the soldiers to Bangor, the sixth graders from Ellsworth clustered by the lectern and sang along as Lee Greenwood pronounced, "God Bless the USA." A Sgt. Louis Cortez sang, too, as he munched a cookie.

A public-safety officer at the St. Francis Medical Center in Topeka, Cortez had been activated in December 1990, along with other Army Reservists from the 403rd Military Police Co. (POW Camp). Cortez, who had belonged to the unit for eight years, was the compound sergeant, a squad leader, and retention NCO. He had counted off the days before the 403rd left for the Gulf. "You see, my wife, Frances, was pregnant with our first child, and she was due about the time they called us up," Cortez explained. "I was afraid we would leave before the baby was born. I guess God was good to me, because I was there when my daughter was born on Dec. 28."

Cortez shipped for Saudi Arabia on Jan. 13 and landed at Al Khubar on Jan. 15. "I've missed the first five months of my little girl's life. Frances has had to do all the work, so when I get home, it's my turn to change the diapers," he said. His unit had operated a prisoner-of-war camp outside Al Sarrar. Located about six hours east of the camp run by the 301st Military Police Co., the 403rd's facility was known as "the Bronx." The 301st's camp was called "Brooklyn."

Jack Dragoo and the 745th Military Police Co. (Guard) of the Oklahoma Army National Guard had been assigned to the Bronx. "I remember those Oklahoma boys. They're good men," Cortez commented. "The Iraqis were coming in without uniforms or shoes or boots," he recalled. "Some of them had tied sandbags around their feet in place of shoes. They were in kind of sad shape. They didn't give us much hassle. The most problems we had were feeding them, because they were real hungry."

The Iraqis got wound up if they didn't get bread or cigarettes, he said. "At times, they might get rowdy because they wanted an extra scoop of rice, but they didn't threaten us. They'd just make noise."

The Army Reservists from Kansas faced their greatest challenge when 10 trucks would show up carrying 200 prisoners apiece, Cortez said. The Bronx had 30 prisoner cages and three compounds, each capable of housing 2,500 to 2,800 POWs. "Yeah, we got crowded at times," Cortez observed, "but we kept a handle on everything."

Marianne Mitchell announced the first boarding call at 12:35 p.m. Seeking last-minute autographs, schoolkids raced from soldier to soldier.

"Hey, I was really touched by this greeting you folks gave us," Cortez said as he shook hands with troop greeters. "They told us to expect people, but this is incredible!"

By 12:45 p.m., the last soldiers had vanished up the ramp. The students gathered to compare autographs and souvenirs. Saudi and Kuwaiti currency appeared in abundance. Some Ellsworth kids displayed rank insignias and a few patches, and Suzanne Shaw showed off her autograph-laden T-shirt. Less than an hour after American Trans Air Flight 8750 departed BIA, a spring monsoon drenched eastern Maine. The schoolkids boarded their buses beneath an overcast, but rainless sky. A few minutes later, a pouring rain doused all hopes for a nice day. A Hawaiian Airlines L-1011, bound with 206 passengers for Fort Campbell in Kentucky, landed at 1:30 p.m. The rain intensified while the airliner rolled to a halt beside Gate 6 just five minutes later. Inside the domestic terminal, raindrops thundered on the inadequate skylights and streaked the windows overlooking the runway. A leak had developed above the escalator. The people arriving late to catch the troop flight took a brief shower as they rode the escalator to the second floor. A dark-haired man, perhaps in his late 30s, bounded upstairs in the international terminal. His young daughter followed him. The HAL jet had already reached Gate 6.

"Are we too late?" the daughter asked a passenger-service agent. "For the troops?" the woman responded. "Oh, no, they'll be right along."

"Gosh, Dad, Mom's gonna be late," the girl said to her father. "She's just parking the car," he replied while collapsing his umbrella. "She'll join us in time."

A minute later, a wavy-haired woman entered the terminal. "Hurry, Mom!" the teen-aged girl shouted downstairs while signaling the woman by hand. "They're coming right out!"

As the woman joined her family behind Carl Lindh on the ramp, the daughter displayed a sign that read "Richard L. Baker III." Suddenly, soldiers marched through the double-glass doors leading to the ramp.

Nervously chewing at her lower lip, the woman stooped and peered through the glass. As she struggled to maintain her composure, tears welled in her eyes. Whoever Richard L. Baker III was, he meant quite a bit to the woman tightly clutching her purse on the ramp.

Soldiers filed past with surprise etched on their faces. Though the crowd numbered no more than 75 people, the noise welling up the ramp from the domestic terminal told these Alabama National Guardsmen that they were welcome in Maine. The L-1011 carried troops from other units, of course, but most soldiers belonged to the 123rd Supply and Service Battalion, an Army National Guard outfit based in Goodwater, Ala. Soft Southern accents intoned "how're y'all" as the troops reached Carl Lindh at the head of the official receiving line.

Fighting back tears, a Maine woman and her family (left) awaited a soldier named Richard L. Baker III at BIA on May 17, 1991. Moments later, the woman launched herself into her brother's arms (right) as he entered the terminal.

"My God, Richard!" The woman exploded into tears and vaulted into the arms of her brother, a tall, brawny, mustachioed sergeant with an enormous smile on his face. She sobbed on his shoulder as the couple rejoined her family.

Outside the terminal, raindrops splattered on the pavement and drummed on the roof above the ramp. Inside the terminal, the sister of Richard L. Baker III cried her joy until she could cry no more.

Her brother had come home safely from war. That was all she wanted on this rainy Friday.

SEEING DOUBLE

If Lord Tennyson had witnessed the tumult surrounding United Airlines Flight 6405, he might have written "twins to the left of them, twins to the right of them, twins all around them."

As UAL Flight 6405 sped toward BIA very early on Monday, May 20, no one imagined that United would never land another troop flight in Bangor. A tradition that began with UAL Flight 6401 on March 9 would end long before sunrise on May 20.

Nor did the bleary-eyed troop greeters who straggled into the domestic terminal about 1 a.m. realize that by Wednesday, BIA would officially end the troop flights. UAL Flight 6405 was next to the last.

At 1:13 a.m., passengers from Monarch and Air Belgium jets packed the terminal wall-to-wall. Scottish burrs mixed with softer accents from the Midlands as Britons en route home on the Monarch jet talked about Disneyworld and Epcot Center. Passengers flying to Fort Lauderdale and Cancun on the Air Belgium airliner spoke in words alien to the ears of most Mainers.

A BIA employee used the PA system to call the Monarch passengers to their plane. Tourists stamped on to the ramp and emptied the terminal.

At 1:28 a.m., a bright-eyed Gary Leighton stepped to the lectern. "Good morning, Bangor!" he greeted the 40 or so people who'd formed a staggered wire after the Monarch passengers left.

Leighton was talking about updating the message on the airport's answering machine when he froze in mid-sentence. His eyes widened as he gazed out the terminal windows.

"And there he is," Leighton told the crowd. The flashing lights of UAL Flight 6405 glided through the darkness as the red-and-white 747 touched down safely at 1:35 a.m.

"We can expect about 330 soldiers on this flight," Leighton said. "The plane's headed for Hunter Army Air Field in Savannah, and everyone on board should be out here in the terminal within 15 minutes."

About 1:50 p.m., two soldiers stepped through the doors leading to the security corridor. One trooper proudly bore an American flag, which gently wafted in the air currents passing along the corridor. Other soldiers marched in columns left behind their color guard and poured into the ramp. Soldiers, exuberant, rejoicing soldiers, kept coming...and coming...and coming, until they clogged the ramp.

Men and women from the 38th Ordnance Detachment, 112th Military Police Battalion, 786th Transportation Co., and 1208th Quartermaster Co. patiently waited their turn to greet the civilians who'd turned out so early to cheer them home.

Faced with a growing delay, Gary Leighton poked his head around the corner and beckoned soldiers to form another column. Anxious to reach the phones and the beer, many soldiers willingly bypassed the wire and bolted into the terminal.

Minutes later, the ramp plugged again, so Valerie Bellomy served as traffic cop, steering some troops past the slow-moving greeting line and telling others where to find the phones. By 2:10 a.m., the ramp sufficiently cleared for Bellomy to resume her duty as guardian of the tape player.

On his upper left arm, Command Sgt. Maj. Allen Kelly wore a hard plastic, sandstone-covered pauldron emblazoned with the seal of the 89th Military Police Brigade. The 112th Military Police Battalion of the Mississippi Army National Guard, to which Kelly belonged as the senior NCO, had been assigned to the 89th during the Gulf War. Based in Jackson, Miss., the 112th was activated in September 1990. "We've been in Saudi Arabia since last October. They didn't waste any time getting us over there," Kelly said. The 112th departed the United States from Fort Benning, Ga., and landed in Dammam.

According to Kelly, the unit's primary missions were providing security for the MSRs and for vital installations. There was some concern over the terrorist threat, and there were only certain roads that were capable of handling the heavy traffic going north to the border. Watching over those roads was important.

A woman offered Kelly his choice of homemade brownies. Making his selection, he bit into one and savored the taste. "Those are good brownies. I haven't had one like that since September," he complimented the Maine woman.

"Yes, we provided security - rode shotgun, if you will - for ammo convoys and guarded quite a few generals and command posts. We were armed and ready for anything," Kelly recalled.

The Mississippi Guardsmen encountered no terrorism during all the months they guarded Allied facilities, convoys, and personnel. A few soldiers crossed into Kuwait and Iraq while escorting convoys during and after the ground war, but none of the guardsmen people were shot at.

"All in all, it's been an interesting tour, being exposed to the Saudi culture and their lifestyles. I will say, it's quite different than Europe, even southern Europe, where they're closest to the Moslem countries," Kelly said.

According to Kelly, American women experienced the greatest culture shock. "The Saudis treated our women as the American soldiers they were. There were requirements to keep their sleeves rolled down when they went into built-up areas, and the Saudi men had an annoying habit of being fascinated with our women, but overall, no one got into trouble," Kelly said.

He anticipated returning to his civilian occupation as manager of technical support for the Methodist Medical Center in Jackson. "It is great to be coming home," Kelly said. "We were called to do a mission (in the Gulf), and we stayed until our mission was up. I would like to thank the town of Bangor for the turnout." A newspaper reporter turned and collided with three soldiers named Green, Green, and Moore. Green and Green sported moustaches, floppy desert hats, and and sergeant's stripes. Moore wore a specialist's insignia and stood half-a-head taller than the Greens.

Identical twin sergeants Ronald (left) and Donald Green, assigned to the 1208th Quartermaster Co. of Lineville, Ala., raised havoc with Bangor troop greeters on May 20, 1991. A nephew, Specialist Danny Moore, served as the Greens' spokesman.

Handling the introductions with aplomb, the reporter studied the Greens and asked, "Which of you is which?"

Four matching eyes blinked at him from two faces poured from the same mold.

"I'm Danny Moore," the taller soldier spoke.

"You're not the third member of this trio, are you?" the reporter inquired.

"Oh, no, we're not triplets!" Moore grinned. "Gosh, I hope not! These are my uncles, Donald and Ronald Green," Moore explained, introducing the twin sergeants.

"Hi, I'm Donald," the right Green responded. "And I'm Ronald, except when I'm Donald," the left Green said. "How can you tell them apart?" the reporter asked Moore. "Oh, it's hard at times," Moore replied. "Especially when they play tricks on the officers, like sneaking through the chow line twice."

"That's always fun," Ron Green chuckled. Or was he Don Green? "No, I'm Don. He's Ron," one Green pointed to the other.

The men belonged to the 1208th Quartermaster Co., an Army National Guard water-purification outfit from Lineville, Ala. Ron Green was returning from his fourth foreign excursion after 20 years in the guard. He'd twice been to Germany and once to Egypt.

Don Green, a 15-year veteran of the guard, had traveled to Ecuador, Honduras, the Gulf, Germany, and Egypt. He and Ron occasionally went together, which only amplified their opportunities to raise cain with unwitting local populaces.

They'd been separated in Saudi Arabia, however, and hadn't reunited until two weeks ago. "Not much chance for mischief over there," a smiling Don Green said.

Or was he Ron Green?

"No, no, I'm Ron. He's Don," Ron confused the reporter. "I'm Don? I thought you were Don!" the other Green responded.

"Well, if I'm Ron, you must be Don," Ron commented.

Danny Moore sheepishly grinned and explained, "They do this wherever we go. Geez, they'll work the crowd tonight."

"I hope they're the only twins in your outfit."

"Oh, no!" Danny exclaimed. "Let's see, the Hearns are right over there." He pointed farther into the terminal.

After photographing Green, Green, and Moore, the reporter introduced himself to Specialists Gene and Joe Hearn. He had no difficulty in identifying the brothers. They were fraternal twins. Joe stood at least three or four inches taller than Gene.

Ron and Don Green passed into the crowd, where they kept performing their "Darrell and Darrell" routine. "We enjoy doing things together," Gene Hearn said. "Joe and I joined the 1208th at the same time, and we were both seniors at Jacksonville State University until this Gulf mess started. I was majoring in forensic science."

"My major was medical technology," the taciturn Joe Hearn said. "We had to drop out of school, because we were called up on September 12th," Gene said. "The Army sent us to Fort Rucker on the 14th, and we got to Saudi Arabia on Sept. 22nd."

After the Hearns' grandmother died on Oct. 4, 1990, their parents notified the American Red Cross, which forwarded the message to Saudi Arabia. That evening, the battalion chaplain informed Gene and Joe about the death.

The boys applied for emergency leave. "They refused our request. They told us it didn't qualify as emergency leave because it wasn't immediate family," Gene glowered.

"How could they say that?" he asked, the painful memory burning in his eyes. "When we were growin' up, we spent a lot of summers at her home. She was like a second mother to us. "We couldn't understand why they wouldn't let us go home, bury her, and come back. It's not like we were the only soldiers in the desert. I don't think it was right," Gene said.

"It really hurt me, too," Joe buttressed his brother's words. The Hearns pursued their request "up the chain-of-command, but it didn't do any good. `You gotta stay here,' everyone told us, and the family buried our grandmother without us there," Gene growled. "That made me angry."

Fire flamed in Joe's eyes. "I don't talk about if often, because I get so angry," he commented. "We only needed a week, maybe less."

Besides the Greens and Hearns, the 1208th Quartermaster Co. contained other families. The Woods were well-represented by Sgt. Timothy Wood and his brother, Spec. James Richard Wood - or "Wood, JR," as his name tag indicated.

Timothy worked as a district manager for the United Inns out of Atlanta, while JR worked for Allied Signal in Anniston, Ala., the town where he lived. Timothy hailed from Austell, Ga.

"We're not all the Woods in the 1208th," Timothy grinned. A sister, Jennifer Wood, had served in Saudi Arabia with them until she returned home in November 1990.

Their uncle, Monroe Wood Jr., went overseas with the 1208th and his son, Irving Monroe Wood, and "his daughter, she'd be our cousin, Cassandra Wood, had joined the 1208th, but she was away at AIT (Advanced Infantry Training) when we were activated," Timothy said.

The Woods also had second and third cousins in the 1208th. "The whole unit's like a big family," Timothy said.

"When you're out there in a war zone, it was kind of scary having your brother out there with you," JR noted. "What if something happened to him - or you?"

"It was good, having the family there to talk to," Timothy commented. "Our uncle was often called `Uncle Junior,' because he was a Vietnam vet and was one of the older troops in the outfit. He'd sort of look after everybody, especially us young guys. He'd give advice, good advice, if you asked him."

According to the Woods, their grandfather planned to hold a big family cookout at his farm in Delta, Ala., on June 1. "I cannot wait!" JR laughed. "Everybody's going to get together. We'll have all sorts of stories to tell."

LAST FLIGHT

"Whaddya mean, it's the last flight?" an angry woman asked during a May 22 phone call to the Bangor Daily News.

She referred to the notice printed on page 7 that Wednesday morning. In the "Maine Page" box dedicated to troop-flight schedules, the headline blared: "Last troop flight."

According to the box, "Wednesday's Hawaiian Airlines troop flight will be the last scheduled arrival of U.S. troops returning from the Persian Gulf. The flight is expected to arrive at the airport at 4:10 p.m. The flight will go to Philadelphia, Pa., after its Bangor stopover."

The notice explained that "the military has placed the three major charter airlines on `hold,' and many of these aircraft have been returned to their regular fleets. Airport officials anticipate (that) remaining troops will be returned to the U.S. via military aircraft and ad hoc charters."

The notice shocked and angered many troop greeters. How can this be? They commiserated over the phone. Aren't there still troops over there? We can't stop this now!

Some people charged collusion and conspiracy by Bangor municipal officials, presumably because they wanted to stop disrupting the lucrative international flights at the airport. But, according to the Associated Press, the government no longer needed charter aircraft. Apparently the Air Force could handle the remaining troops in the Gulf with its C-5s and C-141s.

Throughout the morning, people contacted the paper and expressed their disbelief at the notice. Then Valerie Bellomy called the paper to announce that the final flight had been confirmed for 1:30 p.m. "We're trying to tell as many people as we can!" she said.

People flocked to BIA that afternoon. According to the security detail from the Bangor Police Department, about 600 people packed the wire when Hawaiian Airlines Flight 890 landed at 1:22 p.m.

Despite the short notice, airport officials had organized a "last flight" ceremony that included local dignitaries, the Milford Junior High School band, and personnel from the Maine Air National Guard and the 776th Radar Squadron, the Air Force unit that operated the Backscatter radar located at BIA.

Legionnaires, Air Force personnel, and VFWers formed two lines on the ramp. News media circulated in the domestic terminal, where smiling children and flag-waving adults made for good sound bites and TV footage. The Milford students supplied the background music, not in a patriotic strain, but in a competent jazz beat.

Airport officials appropriately let Gary Leighton handle the last flight. Shielding his disappointment behind his businesslike approach to the ceremony, Leighton read several handwritten "thank you" notes from the troops to the crowd and "everyone who made the troop receptions possible."

Acknowledging that the day's flight would be the last, Leighton invited people to return in the future and, in reference to the myriad signs that plastered the terminal, "read our walls, and I don't mean our bathroom walls."

Despite its size, the crowd remained fairly quiet...until the troops entered the ramp.

People went nuts as the soldiers shook hands along the official reception line before reaching the gift table. Stunned by the noise echoing up the ramp, soldiers blinked hard as they marched into the terminal and encountered the 650 Maine residents waiting for them.

The HAL L-1011 carried a conglomeration of units: the 27th Chemical Co., 3rd Armored Division headquarters, the 518th Infantry Battalion, and other 3rd Armored components.

Capt. Nathaniel Johnson Jr., assigned to the 3rd Brigade, 3rd Armored Division, came from Greenville, S.C. He had been attending the Infantry Officers' Advanced Course at Fort Benning, Ga.,, when the Gulf Crisis erupted.

The Army tapped him as the assistant S-3 (operations officer) for the 518th Infantry Battalion and sent him to Saudi Arabia on Jan. 26. He joined the battalion on Feb. 2.

According to Johnson, the 518th was blended with other outfits to fashion the Spartans, a mechanized-infantry combat team that was the first 3rd Armored Division force into Iraq. The combat team included two companies equipped with Bradleys and M-1A1 Abrams tanks, plus two more companies equipped solely with Bradleys.

The Spartans suffered casualties during the ground war. Johnson, who would soon take his next assignment with the 7th Infantry Division (Light) at Fort Ord in California, beamed as the civilians showered him with souvenirs and well-wishes. "This reception, I think it's great," he said. "We didn't expect this.

A Canadian who had joined the Army during the Vietnam War, Lt. Col. Kendall Russell held back his tears as he addressed troop greeters in Bangor on May 22, 1991.

"As we were taxiing up, we could see the people with the flags in the terminal. It made me think about Lee Greenwood's song, 'God Bless the USA.' I got a really nice feeling as we came in here and met all these people. This is incredible."

Lt. Col. Kendall Russell had been assigned to USA Dentac (United States Army Dental Activity) at Fort Eustis in Virginia before heading for the Gulf. Although born to American citizens living in Lethbridge, Ontario - which made him a Canadian citizen - Russell joined the Army in 1972.

"Everyone (draft dodgers) was going north, and I was headed south to the States," he said. "Nothing patriotic about it. Just felt it was my duty. I joined up and decided to make a career of it."

The Army sent him to care for its soldiers' teeth in the Persian Gulf. "Because of the demographics - mainly young, or at least relatively young soldiers in good physical condition - dental problems I encountered were not quite typical of the population at large," Russell said.

As people celebrated around him, Russell struggled to master his emotions. With soldiers and civilians hugging and crying, many tears flowed that afternoon. The troop greeters cherished the moment, the feeling, the emotion that they believed would never happen again.

A baseball toss away from Russell, a young woman plowed through the crowd and wrapped her arms around a grinning soldier, Pfc. John Michael Hileman of Dover-Foxcroft. He'd deplaned from HAL Flight 890 and immediately phoned his fiancee, Bangor resident Joan Marie Talon.

After working all night, Talon had gone home to catch some badly needed sleep. She vaguely remembered the phone ringing about 2 p.m., and her mother answering it.

"Suddenly, she was screaming, 'Joanie! Joanie! It's for you!'" Talon said. She answered the phone and came instantly awake when she heard Hileman's voice. Learning that he was calling from the airport just a few miles away, Talon hastily dressed and rushed to meet him.

As they held tightly to each other, the young couple said that they intended to marry when Hileman returned home on leave. "He's going to Germany, and I want to go with him," Talon explained.

While Russell signed more autographs for the troop greeters, Gary Leighton announced that the Milford band would play the national anthem. Two soldiers hurried to the lectern, took the proffered American flags, and stood at attention as the band launched into the "Star-Spangled Banner."

Capt. Wendy Butler smiled broadly and blinked back her tears as she proudly held the flag. The operations officer with the 328th Medical Battalion, an Army Reserve unit from Austin, Texas, Butler said afterwards it was her first time as a flagbearer.

She'd joined the Army in August 1980 and had become a full-time AGR in 1987. The 328th, which Butler described as a command-and-control battalion, had left the United States "about Jan. 13, when a lot of medical units were shipping out. The battalion went all together, not piecemeal. We got in-country the day before the war started. We were sound asleep when we got the alert at 2 a.m. That's a heckuva wake-up call!"

The 328th supervised other medical outfits, including evacuation hospitals and dispensaries. According to Butler, the battalion first worked with the 322nd Medical Brigade, which controlled the medical units assigned to the 1st and 3rd Armored Divisions. "I was stationed in the middle of the desert, eating the dust," Butler said. "The dust is real bad, even when you have chapstick on. It pounds at your skin and dries it out and gets in your nose, ears, eyes, and mouth. Before we left - we flew out of KKMC - we had a two day dust storm that didn't want to end. That sand, it's something else. It holds in the air like fog. Heck, our departure was delayed by a dust storm.

The sand doesn't deter the Saudis, she said. "The Saudis drive like bats out of hell, even during a sand storm. If you can survive the Tapline Road and its Saudi drivers, you can survive anything."

The 328th entered Kuwait while Butler remained with the 322nd Medical Brigade at a base not far from Hafr al-Batin. When not working, she often thought about her husband, William, and their 4-year-old son, William Butler II. "I missed his fourth birthday in January," Butler said. "They sent me a copy of the videotape. It took me two days to view the tape, (because) I'd start crying and to shut it off."

Butler searched her wallet for a color photograph of her family. Beaming as she displayed the photo, Butler admitted that "yes, I missed them terribly. They don't know I've left (Saudi Arabia) yet. They're expecting me on May 30. I might call them when we get into Philadelphia." While on the ground in Pennsylvania, Butler also intended to call her in-laws in New Jersey and her mother in South Carolina. As the first boarding call sounded for HAL Flight 890, Lt. Col. Russell stepped to the lectern and commandeered Gary Leighton's microphone. Russell let the tears streak his cheeks as he thanked the crowd for their generosity. He identified himself as the aircraft commander and later as "a GI who really appreciates what you've done here."

Soldiers slowly filtered from the terminal. The civilians wished the troops well and said among themselves, "I can't believe it's all over." A sergeant entered the terminal about 2:50 p.m. and blew his whistle. The signal brought the Tail-End Charlies hustling from concealment in the lounge or deep in the crowd.

When Leighton invited the civilians to take what baked goods and other souvenirs they wanted from the gift table, people crowded the ramp and stripped the table clean. Other troop greeters, primarily those who'd become known as the "regulars," stood and watched. All of them sensed the sadness that such an exciting moment in local history was over. Just like that, with a published notice, the official troop flights had ended.

LOVE ON THE RUN

Fate? Kismet? Luck?

Who knows?

Despite the longshot odds, the diverse paths traversed by a Colorado couple intersected at Bangor International Airport on Monday, June 3. Four days after the last official troop flight departed Bangor, the first unofficial troop flight touched down at BIA. On Friday, May 24, word reached the "regulars" that an American Trans Air flight might stop in Bangor over the Memorial Day weekend. Hoo-rah! troop greeters exclaimed upon hearing the news that AMT finally confirmed the plane's arrival for 8:25 p.m. on Sunday, May 26.

By 8 p.m., people started gathering in the domestic terminal. An Air 2000 jet occupied Gate 6 at the international terminal, leaving room at Gate 5 for the incoming AMT L-1011.

With the troop flights officially over, airport officials had revamped the rules for meeting the troops. No one - absolutely no one could stand on the ramp, and no bands could perform. All the welcoming signs had been removed from the walls. Fortunately, Valerie Bellomy had convinced airport authorities to permit a gift table at the lower ramp entrance.

When she stepped to the lectern at 8:20 p.m., Bellomy delicately discussed a contentious issue. "There have been a lot of rumors going around, and I'd like to clear the air a little bit," she said.

"On Wednesday, the airport was advised by the military that there would be no more scheduled flights coming through Bangor," she said. However, the military would be having flights, and there would be ad hoc flights, meaning flights that perhaps would come to Bangor. "That's what tonight's flight is," Bellomy told the crowd. "Because it's the summer season, and the terminal is only so big and can handle only so many people, it was decided that the contracted international flights would have priority," she explained.

"That has to be recognized. However, the policy that the airport had made on Friday, when I spoke to Mr. Ziegelaar, has been modified some. Military flights that come into the airport are usually going to be allowed into the terminal, into this part, the domestic terminal. If there are a lot of planes on the ground, and the airport is very busy, military flights will be held in the secured area," which is not open to the public, Bellomy said.

"Tonight's flight originally was going to be in a secure area," she ventured, "but because, again, it's busy, the secure area is being used for another flight...that area is now being used, so our troops have to come inside.

"We're allowed to be here, but we have some very definite rules, and tonight's the chance to show that we can be mature, responsible people who want to see our troops, but at the same time abide by the rules," Bellomy declared.

She outlined the tightened rules passed along to her by airport officials. At 8:25 p.m., Bellomy told the crowd, "If you look out the window, you can see the flight coming in."

The crowd went nuts.

The blinking lights from AMT Flight 8835 flashed past the terminal windows as the L-1011 touched down following a long flight from Ireland. The plane carried 201 passengers, whom the crowd had already figured were Marines.

Unfortunately, the L-1011 had broken down after landing in Sigonella, Sicily, so the leathernecks had to reclear customs at BIA. An exasperated Bellomy explained that the leathernecks "would be trickling through here," a practice that some later flights would take.

The aircraft that AMT put through BIA that night did not sport the standard blue-and-white paint scheme, but had a white fuselage with a blue stripe along its horizontal axis. The tail was painted a lawn green.

Excited civilians alternately watched the ramp and listened as Bellomy read the rules for welcoming the troops. The troop greeters wanted Marines, now!

One leatherneck already stood in their midst. Corp. Robert Heavilin from Akron, Ohio, awaited the incoming Marines with Stacie Nevells of Bangor, a young woman whom he'd met when he landed at BIA on April 11. Heavilin had flown to Bangor for the Memorial Day weekend. Just hours ago, while dining out at a local restaurant with Nevells and her parents, he'd proposed to her.

"I had no thoughts of romantic attachments at all," Heavilin recalled his initial visit to Bangor. Assigned to a battalion from the 2nd Marine Division, he'd left for Saudi Arabia on Dec. 18, 1990, and had fought in Kuwait. United Airlines Flight 6448 brought him into Bangor at 10:38 a.m. on April 11.

Nevells, a University of Maine student and a member of the American Legion Auxiliary, had met many troop flights at BIA. She had been there the previous night, greeting the troops, and had gone home in mid-morning to catch some sleep before heading for work. But another jet had rumbled into Bangor before she'd fallen fell asleep. Caught up in all the excitement, Nevells had decided to return to the airport.

When Heavilin reached the official reception line on the ramp, he saw that the third person in line was a lovely brunette. Nevells met him there, but at the time, his face blurred with those of more than 250 other Marines who came past her.

Later that morning, Nevells started directing Marines to the telephones on the first floor in the domestic terminal. Heavilin noticed her as she passed him, time and again. He finally caught her attention and told her, "You've run past me 10 times in the past five minutes. Stand still and talk to me for a second."

They chatted until the Marines were told to return to the secure holding area in the international terminal. A jet carrying a few hundred soldiers was scheduled to land, and airport officials wanted the grunts and the leathernecks separated.

Heavilin quickly asked Nevells for her address, which she provided him before leaving for work. Later, she discovered that her wallet was missing, so she drove back to BIA to search for it.

The Marines had returned to the domestic terminal after the soldiers left. Heavilin saw Nevells looking for her wallet and spoke to her. Thinking he was just another Marine, she stopped to explain her problem. Then she recognized Heavilin from the pin that she had earlier affixed to his uniform.

The boarding call came at last, so Heavilin asked Nevells for her phone number and for an appropriate time to call her. Suspecting that he would not call, Nevells picked two "weird times," either 11:32 or 12:05 in the morning or evening.

En route to North Carolina, Heavilin started writing a letter to Nevells. Back at BIA, a woman found and returned Nevells' wallet.

The clock read almost 11:30 p.m. when the Marines arrived at Camp Lejeune. Heavilin headed for a phone, and "just to be a smart ass, I called her at exactly 12:05 (a.m.)," he said.

There followed a whirlwind courtship. That first phone call lasted about 5-1/2 hours, not a record time for the phone conversations that followed. Even while on leave in Akron, Heavilin called Nevells as often as possible. Quoting their cumulative phone bills, he shyly smiled and said, "AT&T has gotten rich off of us." On April 23, Heavilin flew to Bangor, where "we spent the whole time together," he said. She spent 10 days in North Carolina in mid May, and he, of course, made a special return trip to Bangor just before Memorial Day weekend.

When Heavilin went to dinner on May 26 with Nevells and her family, he asked her parents for permission to marry their daughter.

They replied, "Yes," as did Stacie.

Tonight, Robert Heavilin stood nervously on the far side of the wire and watched as Marines unloaded from AMT Flight 8835. The crowd patiently waited as the passengers aboard the AMT jet offloaded their baggage and carried it into the international terminal. Inside the domestic terminal, Roy and Dody Duplisea of Palmyra anxiously awaited their son, Marine Sgt. David Duplisea. He belonged to the 273rd Marine Wing Support Squadron from Beaufort Marine Corps Air Station in South Carolina, the final destination for AMT Flight 8835. He'd arrived in Saudi Arabia on Christmas Day 1990.

David had called his parents early on May 26 and told them, "My flight is supposed to be landing in Bangor." No, he didn't know the exact time, but "he is most definitely excited" about returning to Maine, his mother smiled.

Minutes later, David Duplisea cleared Customs and tore down the ramp to join his family. His mother met David part way, hugged him, and escorted him toward the terminal, where his father and at least another dozen people met the young Marine.

Four more Marines entered the ramp behind Duplisea, and so they came. Two, three leathernecks here; a few more Marines and a sailor - a Navy corpsman - there. By 8:53 p.m., a steady line of Marines poured down the ramp. "I think someone in Customs opened a floodgate," a bystander commented. Lance Corp. John Dunne entered the terminal weighted down with his baggage, a helmet and its goggles, and his web gear. From Ocala, Fla., he had joined the Marines about two-and-a-half years earlier, shortly after graduating from high school.

Dunne recalled coming home from Okinawa in August 1990 to a billet with Marine Wing Support Group 27 at Cherry Point Marine Corps Air Station. Since he was a military policeman, and the Marines required security specialists in the Gulf, he was temporarily attached to the 273rd Marine Wing Support Squadron from Beaufort Marine Corps Air Station.

"Our unit was deployed back on the 15th of December," Dunne said. He landed at Jubail, then shifted with the 273rd MWSS to a helicopter base at Ra's az Zawr, a peninsula on the Gulf coast slightly north of Jubail.

Dunne described the mission of the 273rd as supporting "a regular wing squadron...we help refuel 'em, we provide security for the base, the flight line, ah, we do all kinds of things. And depending on the mission, sometimes we handle(d)...EPWs. Basically, as far as MPs, we just...are just responsible for security and enforcing the laws."

The 273rd supported a Marine outfit flying UH-1 Hueys, CH-46 Chinooks, AH-1H Sea Cobras, and CH-53 Sea Stallions. When the war heated up during the Battle of Khafji, some Ra's az Zawr helicopters tackled the advancing Iraqi armor.

"We heard that there were several of them from our base that were going over there at that time," Dunne said. Other choppers "used our base as a refueling point. We were told that we were the closest MWSS (to the border) at the time.

"After we were there approximately a month and a week, we moved to a place called Lonesome Dove. I'm not sure where that was on the map," he recalled. "We were told it was anywhere between 10 and 12 miles. We were parallel with the Iraqi-Kuwait border." During the ground war, the unit was on stand-by, to go into Kuwait while providing security for Lonesome Dove.

The military police kept a constant vigil for terrorists and infiltrators. "Most of the infiltrators who we came up on were people who were surrendering. We didn't have any problems with them," Dunne stated.

The infiltrators who surrendered to the Marines actually crossed the border before the ground war started. "Most of the ones we had, had already surrendered to a major grunt unit or to some Navy Seals. After that, we pretty much processed them and searched them," Dunne said.

"Most of them (Iraqi EPWs) were in pretty bad shape," he stated. "They hadn't been fed in a month. They were feeding off the grass and what water they could find. Their morale was very, very low. They didn't even want to fight."

Although afraid that the Americans would hurt them, many Iraqis still surrendered. "A couple of them told us that some of Saddam's suicide squads were going around and threatening them to hold their positions, or they'd be shot if they tried to desert," Dunne stated. "Once they found out they were going to be treated right, they were very happy that it was over for them at that point."

Dunne and his comrades lived in general-purpose tents that were designed to sleep 12 men, "but we had up to 24 at any one time. The way we had the cots set up, there wasn't much room for privacy or for moving around." The Marines living in Dunne's tent worked on different shifts, so usually there was sufficient space and quiet to catch some sleep.

The Marines received mail, but occasionally not in a volume that they desired. "A lot of the letters that did make it through were people writing to 'Dear Any Service Member.' My home town paper (the Ocala Star Banner) had put in an article for people to write to us," Dunne said, "and I received a lot of letters from that."

The 273rd MWSS finally returned to Jubail from Lonesome Dove and awaited orders to ship home. "Our advance party went home right around the 1st of May, and the main body went home on the 15th of May," Dunne said. "The flight crew told us when we left Shannon that people here usually welcomed the troops home," he said. "We weren't expecting this. As we pulled up, we could see people up on the roof. I saw flags. I was flashing my camera, hoping they'd see that we were waving back. We really appreciate this."

At 9:15 p.m., Valerie Bellomy announced, "May I have your attention, American Trans Air passengers? Your plane is ready, and it's time to go home!"

Marines thundered from the terminal as the tape player kicked into "Anchors Aweigh."

For some reason, troop greeters sensed the possibility that this troop flight was not the last one after all. As the Marines departed BIA, the "regulars" gathered along the wire and bid the leathernecks "adieu." John Dunne, who received a royal send-off, left with additional equipment, including an Ursus Berrie. "Glad to have you home, son!" Everett Steele exclaimed as Dunne passed him on the ramp.

People kept cheering and applauding until Bellomy leaned into her microphone and announced, "I think we did it!" Then bedlam broke loose as the troop greeters applauded a successful transition to nonofficial flight status.

The troop flights crossed a threshold that Sunday night. Through May 22, the troop greeters always knew they could rely on BIA staff to assist them in a jam. The Chamber and Red Cross volunteers would be there to run the gift table, and everything would go right, because the powers-that-be would ensure that the homecomings really happened.

On May 26 - and every time a troop flight landed through the upcoming winter - the "regulars" assumed responsibility for making the homecomings work. Before May 26, the "regulars" had wondered if they had what it took.

After May 26, they never doubted that they did.

Sheila Dean wheeled across the terminal wearing a floppy fatigue hat weighted down with military insignia. A shiny silver star glistened atop the campaign hat.

"One of the guys gave it to me," Sheila chuckled. "He got it from an Italian general in Sigonella, Sicily. It's a star! That's all that counts!"

As Robert Heavilin and Stacie Nevells held hands and watched the unremitting chaos from a safe distance, the tape player sounded Lee Greenwood's "God Bless the USA." The troop greeters began singing with Greenwood.

Their numbers swelled as the minutes passed. People who had been complete strangers on March 8 wrapped their arms around each other's waists and formed a line at the lower ramp entrance. The amateur musicians, the people who'd formed the very core of the American homecomings, swayed from left to right and right to left as they invoked God's blessing on the United States. When they finished singing, the civilians wildly cheered.

There wasn't a Gulf vet in sight, except for Robert Heavilin. He was busy sneaking a few kisses with his fiancee. The troop greeters sang "God Bless the USA" again. Whenever the music paused, women applauded and cheered before launching into the next verse. "This is a moment you'll never see again," a troop greeter told Valerie Bellomy.

"Right," she replied.

People lingered to sing the national anthem. Robert Heavilin stood at attention and quietly sang with the Maine residents who surrounded him. As the music finished, the troop greeters went bonkers one last time.

Valerie Bellomy stopped to chat with some volunteers. "Tomorrow is Memorial Day. Fifty-eight thousand people (Americans) were killed in Vietnam. We've welcomed 58,000 people here whom we've gotten to know one-on-one and gotten to know their story. It's kind of a sobering thought, don't you think?" she asked. "As many people were killed in the last war as have come through Bangor." A sobering thought, indeed, on Sunday, May 26, the day that the unofficial troop flights began landing in Bangor.

About 5:30 p.m. on Monday, June, more than 100 performers traveling with an "Up

With People" troupe arrived in Bangor to prepare for a June 5th concert at the Bangor Auditorium. Accompanying the troupe was Melanie Sena, a young dancer from Pueblo, Colo.

After being introduced to their host families, the "Up With People" people learned that a troop flight would land at BIA later that night. Some performers expressed a desire to see the troops, so the host families agreed to take them out to the airport.

Sena had a special reason for meeting the American Trans Air L1011. Her fiance, Marine Lance Corp. Kevin Williams, had fought his way into Kuwait with the 2nd Amphibious Assault Battalion. He also came from Pueblo.

When she arrived in Bangor with an "Up With People" entourage in June 1991, Melanie Sena of Pueblo, Colo., did not realize she would meet the flight bringing home her fiance, USMC Lance Corporal Kevin Williams.

"We got here for our host drop-off, and they announced there was a flight coming in at 10 o'clock, and I knew he (Williams) was leaving on Sunday and would be in some time today," Sena said. "I was just hoping that he would be here." By 9:10 p.m., only 30 people awaited AMT Flight 8865, which was headed for Cherry Point Marine Corps Air Station. Some women set up the gift table at its former location adjacent Gate 2. Other regulars acted as scouts, watching for the approaching L-1011 from the terminal windows.

About 9:30 p.m., a few "Up With People" people and their hosts entered the terminal. Within 15 minutes, performers from the United States and other countries, including Denmark and Belgium, swelled the crowd to 150 people.

AMT Flight 8865 touched down at 9:50 p.m.

Free to create their own wire, troop greeters hastily formed two columns that would guide the incoming troops straight down the ramp and past the windows. Excited young women, with Sena in their midst, edged to the lower ramp entrance and displaced some regulars, who simply moved across the corridor. As the L-1011 taxied past the domestic terminal, people pressed their faces against the glass and cheered and waved American flags. Then, after a Bangor police officer informed her that the crowd had crept too far into the ramp, Valerie Bellomy asked everyone "to move back four giant steps." The crowd complied with her request.

As Marines appeared atop the ramp, the crowd went wild. Sena and several other women from "Up With People" moved even farther toward the head of their line, where they cheered as loudly as the regulars did.

Sena watched for Williams. "He was one of probably the first five or six, and I was standing in the front line, and I spotted him immediately," she said.

Confronted by 150 cheering, flag-waving civilians, Williams did not notice Sena standing at the edge of the crowd. "She spotted me first, and then I saw her running up toward me,' he said. To say the least, he was pleasantly surprised to meet his fiancee at an airport in Maine.

As Sena watched the Marines approach her, "all kinds of different things raced through my mind," she said. "I couldn't believe that our luck was that great, that it was actually him." Once Sena recognized Williams, she rushed into his arms. Williams, who had been in the Marines for 20 months, planned to return to Pueblo on leave in July, when Sena would also take a break from her year-long road trip and return home. Sena, who planned to study elementary education in college, said that she and Williams had set their wedding date for July 1992.

As the Marines checked out the beer and the phones, the "Up With People" people chatted with them. A few women sang "Happy Birthday" to a young Marine, and when an officer strolled through the terminal at 10:27 p.m. and announced the first boarding call, the performers gathered to sing to the departing leathernecks.

Civilians clapped in time to the "Marine Corps Hymn" as the Marines passed along the wire. A short, blond, and burly leatherneck snatched a pretty young woman from the crowd, slipped an arm around her waist, and said, "Good-bye, sweetheart," before hugging her.

She laughed and hugged him, too.

Michelle Wallace, a performer with "Up With People," bounded on to the ramp and asked Marines to autograph her red-and-white T-shirt. Her comrades clustered along the imaginary wire and applauded as the last Marines drifted from the terminal.

Wallace, who hailed from Portland, Ore., bubbled with joy while shaking hands with the outgoing Marines. "A lot of our people from 15 different countries turned out for it (the flight). Europeans, Americans, Canadian, whatever the country is, everybody supported this," she said. As she watched the Marines enter the terminal, "the first thing that I thought of was, I saw the American flag, and I just thought about all we stood for here, what we were all for," Wallace stated.

Her fiance, Chris Fadness, had served in the Gulf War with the Army and had returned home through Bangor a month-and-a-half ago with the 82nd Airborne.

Fadness had told Wallace about his reception at BIA. "From what I hear, it was the same type of thing, flags, autographs, a lot of rushing to the phones and waiting in line for hours and only being able to call home for only a minute or two," she said. "I just can't believe it," Wallace commented about the homecoming. "This is something I'll never forget. Everybody here, no matter what country we were from...the thought of the United Nations working together and how they did it and how fast this was done.

"We owe a big salute to the troops, (and) President Bush handled it very well. We got this over very quick, and that's how it needed to be done," Wallace said.

Louise Ladefoged of Denmark said, "This is the first time I have seen anything like this...this is amazing. I mean, I talked to a guy here, and he found out that I was from Denmark and said, `Oh, no way! My mother originally came from Copenhagen.'"

Diane Emdin, who came from Mons, Belgium, proclaimed that "when I heard that (about the troop flight), I said, `Gosh, I want to go,' and that was the first thing I said to my host family today.

"It's wonderful," she said.

"It was like, so amazing, because the day we were split up into groups, was the day the war started," Ladefoged observed. "It started out together with us, and now we're here, and people are going back (home) again.

"Everybody was kind of happy, and then they came in and told us about the war, and we were really down," she said. "We were really bonded together at that time."

By now, Michelle Sena had rejoined her friends. She and Kevin Williams had strolled arm-in-arm through the chaos by the gift table as if they walked alone through a quiet forest. They bid each other farewell farther up the ramp, then went their separate ways, perhaps not expecting to meet again until July.

Two nights later, when Sena performed with "Up With People" before a large crowd at the Bangor Auditorium, Williams sat in the audience. He'd caught a flight from North Carolina just to spend more time with his fiancee.

GRADE A U.S. ARMY JUNK

"One man's trash is another man's treasure" seems applicable to Maine, where people just love yard sales.

From what they learned on Thursday, June 6, troop greeters realized that Uncle Sam could have thrown a humongous yard sale in Germany during the Gulf War. Over there, soldiers were classifying military equipment: To repair or not to repair, that was the question.

Some of the stuff was deemed Grade A U.S. Army junk.

American Trans Air Flight 8890 was en route from Frankfurt, Germany, to England Air Force Base in Louisiana as troop greeters drove to BIA before midnight on June 5. At 11:50 p.m., Valerie Bellomy hit a button on a decrepit record player, and the Beach Boys sang "Kokomo" for the weary crowd.

American Red Cross volunteers advertised their outfit that night by pinning a large Red Cross flag on the wall behind the gift table. They planned to swamp the 93 troops aboard the AMT flight with every teddy bear and homemade cookie they could find. "We want 'em to know who we are," an ARC volunteer explained the flag. The AMT jet touched down at 12:05 a.m. and taxied past the terminal. Blinking red lights reflecting off their faces, troop greeters pressed their noses against the windows and waved to the plane.

"There's a problem tonight," Bellomy told the crowd. "The soldiers didn't clear customs in Europe, so they've got to do so here. They will probably come upstairs a few at a time." A strange arrangement, customs' inspections at BIA. If they had cleared customs overseas, troops simply deplaned through a gateway and entered the international terminal on the same level. The soldiers who hadn't cleared customs had to go downstairs in the terminal, talk their way past the inspectors, and return upstairs if they wanted to find a cold beer or a friendly ear.

That's what the soldiers aboard AMT Flight 8890 did on June 6. While Dottie Thibodeau waited by the passenger-service desk with flag in hand, three blond-haired flight attendants from Air Belgium exited the international terminal via the ramp and passed through a delighted crowd. Men and women cheered, the former enthusiastically. Then an AMT flight attendant entered the domestic terminal from the ramp. She drew some applause, too.

After clearing customs, another AMT attendant rode the escalator to the upper ramp entrance. Fatigue etched on her face, the brunette wearily smiled and explained, "A seven-hour flight. I'm tired. They are great people, but it's been a long day."

The soldiers would be a while; the Customs' inspectors were going through everything. Then she and an AMT comrade wandered down the ramp. People cheered them through the domestic terminal. The Air Belgium stewardesses soon returned to the international terminal. Three women clustered near the passenger-service desk and asked, "Are they coming?"

George Nye raised an eyebrow. "I sure hope they do, or I'm going to have a heart attack," he whispered, his eyes on the stewardesses.

Minutes later, Staff Sgt. Jerry Herrington rode the escalator to a rousing welcome from Nye, Thibodeau, and a few BIA employees. Giving Harrington an escort as far as a noisy terminal, Thibodeau took a position some distance up the ramp from the gift table.

Five minutes passed before the next soldiers appeared upstairs. His eyes widened in surprise when he spotted the pretty Air Belgium women. "Quite a welcome!" he later told Nye.

Two women scooted into the downstairs' ladies' room in the international terminal. They then rode the escalator upstairs behind an exhausted lieutenant, who blinked and shielded his eyes as a camcorder cast its bright light across his face.

"What's that for?" the lieutenant brusquely asked. "This is for you," the cameraman replied. "There's a reception waiting for you down the ramp."

Jerry Herrington belonged to an Army National Guard outfit, the 623rd Service and Classification Co. from Collins, Miss. The company had been activated on Jan. 7. The guardsmen reported initially to their armory, then to Fort Polk, La. They left the United States on Feb. 5 and flew to Frankfurt, Germany.

"I'm an armament inspector," Herrington explained, "checking anything to do with weapons, from small arms to tanks." He settled onto a seat outside America To Go and chatted with a young boy wearing a green Boston Celtics sweatshirt.

"Come here, son," Herrington said. He removed his metal stripes from his floppy hat and pinned them to the boy's sweatshirt. "A memento from Germany," the soldier explained.

"We're kinduva a little outfit, but they had us doing some really important work," Herrington said. "When all those Army units went to the Gulf from Germany, they left behind a lot of equipment not in workin' order, or maybe it was old, or maybe it was excess stuff.

"Our job was to 'classify' it. I would inspect a piece of equipment. I'd look it over and financially evaluate it. Would the Army pay more to repair or replace it? "We'd decide either way. Most combat gear was repairable. I'm talking about stuff like tanks, big stuff," he said.

There were some old trucks that were rusted all out, or had engines and transmissions in bad shape, he recalled. The soldiers also junked generators, trailers, and ancient electronic equipment that had not worked in years.

All inspected equipment was moved to a consolidation point to be disposed of, Herrington said. "I'm not exactly sure of what they did with the junked stuff. I don't know if a local scrap-metal dealer got it, or not. Seems to me it would cost way too much to ship to the States."

The 623rd scattered detachments to various German cities, including Hanau, just east of Frankfurt, and Stuttgart. Herrington was stationed in Kitzingen, some distance south of Schweinfurt.

While he was stationed in Germany, Herrington was joined for almost three months by his wife, Helga. She hailed from Weissenburg, a city south of Nurnberg in Bavaria. As the Mississippi Guardsmen flew home on June 6, central European time, Herrington had no idea that he'd be the center of attention when he landed in Bangor. "My bag came off the ramp first, so I guess that's why I was the first one up the escalator," he said.

"When I turned the corner and headed down here to all the noise, I thought you were cheering the wrong person!" he said. "I thought I was in the wrong place and had walked into somebody else's party! It sure makes you feel good, knowing you were here."

The PA system announced the first boarding call even as soldiers staggered into the terminal under the weight of their duffle bags. A startled Valerie Bellomy slipped the national anthem into the tape player, but by this time, many soldiers had already disappeared into the ramp. A while later, six or seven soldiers wandered into the terminal after clearing customs. "Hey, man, where is everybody?" a young private asked some women standing along the wire. "They've all reboarded the plane," the women responded. "You'd better hurry if you want to catch them!"

Minutes ticked off the terminal clock. Then Carl Lindh announced, "Here comes another one!" Bent beneath the weight of his overstuffed duffle bag, a very young trooper staggered down the ramp. The Red Cross volunteers captured him by the gift table, crammed a plastic bag with edible goodies, gave him some hugs and kisses, and spun him around and back up the ramp.

The soldier paused halfway up the ramp, then smiled and waved to the crowd. The troop greeters cheered his departure. By Monday, June 10, realization dawned among the troop greeters that "hey, maybe it isn't all over."

When word reached them that American Trans Air Flight 8910 would land in Bangor about 9 p.m. on June 10, troop greeters could not envision the flights lasting much longer. They were wrong.

About 100 people gathered to meet the AMT L-1011, which touched down at 8:47 p.m. while en route to Forbes Field in Topeka, Kansas. According to AMT rep Mike Stott, Flight 8910 had originated in Germany, Frankfurt-am-Main to be specific. Like their counterparts on AMT Flight 8890, the soldiers aboard the jet must clear customs before entering the domestic terminal.

The troop greeters resigned themselves to a long wait. Bellomy, the summertime sparkplug for the troop flights, told the crowd "there are two other flights on the ground at the same time, and our troops are in the terminal, so our military is getting a little bit of respect back."

Her words drew applause.

Minutes later, a half dozen soldiers wandered upstairs into the international terminal, swung left onto the ramp, and stared incredulously at the people cheering their appearance. Clad in jungle fatigues, the troops strode down the ramp and passed the gift table.

The crowd went wild.

As they cleared customs, other soldiers hauled their gear up the escalator or stairs and walked straight into the ambush laid by the troop greeters. A soldier apparently too young to shave broke grandmothers' hearts as he hugged the older women standing along the wire. Other soldiers exchanged high fives or shook hands.

Pfc. Danny McCrary came from Stewartsville, Mo. A member of the 189th Ordnance Co., an Army Reserve outfit from St. Joseph, Mo., he had been activated a week before Christmas.

"We left (St. Joseph) the 3rd of January" and went to Fort Riley, McCrary said. The 189th flew to Rhine-Main Air Base in Germany, landing there on Jan. 17 before heading to an Army base in Crailsheim, near Nuremburg, McCrary recalled. The Missouri Army Reservists replaced a regular Army outfit that had gone to Saudi Arabia.

From the base in Crailsheim, they shipped ammunition to the Gulf, McCrary said. The Army sent "Stingers, multiple-launch systems, grenades, M-16 rounds, M-60 rounds, everything" to Saudi Arabia via the 189th, he said.

Once the war ended, "we've mostly been moving it (ammunition) out of ASPs (ammunition supply points), where we store ammunition. We've been moving it from site to site until we got ready to leave.

"We've been staying at American bases in old barracks, World War II barracks," McCrary said. "They were in pretty rough shape. Living standards weren't the best in the world."

When his plane landed in Bangor, McCrary had "no idea (about the reception awaiting the troops). It was a shock...well, we'd done our job, and it's nice to know people are proud of us and recognize us. It took my breath away to see all those people cheering. There was a warm feeling inside. It made me feel proud."

From Fort Riley, McCrary planned to return home within a week or so. Some relatives would probably meet him in Kansas. He had a job awaiting when he got back to Missouri.

By 9:45 p.m., soldiers were still entering the terminal. An older man yelled to a Missouri soldier, "Welcome home, son!" Somewhere behind him, a tall soldier slapped high fives with the younger civilians standing along the wire, and a trooper whose service dated at least to Vietnam grinned from ear to ear as a woman his age gave him a friendly hug. At 9:55 p.m., the crowd remained only one row deep on the wire. While thin in numbers, the troop greeters never faltered in making noise, in applauding and cheering every soldier who ventured as far as the domestic terminal.

Three minutes later, a boarding call summoned the soldiers back to their plane. Off in the crowd, the last souvenir hunter to haunt a troop flight encountered a cop. Far across the terminal near America To Go, a civilian woman in her mid-30s approached a woman soldier named Logan and requested a dog tag. The startled soldier replied, "Yeah, sure," and worked the silver chain around her neck until she located her dog tags. Unhooking the chain, Logan removed a red tag and gave it to the civilian, then refastened the chain and let the remaining silver tag drop beneath her fatigue blouse.

As the Missouri soldiers exited the terminal, a few soldiers entered the building after clearing customs. Consternation written on their faces, the incoming soldiers abandoned thoughts of phones and beer, wheeled about, and dragged up the ramp.

Like a hawk riding the air currents above its prey, the souvenir hunter espied another woman soldier standing outside the lounge. Although several civilians surrounded the soldier, the Maine woman insisted on speaking to her. When the Kansas-bound trooper turned and spoke to the souvenir hunter, a police officer watched from an inconspicuous distance.

He moved after the woman soldier dug deeply into her duffle bag and found something to give the souvenir hunter. Words passed quietly between the police officer and the Maine woman. He threw her out of the terminal.

Two or three soldiers lingered inside the lounge to polish off a cold beer, then bolted for their plane. Troop greeters shifted position to the lower ramp entrance and waved and hollered as the stragglers bounded for the L-1011.

"It's too bad they're gone so soon," Joy Brown murmured to Dick Shaw. Other civilians shared similar sentiments. As people discussed their feelings, a light bulb flicked on in someone's mind: Why don't we see them off from the observation deck?

About 20 people rushed up the twisting, poorly lit steps to the observation deck, a narrow rectangular expanse of concrete stretching half the length of the domestic terminal. A warm southwesterly breeze blew into their faces as the troop greeters spread themselves along a waist-high parapet and waved to the AMT L-1011. The breeze caught and whipped a large American flag in the darkness.

As a tug backed the plane from Gate 5, a soldier noticed the people standing atop the observation deck. "Hey, look, they're signaling us!" a civilian exclaimed, indicating a flashlight blinking through a window on the L-1011. The troop greeters waved all the harder as flashlights winked and blinked from four or five windows along the port side of the plane.

Civilians lingered on the observation deck until the L-1011 rumbled down the runway and vanished into the night sky.

The scene repeated itself nine nights later, when people gathered to meet AMT Flight 8938, another L-1011 en route home from Frankfurt, Germany. This time, however, the blue-and-white jet carried 172 leathernecks bound for Cherry Point Marine Corps Air Station.

"Marines? From Europe?" a woman asked Carl Lindh. Carl tried to explain to the woman concerned about Europe-based Marines that "there are Navy bases over there, and wherever you find sailors, you'll find Marines."

Sans his trademark beard, but with his moustache still intact, a yawning Tom Dean rolled past the wire about 7:40 p.m. "We've really got another flight?" he asked Carl Lindh. "I thought they'd be over by now."

"Apparently not," Carl replied, shrugging his shoulders. "That's the military for you: They tell you the troops flights are done, but the planes keep coming."

His trusty camcorder already slung over his shoulder, the Cable Guy, a.k.a. Bob Jones, worked his way through the gathering crowd at 7:47 p.m. People complimented him on the Channel 35 broadcasts they had seen since June 10.

By 8:10 p.m., about 100 people packed the imaginary wire all the way from the lower ramp entrance to the weather kiosk. People talked with their friends, occasionally looked out the window, and speculated as to when AMT Flight 8938 would land.

Outside the terminal, the glorious Maine spring neared its peak. The sun would not set for a while, and twilight would linger beyond 9 p.m. Bangor-area residents thrived on such nights, when lawnmowers ran until dark, and people enjoyed long, leisurely strolls through a countryside buzzing with life - including blackflies and mosquitoes.

Mike Stott took a walk through the domestic terminal that night to check out the crowd. He tossed out some facts about the L-1011:

* A normal crew comprised three officers and seven flight attendants;
* Flight 8938 should take one hour and 47 minutes to reach Cherry Point from BIA;
* In doing so, the plane would burn about 29,400 pounds of fuel.

"You can see the economic benefit the airport receives whenever we bring a troop flight through here," Stott pointed out. "We've got two crews spending at least one night apiece in Bangor, not to mention the fuel that Trans Air buys and the other supplies like meals. It all adds up."

Perhaps 200 people jammed the wire by 8:25 p.m., five minutes after AMT Flight 8938 greased its wheels on the BIA pavement. Word rippled through the crowd that the Marines had cleared customs already.

Marines suddenly burst through the double-glass doors beside the passenger-service desk. A horde of desert fatigues rolled downhill, overwhelming the Red Cross volunteers at the gift table and encountering the homecoming crowd just as it shifted into high gear. A blond Marine cried as she hugged civilians standing along the wire. Other Marines laughed as they exchanged greetings with civilians. Indelible markers flew across T-shirts and notebooks, fingers pointed the way to the beer and phones, and flash attachments furiously winked while Marines still remained on the wire.

Lance Corp. Arthur Briggs, who came from Portsmouth, Va., reported that he'd been assigned to the 2nd Supply Battalion of the 2nd FSSG (Field Service Support Group). He'd been stationed at Camp Lejeune before heading off to war on Dec. 8.

"Then you folks were in the Gulf?" a man asked. "For sure," Briggs replied. His black hair cropped close to his skull, he grinned and said that "we were definitely in the desert. I don't ever want to see sand again, as long as I live."

"Not even at a North Carolina beach?" a woman inquired. Briggs smiled and responded, "Oh, well, maybe, as long as there are no camels wanderin' around."

During the Gulf War, the 2nd Supply Battalion had supplied ammunition to the two Marine divisions operating along the Kuwait-Saudi border. The Marines established a major ammo dump "about three miles from the border, about where it bends on the map," Briggs said. The dump stored ammunition for "everything the Marines fired, like tanks and M-16s." He said his unit was stationed 30 or 34 miles from the airport in Kuwait City.

The Marines aboard AMT Flight 8938 enjoyed only a short visit to Maine that night. Arthur Briggs was still talking about the war when Bellomy ran into the terminal about 9 p.m. and shouted, "This is the first boarding call! Time for the Marines to go home!"

"I gotta go," Briggs said, pausing to shake hands with the civilians gathered around him.

Troop greeters formed a ragged gauntlet beside the duty-free shop and applauded as the Marines filtered from the terminal. A few corpsmen passed along the dual wire, where troops found hands thrust from every direction. A Marine would shake one hand, turn and shake another hand across the aisle, then find himself facing more right hands a short distance away.

Among the Marines who lingered to roust the Tail-End Chucks from the gift shops and Red Baron Lounge was Chief Warrant Officer Third Class James McCormack, a member of the 2nd Supply Battalion. Speaking briefly with Bellomy, he thanked her for the warm welcome given his leathernecks. By 9:10 p.m., most Marines had departed the terminal. McCormack and other ranking Marines flushed their last charges from cover and headed for their plane. Once the troops cleared the ramp, the troop greeters headed for the observation deck.

SADDAM GETS THE BOOT

Even Saddam Hussein turned out to meet the returning troops at BIA.

Phones started ringing in various Bangor-area homes about 9 p.m. on Monday, June 24. Word spread along the well-organized network of troop greeters that American Trans Air Flight 8946 would land at BIA after midnight. The L-1011 carried 152 soldiers and airmen bound for Columbia, S.C.

Someone apparently called Baghdad that evening and told Mr. Hussein that if he wanted to catch a troop flight in Maine, he'd better get his butt in gear.

He did.

By 11:55 p.m., about 50 people awaited the arriving AMT jet. Six or seven volunteers, including a few still wearing their ARC badges, hastily organized the greeting table. Other people stood and chatted with airport acquaintances. Then a woman whispered to a man next to her, "Do you see who's here?," and pointed to a man sitting near the weather station.

A quick glance and then a doubletake confirmed the man to be the likeness of Mr. Saddam Hussein himself. Clad in green fatigues and a pair of combat boots and looking slightly more wrinkled around the edges, the "Iraqi leader" sprawled in an airport chair and watched the crowd form for the incoming AMT flight.

Ol' Saddam also wore a hangman's noose around his neck.

Just as his appearance in Kuwait disturbed the Arab inhabitants, so did Hussein's appearance at BIA upset the troop greeters. Conversation immediately shifted to such topics as "I wonder why he's here?," and "He really frightens me."

"Hussein" ignored the worried glances cast in his direction. Back in January, of course, the real Hussein had ignored the UN directives to get out of Kuwait.

The consequences proved the same.

He got the boot. A quick check with employees at the passenger-service desk confirmed that "yes, we know he's here." Because the announced arrival of the AMT flight had come so late, however, no police officers had yet reported for duty at the airport. Apparently everyone at BIA believed that just like in January 1991, Hussein would move only for a man wearing a gun. Besides, he was just sitting there, minding his business.

The crowd didn't appreciate Hussein's presence, though. Conversation turned to concern for the troops aboard the AMT L-1011. What would they think, how would they respond on meeting their nemesis 8,000 miles from the Persian Gulf? A Bangor police officer strode into the domestic terminal about 12:13 a.m. He'd apparently discussed "Mr. Hussein" with airport staff. Spotting the bogus Iraqi dictator across the terminal, the police officer passed through the crowd to confront him. The man with the gun told "Mr. Hussein" to remove his mask. He declined the offer.

This "Saddam" wore a rubber mask that convincingly recaptured the dictator's middleaged face right down to the black moustache and bulbous nose. The mask had worried the civilian troop greeters more than an appearance by the real Hussein would have. Zorro, the Ninja Turtles, and the Lone Ranger to the contrary, wearing a mask still suggested something sinister.

In another time and another place, a confrontation between a police officer and Saddam Hussein would have drawn a large crowd. Even in Maine, a typical public confrontation between police and bad guys often attracts onlookers, many of whom routinely jeer the men and women wearing the badges.

Nobody jeered the Bangor police that night. Nobody ventured close to the meeting of the minds at center court, either.

Several slightly tense minutes passed while "Hussein" refused to remove his mask. Unsure of whom he faced, the police officer stood perhaps a yard from the noose-wearing Iraqi dictator, who finally and half-heartedly attempted to lift the mask to reveal his face. That's not acceptable, the police officer's response indicated. It's all or nothing, buddy. At 12:18 a.m., two more Bangor police officers appeared not far from Mr. Hussein's elbows. "Saddam" then removed his mask and revealed his true identity as an older man with grayish-white hair -a veteran from a past war who'd believed his disguise an appropriate way to welcome home the troops. They'd left the real Hussein hanging in the wind, hadn't they?

The veteran's attempted humor soured that night. The sergeant commanding the police detail summoned Marianne Mitchell, the shift supervisor for passenger service. She spoke briefly with the man, then the police officers escorted him from the terminal.

The AMT flight touched down moments later.

Forgetting about Saddam Hussein, the crowd formed an imaginary wire and waited for the troops to enter the terminal. An early, unconfirmed scenario had the soldiers passing through Customs. Before the soldiers reached the top of the ramp, however, word spread that these people had been precleared and would exit their L-1011 en masse.

Soldiers clad in desert fatigues, airmen wearing jungle fatigues, and civilian technicians sporting beards and baseball caps poured down the ramp. The crowd, now numbering about 75 people, wildly cheered and applauded.

Young women soldiers openly cried. A grandmother wearing slacks and a sweatshirt reached out, hauled in every male soldier she could reach, and kissed him on the lips. A handsome soldier got a particularly enthusiastic kiss.

The AMT passengers turned the corner of the wire and worked their way toward Mr. Paperback and America To Go. Somewhere along the way, a civilian technician picked up a Dysart's Truck Stop cap. Two soldiers removed the insignia from their uniforms and pinned it on the desert-fatigue pajamas worn by a young boy.

A young soldier reached into the crowd and hugged an older woman for several moments. His eyes remained closed the whole time.

Standing near the cafeteria entrance, 1st Lt. Frank Roberson of the 22nd Support Command watched the interaction between civilians and soldiers. He'd hopped a flight home from Dhahran, Saudi Arabia, to enjoy "only a couple of days (of leave) to see my wife, Jill, in Atlanta, but it's better than nothing."

Before the Gulf War, Roberson had been assigned to the 547th Engineer Battalion in Germany. He arrived in Dhahran in early February to work with the engineer staff of the 22nd Support Command. The Army intended Roberson and other newly arrived soldiers as replacements for people wounded or killed during the war. "The low number of casualties ended that assignment," Roberson said. "They found us jobs because we didn't have anyone to replace." He helped build various facilities and roads in Dhahran to support the troops entering or leaving Saudi Arabia. Roberson told how the 864th Engineer Battalion of Fort Lewis, Wash., constructed an APOE (Aerial Point of Entry) from six K-spans, large quonset huts set "four in a row, and two the other way."

The APOE housed U.S. Customs and provided departing troops someplace to store their gear before boarding their aircraft. Soldiers could watch a movie or buy refreshments in the air-conditioned Kspans.

The 22nd Support Command served as higher headquarters for the 864th and similar units. As the subordinate battalions shipped out, the 22nd staff let some of its soldiers go home on leave. Roberson flew home with Col. Charles Ingram, chief of staff for the 22nd.

AMT Flight 8946 carried personnel from several units. Some soldiers like Roberson had to return to the Gulf; others came home for good. Most civilian technicians were back to stay.

Roberson didn't mind catching a return flight from South Carolina on June 29. After her husband had gone to the Gulf in February, Jill Roberson returned home to the States and stayed with friends. Roberson planned to return to Germany on Aug. 1, then depart the Army in September. He and Jill would live in the Southeast, where he had lined up a slot with an Army Reserve unit in Alabama.

About 12:55 a.m., civilians in the terminal started passing word of the first boarding call by mouth. Even as word spread that "it's time to go home," two or three soldiers boogied to a Michael Jackson record. The slow response to the boarding call suggested that many soldiers didn't want to leave Bangor.

Then a taped Whitney Houston launched into her elongated version of the "Star-Spangled Banner."

Played fairly quietly, the music slowly filtered across the terminal. As more soldiers and civilians stood at attention, a respectful silence overspread the building. To one side, Tom Dean had been videotaping an interview with an Army officer. As the first strains of the national anthem reached his ears, the officer turned from the camera and toward the flag and raised his right hand in salute.

He held the salute the length of Houston's music.

Word came again that the soldiers must reboard their L-1011. As weary, but smiling soldiers and airmen departed the terminal, Spec. Anthony Mitchell of New York City photographed everyone standing on the wire. He grouped four or five civilians together at a time, snapped a photo, and asked the next group of civilians to gather for a photo. In this manner, Mitchell "shot" his way along the wire and made the turn into the ramp.

The troop greeters cheered him as he departed. By 1:13 a.m., a few soldiers still trailed out of the terminal. They left not knowing that a veteran in the guise of Saddam Hussein had been booted from BIA just before they arrived.

The disguise might have worked if the veteran had included in his act an American soldier holding the other end of the noose.

THE GEORGIA WILD CATS

In Maine, a bobcat's considered a wild cat, unless the wild cat's a lynx, in which case it can still be a wild cat, but not a bobcat.

The Georgia Wild Cats are another animal altogether.

American Trans Air Flight 8948 landed in Bangor at 1:38 a.m. on June 27 while en route to Augusta, Ga. The L-1011 carried 152 soldiers and airmen on their way home from the Persian Gulf.

Thirteen minutes before the airliner touched down at BIA, about 40 people formed a rudimentary wire in the domestic terminal. Still promising to meet every troop flight, Sheila Dean arrived with nine colorful balloons tied to her wheelchair. Other civilians turned out wearing red, white, and blue in assorted clothing styles. The regulars greeted each other with comments like "It's another one!" and "We get another chance!" As the L-1011 taxied past the terminal at 1:45 a.m., more people arrived to swell the crowd's numbers to about 50. The regulars made room for a few newcomers. Although wide awake at this ungodly hour, most people standing along the wire talked quietly, as if conserving their energy.

Soldiers appeared at the door in the international terminal. "Holy smoke!" someone exclaimed. "They're here already!" Cheers echoed up the ramp while civilians scrambled to find a place along the wire. The photographer or two present that night hastily backpedaled as the soldiers and airmen - far more Army personnel than people in jungle fatigues - swept into the terminal.

Uniforms and civvies intermingled once again at BIA. Definitely affected by the hour, the troop greeters applauded quietly. The cheering dwindled as more passengers from AMT Flight 8948 lined up along the wire and waited their turn to meet their fans.

Content to let other people hug and kiss the soldiers, Valerie Bellomy stood near the terminal windows and waved a large American flag. Just a few yards away, a soldier passed among the civilians while carrying a briefcase marked "MI: Musical Institute." After reaching the end of the wire, two women soldiers slipped back to the gift table and soon reappeared with teddy bears in hand. Unable to offer the returning soldiers many baked goods, the people staffing the gift table handed out teddy bears by the score. Later, as the national anthem sounded in the domestic terminal, Spec. Madlin Patterson borrowed the American flag from Bellomy. Assigned to the 1015th Maintenance Co. (Army Reserve) at Fort Gillim in Atlanta, Ga., Patterson stood near the duty-free shop and proudly lifted the big flag ceilingward. The 1015th, known as the "Wild Cats" for the symbolic black cat mounted on the its shoulder patches, left Fort Gordon, Ga., on Oct. 31, 1990, "a fitting Halloween for us," Patterson said. The soldiers arrived in Dhahran, Saudi Arabia, the next day.

The members of the 1015th spent two weeks acclimatizing to the harsh desert climate. Wednesdays, Patterson said, were reserved for NBC drills.

Once accustomed to hot days and cold nights, the Georgia soldiers worked on bunkers and concertina emplacements. "Our main mission was maintenance, of course," Patterson pointed out. Soon attached to the 80th Ordnance Battalion of Fort Lewis, Wash., the 1015th started repairing bulldozers, forklifts, five-ton trucks, and other vehicles used by Army engineers.

Patterson worked as a mechanic, a skill and interest she had developed back home in Georgia. Out in the Saudi desert, however, mechanics also learned the skills needed for guard duty, an assignment that Patterson described with relish.

The soldiers pulled guard duty in 24-hour shifts, she said. Some soldiers escorted visitors to the military bases. Escort duty "usually meant some sleep, because you were up all day with visitors," Patterson recalled.

"If you didn't have escort (duty), you stayed up all night guarding your assigned area," she said. "You still had to work your normal job, no matter if you slept or not."

Guards carried loaded M-16s, but could not fire them without permission from a superior officer. Someone shooting at you might excuse your shooting back without authorization, Patterson confirmed, but even then, maybe you'd better get permission.

The 1015th sent detachments as far afield as King Khalid Military City and Khubar. Patterson remained in Dhahran, "watching the Scuds go by. It was like a flash going over — scary, yet amazing. You never expect to see anything like that go overhead, a missile coming after soldiers like you."

As the first boarding call sounded, Patterson said that duty in the Gulf had cost her a year at Savannah State College, where she majored in physical therapy. Also an employee for the City of Atlanta Parks and Recreation Department, she had joined the Army Reserve in 1989 for an eight-year hitch. "Military duty helps pay for my college," she explained. "I completed my junior year before this mess started. I'll just pick up where I left off, I hope."

After excusing herself and starting up the ramp, Patterson quickly returned, removed the Wild Cat patch from her sleeve, and gave it to Bellomy. Supposedly the first Army-issued patch, the Wild Cat patch remains green on all uniforms.

"As far as I know, it's the only patch that doesn't change colors between uniforms," Patterson explained. "We're proud to wear it."

She quietly bade farewell to Bellomy, stopped once on the ramp to wave, and vanished among the soldiers and airmen now crowding toward their L-1011. Within a few minutes, the last Georgia Wild Cats vanished from the terminal.

VALERIE

Thursday, July 4, dawned clear and warm, promising a hot day. No troop flights, either...just a parade.

Bangor and Brewer threw a big parade every Fourth of July. Today was no exception. By 9:30 a.m., vehicles and marchers jammed parking lots and side streets near the Brewer Auditorium. Fire trucks, units from the Anah Temple Shrine, and floats lined up to roll across the Penobscot River into Bangor.

About 25 troop greeters descended on a flatbed parked behind the old Brewer Post Office. The previous evening, the civilians had converted the trailer into a reasonable facsimile of an American Trans Air L-1011. Men and women packed the float, which included a genuine Maine Gulf vet standing in the cockpit. The aviator from the Air National Guard wore his green flight suit and held aloft a large American flag as the truck-towed trailer wound its way to Bangor.

Valerie Bellomy joined the troop greeters that day. For once, no troop flight intruded on her schedule. She could relax, knowing that she had no calls to make and no plane to greet.

When Hawaiian Airlines Flight 890 departed BIA on May 22, nobody anticipated further troop flights. Believing the flights were over, airport employees ended their involvement with the homecomings. That left no designated liaison between airport and troop greeters.

Bellomy filled the gap during late May, June, and July. Another troop greeter, Sylvia Thompson, took over after that.

Greeting the troops in March had seemed natural for Bellomy. Her husband, David, worked in BIA dispatch and often informed his family about incoming flights. She and her daughters had turned out to meet the initial flight, American Trans Air Flight 7254. "We set the alarm clock for about quarter-past five, because we were going to get up and go to the airport," Bellomy recalled.

"David called Mike (another BIA employee) in the dispatch. Mike says, 'If you're going to be here, you'd better hurry, because the plane's circling the airport.'

"So we didn't get there when the plane touched down, but we were there as they were coming into the terminal," she said. "We came up the escalator in the international (arrivals) building, clapping as they all came through. "I guess my first reaction was that they were so young. We went into the terminal after they all went by, and it was weird," Bellomy described that first encounter between civilians and soldiers. "The troops were over here, people were over here, and they wasn't really mingling.

"My sister was with me. We were standing over by the television sets...there were troops here and there, a lot of them on the phones. Prudie (Prudence Bradford) says, 'Come on, let's go go shake hands, let's go meet 'em.'

"And that's what she did...so we followed along with her," Bellomy said. "The first person we met was named Perez. (He) was the one who had all the personality."

Before a new job at Dysart's Truckstop called her away in summer 1991, Bellomy estimated that her family had met "well over half" of the troop flights. "When we first went, it was because I had been at the airport in August and September, when the troops were outbound," she said. "I did that twice...and it was just so somber. It was sad. I knew when they came back that I was going to be there," she explained her decision to meet the incoming flights in late winter. "We'd read about it (the Gulf War), watched it on TV. I'd go to bed after Channel 7 and 'Nightline' went off the air (late at night), and the first thing you'd do at six o'clock in the morning is to turn on the national news to see what was going on.

"That was the first couple of flights. But, then, it was fun! It was addictive. Waving the flag, patriotism, that is fun," she stated.

"And then, after a while, you just became committed. You had to be there. You had to give the 63rd flight the same greeting, and the 72nd flight.

"The beginning flights, everybody was happy. Then when April came, the mood had kind of changed," Bellomy said. "When April came, people were really relieved to be home. We became listeners. We listened a lot. People coming home the end of April, they had seen the effects of war. Those people had tough stories...it was important for those guys and girls (to talk to people in Bangor)."

Bellomy said there was also another impression: "There were so many women! Not just young girls who were in the Army because that was the thing to do, but older women (too). I remember thinking that the people on the airplanes needed to have people there (at the terminal) to know that they were decent human beings, that they had done a job and had done it well. I think it worked out well, because when they came to Bangor, and they came down the ramp and saw people very glad to see them, they were able to get their worries and concerns out of their systems. Tom Dean says it was like 'emotional therapy,' that they were worked on before they got home to their loved ones."

Bellomy remained with the troop flights until July 28, when she took a full-time position as a waitress as Dysart's, the popular restaurant and truck stop in Hermon. Through Jan. 11, 1992, she did not meet many more flights, but she'd already done her duty. "May 22 was the last official flight that the government-recognized (Civil Reserve Air) fleet needed commercial carriers. And then the following week, AT&T took their phones back (the additional pay phones installed in the terminals)," Bellomy said. The phone that people could dial to receive flight updates vanished in late May.

"People didn't have any idea when a troop flight was coming. It turned out the flights were mostly American Trans Air," and aircraft often arrived with a short-term notice.

"Because of David's job at the airport, I was the contact person, and that was approved with Bob Ziegelaar," she said. "All the dispatchers on all the shifts would call and let me know that there was something on the schedule. When it had been confirmed, I did the telephone tree, calling 18 people who would call everybody else."

Looking back six months later, Bellomy would wonder why the flights, specifically the troop greetings, occurred in Bangor. BIA's location made sense geographically, of course, but what about the human element?

"There's a sign out at the airport that says, 'Welcome to Maine, The Way Life Should Be,'" she observed. "I think a lot of people in Maine, in Bangor, were compassionate, caring people, that we weren't so busy and so wrapped up in just trying to get through today and tomorrow.

"Our lifestyle's is so laid back. We've got extra time," Bellomy said. "It's not that we're just lazy people looking for something to do, but we care. And here was a real outlet for caring, and we did it."

THE LAST OF MISSISSIPPI

One time when the 1355th Supply and Service Co., Mississippi Army National Guard, landed in Bangor during the late 1980s, the soldiers weren't allowed off the plane. They'd cleared customs somewhere else in the States, so they remained aboard their aircraft.

The National Guardsmen received a different reception on July 23, 1991, when they touched down at BIA while heading home from the Persian Gulf. This time, they'd cleared customs before heading out from Saudi Arabia to Sicily, Ireland, and Maine.

Mike Stott had confirmed American Trans Air Flight 8980 to land at 8:35 a.m. on a day that dawned to a steady downpour. Troop greeters shook raindrops from their umbrellas and raincoats as they straggled into the terminal in time to meet the AMT L-1011, which touched down at 8:40 a.m.

About 50 people cheered the 155 soldiers and one hitchhiker, a Navy corpsman. The troops shook hands along the wire and graciously accepted American flags and hugs from their hosts.

According to 1st Sgt. Henry LeTort of Poplarville, Miss., the 1355th Supply and Service Co. had been called to active duty on Nov. 17, 1990. Based in Ocean Springs, Miss., the company reported to Fort Rucker, Ala., on Nov. 20, 1990, and finally got to Dhahran on Jan. 6. The soldiers did go home for Christmas.

Desert heat "isn't the same as the heat back home," LeTort said. "We get it hot and humid back in Mississippi, but over there in the desert, it gets real hot, a dry heat."

The troops lived in tents on the beach in Dhahran for three days, then went on with their missions, he said.

The 1355th sent detachments across the Persian Gulf, especially to the logistics bases spread across the desert toward KKMC, to handle petroleum and water-purification. The Mississippi Guardsmen traveled into Kuwait, a country that LeTort described as devastated.

"There are mines everywhere, ammunition being dug out of all the beaches on the Gulf," he recalled. "It's really bad, especially up where Death Valley is. That's where all the Iraqi vehicles were shot to pieces when they were trying to get away. The Air Force and Navy, I guess they were everywhere up there.

"We heard there were 600 oil fires still burning. I saw one gushing up in the air, not fire, but oil gushing up. Can you imagine how that would go over in this country?"

A child asked LeTort for his autograph. "Certainly, sweetheart," he responded, scrolling his name onto the little girl's T-shirt. "I am so glad to see you.

"I'm glad to see everyone here," the first sergeant stated. "You look out there, through those windows, and you probably see the rain and think, 'Hey, no sunshine today.'

"Well, we haven't seen rain since February, nothing but the hot sand and hot wind," LeTort grimaced. "I'm sick of sand. I think your rain and trees are great, almost like home.

"And the air looks clean. Over in Kuwait, everything is covered with soot. When the wind's right, it blows smoke across the road. I remember times when it was so dark - this in the middle of a sunny day - it was hard to see the man sitting beside you," he said. "The sun looked like the moon at night."

A Mississippi state trooper in civilian life, the first sergeant drove a Cutvee (a militarized Chevy Blazer) in Saudi Arabia. "Geez, I put 20,000 miles on the odometer, ridin' all over the desert," he chuckled. "I don't drive 20,000 miles in seven months on the job in Mississippi.

"They had us covering some ground over there. We put over 500,000 miles on our vehicles, and we came through slick; with no casualties, no one hurt," the first sergeant said.

According to LeTort, 33 Mississippi state troopers had been activated for duty in Operation Desert Storm. He was the last trooper to return home. The 1355th was the last Mississippi Army National Guard outfit to return from the Gulf, too, LeTort said. The company commander, Capt. Johnny McKay, confirmed LeTort's assessment. We've been through Bangor before, "a couple of years back while we were headed for Germany," McKay said.

"We stayed on the plane. They refueled us and sent us on our way without letting us off. It's much better this time around," he said, "getting off and mingling with all you folks."

After the tape player finished with the national anthem, soldiers drifted to the gift table and stripped it clean of Ursus Berries teddy bears. LeTort estimated that the Mississippi soldiers would land at Lawson Army Airfield in Savannah between 11 a.m. and 12 noon.

"I'm really excited about gettin' home to see Sheila - she's my wife - and our two girls. One's 6, the other's 13, beautiful girls," he said. "Can't wait to see them again."

"We were supposed to be over there until the 27th of September," LeTort commented, "but they told us two weeks ago (that) we would be leavin' by the end of July. Believe me, people were ready to leave."

Sgt. Edward Webb wanted to leave Bangor ASAP. "No offense to you great folks," he explained. "I think what you've done for us here is fantastic. It's just that my wife, well, just five days ago, she had a seven-pound, 12-ounce baby girl!

"We named her Maria Dante Webb. Pretty name, isn't it?" he asked, grinning as gray-haired Maine women pumped his right hand or patted his shoulder and extended him their warm congratulations.

"She's our first child. Man, I missed her being born! I'm so anxious to get there to see her! Say, what time does this plane leave, anyway?" Webb asked the troop greeters.

All the Mississippi Guardsmen wanted to return home, McKay said. "We've been gone long enough. Everyone misses their families. We've done our duty, they're sending us home, so we figure it must be our turn to hug our loved ones."

A boarding call summoned the Mississippi soldiers to the L-1011. Guardsmen rushed from the terminal, though not without offering profuse "thank yous" to their Yankee hosts.

When Sylvia Thompson handed a woman soldier a July 23 newspaper, the trooper cried, "Today's paper! Thank you! Thank you!" Then she hugged a startled Thompson. LeTort and Webb swept along the wire and into the ramp. After a stop at the gift table, McKay bounced back into the terminal to find his Tail-End Charlies. As the last of Mississippi vaulted toward the AMT jet, a visibly moved McKay thanked the crowd for their support.

A BUSY AUGUST MORNING

Four events coincided at BIA on Aug. 5.

For the last month, the troop greeters had planned an informal get-together for this Monday. A loose consensus developed that the regulars wanted to hold a breakfast at the airport. After comparing schedules, most people opted for 9 a.m.

William Gardiner, who owned the airport coffee shop and the Red Baron Lounge, offered to serve the meal gratis. He confirmed the 9 a.m. start time for the breakfast, which would be cooked in the coffee shop.

Then word got out the previous weekend that a troop flight might land in Bangor Monday morning. American Trans Air planned to land an L-1011 at 4:30 a.m., then rescheduled the landing for 9 a.m.

Free or not, no breakfast could conflict with a troop flight. By Sunday afternoon, the telephone network told the troop greeters that their breakfast would start at 7:30 a.m. on Monday.

During the night, a low pressure system moved across New England and doused central Maine with more than an inch of rain. No one complained about the precipitation; the bone-dry fields and woods needed rain. The fire danger remained high in the forests.

By morning, however, the gun-metal gray ceiling descended as the rain fell harder. Although horizontal visibility reached more than a mile, the low ceiling concerned some troop greeters. On Aug. 1, a fog that lasted only a few hours forced another AMT jet to divert to Boston with its military passengers. At 4:30 a.m. that Thursday, the fog extended perhaps several hundred feet upward. People spotted the moon glowing above the fog.

Would similar conditions divert another troop flight today?

As troop greeters gathered for the breakfast, knowledgeable heads among the veterans studied the sky from the terminal windows and predicted that the rain would not mess up any landings.

About 75 people met that morning to enjoy scrambled eggs, sliced ham, toast, muffins, coffee, and juice. The long line that formed in the coffee shop soon backed out the door and snaked past the entrance to the lounge. People sat wherever they found space, ate breakfast, and caught up on the news.

A Canadian couple catching a flight from BIA with their children accidentally lined up for the breakfast. Noting the tired parents, a troop greeter told them to "pretend you're one of us" and eat a warm breakfast.

As the meal wound down, Mildred Bowden asked Bob Jones from Cablevision to join her near the rear wall of the Red Baron Lounge. The unsuspecting Jones never questioned the wrapped packages stacked atop the table.

Commenting on the Cable Guy's new status as a bachelor and as a resident of a town 45 miles from Bangor, Bowden said, "Because we couldn't go to Lincoln, your housewarming is here." She gestured to the wrapped packages and told Jones that his friends among the troop greeters had decided to throw a housewarming party for him.

For the next hour or so, Jones unwrapped towels, silverware, and other household necessities. He joked with people and thanked them for their kindness. As he'd discovered while taping so many troop flights, he'd been accepted into the community with open arms.

By 9 a.m., people started drifting away from the breakfast to do a few chores before the AMT jet landed. A while later, the remaining troop greeters held an impromptu awards ceremony to honor the volunteers whose efforts had kept the troop receptions going since May 22. About the same time, Maine's Democratic senator, George Mitchell, held a press conference at the Bangor Hilton to announce a Congressional investigation into the timing of the release of the Iran hostages. The media sent reporters and cameramen. The breakfast, the "unofficial" awards ceremony, and the arriving troop flight attracted a far larger audience than did the press conference.

Many troop greeters who attended the breakfast lingered to meet American Trans Air Flight 8989, en route from Saudi Arabia to Altus Air Force Base in Oklahoma. The schedule now called for the L-1011 and its 152 passengers to land at 11:25 a.m.

Any concerns about a low ceiling had evaporated as the heaviest rain ended about 8:45 a.m. The solid overcast broke into thick puffballs, a weather trend that usually signifies a storm's passage in New England. The ceiling lifted as the clouds swirled over BIA.

Troop greeters arriving by 11 a.m. noticed that a 757 belonging to Air 2000 was parked at the international terminal. Such aircraft passed through BIA all the time, their arrivals and departures hardly noticed by the public.

Everyone would notice today. At 11:17 a.m., the AMT relief crew crossed the skywalk between the Bangor Hilton and the domestic terminal and walked up the ramp. Six minutes later, another Air 2000 757 landed. Heidi Suletzski announced the plane's arrival over the PA system and said that the flight had originated in Manchester, England. At 11:25 a.m., another relief crew exited the Hilton and walked across the domestic terminal to the ramp. Unlike the blue-clad AMT crew, this crew wore white uniforms emblazoned with black designs. At 11:28 a.m., a KC-135 Stratotanker from the Maine Air National Guard landed at BIA. For the last half hour, the sound system set up at the entrance to the ramp had been playing music best described as "generic." A subdued crowd reflected the lifeless songs that emanated from the tape player. Not until "God Bless the USA" rumbled through the speakers at 11:30 a.m. did people stir and start to form a human wire. A disguised AMT L-1011 touched down at 11:35 a.m. Few people in the crowd recognized the jet as AMT property. It sported a bright Irish green tail and a white fuselage with a blue band painted horizontally along the windows.

At 11.37 a.m., a Monarch jet landed at BIA. Suletzski later confirmed this plane's point of departure as Newcastle, England.

With three airliners vying for space at the international terminal, some troop greeters worried about the AMT passengers. Would they be allowed off the plane or kept in security holding? The airport staff wouldn't dare let foreigners into the terminal, but not our boys, would they?

Throughout the troop flights, no American troops were ever confined to security holding. Time and again, the airport staff somehow made room for the troops. As word spread across the domestic terminal that the AMT L-1011 had landed, people arose from their seats and extended the wire past the weather station and almost as far as the Mr. Paperback shop. About a dozen people squeezed past the crowd to stand in the ramp next to the duty-free shop.

Another homecoming for a weary soldier?

Yes.

While three male relatives unfolded a brown kraft banner printed with the phrase, "Welcome home Dan and Audrey and 304 Combat Support Co.," Susan Oliver of Deer Isle said that her sister, Audrey Stone, was aboard the AMT jet. Accompanying Audrey was her husband, Dan.

Chris Kornkven of Oklahoma was called to war with the 304th Combat Support Co.

The Stones belonged to the 304th Combat Support Co., an Army Reserve unit based in Bartlesville, Okla. They were married just before the company left for the Persian Gulf in February 1991. Oliver said that no one in her family had met Dan.

Like the family from Worcester, Mass., that had driven to Bangor on Aug. 1 to meet a relative aboard the diverted troop flight, Oliver and her relatives knew their kin was aboard the L-1011. Audrey had called from Ireland about 4:30 a.m., Oliver said.

Four days earlier, the family from Worcester learned after driving through the night that the fog had sent their relative's flight to Boston.

So close, and yet so far. The weather cooperated with Audrey and Dan Stone, however.

The crowded conditions outside the international terminal forced the AMT L-1011 to park some distance from a boarding gate. The soldiers had to walk across an open ramp to enter the terminal. Fortunately, the rain held off long enough for the Oklahoma-bound troops to exit their aircraft.

This time, the soldiers did not pass through the glass doors adjacent the passenger-service desk. As the Legionnaires and VFW members stood restlessly in the receiving line along the ramp, an airport employee suddenly popped out of the waiting room overlooking Gate 6. Behind him appeared two young soldiers whose eyes widened when they saw the crowd.

"Here they are!" someone shouted. People applauded and cheered as the soldiers descended the ramp.

About 11:50 a.m., Audrey and Dan Stone stepped into the waiting arms of their relatives. The self-conscious teen-agers and children who'd come to BIA with Susan Oliver initially let the adults do all the greeting.

Within five minutes, the Oklahoma soldiers plugged the ramp. In the past, troops often bypassed the welcoming crowd to head for the phones. Today, the tired soldiers stood patiently in line and awaited their turns for hugs and handshakes.

Another KC-135 Stratotanker put down at BIA.

After passing along the wire, Staff Sgt. Chris Kornkven sat down in a lounge chair and watched the civilians greet his comrades. Some civilians spotted him and stopped to chat. Before long, he stood and talked about the Gulf War as experienced by the 304th Combat Support Co.

On Dec. 6, 1990, the approximately 150 members of the 304th reported for active duty at their armory in Bartlesville, a city due north of Tulsa. The company had a detachment in Norman.

The soldiers reported to Fort Sill and remained there until shipping for the Gulf on Feb. 8, 1991. Kornkven spent his Christmas at home. "My wife was up visiting her folks in Wisconsin. We didn't know if we'd have time off or not, so I was in Oklahoma alone, but the rest of the fellows got to visit," he said. In February, the 304th flew from Altus Air Force Base aboard an Air Force C-141 Starlifter, a plane not designed with passenger comfort in mind. Comparing the C-141 to the L-1011 that brought him out of Saudi Arabia, Kornkven said, "It was a luxury flight coming back here. The big difference was just the climate control, and the comfort in just being able to stretch out."

"If you were in certain sections of the 141, it was either freezing cold, or so hot you couldn't stand it," he said.

The C-141 landed at Al Khubar, a town near Dhahran on the Persian Gulf. After staying at Khubar Towers for a week, the 304th went north to an outpost 22 miles north of Hafr al-Batin. The company supported the 18th Airborne Corps and the 7th Corps.

The 304th "is a general support maintenance unit," Kornkven said. "Our ability is to repair just about anything electronic," including generators. Not a transportation company in itself, the 304th saw a heavy equipment detachment from Phoenix, Ariz., added to its ranks. In fact, the Army filled out the company with National Guardsmen and regular soldiers, a practice followed for many other units stationed in Saudi Arabia. "We were up at the front when the ground war started," Kornkven recalled. "Rumor spread around the company that we were so close to the front, that the 101st Airborne had to go over us (when they attacked Iraq)."

Although not based close enough to Iraq to hear artillery fire, the Oklahoma soldiers realized that a war raged nearby. "Some of the guards who were on duty at night said they had seen some flashes off in the distance, and they said that a Scud was blowing up maybe a thousand meters outside our perimeter," Kornkven said.

Before returning to the United States, many members of the 304th traveled to Iraq and Kuwait. Kornkven visited Iraq once, driving 10 miles into the country, and went into Kuwait four times.

"We saw the big sand berm that they had built up along the border (between Saudi Arabia and its neighbors)," he said. "It had a lot of tank traps and everything. Right where we crossed over the berm, there was an outpost or something. Whoever had hit it had really blew the hell out of the whole outpost. It wasn't very sizeable, but still they blew it up pretty good." He described one trip into Kuwait City, when he counted 68 oil fires burning about 10 kilometers away. "Soon after the ground war was over, everyone wanted to go up to Kuwait," he said. "Witnessing a battlefield, that's a once-in-a-lifetime thing. I wish the war protesters could see the destruction that the Iraqis did up there."

He explained that "you couldn't really tell too much on the outside of all the buildings. There were a lot of explosions and fires and everything, and that was obvious, and there was a lot of destruction on the streets.

"You couldn't really tell anything unless you walked around the streets and saw where they (the Iraqis) had gone through and just totally trashed all the stores and stolen everything out of them," the Army Reservist recalled.

"These protesters are saying that it's wrong for American troops to be over there, and then you look at Kuwait City and it's like, well, if that ever happened over here in America, I hope someone would come to our defense," Kornkven said.

During their journeys to Iraq and Kuwait, the Oklahoma soldiers saw other evidence of the war. "Even before you got into Kuwait City, you started seeing destruction all over the place," he said. "Then you got into Kuwait City, and there were trashed vehicles everywhere, and a lot of buildings blown up or burned up or whatever."

Kornkven saw abandoned Iraqi equipment, including "a lot of Russian T-54 tanks, a lot of armored personnel carriers, infantry fighting vehicles, a lot of artillery. We saw five or six Scud missiles."

People living in Kuwait City celebrated their freedom by turning out and lining the streets whenever allied troops passed by. "The Kuwaitis were real happy to see any of the Americans," Kornkven stated.

The GIs tossed food to the Kuwaiti children, even throwing some cases of MREs to them. "Then when we got further into Kuwait City, a lot of the parents came around. We stopped somewhere to look at a Russian tank or something, they (the adult Kuwaitis) would bring their kids up and want to take pictures with us holding their kids," Kornkven recalled. The Kuwaitis "were real generous, giving out sodas to the troops."

Another time in Hafr al-Batin, Kornkven pulled up beside a boy about 2-1/2 years old. "We were going to give him some candy, but a GI must have been there before us, because he just stood there on the side of the street and gave us this cute little salute. "We gave him some bags of M&Ms, and he quickly ran off and hid them, because there were a lot of big kids that were coming toward us," Kornkven said. As Kornkven spoke, the sound system played the national anthem. A male soldier rested the butt of a flagpole against his belt and held the pole with his right hand. A large American flag fluttered from the pole. To the soldier's left stood a smiling woman, an enlisted soldier, who proudly held another American flag high to her left side.

Like soldiers throughout history, the Oklahoma soldiers naturally complained about life in the desert. "Wherever you're putting up with 140-degree heat, and you got nasty chow, filthy latrines, and just poor living conditions compared to what you're used to in the States, you're going to have complaining anyhow," Kornkven said.

Until midsummer, the complaints did not extend that often to the most important issue: going home. "We got over there in February, and a lot of the units had already been there five, six, or seven months. (Those units) were going home, and they (the Army) seemed to stick by their 'first in, first out' policy," Kornkven said.

"We understood that if 'hey, we get out of here in six (or) seven months, that's fine, because our orders say that we could stay here for one year.' A lot of the older, higher-ranking people understood that. It was just a constant exercise to remind the younger people that we'd be going home eventually," he said.

While in Saudi Arabia, the 304th suffered no serious casualties, only "a lot of dislocated shoulders, elbows, no broken bones, nothing real major," Kornkven said. "We're glad to have gotten through this with nothing more serious." By July 4, the Oklahoma soldiers learned that they might be going home sometime in August. They actually flew from Dhahran at 1:40 a.m. Saudi time on Aug. 4. The L-1011 refueled in Sigonella, Sicily, and at Shannon International Airport in Ireland.

Because the plane delayed in leaving Saudi Arabia, its arrival in Oklahoma was pushed back to midafternoon on Aug. 5. According to Kornkven, his wife had already left for Altus Air Force Base before he landed in Bangor. He could not call her and let her know he was on American soil.

By 12:34 p.m., the last members of the 304th left the terminal, with Audrey and Dan Stone lingering to say good-bye to their relatives. Passengers from the Monarch flight had migrated to the terminal during the last hour and occupied every available seat. They watched as the American soldiers departed. One Englishman, perhaps in his late 40s or early 50s, stood and applauded the Yanks. With their relatives in tow, the Stones worked their way up the ramp. Behind them trailed two multi-striped sergeants, apparently sent to roust the "Tail-End Charlies" from the terminal. As a staff sergeant named Vaughn dashed past the gift table, a Red Cross volunteer grabbed him, steered him to the table, and filled his arms with goodies.

By 1 p.m., the Oklahoma soldiers filled the L-1011 and anxiously waited for takeoff. The foreign-flag airliners that had shared space on the tarmac with the AMT jet flew on to their destinations, bringing to an end a busy morning at BIA.

A YEAR GONE

The 551st Transportation Co. finally came home a year after deploying to the Persian Gulf. A year gone...a year away from families and friends...a year in the desert, where the so-called trees resembled roadside bushes back home in Virginia, Minnesota, or Oregon...a year gone.

Sgt. Chris Rakestraw and 231 other passengers flew into BIA on a hot, exceptionally hot Aug. 8. American Trans Air Flight 8990 came into Bangor at 9:30 a.m. while on its way to Langley Air Force Base, Va.

The people waiting to greet the AMT passengers that morning did not know how long the soldiers, Marines, or airmen aboard the L-1011 had been gone. Other units that had deployed to Saudi Arabia in August 1990 had landed in Bangor, particularly during March and April. Most people who visited the airport that hot and sunny Thursday assumed that the men and women aboard the L-1011 had shipped since the fall.

Before the AMT jet landed, Valerie Bellomy and other troop greeters discussed the official flight count. "Since we want to throw a big party for the 200th flight, we don't want to mess up the count," Bellomy pointed out.

"Good," the troop greeters replied. "How many have you counted?" "I'd say 196," Bellomy said. Most people agreed, so that made today's flight the 197th.

Then Tom Dean asked people to gather by the entrance to the ramp. He held aloft two plaques sent to Bangor by Marines who had landed at BIA. In a written commendation that accompanied the plaques, a Maj. C. E. Rodgers, acting commander of the 8th Communications Battalion, referred to Bangor as "the patriotic heartbeat of our great nation." The Bangor City Council accepted the plaques and the commendation at its next meeting.

That morning, troop greeters intermingled with passengers waiting to board a Delta Airlines flight to Washington, D.C. A few passengers inquired about the commotion in the terminal. When told that the AMT L-1011 carried homeward-bound troops, the passengers willingly joined the wire.

"We heard about these flights in Houston," Alan McLaren said. "The TV stations covered them." He and his wife had planned to fly home from Bangor on Aug. 11. He owned McLaren Books, which specialized in locating out-of-print, rare, or used books.

"The plane's got 232 people on it," a troop greeter told McLaren. "Do you want to meet them? You probably won't get another chance."

McLaren asked his wife for their boarding time. "I think we have enough time," he replied. "Where's the best place to stand?" A volunteer positioned McLaren a few feet from the gift table, where he would be in a great position to shake hands and talk with the troops.

Anxious to spend their first minutes on American soil in the past year, the soldiers aboard the L-1011 flooded the ramp. People in the crowd cheered, applauded, laughed, and cried as the soldiers worked the wire.

Among the first civilians to greet the soldiers was McLaren, who smiled broadly and thrust out his right hand as he leaned on his cane with his left hand. He proudly stood at the entrance to the United Airlines gate for 10 to 15 minutes before leaving to catch his own flight.

Sgt. Chris Rakestraw walked among the soldiers who landed at BIA that morning. A tall, blond Tennessean who smiled easily, he reported that he belonged to the 551st Transportation Co. from Fort Eustis, Va.

The 551st arrived in Saudi Arabia on Aug. 11, 1990, Rakestraw said. At the time, he'd been attending a primary leadership development course at Fort Knox, Ky. - not far removed from Rakestraw's hometown of Surgoinsville, Tenn.

The Army let Rakestraw finish the leadership course before shipping him from Langley Air Force Base on Sept. 10, 1990, aboard a C-5B Galaxy. The plane took him into Dhahran the next day.

Rakestraw rejoined his unit three hours later.

The 551st initially unloaded planes at Dhahran, then transferred to Aziz, a port on the Persian Gulf. "Ammo, trucks, tanks, anything that was on the ship, we unloaded it," Rakestraw recalled.

After the war ended, about two-thirds of the soldiers assigned to the 551st went to Kuwait International Airport. They helped to set up facilities for Americans flying home from the Gulf.

Rakestraw and other soldiers remained in Aziz. He made a two-day trip with a fuel tanker to Kuwait International Airport and also went to King Khalid Military City.

The 551st remained on duty as other units shipped home. "Yeah, we noticed all the people leaving," Rakestraw said, "but we had a job to do. Working kept our minds off other people going home." By summer, "we had big duststorms constantly (and) heat of 115 degrees every day," Rakestraw said. "But we had nice accommodations at KKMC and at Aziz. That probably made a difference."

The soldiers noted the passing days as July gave way to August. The Army rumor mill suggested a departure date for the 551st. "Not until we got the final okay that, 'Hey, pack up your gear,' did we really believe that we were going home," Rakestraw said.

He laughed as he described "how serious we got when we started loading our own equipment on ships. We figured that if we got everything stowed away faster, we'd get home faster. I'm not sure that's how it worked out, but, here we are, and I can't tell you how happy we are to be here."

Besides the ecological shock he experienced from boarding the L-1011 in searing heat and windblown desert and deplaning to cooler temperatures and green grass and trees in Maine, Rakestraw encountered a culture shock.

"It's different, it's kind of shocking," he said. "All the people speak your language. You can understand what you're reading. I don't suppose you folks have a McDonald's around here, do you?"

Go out the front door and take a right at the second light, someone told him. "Well, then, I guess we're really home," Rakestraw smiled.

He wanted to get home to Virginia and his wife Teri, their 2-1/2year-old twin daughters, and their 1-year-old son. "His birthday was in July," Rakestraw said. "He was two months old when I left." The joy momentarily dimmed in his eyes. "Oh, man, I missed them bad, real bad," he said. "That's the worst part of it."

As the sound system played the "Star-Spangled Banner," Rakestraw stood at attention and faced the flag. Then Valerie Bellomy issued a boarding call by word-of-mouth. As the soldiers stampeded toward the ramp, Rakestraw shook hands with a troop greeter, thanked him for the welcome, and vanished into the fatigue-clad ranks.

The soldiers and three Air Force hitchhikers exited the terminal along the wire. "Welcome home! Welcome home!" people called. "We're glad you're back!"

A year gone, yet never far from the hearts of their fellow Americans: When they left Bangor about 10:30 a.m., the 232 passengers on AMT Flight 8990 knew they'd landed on American soil.

TOURISTS ON BOTH SIDES OF THE WIRE

Two tourists to Maine arrived via Saudi Arabia in mid-August. On Sunday, Aug. 11, American Trans Air Flight 8994 intended to stop at Langley Air Force Base in Virginia before flying on to DavisMonthan Air Force Base in Tucson, Ariz. Most of the 115 soldiers aboard the L-1011 belonged to the 1404th Transportation Co., Arizona Army National Guard.

Soldiers? Not all were soldiers — not by a long shot.

The day promised sunshine and low humidity as people trickled into the domestic terminal by 9 a.m. Within a half hour, about 120 people gathered to meet the AMT flight. That number included a Gulf War veteran who'd passed through Bangor and returned to Maine to vacation on Mount Desert Island. After hearing a radio announcement about the troop flight, he decided to join the celebration.

Two women from California had also heard a radio announcement as they vacationed near Bangor. "Yes, we watched news reports about this on CNN," they said, "so we had to see it for ourselves." A few troop greeters noticed that several Marines clad in their dress-black uniforms had entered the terminal. Would there be an honor guard for today?

Yes, but not for the troops aboard AMT Flight 8994.

Passengers waiting to board outgoing flights watched the goingson with detached interest. Piero Filipponi, a research mathematician with the Foundation U. Bordoni in Rome, Italy, sat with his wife in the smoking area near America To Go.

Filipponi had been invited to attend a mathematics conference at the University of Maine. The conference, which focused on number theory, had been sponsored by the United States Military Academy at West Point. He had previously visited the United

States twice, again for mathematics conferences. The USMA conference brought him to Maine for the first time, and he had eaten his first lobster.

He stood and watched the excited troop greeters form their imaginary wire across from him. Yes, he'd heard how the Americans greeted their homecoming soldiers, if not in Bangor, at least elsewhere. Filipponi quickly checked the time; if the L-1011 landed at 9:30 a.m. as anticipated, he and his wife might catch a few minutes of an American homecoming before boarding their plane for New York.

"I expect some commotion," Filipponi commented. "I think the people, what is the English word, will be moved."

The Filipponis did have the opportunity to witness how Maine welcomed back the Gulf vets. The L-1011 touched down right on time, taxied to the international terminal, and promptly discharged its tired passengers.

The soldiers swarmed down the ramp and quickly mingled with their greeters. At the first turn on the wire, Spec. Erik Schools, a young soldier from Gray, Maine, encountered his parents, Clifford and Mary Schools. He hollered for pure joy and hugged his parents tight.

Schools, a 1988 graduate of Gray-New Gloucester High School, had gone to Saudi Arabia as a member of the 9th Infantry Division at Fort Lewis, Wash. He'd been attached to the 1404th during the past several months and had flown home with the Arizona Guardsmen.

"The problem is," Schools pointed out, "the 9th Infantry's being deactivated, and I don't know where I'm going next." "Don't worry," his mom blinked back her tears of joy. "You're here right now. That's all that counts." Sgt. Roger Metz of Payson, Ariz., said that the 1404th was activated on Dec. 11, 1990. The guardsmen went to Fort Huachuca to process into the Army, then flew from Tucson on Dec. 31, 1990.

The 1404th landed at Dhahran before moving to the port at Dammam. The company transported supplies and equipment to Log Base Alpha (located near King Khalid Military City) and later went into Kuwait and Iraq to pick up Iraqi prisoners-of-war. The Arizona Guardsmen brought about 3,000 Iraqis to POW camps in Saudi Arabia, Payson said.

The 1404th subsequently returned to Dammam and operated six sterile staging areas for vehicles being shipped to the United States. In their last months in the Gulf, the guardsmen also loaded gear aboard four ships sailing for American ports.

Metz looked forward to returning to his jobs as a carpenter and a reserve deputy sheriff for the Gila County Sheriff's Department. "I can't wait to get home," he said, a big smile on his face. Two Marines wearing knife-creased dress uniforms re-entered the terminal. The honor guard had formed to meet the homeward-bound casket of a young Marine killed in an accident far from Maine.

A problem arose for some passengers aboard the L-1011. A decision made somewhere away from Bangor ordered the plane to bypass Virginia and head straight for Arizona.

The members of the 1404th didn't mind, of course, but the people intending to deplane at Langley sure did.

Several soldiers and a Marine sought assistance at the passenger-service desk, asking if they could book other flights to East Coast destinations.

"Depends on what your government orders permit," responded the BIA staff. Under certain conditions, the Pentagon would authorize travel at government expense. These troops did not qualify, however, and were told that if they did not reboard the L-1011, they'd have to pay their own way home.

"Aw, nuts," the soldiers responded.

In the end, only Marine 1st Lt. Julian Marcus (Mark) Willis from Lusby, Md., and Army Pfc. Gerald Russell of Columbus, Ohio, remained standing by the passenger-service desk. They were coming home on emergency leave, and their orders apparently qualified them to travel at government expense. BIA staffers called the 101st Air Refueling Wing, Maine Air National Guard, and requested that someone look at the travel orders. Driving to the airport on her day off, a woman from the 101st came to the international terminal, checked the appropriate paperwork, and determined that Willis and Russell did indeed qualify for assistance.

She took the former AMT Flight 8994 passengers to the Bangor Air National Guard Base, processed their paperwork, and returned them to the domestic terminal. The two men booked passage on Delta Airlines Flight 663 (Bangor-Boston-Washington, D.C.). Willis would stay on the plane to Washington; Russell would change planes in Boston, fly to Cincinnati, then change planes to fly to Columbus.

Unfortunately, Delta Flight 663 would not depart BIA until 7 p.m. While Willis and Russell sought other transportation, the passengers on AMT Flight 8994 reboarded their aircraft. Bellomy and an Army officer rechecked the domestic terminal about 11 a.m.

Pfc. Gerry Russell made two trips home from the Gulf via Bangor International Airport.

"Nope, nobody out here," they reported to passenger service. "You've got 'em all." Everyone overlooked the first floor - everyone, that is, except for Elaine Gustafson, a Red Cross volunteer.

The AMT passengers had settled into their seats, and the L-1011's hatch had been shut, when Gustafson headed downstairs in the domestic terminal. She spotted a soldier, Bradley McNair of Lexington, Ky., standing near the airline counter with discouragement written on his face.

"I just don't believe it," McNair answered Gustafson's first question. "I can't get a flight with anyone from Bangor to Kentucky today. Can't you get there from here?"

Visitors to Maine have asked that question for years. "Do you know that your plane's all boarded?" came Gustafson's next question.

"No," McNair replied.

"Maybe there's still time to get you aboard," Gustafson said. Turning to a passing troop greeter, she explained the situation. The man grabbed a heavy dufflebag, McNair latched onto his remaining luggage, and both bolted upstairs with Gustafson in pursuit.

As McNair and the man charged the ramp, Gustafson trailed a step behind. "Hold the plane! Hold the plane!" she yelled as the two men huffed and puffed toward the passenger-service desk. "We've got another passenger!"

Consternation lined the faces at the passenger-service desk when McNair and the volunteer thudded the luggage onto the floor. While McNair explained his situation, and his helper regained his breath, Gustafson vanished.

She returned within minutes with news that she'd booked McNair a series of flights from Tucson to Dallas to Lexington. "Just show your ID card or whatever at the airport in Tucson," Gustafson told McNair. "They're holding your tickets there for you."

McNair thanked Gustafson for what was probably the only good news he had heard that sunny Sunday.

Displaying their ability to handle any problems that arose during the troop greetings, the passenger-service employees held the L-1011 until McNair and his luggage reboarded.

"Hey, it's no big deal," a young woman explained. "We do this all the time with foreign tourists who miss their boarding calls."

By the time the AMT L-1011 finally pulled away from its gate, all of the troop greeters except the man who had helped McNair with his luggage had left the airport. The volunteer had decided to await the return of Willis and Russell from the Air Guard base and invite them to spend time with his family until their flights home.

The men accepted, although Russell was cool to the idea until he learned that he could see author Stephen King's impressive Bangor home. He described himself as a devoted King fan who had always wanted to meet the master of horror. "What's he like? Is he as weird in real life as he writes?" the young soldier asked.

Driving past King's turreted West Broadway home, the host fielded the same questions that had been asked about King by hundreds of other tourists and then, after taking his military passengers to meet his children and dine on pizza, drove his guests back to the King mansion.

Russell was in seventh heaven. He photographed the wine-red mansion and touched the bats and spiders welded into the wrought-iron fence separating the Kings' yard from the sidewalk. Even Willis, who acknowledged that he was not a fan of the horror genre, consented to having his photograph taken in front of the landmark. People driving past paid the tourists no mind. Natives were accustomed to people stopping outside Stephen King's house at any hour of the day.

The guided tour of the Bangor area continued and even included the Penobscot Indian Reservation in Old Town. Then the host and his two guests returned home, where Willis and Russell relaxed before heading for BIA to catch Delta Flight 663.

Willis, who called Lusby, Md., his home, was actually returning the second time from the Persian Gulf. In August 1990, he'd gone to Jubail, Sauai Arabia, with the 2nd Landing Support Battalion, 2nd Marine Division. Wearing the red patch that denoted a landing support specialist, Willis spent the next eight months unloading the ships that ferried Marine Corps equipment to the Gulf.

He returned home in spring 1990, but later volunteered to return to Saudi Arabia as a member of the Landing Support Detachment, Combat Service Support Element (CSSE). These Marines loaded outgoing Marine gear onto the ships bringing the equipment home to the United States.

Before he caught AMT Flight 8994 for the States in August, Willis was serving as the port officer in Jubail. He'd done similar work at ports in Bahrain and at Al Mish'ab, a city just a few miles down the Saudi coast from Khafji.

His work often took him from vessel to vessel, since his Marines were the men who loaded and attached the cargo nets that helicopters used for hauling supplies to waiting ships. "I've spent a lot of time on a lot of different ships," he said. "We operated pretty much day and night, especially during the buildup before the war."

He'd assumed that when he returned to Saudi Arabia, he'd probably be there until the last Marine gear sailed for home. But when his mom faced open-heart surgery at a

Washington, D.C., hospital, the Marine Corps granted Willis a 14-day emergency leave and sent him home. Russell had arrived in Saudi Arabia in late June 1991. He'd joined the Army before graduating from high school in Columbus, Ohio, then reported for basic training in September 1990. He later trained as a 63H ("63-Hotel," or tracked-vehicle mechanic) and as a recovery specialist.

On June 1, 1991, Russell reported to Fort Polk, La., for duty with the 539th HEMCO (Heavy Equipment Maintenance Co.). The unit left for the Gulf on June 22, landed at Riyadh, then stayed a few days in Dhahran while en route to King Khalid Military City. Before he left the States, Russell married his sweetheart. The 539th belonged to CEGSWA (Combat Equipment Group, Southwest Asia). "The main mission of CEGSWA was to repair vehicles left from the war to 10-20 standards, so they shoot, move, and communicate," Russell said. The other units comprising CEGSWA were the headquarters company, the 506th HEMCO, and the 304th LEMCO (Light Equipment Maintenance Co.)

Russell's work involved "downloading" outgoing American vehicles, including tanks and Bradley fighting vehicles. Downloading meant removing the BII (basic initial issue), or "everything that needs to be accounted for" (i.e., firearms, binoculars), he said. The Army mechanics then examined the vehicles with a fine-tooth comb before "uploading" them (returning the gear that had been downloaded).

The uploaded vehicles went through further tests and analyses. Then the soldiers towed the vehicles to a large storage yard, where they would remain until being moved to a port for transshipment to the United States or Europe.

Although he arrived in the Gulf some four months after the war, Russell still saw what damage that explosives could do to vehicles. On July 11, an electrical short on a truck laden with howitzer shells apparently started a fire at Camp Doha, an Army base about 12 miles north of Kuwait City.

The fire touched off a massive explosion that shattered vehicles and men. The disaster destroyed more M-1 tanks than were lost during the Gulf War and injured 53 American and six British soldiers.

At the time, the 11th Armored Cavalry Regiment assigned to Fulda, Germany, was based at Camp Doha. The cavalrymen were planning to return to Europe by late September, so their equipment would be sent to CEGSWA for downloading.

After the July 11th explosion, Russell saw 11th Armored Cav Hemmets (large Army trucks) brought to the CEGSWA facility "peeled right down to their frames. It was like you'd stripped off all the truck parts."

Instead of receiving 11th Armored Cav vehicles in mid-July, CEGSAW found itself sending replacement vehicles to Camp Doha. The vehicles were subsequently returned, since the cavalrymen left Kuwait on schedule in September 1991.

At 2 p.m. on Tuesday, July 23, more ammunition accidentally blew up at Camp Doha. Three soldiers who were cleaning the ammunition that had survived the July 11th explosion died in the blast. The 539th HEMCO sent a detachment to Camp Doha on Aug. 12. Russell had been assigned to the detachment, but he came home on emergency leave instead. The clock was ticking toward 6 p.m. when Willis and Russell returned to BIA to check their luggage and wait for their plane. Anxious to get home, they talked a while longer with their host, posed for a few more photographs, and boarded their Boeing 727 about 6:30 p.m.

The two visitors lifted from Maine soil about 7 p.m. They probably would never return, but they'd at least enjoyed a tourist's view of Bangor.

THE 200TH

Driven by a northeast wind, a steady drizzle fell as Sue Bradman of Bangor and another troop greeter entered the BIA domestic terminal at 7 a.m. on Aug. 21.

They'd arrived to meet American Trans Air Flight 8998, scheduled to land at 7:30 a.m. while on its way to Volk Field at Fort McCoy in Wisconsin. A day earlier, AMT representative Mike Stott had estimated the arrival time at 6:15 a.m. He'd guessed well, considering that the L-1011 had not yet left Saudi Arabia when he made the prediction.

The pair circumvented the long walk to the escalator by climbing the north stairs in the terminal. As they made the turn halfway between the terminal walls, they realized that desert fatigues filled the second floor of the terminal. Everywhere that Bradman and her companion looked, soldiers lounged in the chairs, stood talking to civilians, and chug-a-lugged beers. "How did this happen?" Bradman asked. "Was the plane early?" Another troop greeter explained, "It's another flight! They got in a few hours ago!"

That would explain the gray and white C-141B Starlifter parked midway between the international terminal and the KC-135 Stratotankers belonging to the Maine Air National Guard. Other C-141Bs seen at BIA since August 1990 had been painted green camouflage. The military plane was en route to California with seven crew members and 124 passengers aboard, a BIA employee said. Pfc. Kent Senalik set the facts straight. A member of the 4th Infantry Battalion, 21st Infantry Brigade, 7th Infantry Division (Light) in Fort Ord, Calif., Senalik came from Springfield, Ill. He'd joined the Army two years earlier. Although Senalik had been to the Mideast, the patch on his right shoulder didn't belong to any American unit that had passed through Bangor. The patch read: "Multinational Force & Observers." Senalik and his comrades had kept the peace in the Sinai Peninsula, the site of four wars fought between Egypt and Israel. The 7th Infantry troops had shipped to the Mideast in February 1991, passing through McGuire Air Force Base in New Jersey and Torrejon Air Base in Spain before landing at South Camp, a peacekeeper base near Sharm el Sheikh on the southern tip of the Sinai. As part of the United Nations Multinational Peacekeeping Force, the American soldiers patrolled the Sinai Peninsula to monitor the peace treaty between Egypt and Israel. Eleven other nations contributed troops to the peacekeeping force, Senalik said. "We have observation posts throughout the Sinai Peninsula," he said. "We just sit in those observation posts and monitor the area and aircraft flying over. We call it in and report it. If we see any big movements, or the Bedouins, or anything suspicious, we just report it."

Most observation posts housed nine to 12 men, who were armed with M-16s and M-60s, but no larger weapons. Various-sized trucks provided transportation.

The greatest danger facing the peacekeeping troops came from the minefields left over from the Arab-Israeli wars fought in 1948, 1956, 1967, and 1973. The Americans had maps pinpointing known minefields, Senalik said.

"We basically stay away from those (mapped minefields)," he said. "If we find a new one, we report that." His outfit found no hidden minefields. Other peacekeeping troops apparently had.

Life in the desert proved quiet for the Americans. Senalik visited Cairo, Eilat, and Tel Aviv and experienced little if any hostility from the Egyptians and Israelis. The Americans lived in air-conditioned barracks with running water, working toilets, and food that "was better than I expected," Senalik said.

As he spoke, a multistriped sergeant appeared at his right elbow and said, "Final boarding call. Let's go." Senalik thanked the people standing near him for their reception and hurried to board the C-141.

Attention now turned to the incoming AMT flight.

For a few moments, confusion reigned as to whether or not the AMT L-1011 would be the 200th troop flight to land in Bangor. People compared notes and consulted the chart at passenger service. Yep, everyone finally agreed, this is No. 200.

About 60 people hustled to form a rudimentary wire or help spread a few decorations around the terminal. A woman supplied a computer-generated banner that read "Welcome Home Troops - 200th Flight." She hung the banner at the bottom of the ramp.

"Music? Where's the music?" someone asked.

Since Valerie Bellomy had started working at Dysart's Restaurant in Hermon, music had proved hit or miss for the troop flights. Later that day, she expressed her regret at missing the two flights. "I was so tired when I got home, I went to bed at 3 a.m.," she said.

American Trans Air Flight 8998, an L-1011, taxis toward a BIA ramp on Aug. 21, 1991. This was the 200th troop flight to pass through Bangor.

For her unflagging dedication to the troops, Bellomy deserved to sleep as long as she wished. Unfortunately, no one took up the music slack.

The soldiers aboard the AMT jet never noticed.

The L-1011 flared out and greased its wheels on the BIA runway at 7:35 a.m., just five minutes late after a long flight from the Gulf. The follow-me truck buzzed to the taxiway and guided the airliner to the international terminal in a driving rain.

As the L-1011 rounded the turn from the taxiway to the ramp, a tug hurriedly backed a departing United Airlines 737 out of the way. The L-1011 taxied between the 737 and the domestic terminal and halted at a gate.

By 7:45 a.m., perhaps 60 to 70 people awaited the 132 soldiers aboard the L-1011. The civilians figured they'd have ample warning before the soldiers reached the upper ramp.

On this morning filled with surprises, guess what?

A young soldier coalesced on the ramp beside the security-screening area. He absorbed the few cheers that announced his arrival, then yelled, "Here I am!"

The cheers straggled for several moments until the troop greeters realized that the soldiers had truly appeared in the terminal. Desert camouflage blended quickly with T-shirts, sweatshirts, and rain gear. Voices exchanged greetings as civilians shouted, "Welcome home!," and soldiers responded, "It's great to be here."

The arriving soldiers packed the wire by 7:50 a.m. One tall young man, his hair cropped into a flat top, wore sunglasses and carried a large metal case. Behind him walked two young women soldiers, one of whom cried as she hugged the grandmothers in the crowd.

A fairly young soldier left the receiving line and headed for the Red Baron Lounge. "The bar's open!" another soldier called while pointing toward the lounge. A friend followed his pointing finger and exclaimed, "Yes!" The two soldiers immediately decamped for the lounge and some cold beers. Along the wire, a rugged linebacker disguised as a soldier placed his arms around a young blonde in the crowd, tightly hugged her, and lifted her off her feet. Her cheeks flushed as the jubilant soldier squeezed her as hard as he could. People standing nearby cheered and shouted their approval. The shoulder patches worn by the incoming soldiers indicated at least four different units. Surprisingly, only a few women wore the Army uniform this morning. One of them was Sgt. Pamela Lessner, who belonged to the 822nd Military Police Co. This Army Reserve company was based in Rosemont, Ill., a Chicago suburb near O'Hare International Airport.

Lessner, a brunette with a pleasant smile, said that the members of the 822nd were activated on Jan. 3, 1991. They left Volk Field in mid-February and arrived at King Fahd International Airport near Dhahran, Saudi Arabia, on Feb. 15.

As she stepped off the airliner, Lessner noticed the first major difference between the Midwest and Saudi Arabia. The troops had left Wisconsin with the temperature at minus 40 degrees Fahrenheit; they deplaned in the Saudi desert to a temperature of 78 degrees Fahrenheit.

After landing in Saudi Arabia, the 822nd went to the already infamous (Al) Khubar Towers and acclimated to the environment for two weeks. The company arrived at a prisoner-of-war camp in late February. This facility, called East Camp (Louis Cortez's "Bronx) as opposed to West Camp ("Brooklyn") near King Khalid Military City, was located near Al Sarrar.

Lessner said that the Iraqi prisoners-of-war proved cooperative. "There were the choice few that would bother their guards, but basically they were real nice people," she recalled.

Encountering women soldiers among their guards shocked the captured Iraqis. "They were really surprised to see the females working, carrying weapons and stuff. A lot of people were real nice to us, and other people, like with any religion, were a little more skeptical than others," Lessner said.

Saudi men reacted in similar fashion to the women soldiers. "They kind of looked at you," Lessner stated, "but I think after a couple of months, they got used to us being there."

While traveling along the Kuwait border, she encountered the environmental damage caused by the burning oil wells. "You come back, and you've got oil all over your vehicle, yourself, your uniform," Lessner said, describing the soot that fell from the sky.

During their last five months overseas, the military police performed customs inspections.

"In customs, basically what we do is we take care of everybody's baggage and make sure they're not taking home anything they're not supposed to," Lessner said.

"You can't take anything agricultural home," Lessner pointed out. "You've got to be constantly aware of what people are taking home so it doesn't affect our agriculture over here. Of course, you want the planes to be safe, so nobody's carrying any weapons or ammunition."

United States Customs sent agents to train the military police in correct inspection procedures and to serve as advisers. The 822nd did customs inspections for troops departing Saudi Arabia from King Khalid Military City and Dhahran.

Although the military police checked soldiers moving in-country, "our real main concern was people going out, back to the States or Germany," Lessner said.

Soldiers could not carry fruits, vegetables, sand, soil, ammunition, or loaded weapons aboard their aircraft. The outgoing soldiers cooperated, especially after "the incident where the bomb went off, where someone tried to take a (cluster) bomb on a plane. It went off, and I'm not sure, but it killed one (soldier) and injured a couple," Lessner recalled. "After that on the news, no one basically bothered" trying to smuggle cluster bombs again.

The 822nd initially learned that it would be coming home June 5. "Then they said July, and they kept going because they needed customs and MPs," Lessner said.

Final notification came Aug. 19. "We were told at six o'clock at night, and we were ready for the next morning," she said. Takeoff came none too soon for the Illinois soldiers, who hadn't seen green grass in months, and no rain since March.

They discovered both in Bangor. Even as Lessner talked about her work as a police officer for the Will County (Illinois) Sheriff's Department, a heavy downpour splattered against the terminal windows. A soldier raised his arms to form a V and cried, "Let it rain!"

Capt. Jeff Sacks, the commander of the 822nd, worked as a police officer for the Chicago Police Department in civilian life. "I'm a patrolman, and it's a real change to be in management," he grinned.

Sacks talked about guarding the Iraqi prisoners-of-war at East Camp, "which was a desert location, totally a tent city.

"The camps themselves were big berms of sand which the engineers bulldozed around the camp. They held up to 12,000 prisoners each," he said. Concertina wire surrounded the camps. "The food kept them happy. They were happy to be alive. I think anybody coming out of a war is happy to be alive," Sacks observed. Despite the Moslem beliefs against eating pork, the Iraqis "were happy to have whatever we gave them at the time. We gave them MREs with pork, and German field rations that had pork pies," he said. As the Americans organized the supplies flowing to the prisoner-of-war camps, the Iraqis received more chicken and rice. The Iraqis cooked for themselves and provided "meals that were more in keeping with their religion," Sacks said.

The Americans maintained the daily meal schedule during the holy month of Ramadan, when devout Moslems fast from dawn to dusk.

"They weren't as religious as you think, not the Iraqis anyway," Sacks commented. "The Saudis working on our side are very religious. It's just like any other religion. I think you're going to find a certain percentage of the people who keep the faith, and the other people were really just born into it."

The 822nd transferred from Al Sarrar to KKMC in late March. Besides working with Customs agents, the military police dealt with an adviser from the United States Agriculture Department. The soldiers learned about Customs through classwork "and a lot of OJT," Sacks stated. "We moved 50,000 people from KKMC back home by working around the clock, seven days a week."

Agricultural inspections even extended to the meals sold to the airlines for consumption en route to Europe. There was great concern about exporting a plant disease or insect pest to the United States, Sacks pointed out, and the military police wanted to know where all the prepared airliner meals originated.

Keeping munitions off the outbound airliners meant checking each soldier's baggage. The 822nd set up "amnesty boxes" where the soldiers passed through customs. Departing troops could leave explosives and weapons in these boxes without recrimination. To keep the abandoned munitions from causing much damage if they detonated, the military police heavily sandbagged the amnesty boxes.

Sacks said "we caught a guy with three guns in his waistband one time. The embarrassed soldier left the weapons in Saudi Arabia and received some discipline from his company commander."

For a time, cluster bombs remained a favorite souvenir for inexperienced soldiers who could not tell a CB from a golf ball. "There were some bad stories about that happening in the beginning of the redeployment," Sacks said. "That got around to the troops quickly, and they knew we were looking for that, and that the repercussions would be serious."

The tight customs inspections "caught just about everything" that soldiers tried to smuggle from Saudi Arabia, Sacks said. Unfortunately, some weapons probably did get through in such a largescale operation, he admitted.

Outgoing soldiers could bring back "anything that I can buy in a military surplus store," Sacks said. These items included bayonets, clothing, and other non-lethal items.

After a soldier leaned over the captain's shoulder and said, "Excuse me, sir, the second boarding call's been called," Sacks spoke a few minutes longer. He mentioned that the 822nd had been converted to a military police (guard) company. The company's ranks were augmented with military police from the regular Army and the National Guard.

Sacks described the reception in Bangor as "great. We didn't expect people to even remember us. When we came off and saw these folks from this area here, I couldn't believe it. It was just real nice.

"I was really impressed with the folks who came out and met us," he said. "I was just surprised that anyone remembered we were still coming home, it's been so long now. We just expected to see Customs folks here, and that was it."

Sacks left to chase his remaining troops from the terminal. Pamela Lessner walked into the ramp carrying a teddy bear and eating a cookie. The soldier who had entered the terminal with a large metal case in hand departed with his fatigue hat redesigned into a kepi.

Capt. Sacks finally flushed a few stragglers from the terminal. He waved to the crowd as he entered the ramp and encouraged the soldiers to get home. The 200th troop flight into Bangor International Airport passed into history.

THE BOYS ARE BACK IN TOWN

The troops came back the last full weekend in August 1991.

Since early summer, Scottie Bell, Sharon Albert, and other people from the Greater Bangor Chamber of Commerce had been planning "Operation Thank You," a daylong party intended to honor the people who had welcomed the troops home. After playing with various dates, Bell targeted Sunday, Aug. 25.

Many people volunteered their time during July and August to make sure Operation Thank You went well. Official invitations went to the politicos, of course, including President Bush. He demurred, but his sister did attend.

Many other invitations hit the mail and the phone lines, too, but these went to the troops who'd come home through BIA. Most people did not care if the president stopped by Bangor on Aug. 25, but if the boys weren't back in town, well, a celebration wouldn't be right.

By late August, the plans for Operation Thank You hit high gear. Volunteers hauled banners, photographs, uniforms, newspaper and magazine clippings, and other memorabilia to the grandstand at Bass Park, where several people, including Albert, Paul Tower, George Nye, Carol Eremita, and Ed Maxsimic, spent more than two days creating a museum.

Other people coordinated the "official" troop movements into Bangor. Lt. Gen. John Yeosock planned to attend, as did Lt. Gen. Charles Horner, who'd commanded Air

Force operations during the Gulf War. The generals would bring some support personnel with them. They all would need ground transportation to and from the airport.

Ditto the musicians provided for Operation Thank You. Oh, the local bands - John Bapst Memorial High School, Desperado, Sound Dimensions, and that impromptu airport duo, Rick Aiken and Bill Trowell, could get themselves to Bass Park. Not so the military musicians, including the 77th Army Band from Fort Sill, Okla., Sgt. Butler Hodges from the Alabama Army National Guard, and possibly that Airborne saxophone virtuoso, Sgt. Kevin Tillman. They would require transportation, too, during their stay in Bangor.

Tillman had returned to Bangor twice since his March 8th performance at BIA. In April, he'd performed with the John Bapst band during its spring concert. Then he flew into BIA late on July 3, donned his dress greens the next day, and participated in the Bangor-Brewer July Fourth festivities as the parade marshal.

When the parade ended, Tillman mounted the reviewing stand set up in downtown Bangor, unlimbered his saxophone, and repeated his moving performance of the national anthem.

Many people had anticipated Tillman's third return to Bangor for Operation Thank You, but just days before he was supposed to catch a flight north, his outfit went on alert status. Though he could have sought official permission for a few days' leave, Tillman decided to remain with his comrades. Disappointed Bangor-area residents cheered his decision, of course — duty's duty, after all.

From Maine to California, Florida, and points in between, people made plans to return to Bangor for Operation Thank You. As the weekend approached, the troop movement through BIA gradually shifted direction. By Friday, Aug. 23, the desert fatigues moved through the airport from south and west to north, not from east to west.

According to the local newscasts that night, the boys were back in town. And not only the out-of-state boys: Sometime Sunday morning, the boys and girls from the 112th Medical Co. (Air Ambulance), Maine Army National Guard, would return to Bangor, the hometown they'd left months earlier for duty in Europe or the Gulf.

That Saturday, Tom Dean hosted some troop greeters and Major Carl Andrews, a Marine officer who'd come through BIA as the acting CO of the 8th Communications Battalion, 2nd Marine Division. Dean, who actually lived near author Stephen King in Bangor, invited many people to his camp on Phillips Lake in Dedham.

Helen Schact threw a big party that night at her home in Hampden. Elizabeth Smentkowski and Francine Gerardi flew into Bangor from California just for Helen's party and Operation Thank You. Introduced to the assembled troop greeters by Valerie Bellomy, Smentkowski and Gerardi met many people who'd always wanted to thank some flight attendants for bringing the troops home safely from the Gulf.

Among the people attending Schact's bash that night was Tech Sgt. Russell Chamberlain, an Air Force Reservist from Eglin Air Force Base in Florida. He'd passed through BIA on March 17, when he'd met Galen and Karen Cousins from Orland.

From Ridgefield, N.J., Chamberlain now lived in Crestview, Fla. He worked as a communications-navigation technician for the Air Force civil service during the week and was a member of the Air Force Reserve.

"I'm with the 919th Special Operations Group, and we fly the AC-130 gunship," Chamberlain said. "We're based at Duke Field, which is part of Eglin Air Force Base."

As the Gulf Crisis passed into January, the reservists suspected they'd be leaving soon for the Saudi sands. "We'd heard rumors for quite a while; we were expecting to be called up," the tech sergeant recalled.

The Pentagon activated the 919th "the day the air war started," Chamberlain commented. Two weeks later, "we went over on C-141 cargo cargo planes."

He landed in Saudi Arabia about Feb. 2nd at an undisclosed base. The 919th Special Operations Group began flying missions soon after arriving in the Gulf, particularly missions providing fire support for Allied ground troops.

The AC-130s flew their missions all at night. "The C-130 flies kind of slow. They normally fly at between nine and 10,000 feet when they're on their missions, so you're fairly low to the ground, also," Chamberlain said.

The gunships flew missions only against land-based targets. "Everything we did was inside Kuwait, or once they started pulling out, on the road back to Basra, we hit targets along that main highway," Chamberlain said. Of course, all was not work in the Gulf. The troops listened to the radio when they could, a difficult feat for a generation weaned on MTV and game shows. Music proved an important staple in the military diet, Chamberlain said, with "the No. 1 song (which) was Bette Midler, `From a Distance.' And No. 2 was the record that's playing right now, (Lee Greenwood with `God Bless the USA).'" The Armed Forces Radio Network had an FM station running out of Dhahran. "That was mostly rock 'n roll for the younger troops," he said.

The 919th Special Operations Group returned from the war with no casualties, although air crews did encounter some antiaircraft fire. The reservists learned on March 15 that they would leave the Gulf in a day. On March 16, Chamberlain was headed home aboard a World Airways flight, a DC-10 (WOA Flight 7411).

The DC-10 refueled in Rome, then put into Shannon Airport in Ireland just in time for St. Patrick's Day. "We were on the ground there for a couple of hours. When we got there it was just after midnight, the start of St. Patrick's Day, so that was a pretty wild place...a lot of beer, and just everybody glad to see us. There were a lot of signs up," as well as "a band there to meet us, playing Irish music."

The DC-10 soon left Ireland for the States, landing at BIA about 2:30 a.m. "When we got off the plane, they were coming down the sky ramp, whatever you want to call it, and there was a bunch of Army guys coming out to get on a Hawaiian Airlines flight (7852) leaving," he said, "and all they kept saying was, `You won't believe what is going to happen to you when you walk through those doors.' They were right, because I would never have dreamed of such a thing."

He could not imagine what the soldiers meant. "We figured it was good, but we never dreamed there'd be that many people in the middle of the night," Chamberlain explained.

"I was pretty far back. There were about 300 of us on the plane," he recalled. "We could hear noise, but still, you couldn't tell what was going on, other than you could tell they were cheering.

"It was a very emotional experience. I don't think there are too many people with a dry eye. They had the American Legion there, and they were lined up shaking everybody's hand before you got into the main part (of the terminal)," Chamberlain said. "The place was packed. We were told they'd turned people away," the tech sergeant remembered.

"Every woman had to give you a hug and a kiss, and I must have signed I don't know how many hundreds of T-shirts," Chamberlain commented. He did give away some souvenirs, including "some Saudi Arabian money, little things like that. "We just didn't believe the amount of people, and how glad they were to see us," he said. WOA Flight 7852 touched down at Eglin at 6 a.m. About 10 people turned out to meet the plane, Chamberlain said. "The weather was lousy," so the DC-10 put into Eglin while "all the families were out at Duke...So, there was a whole bunch of generals and colonels...They had the honor guard out, and they put us on buses and bussed us back to where the families were. It was somewhat of a letdown after what we went through in Bangor, but, that's just the way that things happen."

The 919th Special Operations Group did not return immediately to civilian status. "I got out April 5. The first week they gave us off just to recuperate. I was like a walking zombie for the first three days I was home," Chamberlain said. "Then we came back and processed our paperwork."

Chamberlain had not planned to return to Bangor, but "just over two weeks ago, one of the guys I work with got an invitation in the mail. He'd written a letter to the newspaper to thank everybody, and I guess the paper or the Chamber of Commerce kept a list people who had written, and they sent invitations out.

"But he's TDY'ed (gone on temporary duty) to Texas, so he could not come, and he brought it into work and showed it to me. I went to our commander. Originally, we were going to bring an aircraft up here with at least a dozen, two dozen people, but we had a change in some commitments, and we had to send the aircraft somewhere else this weekend," Chamberlain said.

But the commander still wanted someone to represent the 919th at Operation Thank You, so Chamberlain flew to BIA via "three different airlines that are all connected to Delta."

He'd anticipated that the Cousins would meet him, since "they're the people I'm staying with here. But they made a couple of phone calls, and there was like 25 people there. It was something else. It was really amazing."

Before they arrived at Helen Schacht's party that night, the Cousins took their Air Force guests to Acadia National Park and stopped at Fort Knox State Park. "They had a Civil War re-enactment there... I'm interested in that. My interest is military history," Chamberlain said.

He planned to attend Operation Thank You as an official representative of the 919th Special Operations Group. Little did he know that Saturday night, however, that within 12 hours, he'd be meeting another troop flight, the one bringing the Maine men and women back to town.

About 9:30 p.m., someone slid another tape into the player mounted on the Schachts' deck. As the haunting, mournful notes from "Taps" echoed across the backyard, adults respectfully and quietly stood to attention. The children kept playing. They knew not this sad music, a trumpet solo written to honor America's war dead.

A deathly silence fell over the Hampden neighborhood. Afterwards, the national anthem blared from the tape player. This time, people sang along, then cheered when the music finished.

At 7:10 a.m. on Sunday, Aug. 25, a C-141 carrying 96 members of the 112th Medical Co. (Air Ambulance), Maine Army National Guard, approached the BIA runway and flared to a safe landing beneath a sunlit sky. Word had not reached all guard families that a mechanical failure had disrupted the original flight schedule. Plans had called for two C-5 Galaxys to ferry the Army aviators and their personal gear home, with the planes landing maybe an hour or two apart Sunday morning. A C-5 broke down, however, so the Maine Guardsmen transferred to a C141 Starlifter at Rhine-Main Air Base in Germany and beat their gear home to Bangor.

For a Sunday flight, the domestic terminal seemed alarmingly empty. Passenger service soon explained that family members waiting for people on the C-141 had already moved into the security-holding area. The 200 civilians stuffed into the under-sized room mobbed their soldiers.

Still clad in jungle fatigues, Sgt. Wendell Stadig hugged Linda, his wife. A helicopter mechanic with the 112th, Stadig said that he had been gone nine months. He felt "great" to be home.

Staff Sgt. Gordon Burnham noted "that we were supposed to leave Rhine-Main on two C-5s, but one of them apparently experienced mechanical problems, and the decision was made that we'd all come on the C-141 that was substituted, and all our gear would be coming on the C-5 later."

Burnham's wife, Patricia, never strayed from his side as he conversed with the press.

One guardsman, Capt. David Smith of Hampden, had returned home a second time to his wife, Julie, and their 9-month old son, David II. According to Smith's sister, Debbie Sleight, the captain had shipped to the United States in June to attend an Army school in Alabama. He "was back here just a couple of days, and then he had to go to Alabama," Sleight said.

Smith had left with the 112th when his son was two weeks old. "It was extremely hard on the whole family," Sleight said. The knowledge that he would serve in Germany and not Saudi Arabia really did not ease the pain, she admitted.

Another aviator, Chief Warrant Officer Second Class Cheryl Burr-Clark of Bangor, sat next to her husband, Richard, and cradled their two daughters in her arms. Chelsea snuggled as close as possible beneath her mother's right arm, while Courtney leaned against Cheryl's left side. She closed her eyes and sighed deeply when mom kissed her forehead.

Returning from duty in Europe during the Gulf War, CW2 Cheryl Burr-Clark of the Maine Army National Guard hugs her daughters, Chelsea (left) and Courtney.

As the guardsmen and their families mingled inside the security holding area, more people gathered to meet them in the domestic terminal. Under the direction of Stan Buchanan, the 195th Army Band of the Maine Army National Guard opened their folding metal chairs and set up beside the windows. They entertained the more than 500 people awaiting the returning aviators.

Dignitaries quietly graced that morning's reception, too. Representing the governor, Maine Adjutant General Nelson Durgin watched as the aviators mingled with their families. Somewhere in the terminal, Karen Cousins collared Sen. William Cohen and introduced him to Tech. Sgt. Russell Chamberlain.

About 8 a.m., guard families started filtering from the security-holding area. Someone had laid down a good breakfast spread in a room adjacent to the holding area. Hungry after their workshiftlength flight from Germany, the soldiers devoured the finger sandwiches and other treats.

Once they'd been debriefed, the aviators left the holding area. Some immediately departed the terminal with their families. Others, perhaps half their number, received their own American greeting by descending the ramp and working the hands along the wire.

As the Red Cross volunteers handed out myriad Ursus Berries bears, a patriotic canine appeared at the crowd's edge and woofed in rhythm to the music from the 195th Army Band. Every time a guardsman took the corner by the duty-free shop, the crowd applauded.

And so went the final BIA homecoming for Maine Army Guardsmen. The 195th played a stirring national anthem - which people applauded - and everyone finally went home.

Russell Chamberlain had watched the homecoming with great interest. "We got a call about 5:20," he said. He and the Cousins arrived about 6:10 a.m.

Among the military dignitaries attending Operation Thank You in Bangor on Aug. 25, 1991, were Army Lt. Gen. John J. Yeosock (left) and Air Force Lt. Gen. Charles Horner.

"Things like this have been going for months now, to get a phone call in the middle of the night, and they throw some clothes on and rush down here to greet everybody coming back," Chamberlain said. "I pinned some 'welcome home' pins on (the troops) and explained how I had come through here in March.

"It was just great to see everybody coming back. I think it was almost as emotional as when I went through myself, knowing what everybody went through," he said.

Many people who met the Maine Guardsmen that morning soon drifted southward to Bass Park, where the parking lots started filling by 11 a.m. On a day when the Chamber had hoped for 10,000 visitors, only 1,500 to 1,800 people actually caught the festivities for Operation Thank You.

They weren't disappointed, however.

Spec. Tim Simpson and Spec. Christopher Brandon had come to Bangor from Fort Sill, Okla. "The Chamber of Commerce asked us to come up here for Operation Thank You," Brandon said. "We're from the same post (as the 77th Army Band), but we were just soldiers who went over to Saudi and came back through Bangor. "We are really enjoying all the hospitality that Bangor and the Chamber of Commerce have put forth," he said.

Their troop flight had landed in Bangor on May 16. "We couldn't believe the reception that we got. It was great; it was perfect," he recalled.

Operation Thank You went well. The honor guard from American Legion Post 84 presented the colors. Then the John Bapst band and chorus performed the national anthem and other patriotic music.

Slightly surprising some people in the crowd, Bangor Mayor Richard Stone introduced the president's sister, Nancy Bush Ellis, a delightful woman who passed on the president's thanks "for their spirit, which has helped transform the spirit of this, our beloved country." She later endured some gentle politicking as Maine residents sought her autograph and photo.

Perhaps the two people who the troop greeters really wanted to see on this perfect summer afternoon were the guest speakers, Gens. Yeosock and Horner. Everybody who had been at BIA on May 12, the "Day of the Generals," enjoyed a special affinity for Lt. Gen. Yeosock. Of course, everyone who'd watched the bomb strikes as shown on national TV during the Gulf War knew what the Air Force had accomplished. If Lt. Gen. Horner had commanded the Air Force effort over there, well, then, he was welcome in Bangor any time.

Brig. Gen. Nicholas Eremita of the Maine Air National Guard introduced the generals, "who are the lightning and the thunder of Desert Storm."

Yeosock stood, spoke briefly to Eremita, and stepped to the lectern. He'd come strictly informal to Bangor this day, desert fatigues and combat boots and all, and the crowd loved him for his casual attitude.

"I'm most appreciative of having this opportunity to again return to Bangor," the general said, rekindling the special relationship he would always enjoy with Bangor.

"Earlier during the month of August (1990), as Gen. Chuck Horner and I sat in Saudi Arabia," Yeosock harkened to those dark days just 12 months ago, "I knew that we could probably draw on whatever military strength we would need to (do the job)...

"What I was concerned about is, would the United States lose interest in what it was we were about to do?" Yeosock told the crowd. "Very quickly, there began a groundswell of support, coming in from every corner of this great nation of ours." He described the mail, cookies, "and whatever else it might be, but nonetheless, it was still rather difficult to completely, totally, and entirely understand or comprehend exactly what was going on here in the United States.

"But, I'll tell you folks, when I returned to the United States on Mother's Day of this year, here in Bangor," Yeosock said, "there was no doubt in my mind that you folks manifested the totality of what it was that this great nation of ours came to believe, feel, understand, and do.

"I must admit, folks, there are few things that will bring a tear to my eye, but, by golly, that day you brought tears to mine," he admitted. "I'm extremely grateful to you folks."

The general acknowledged the applause and whistles from his fans, "and for the tens of thousands of those who were greeted here back on American soil, as their first return to the United States," he said. The crowd went wild.

Clad in his green flight suit with its attached pilot's wings, a smiling Chuck Horner patiently waited while Eremita read his resume to the crowd. A fighter pilot by trade, Horner had not returned from the Gulf via BIA. He had apparently heard about the homecomings, however.

Horner described the Gulf War as "a great victory. It was a victory we can attribute to several factors, the first being the youth of America. They're absolutely selfless...they're dedicated to this nation. They're good, loyal people, hard-working...they are the single greatest tribute to our nation that exists today."

He then praised the leadership of President Bush and the technological superiority of American industry.

"What we didn't realize was what was going on back here. We were like Martians; we were in another world, doing our thing...and when we came back, the reception at Bangor, Maine..." was shown to him on a videotape provided by an airman who'd come through BIA in March.

"I cried," Horner said. "It was 1:33 in the morning on March 15, and your airport was crowded with the most enthusiastic, wonderful, loving people I have ever seen in my entire life. God bless you for that."

His remarks drew warm applause from the crowd.

For the next few minutes, Horner revealed his private life, mentioning the "welcome home" sign that his family had erected in their front yard and reminiscing about participating in various parades in the United States. A dedicated pilot who said that he flew and not marched to war, Horner recalled that at some moment during all those parades, "What happened is that I became a spectator, and I looked at millions and millions and millions of Americans from all walks of life and every color, creed, every economic (and) social level, whatever.

"And you know what we saw?" the general asked the troop greeters. "We saw people cheering the troops, and we should.

"And we saw people cheering the United States of America...most of all, they were cheering themselves," he said, "and that's exactly whom we should be cheering, because America did something..".

The crowd went nuts, again.

Later that afternoon, the generals directed the John Bapst band in a fast-paced version of "The Horse," that familiar gridiron number. Surprised by the request, Yeosock and Horner took up their batons and guided the Bapst musicians through the music. When the impromptu impresarios finished, they gratefully waved to the cheering musicians and audience before plunging into another song. Then the band presented their generals with John Bapst baseball caps.

Music concluded Operation Thank You. Sgt. Butler Hodges, a member of the Alabama National Guard, performed his recently released country hit, "Thank You, America." Maine residents respectfully listened as Hodges sang. When he mentioned "the reception up in Bangor, Maine," the troop greeters wildly applauded. The cassette tapes that the sergeant had brought with him that afternoon all but sold out.

The 77th Army Band, a highly polished and enthusiastic company from Fort Sill, lifted the crowd to its feet with an excellent performance that ended about 4:30 p.m. Operation Thank You ended shortly afterwards, as civilians headed home to fix supper, and soldiers gradually returned to their motels. The troops who were back in town that weekend came from several bases, including Shaw in South Carolina; Lejeune in North Carolina; Sill in Oklahoma; Florida's Eglin, of course; McPherson and Gordon, army posts in Georgia; Hill in Utah; the Greater Wilmington Airport in Delaware (the Hitchhiker's home port); San Antonio; and even the Pentagon. For three short days, the men and women were back; hopefully, they'd never have to return to the Gulf and receive a second homecoming at BIA.

ANOTHER SCHWARTZ

In the movie "Spaceballs," the science-fiction spoof produced by Mel Brooks, the good guys warped a familiar "Star Wars" phrase into "may the schwartz be with you."

The Schwartz was with the military police who landed in Bangor on Sept. 3.

Under a satin blue sky and a warm sun, American Trans Air Flight 1009 touched down at Bangor International Airport at 11:08 a.m. and some-odd seconds by Michael Stott's watch. "Seven minutes early," he noted while waiting for the AMT relief crew to appear on the ramp. Moments later, the blue-uniformed AMT crew advanced into the international terminal with their baggage in tow.

Out on the taxiway, the AMT L-1011 rolled to a stop at Gate 4, a location not conducive to taxiing past the domestic terminal. People waiting for the plane to appear diverted their attention to Tom Dean as he unveiled a congratulatory plaque from the 414th Civil Affairs Co., an Army Reserve outfit in New York. When the first soldiers suddenly appeared on the ramp, many people among the 75 civilians in the crowd did not realize that the L-1011 had landed.

Yet everyone knew that the airliner carried 157 soldiers on their way to Louisville, Ky.

Almost like old times, Gary Leighton donned his official blue BIA sports jacket and joined the troop greeters awaiting the AMT flight. "It's good to be out here and see such a crowd," he said as Valerie Bellomy and her daughters fired up the patriotic music.

At 11:17 a.m. - just nine minutes since their plane had landed the first soldiers swarmed down the ramp to shake hands with the Legionnaires and VFWers. With George Nye and an American flag leading the way, a Capt. Scully passed the gift table and entered the domestic terminal.

The crowd, mainly women with a smatter-ing of men, went absolutely bonkers. Hands reached out to touch Scully, who grinned and chatted with his fans as he worked his way along the wire.

Some soldiers sported broad tan armbands emblazoned with "89th MP Bgde." Since law-enforcement types remained popular with this crowd, more than one burly Army cop found himself warmly hugged by an older woman two-thirds or half his size. The women soldiers received gentler hugs, of course. As the soldiers worked their way toward America To Go, a Master Sgt. Henry stood videotaping the recep-tion. Beside him stood a girl seeking every sol-dier's autograph. Soldiers clustered about the girl while waiting their turn at her indelible marker.

Within minutes, Master Sgt. Peter Schwartz found himself standing beside the ter-minal windows as he answered questions from troop greeters. A 22-1/2-year veteran of the

Called up with his Army Guard outfit, Master Sgt. Peter Schwartz of Detroit, Mich., left behind a civilian job as a police officer.

Detroit Police Department, Schwartz had been activated in late November. He belonged to the 210th Military Police Battalion, Headquarters and Headquarters Detachment, of the Michigan Army National Guard. Also aboard AMT Flight 1009 were soldiers from the 438th Military Police Co., an Army Guard unit from Louisville, Ky.

The 210th was based in Detroit, a city that had recently surrendered the doubtful honor as the nation's murder capital. Schwartz had kept touch with the Motor City's crime problem while in Saudi Arabia, a place that even during wartime sometimes appeared safer than home.

"Yeah, I was safer over there, you know," Schwartz chuckled. "I'm coming back, and now I'm going to be going back into a more hostile environment, and they don't give combat pay. I don't understand it. "When I left, I was a member of the traffic-enforce-ment unit, motorcycle,," Schwartz said, "and presently they closed the unit because of budget cuts. I don't know what I'm going to do when I go back."

Schwartz, a section leader with the 210th, said that the remaining members of the battalion reported for active duty in early December 1990. The Michigan Guardsmen traveled to Fort Knox, Ky., for introduction to Army life. They arrived in Saudi Arabia on Jan. 8.

The 210th "was responsible (for the security) for the entire Dammam area," including the port at Dammam, the airfield at Dhahran, and the military supply routes (MSRs) leading out of the area, Schwartz said.

"In the rear area, which we were, the MPs are the only ones that have the capability to respond to any type of emergency," he stated. "In other words, we fight the rear battle. There is nobody else."

Despite the potential threat from terrorists and the Iraqi military, "I think our own worst enemies were the way our people drove," Schwartz said.

"Ooh, you ought to see the way those Saudis drive. Very bad. You can't imagine. If it can be done illegally, they'll do it," he said. "Red lights, they'll make left turns from the right lane. They'll be at a traffic light, and they'll be in the right lane, and they will make a left turn and go the opposite way. There's no turn on red over there, but they'll do it."

Referring to the myriad traffic accidents involving American soldiers, Schwartz said, "Close to as many were lost in traffic fatalities as were lost in the war."

Relaxing in the warm sunlight that streamed through the terminal windows, Schwartz reflected on the Scud attacks that struck Dammam in January. "The first night, I think it all started about two or three o'clock in the morning," he said. "We woke up and went into full MOP (gear).

"At that time, they didn't know what might be coming over. And it was exciting, you know, and it was funny," Schwartz recalled. "Well, now, you can look back on it, and it was sort of funny, but at the time, it was dead serious.

"Everybody was turning out the lights," he laughed, "and naturally a Scud can't see where you're at. This ain't World War II. Leave the lights on — it doesn't make any difference! The way I look at it, if your number is up, no matter what you're doing, that's it."

At one time, the 210th comprised seven military police companies. During the battalion's stay in the Gulf, its complement included two Army Reserve outfits - the 94th from Maine and New Hampshire and the 301st from Puerto Rico - and such Army National Guard units as the 115th from Rhode Island, the 855th from Arizona, and the 270th from California. "To be honest with you, after the war was over, it wasn't bad," Schwartz said. "There were a lot of Americans living over there, working for foreign companies. One of the companies that I really want to tip my hat to is the Aramco people. They brought us into their homes and treated us great, just fantastic. It's just wonderful to be an American. The feeling, I can't describe."

A five-year Navy veteran, Schwartz had never expected to see the Persian Gulf as a ground-pounder. "I joined the Guard originally (in 1976) to go to Germany and to get some kind of training," he said, "hopefully never (to use) for war. As it turned out, (I went to) Saudi Arabia. I'd never heard of the country of Bahrain."

Schwartz enjoyed his seven-month contact with the Saudi culture. "Basically, the Arab people are pretty good, the ones that we dealt with. It's a different culture, a completely different culture, especially with women. But, it seems to work for them, and you can't knock success," he said.

"You would be amazed at that country, how it's developed (with) the freeways," Schwartz said. "The food, ooh, some of the best food I've eaten is over there. They imported a German restaurant and rebuilt it. A Mexican restaurant. They love Chinese."

Schwartz, who would turn 51 in December 1991, wanted to get home as soon as possible. The Michigan Guardsmen would process out of the Army at Fort Knox, then fly home aboard Air National Guard C-130s by Saturday, Sept. 7.

The 210th would return home to a new armory in Taylor. The Michigan Guardsmen had never seen the armory.

More than a new job and a new armory awaited Schwartz back home in Michigan. "I've got two grandkids (a boy and a girl) waiting for me. I missed their first Christmas. They're just over 1 (year old)," he said. Schwartz unfolded an envelope and displayed two color photographs of his family. His wife, a registered nurse in Detroit, had made special plans for his homecoming. "My 30th anniversary will be on the 9th of September," Schwartz explained. "I'm getting home next Saturday, and Sunday, she's dragging me before the priest, and we're going to renew our vows," he smiled. "She's a wonderful lady."

Despite having spent more than eight months on active duty, the master sergeant intended to remain in the National Guard, which he described as being community-oriented. "I don't know if it's patriotic or what, but it's just fun to be in," he said.

Schwartz had not expected the reception that awaited him in Bangor. "As the plane landed, they said there were a few people waiting to meet us. I couldn't think of anybody I know of, of course not, but, no, this is great," he said.

Based on their reaction, many other soldiers on the L-1011 felt the same way. They took their time leaving the terminal, opting instead to sign autographs, grab another hug from a female troop greeter, and swig the last beer.

A Spec. Bosan sported a Screaming Eagles patch on his right shoulder. Exchanging hugs and shaking hands, he worked his way along the wire. As he reached the entrance to the ramp, Bosan turned, raised an arm, and shouted to the crowd, "I'm a Vietnam veteran! Two wars!"

MARINES WEAR NAME TAGS?

The troop greeter did a double take. There, emblazoned in big, bold letters above the pockets on the Marine's desert blouse, were the words "Williams" and "U.S. Marines."

Marines wear name tags? Since when?

By 7:57 p.m. on a rainy Sunday, Sept. 15, several dozen people had gathered at BIA to meet World Airways Flight 31028, a DC-10 inbound from Saudi Arabia. Apparently the plane had refueled in Sicily and Ireland, then developed a fuel leak over the North Atlantic. Bangor seemed as good a place as any to land for repairs.

According to passenger service, the airliner carried 151 troops headed for El Toro Marine Corps Air Station, Calif. "No one anticipated this flight tonight," a woman agent said.

At 8:10 p.m., WOA Flight 31028 eased its bulk from the wet night sky and flashed past the terminals. Some Legionnaires and VFWers entered the ramp and pretended they were busy examining the wall art. According to the official rules, no one was supposed to greet troops on the ramp. The crowd patiently waited. At 8:26 p.m., some Marines appeared atop the ramp, and the civilians cheered.

As the leathernecks entered the terminal, the troop greeter spotted a name tag on a Staff Sgt. Williams, who wore a green MP pauldron on his left shoulder. Other Marines, but not all, sported the name tags and "U.S. Marines" identification. Some Navy corpsmen passed along the wire, as did a hitchhiking soldier.

When asked about the name tags, Gunnery Sgt. Mike Muttoni smiled and explained, "It's a transition period. We're starting to come out with it. They just came out in the past few months. Marines have never worn name tags before," he confirmed the civilian's suspicions. Muttoni, who came from Seattle, Wash., said that he'd been in the Marines for 21 years. He was flying to Camp Pendleton, Calif., where he had been assigned to EOD (explosives ordnance disposal), 1st FSSG.

Muttoni had arrived in Saudi Arabia in the first part of May, after "trying to get over there (real) hard" during the Gulf War. He had been "in charge of Marine EOD in-country, that being Saudi Arabia." He operated out of Jubail.

Marine EOD teams worked at various sites in the Gulf, destroying old ammunition unfit for shipment to the States. The Marines tackled any bomb threats, too, but Muttoni described these as minor, since a diligent Saudi security apparatus kept the lid on terrorists. Islamic courts would pass a death sentence on captured terrorists, too. "I think this was a potent deterrent," Muttoni intimated.

The five EOD teams under Muttoni's supervision primarily blew up aging American explosives. "You take an artillery round, you take a tank round that you put in a tank and drive around in the desert and the sand and everything else for three or four months, which is what really happened," Muttoni explained, "and when you take that out and download it, it's no good.

"Either it's past life-expectancy, (or) it's been abused, which just carrying it around is, small-arms ammunition, things like that,

A young Marine snoozes at BIA about 11 p.m. on Sept. 15, 1991.

it's either too hazardous to transport back here, or it's just not worth the cost" to ship it home, he pointed out. That didn't mean all the ammunition sent to the Gulf was in bad shape. Muttoni estimated that the Marine Corps had shipped 150,000 tons of ammunition stateside and that "they blew up 7,000 to 8,000 tons, around there. That's well within standards." The Marines also shipped home captured Iraqi munitions, including "guided missiles, artillery, grenades, rockets, land mines. The Iraqis used a smorgasbord of international munitions," he said. "We picked up Jordanian-marked boxes `tractor parts' that had grenades (in them), rifle grenades."

The gunnery sergeant appreciated his welcome in Bangor. On one occasion when coming home from Vietnam - where he served two tours - his arrival was "secretive, to be quite honest with you. They didn't want to come into various places where people either ignored you or protested against you. "I came into California, Los Angeles. There were 14 of us on a commercial flight out of Daha in Okinawa, and this was right before Christmas," Muttoni recalled that particular homecoming.

"There is a massive difference in these welcomes," he said. "We had gotten word (this time) that we were going to Bangor, Maine, that we would be met by people...this (the BIA greetings) has been known from people who were over there in the war and came back to the States and who want back over there because they had certain specialties that were required."

Gary Leighton chose that moment to welcome the leathernecks to BIA. The Marines cheered him, then sobered when Leighton said that they'd be served a warm meal in the coffee shop.

Muttoni said he was "grinning from ear to ear" when he came down the ramp into the domestic terminal. "The expressions on some of the younger Marines' faces: I saw a lot of fatigue lines just disappear, and all of a sudden the grins started coming up, and they're still in a good mood."

His name tag identified Staff Sgt. Calvin Harper, who came from Omaha, Neb. With 18 years in the Corps, Harper worked as an ammunition technician, assigned to Combat Service Support Detachment 12 at Twenty-Nine Palms in California.

Harper had shipped for the Persian Gulf on May 21. "Primarily we were sent over to reconfigure and return the ammunition that had been taken over there," he explained. The Marines set aside the ammunition that could be returned to the States. "Anything that was unserviceable or unsafe to ship back, we turned over to EOD for destruction."

CSSD 12 loaded four ships outbound for the United States and also loaded ammunition on MPS (maritime prepositioning) ships, vessels anchored near various hot spots around the world. The first Marines to reach the Persian Gulf in August 1990 had drawn their heavy weaponry from one or more MPS ships assigned to the Indian Ocean.

Harper said that CSSD 12 had been stationed at ASP 3 (ammunition supply point 3), "which was at Al Mishab...about 30 miles south of the Kuwaiti border." He was asked if the troops were ever in any danger as far as ammunition blowing up accidentally. "That's one of our primary worries," Harper responded. "Any time you have ammunition stored anywhere, you have a fire hazard, no matter what. The stuff could blow up."

Harper was glad to be back in America. "It's clean," he grinned. "There's no sand. I was glad to see rain. We haven't seen rain since we left."

The cool temperature outside the terminal would not bother him, either. "It's been immensely hot," Harper said. "I know we topped 120 on several occasions at Al Mishab. The thermostat we had on the wall topped 120, and that was in the shade."

He hadn't worried about physical training, especially when wrestling with heavy ammunition. "I lost about 18 pounds over there," Harper observed. "You sweat out a lot, you drink a lot of water. You try to drink at least a liter every hour."

Before he shipped to Saudi Arabia, Harper heard about Bangor from Marines returning from the war. "A lot of them said it was great, 'it was like everybody in town had come out to greet us. They were giving us things, shaking our hands.' "A lot of the Vietnam vets said that `this is totally different from when I came back from Nam.' I knew that Bangor really liked to greet our troops, (so) I kind of expected this," the sergeant said.

Told how popular Marines were with the Bangor crowd. Harper smiled, then chuckled, "Everybody loves Marines! You have to love 'em! We're cute!"

The Marines remained at BIA perhaps another hour. They endured a long rendition of the Marine Hymn that played about 9:40 p.m. Leathernecks across the terminal stood at attention and faced the music. An hour later, the WOA relief crew boarded their DC-10 and prepared it for departure. Sylvia Thompson announced at 10:40 p.m. the jet's imminent exit from Bangor. Marines cheered and poured into the ramp.

Within four weeks, the last Marines would pass through BIA while headed home from the Gulf. Those Marines, too, would sport name tags and Marine identification.

EAGLE PILOTS

World Airways Flight 31033, headed with 265 passengers for Holloman Air Force Base in New Mexico, put down through a thickening overcast and landed at BIA at on Tuesday, Oct. 1. The jet's arrival at 6:55 a.m. placed it just minutes behind the morning's departures for United and Delta.

Perhaps 50 people watched as the plane rolled past the terminals. A few veterans and their spouses moved into the ramp to greet the incoming troops, who deplaned shortly after their airliner reached the international terminal.

Two families awaited today's flight. Pamela DeWitt, who lived in Richmond, Maine, had driven to Bangor that morning with her husband, Tom, and their three children to meet her nephew, Trevor Bell. She'd learned "the day before yesterday, Sunday," that Bell would land in Bangor. "His wife called us from New Mexico," DeWitt explained.

Since Bell belonged to the Air Force, his presence on the plane suggested an Air Force contingent.

Nearby stood Roberta Doughty, a Hermon resident waiting to greet her brother. He'd called her from the Gulf on Sept. 29 and said that he'd probably land in Bangor about 4 a.m. on Tuesday.

"This reunion means a lot to us," Doughty stated after introducing her family. "I haven't seen him for three years. We've greeted a lot of troop flights sort of because we knew he was there, and so I woke my son up this morning and said, `Do you want to greet a troop flight with me?'" Her's son initial resistance to the proposal melted when he realized that his Uncle Steve would be aboard the plane.

About 7:10 a.m., desert fatigue-clad Air Force personnel started pouring down the ramp. Roberta Doughty's brother, Steve McCutcheon, quickly located her standing beside the duty-free shop. The DeWitts waited and watched until a blond-haired Sgt. Trevor Bell leaned over the wire well up the ramp and waved to them.

"There he is!" Pamela DeWitt exclaimed, wildly pointing and waving. Her nephew slipped from line and joined the DeWitts for a noisy and happy reunion.

The wings on his flight suit blurred by the metallic flag decal that someone had pinned to his name patch, Capt. Paul Chapman stated that he hailed from St. Louis. Assigned to the 9th Tactical Fighter Squadron at Holloman, he'd just spent the last several months in Saudi Arabia with the 4404th Composite Wing, an outfit created to coordinate the activities of various Air Force aircraft still flying in the Gulf.

Chapman flew the F-15A Eagle, an "air-to-air superiority" fighter. A 1984 graduate of the Air Force Academy, he explained that the Eagle, although larger than the F-16, carried "weaponry that allows us to do our job, which is maintaining air superiority. You can take out other airplanes before you get into that arena where the size (and an aircraft's enhanced visibility) becomes a deterrent."

According to the captain, the F-15A normally carried four AIM-7 radar-guided Sparrow missiles, four AIM-9 heat-seeking Sidewinder missiles, and "approximately 940 rounds of ammunition in the gun." He described that weapon as a six-barreled, 20 mm. Gatling gun common to various American jet fighters.

Chapman had deployed to the Gulf in June, too late for the war, yet safely beyond any potential for combat. "It was kind of a double edged sword," he said. "It's something you train for every day, and, well, you don't want to do it (fight a war), but you have to do what you have to do."

Only half the squadron had deployed to Saudi Arabia, Chapman recalled. "I flew every other day. We had a commitment that we had to maintain 24 hours a day in the wing, and we flew seven days a week," he said.

Missions took him over Saudi Arabia. For two weeks, Chapman went with a detachment that flew with the Bahraini air force. "They have F-5 and F-16 aircraft. We flew with them, and there's a U.S. naval presence in the Gulf. There's no secret to that," he said.

Chapman noticed differences in flying over the New Mexican and Saudi deserts. "The big difference is the limited visibility over there due to all the (oil) wells that the Iraqis set on fire," he said. "That and the blowing dust and the haze that's just normal for that area do reduce visibility quite a bit. The horizon is not as discernible as you normally have it." He said he flew more instruments than he normally would fly in New Mexico. The Air Force was reconfiguring his squadron's parent wing, the 49th Tactical Fighter, to fly the F-117A Stealth. "They're going to come from Tonopah, Nevada," Chapman explained. He would not transit to the F-117A, but would remain an F-15A pilot. In fact, his latest assignment would take him to Tyndall Air Force Base in Florida to teach other people how to fly the F-15.

Another Air Force pilot, Capt. Jeff Hubbard, said "this is fantastic," referring to the welcome he'd received in Bangor. "It's nice to see the crowd out here today...we didn't expect this at all. It's good to see that the American public is still supporting us over there."

Hubbard, who also flew the F-15A, enjoyed a special tie with Bangor. "I was stationed at Loring (Air Force Base) my first three years in the Air Force," he explained. Flying on a B-52 Stratofortress as a navigator and electronics warfare officer, he'd come into BIA in 1987, when "we brought a B-52 to do an air show that was sponsored by the Air National Guard here."

Hubbard commented on "how sad it was to see the oil fires trashing the skies overhead in Saudi Arabia and how you could see the film of oil all over the place and how much of an environmental disaster it really is.

"That stands out the most (in my memory)," he said, "and the fact that we aren't ravaged by war over here. It's important for us to understand that what we have over here is important to keep and defend."

He looked forward to a reunion with his wife, Tandra, whom he had met while training in F-15s in Florida.

Hubbard appreciated the greetings he had received at BIA and even expressed his delight at watching the stiff southwesterly breeze that tossed the limbs of the pine trees located far across the runway. "We haven't seen rain in 90 days," he confirmed while watching rain drops splatter against the terminal windows.

Captains Chapman and Hubbard joined their comrades along the wire after a boarding call sounded at 7:55 a.m. Air Force personnel passed along the wire, with Trevor Bell lingering to say good-bye to Pamela DeWitt and her family. By 8:03 a.m., every military passenger who was leaving on WOA Flight 31033 had entered the ramp.

Lt. Col. Neil Kacena of Cedar Rapids, Iowa, stopped to chat with Tom Dean and thank the civilians for the reception extended his people. He waved to the people still standing on the ramp and headed for his plane.

MARINES AFLOAT

After the Inchon landing during the Korean War, American troops felt they'd be home by Christmas 1950.

Forty years later, their descendants faced a similar situation. Would they leave the Gulf by Christmas? This time, fortunately, the war was already over, with no Chinese hordes pouring across the Euphrates River. This time, most troops would arrive home before the holidays. In fact, most of the Americans remaining in the Gulf flew home during October.

American Trans Air Flight 1035 touched down at BIA at 10:25 a.m. on Wednesday, Oct. 3. The L-1011 carried 203 passengers en route to El Toro Marine Corps Air Station in California. After taxiing into a light haze, the plane swung past the domestic terminal and put into Gate 5.

After the L-1011 reached its gate, the 10 to 15 people who'd stood on the observation deck moved downstairs into the terminal. Their arrival boosted the crowd to about 60 people. While George Nye took a flag and moved into the ramp, Sylvia Thompson and a veteran from Legion Post 84 carted a record player into the terminal and set it up.

Although they weren't supposed to wait on the ramp, several veterans edged past the gift table and pretended they weren't there. "If I can't see you, you can't see me, right?" a Korean vet joked.

"Ah, yeah," a companion replied.

Marines appeared atop the ramp at 10:35 a.m. The people waiting along the wire spotted those familiar featureless uniforms (no name tags today) and went wild with cheers and applause.

The Marines carried several hitchhikers with them into BIA that day. On her left lapel, an Army first lieutenant named Smith sported a Quartermaster Corps' insignia. An Air Force staff sergeant; an Air Force sergeant wearing jungle fatigues; an Army specialist named Russell; other military personnel, too, intermingled with the Marines.

The incoming AMT flight crew trailed behind the leathernecks. As a flight attendant towed his luggage down the ramp, he spoke quietly to several Marines, "You all take care, y'hear?" The Marines thanked him for a safe flight from Europe.

A tall, muscular Marine strode into the terminal with his floppy campaign cap dangling by its straps from his hand. A teddy bear, actually an Ursus Berrie, bounced and jounced from a perch within the cap.

First Lt. David Glancy, a four-year veteran of the Corps, hailed from Jenks, Okla., a town on the Arkansas River just south of Tulsa. He explained that AMT Flight 1035 brought home "a hodgepodge of people from everywhere. (The Air Force and Army personnel), they just threw them on the flight with us. "I'm at a Marine air base in Tustin, Calif.," Glancy said. He'd shipped for the Gulf "when it all started. Then I came back for a month, and then I volunteered to go back." His initial deployment had taken him to the Persian Gulf with a Marine Expeditionary Unit (MEU).

"We were in the west Pacific. We were around Hong Kong when the war (Iraqi invasion) broke out in August. They sent us to the Gulf. We were there through April," Glancy recalled. "I went back for a month, and they said they needed some people to help retrograde all the tanks, all the equipment, LAVs, parts, even stuff like generators and such," he said. "They had to get that out of Saudi, so we started loading ships."

Glancy rolled his eyes as he remembered the heat. "In July and August, it hit 140 and 150 degrees down in the holds of some of the ships. It was hot. It was a metal ship, and you go down in a hold, and it was unbelievable," he stated. "I guess we had to get all the ammo back. This wasn't like Vietnam, where they were just dumping everything."

The Marines who were loading the ships at Jubail survived on bottled water and Gatorade, Glancy said. He estimated that he'd helped load 30 or 40 ships, work that dragged into the fall.

"We'd have four at the pier at the same time," the lieutenant said, describing port operations in Jubail. "Just load 'em up and get 'em out. Another would come in to be packed with tanks or amphibs, all sorts of tracked vehicles."

The Marines loaded "all the junk, too" aboard the outgoing ships, "stuff like tractors with three wheels on them," Glancy said.

He'd faced a different assignment after his ship arrived off the Saudi coast in late summer 1990. "We would go out and float for about three months up and down the Gulf, up and down the coast, basically off Saudi Arabia," Glancy said. "We went back to the Philippines in December (and) spent Christmas there, then we went right back out."

An aviation-supply officer, Glancy sailed aboard the USS Okinawa, a helicopter assault vessel that the lieutenant described "as like a short aircraft carrier" that handled only helicopters, not VTOL aircraft like the AV-8B Harrier.

"We were an LPH (landing platform, helicopter), which is just a few feet shorter than an LPA (landing platform, aircraft). An LPA is the one that would have the Harriers and stuff," Glancy commented.

The flotilla in which the Okinawa sailed included an LPA "floating right next to us," as well as the battleships USS Wisconsin and USS Missouri, according to Glancy. Although Harriers could operate from the LPA, the Okinawa flew only CH-46 Chinooks, CH-53 Sea Stallions, AH-1W Sea Cobras (similar to a gunship shot down at Khafji), and UH-1H Hueys.

If a helicopter broke down, combat efficiency required the maintenance personnel to get the bird up and running as soon as possible. That's where Glancy's role as an aviation-supply officer was vital.

"I had to make sure that if our helicopters break down, we had the parts to fix them," he said.

Shipboard life kept Glancy busy, stretching his time between performing his routine duties and standing watch. Living inside a steel hull proved monotonous at times. "There really wasn't too much (for entertainment)," he said. "We were glad to get off the ship. It was driving us nuts."

Although the Okinawa's Marines and sailors "really weren't aware of what was going on (with the war)," Glancy admitted that a war actually "made you think.

"When we were first out there floating, it was terrible," Glancy shook his head. "We were just floating out there day after day after day for three straight months."

When the Okinawa returned to the Persian Gulf about the first of January, Glancy and his comrades assumed they'd participate in an amphibious assault on the Kuwaiti coast. News reports during the war placed the battleships off the coastline, where the Missouri, Wisconsin, and New Jersey fired their 16-inch guns at command bunkers, supply sites, and other fixed targets. The shelling apparently convinced the Iraqis that a landing was imminent.

"That was our squadron that did it," Glancy said. "We went within a couple miles of the coast. Electronics technicians eavesdropped on Iraqi communications. They were listening to Iraqis talking, and it was 'Okay, here they come.' So we kept feinting. They thought we were coming."

When the ground war started, "I was up looking for mines on deck. You could hear 'em over the radio," Glancy said. "You could hear the A-6 pilots calling back, saying they couldn't drop their ordnance because the Marines were already there.

"We didn't know what was going on in the war. You could tell we were winning" because the ground troops had already reached intended targets for Navy and Marine Corps aviators. "They were like 10 miles ahead of where they were supposed to be," the lieutenant said.

Not until after the war did the Marines afloat learn that they'd been part of an elaborate deception, in which the United States convinced Iraqi commanders that an amphibious assault would occur somewhere on the Kuwaiti coast. The scheme tied down several Iraqi divisions.

"We thought we would be part of the attack, too," Glancy stated. "We were ready to go. Amphibious landings have always been notorious for (heavy) casualties. We knew what they had waiting for us."

When word reached the Marines that they would not attack Kuwait, "part of the hard-core guys were really disappointed," the lieutenant said. The smarter ones did not mind.

Although the Marines from the Okinawa did not fight in the war, eight Marines were lost in late 1990 when two Hueys collided during night operations.

According to the lieutenant, not that many leathernecks remained in the Gulf. "The last Marines should be shipping home Oct. 10th. It's basically the Army and Air Force there now," he said.

While stationed at Jubail during his second trip to the Persian Gulf, Glancy did not travel to Kuwait. He got as far as Khafji, however, and photographed the scars left from the battle there.

The shattered Iraqi armor that the American press had so photographically splashed across its pages after the Battle of Khafji had been removed, the lieutenant confirmed, but abundant armor remained in Kuwait.

Glancy grinned while discussing his latest return from the Gulf. "This is not what we expected," he explained. When the Okinawa returned to America in April 1991, the Marines were flown off the ship to Tustin, where there was a small celebration featuring mostly family members.

"But this is cool," Glancy commented as he looked around the domestic terminal. "We don't even know these people. They're just really concerned, seems like, making sure everybody has a good welcome home." The first boarding call for AMT Flight 1035 sounded just as the record player offered up the national anthem at 11:08 a.m. A young Marine chatting on a pay phone asked his callee "to wait a minute" so he could stand at attention and salute the flag. Then someone blew a whistle, and George Nye shouted, "Everybody want to go home?"

The Marines collectively groaned, "Oh, no!"

THE MOST WELCOME GATE-CRASHERS
IN THE WORLD

More than 270 sailors "crashed" a banquet being held at the Bangor Airport Hilton on Saturday, Oct. 5. The 150 people attending the banquet didn't mind one bit.

By early afternoon on Friday, Oct. 4, word filtered along the troop greeters' grapevine about a World Airways flight scheduled for a 4 a.m. landing on Saturday. Sylvia Thompson soon learned that the DC-10 would supposedly ferry home soldiers participating in the "Reforger '91" military exercise in Germany.

Not exactly an official troop flight, but Thompson and a few other troop greeters decided to meet it anyway.

About 1 a.m., Thompson discovered that the arrival time had been pushed back to

12 noon. Then the plane delayed until 2:10 p.m....and finally until 6 p.m.

Word did not reach everyone about the 14-hour delay. Christina Stout of Panama City, Fla., had arrived in Maine at Owls Head, two weeks earlier to stay with her parents. Her husband, William, was coming home with Navy Mobile Construction Battalion 133.

He'd called her in the last day or two and said he'd be passing through Bangor. Christina checked the World Airways' flight schedule Saturday morning, learned that William's plane would arrive at noon, and drove up the coast to Bangor in mid-morning. She spent the afternoon cooling her heels in the Queen City.

Dana Marble of Waite, a town of perhaps 150 people on Route 1 far east of Bangor, came to BIA to meet his son, Anthony Zapata. "I really don't mind the delay," Marble commiserated with Christina, "but all the boys on the plane are the ones really being put out. I think they've been in the air about 28 hours."

Earlier in the afternoon, Thompson called many troop greeters in hopes that a few people would meet the so-called Reforger flight. Under a darkening gray sky that threatened rain, people slowly gathered in the domestic terminal.

Four hours earlier, about 150 people had gathered at the Hilton, which was attached to the domestic terminal by a skywalk, for an Amway marketing seminar. Canadians from Price Edward Island, Nova Scotia, and New Brunswick rubbed their elbows with Americans from Maine, New Hampshire, and New York. The Amway distributors sat down to a banquet in late afternoon. About 5:45 p.m., a man left the banquet and walked through the skywalk to the domestic terminal. He went to the coffee shop, where he heard some Legionnaires and VFWers talking about a scheduled 6 p.m. troop flight.

Even as the DC-10 turned into its final approach to BIA, the Amway distributor hustled to the Hilton and spoke to Robert Wengrzynek of Village Business Associates in Old Town. Wengrzynek, the host for the marketing seminar, told his 150 guests about the DC-10's impending arrival.

"As soon as I announced the troop flight, everyone dropped everything and came over, in an orderly fashion, of course," said Wengrzynek. "This is more important than finishing dessert and coffee."

The well-dressed Amway distributors and their spouses decamped to the domestic terminal, where their numbers boosted the waiting crowd to more than 200 people and transformed the assembled troop greeters into the best-dressed crowd ever to meet a troop flight in Bangor.

Unlike the WOA DC-10 that had landed on Oct. 1, the aircraft that taxied to the international terminal tonight sported a gleaming white fuselage with red lettering. George Nye and Paul Tower observed the unusual color scheme from their vantage point at the narrow window beside the gift table.

"Must be a leased aircraft," the sharp-eyed Tower commented as he studied the DC-10 through the darkening shadows. "Those are foreign registration numbers; definitely not American."

According to the people at the passenger-service desk, the WOA jet carried 278 passengers en route from Sigonella, Sicily, to Gulfport, Miss. The Seebees had not pre-cleared customs in Italy, a BIA employee warned a few troop greeters clustered near the desk. They would be coming through Customs at BIA a few at a time. Christina Stout dejectedly shook her head when she learned that William would take longer to leave the plane than she'd anticipated. "Isn't that the military, for you?" Dana Marble told her. "Send 'em all the way to Iraq, but they can't get 'em off the plane real fast here in the States!"

While Christina and Marble stood at the entrance to the ramp and traded observations about military life, more Amway distributors arrived in the domestic terminal. Troop greeters clad in blue jeans and sweatshirts mingled with dark suits and classic dresses. An imaginary wire soon formed its fishhook at the entrance to the coffee shop and ran all the way across the terminal to Mr. Paperback.

Marble appreciated the people waiting to greet the sailors. "Even after (Operation) Desert Storm, I think it's great these people are out here to meet them," he said.

Christina Stout stood nervously on tiptoe and peered up the ramp. She smiled as she told Marble how she and William had met in Spain in April 1989. He'd been stationed there with the Navy, while she'd been living there with her missionary parents. She had married William, a native of Worcester, Mass., in February 1991, between his assignments with the Navy.

"We've been together a total of four weeks since then," Christina wistfully said. She gazed up the ramp, as if by sheer concentration she could materialize her husband right there on the spot.

A ragged cheer echoed into the ramp. Marble looked over his left shoulder, grinned, and reiterated, "I think it's great. I think it's payback time."

Explaining his remark, Marble affixed his gaze on Christina as he recalled coming home from Vietnam and being met "by some hippietypes" not long after he set foot on American soil. "They asked me how many babies I'd killed today," he told Christina.

Then he waved a hand toward the crowd. "Greeting the people from the Gulf is so different than the guys from Vietnam," Marble said. "I think it's a great thing to do."

By 6:25 p.m., the last Amway distributors had entered the terminal and packed the wire two or three people deep in places. "I've never seen so many people all dressed up for a troop flight," a regular troop greeter said.

An airline relief crew clad in navy blue had joined the crowd by now. The seven or eight crew members gathered under the reduced light beside the duty-free shop and cheered and applauded while waiting for the sailors.

At 6:30 p.m., two young women stepped onto the escalator leading to the second floor of the international terminal. Their eyes and attention momentarily elsewhere, the male troop greeters standing near the passenger-service desk didn't notice the young man riding behind the two women.

A day's beard sprouted on his jaw and cheeks, the man also sported a black moustache. The facial hair failed to camouflage the sailor's youth, and the mixed clothing that he wore - part civilian, part military-issue - failed to conceal his Navy identity.

"Heck, they're here!" a troop greeter exclaimed. Someone, possibly Paul Tower, waved down the ramp, where the Red Cross volunteers correctly interpreted the hand signal and started cheering. In turn, the ever-vigilant crowd caught their cue and thundered their welcome for the three sailors who stepped off the escalator.

Christina Stout shifted from foot to foot as the sailors strode past her. She briefly smiled, but riveted her eyes up the ramp. Marble paced impatiently just a few feet away and tried to relieve his excitement by shaking hands with the incoming sailors.

Then Christina blinked hard, perhaps twice, and flew up the ramp and into William's arms. Locked briefly in a warm embrace, they held tightly to each other as they slipped past the Red Cross volunteers and vanished into the crowd.

The logjam at Customs collapsed a moment later, and sailors simply flooded the ramp. Swept into the domestic terminal by the wave of humanity that flowed past the gift table, Marble found a safe haven at the United Airlines gate and kept watch for his son.

Anthony Zapata enveloped his father in his arms at 6:34 p.m. Like the Stouts did perhaps two minutes earlier, Marble and Zapata walked unnoticed through the crowd and located a quiet place to talk. By 6:35 p.m., the Seebees overwhelmed the wire, where Americans and Canadians alike cheered, hugged, and kissed the grinning men in Navy green. The crush pushed a newspaper reporter as far as the entrance to the coffee shop, where he briefly blocked the view enjoyed by a middle-aged man wearing a dark suit. The man applauding the sailors was Sen. George Mitchell of Maine, majority leader of the United States Senate.

Mitchell soon escaped into the coffee shop. Holding a soda cup in one hand and remnants of a hamburger or hot dog in the other, he talked quietly with an aide as civilians and sailors whooped outside the entrance. The senator, who'd been in Bangor to attend a public hearing on the Northern Forest Lands Act of 1991, had planned to catch the evening Delta flight to Washington, D.C. He had not anticipated meeting about 500 celebrating taxpayers.

The din gradually subsided as the last Seebees entered the terminal. The troop greeters scattered to mingle with the sailors, and the senator soon boarded his aircraft.

Then as the traditional Tail-End Charlies - those sailors who had made their phone calls from the international terminal before walking down the ramp - reached the end of the wire, someone started singing "God Bless America."

Words died unspoken on many lips as the sailors turned toward the singing, which intensified near a waving American flag. Civilians who couldn't carry the high notes of the "Star-Spangled Banner" sang loud and proud, and some Seebees joined the chorus.

Two Navy officers, Lt. Robert Donald and Ensign Dan Bramer, listened to the impromptu anthem from their position near the entrance to the skywalk. Donald, the medical doctor assigned to CB-133, said that the 665-man battalion had started moving its equipment to Turkey on April 26, 1991. The battalion had deployed in March from its official home at Gulfport to the naval base at Rota, Spain. With their equipment en route, the sailors flew to Incirlik Air Base in Turkey. Taking their weapons (sidearms, M-16s, machine guns, and even mortars) with them, the Seebees packed into "definitely uncomfortable and crowded" buses for the 400-mile drive across Turkey to the Iraqi border, Donald said.

The Allies had organized Operation Provide Comfort, the multinational effort to return Kurdish refugees to their homes in northern Iraq. Hundreds of thousands of Kurds had fled their suppressed rebellion against Saddam Hussein, Bramer said, and most of them had gone into the mountains.

The living conditions for the refugees were abominable, according to Donald. He described the various diseases that killed many Kurds, particularly women and children.

Along with other American military units, CB-133 had been sent to build refugee camps in northern Iraq. The sailors arrived at Zakho, a town just a few miles inside Iraq, in late April and started building four camps that ultimately housed 5,000 refugees apiece.

The camps contained weatherproof tents, food-distribution points, running water, and sanitation facilities. Refugees slowly came down from the mountains and moved into the camps, Bramer said.

While in Iraq, the Seebees repaired an Iraqi airstrip at Sirsenk, a short distance north of Zakho. Allied aircraft had bombed the strip during the war, Bramer said, but the Seebees repaved the 3,500-foot runway so relief aircraft could land at the airfield.

Although they met many Kurds, Donald and Bramer grew especially fond of the young children. Abandoned military equipment lay everywhere, Donald said, and "even the little kids were trying to sell us mortars, RPGs (rocket-propelled grenades), and AK-47s."

Bramer imitated a child waving a mortar round in mid-air. "They didn't realize how dangerous the munitions were," he said. "We tried to warn them, to educate them, but it was hard when you don't speak their language. And they don't understand English."

Sometimes, the munitions detonated and maimed the children holding them. "It was hard," Donald commented, "seeing the little bitty kids, (who were) not knowing they were holding something explosive in their hands."

The Kurdish children "were so friendly, so hungry for love," Bramer recalled. "They'd wave as we went by and call out, `George Bush No. 1! George Bush No. 1!'"

Donald and Lt. Chris Vockroth, the battalion's dentist, traveled to a Spanish hospital near the Iraq-Iran border and treated many refugees for various medical ailments. Based on all the physical examinations that he conducted, Donald believed that before the war, the Kurds had received adequate, if not excellent medical treatment.

"The war apparently disrupted their medical system, however," he said. "Many Kurds had gone into the mountains, of course, where the living conditions were appalling."

According to Vockroth, the Kurds' patriarchal society apparently placed a greater emphasis on men than on women and children. Men, especially the so-called elders, received attention first in whatever was happening, whether it was food distribution or medical help.

"At the Spanish hospital, we were seeing women and children who'd been at the end of the line when they were handing out medicine up in the mountains," Donald said. "I saw a three-day-old baby die while we were there."

CB-133 spent seven weeks in northern Iraq before egressing the Middle East through Incirlik Air Base. Most of the sailors returned to Rota, but two 60-man detachments went to Sigonella, Sicily, and Suda Bay, Crete. Bramer accompanied the Sigonella-bound detachment as its assistant officer-in-charge and operations officer.

"You know, we're really happy to be on our way home," he said. "Being over there made you grow closer to your loved ones back home. Being out in the desert, well, everyone was writing a lot of letters and talking about their families."

After the PA system announced the first boarding call, the Seebees formed into their respective detachments. A sailor, possibly a chief petty officer, walked past Donald and Bramer and shouted, "Sigonella! Sigonella!"

Sailors fell into squad and detachment formations at three sites in the terminal. The Sigonella detachment formed across the smoking area, while the Crete detachment rough-dressed their ranks nearer the coffee shop. The largest contingent, comprising the sailors who had been stationed at Rota since late June, formed along the windows and faced the ramp.

Then, with their pathway brightened by winking flash attachments, the Seebees marched from the terminal to the loud cheers and "welcome home" cries offered by the crowd. Young sailors grinned and fingered a few "V" signs as they exited the terminal and vanished up the ramp.

Wengrzynek enjoyed a short chat with Donald and Bramer before they ran to retrieve their hand luggage and rejoin their mates. As he watched the last sailors disappear from the terminal, Wengrzynek smiled and said, "We're just glad to see them home safely."

Had the disrupted banquet upset him or his guests?

Wengrzynek smiled. "Are you kidding? Those boys didn't bother us at all. They're more important than any banquet. I believe they could disrupt any function anywhere in the country right now, and the people probably would love it," he replied. "It's not like they crashed our function. We gladly came to theirs', and we'd do it again."

FAMILY FLIGHT

It's not every day that soldiers escort their spouses and carry their children through Bangor International Airport. Such an unusual event occurred after American Trans Air Flight 1044 landed at BIA at 2:58 p.m. on Tuesday, Oct. 8.

The L-1011 arrived four minutes early and taxied to the international terminal. Two Balair aircraft, including a DC-10, lifted off from Bangor just before the AMT jet touched down.

On its way from Frankfurt, Germany, to McChord Air Force Base in Tacoma, Wash., the big L-1011 carried 238 passengers. Its final destination caused some consternation among the troop greeters, who wondered whether the passengers might be Air Force or Army. Fort Lewis isn't too far from Tacoma, an Army vet pointed out. "Well, we know they aren't Marines or Navy," another knowledgeable veteran observed. By the time the plane arrived, about 40 people had gathered to meet it. Other people drifted into the terminal as Everett Steele took a flagpole and its attached American flag in hand and walked past the passenger-service desk.

He found a vantage point beyond the double-glass doors and stood watching the corridor through which the arriving troops must pass. The L-1011 carried both soldiers and their dependents. Airport personnel expressed some doubt as to when anyone would clear Customs. Someone working behind the scenes steered people in the correct direction, however.

Soldiers made the turn from the security corridor and marched toward Steele. Glancing just once over his shoulder, he told the troops to "follow me" and escorted them down the ramp.

Most soldiers wore jungle fatigues. The troops swung into the domestic terminal and warmly responded to the handshakes and hugs that they received.

As more soldiers entered the terminal, family members appeared in their ranks. Husbands and wives walked beside their military spouses, often carrying infants or young children who shied from the chaos. A blond-haired woman soldier held hands with her spitting image, a little girl with hair as light as her mother's. The tie loosened on his dress uniform, a soldier named Almeida tucked a young daughter inside the crook of his left arm and freed his right arm to shake hands. His daughter, no more than 3 years old, merely watched the crowd.

Cpl. Anita Marquis and her husband, Carl, cleared the wire about 3:25 p.m. They'd been married eight years, not long after she had enlisted in the Army. The husband had once been in the Army, but he'd been out "10 or 11 years now."

Marquis had been stationed in Dexheim, "about 45 minutes outside of Frankfurt," with the Patriot-equipped 4th Battalion, 7th Air Defense Artillery Brigade. This battalion had started deploying to Incirlik Air Base, Turkey, by the end of December, and everyone was there by the end of January. She had arrived the first of January as the battalion commander's secretary. "We didn't see as much excitement and activity as everybody had hoped we would," Marquis said. "It was still an experience. I mean, we still were part of it."

The battalion defended Incirlik against possible Scud attacks. We had some threats, Marquis recalled, "but we didn't have any actual interaction with a Scud itself."

The Army confined the soldiers to Incirlik Air Base, particularly after a couple of incidents off base involving murderous assaults on Americans, she said.

Marquis remained in Turkey just under three months, leaving only three days before Operation Provide Comfort began. "I was lucky enough to be one of those sent back early," she said. "I came back the end of March."

While Marquis went off to war, her husband stayed in Germany with their 11-year-old daughter, Cherise. "I was terrified" at the thought of his wife serving in a war zone, Carl admitted. "War's not a joke, so I was real nervous about it. "I was strong for her and my daughter, you know, trying to show no fear, but she knew better," he said. Cherise, of course, had been concerned for her mother, "but, we worked together. It was rough on her at first," Carl observed. "We stayed active: sports, going out to the movies, shopping, just doing things together."

Her parents surmised that Cherise had handled the situation very well. "I think it made her stronger," Marquis commented.

"She weathered the storm with him," she said. "She became the lady of the house, and he was the momma-slash-daddy of the house."

Marquis had tried to keep her return to Dexheim in late March a secret, but word got out ahead of time that she was coming home. Carl left his job early that day.

Marquis laughed as she described her arrival in Dexheim. "The landlord, the dogs, everybody was there, the neighbors. It was nice," she smiled.

The Marquis were anticipating a joyful reunion with Cherise, who went home for the summer in June to visit, Anita noted. "But then we got notification that we were coming here, so we left her in Pennsylvania with my mother. She's joining us on Saturday. We're excited about it."

Stationed in Germany since August 1988, the Marquis were returning to the United States because the Army had transferred their battalion to Fort Lewis, Wash. They were pleased to touch American soil again. "I want to go to 7-11 at three in the morning," Marquis chuckled.

The first boarding call came about 3:35 p.m. The terminal quickly emptied as soldiers and dependents said good-bye to Maine residents and headed for their plane.

SYLVIA

Sometime after American Trans Air Flight 1042 left Shannon, Ireland, well past sunset on Oct. 8, a BIA employee dialed a Bangor phone number and told Sylvia Thompson that the inbound L-1011 should land at 10:20 p.m. The call gave Sylvia a three-hour grace period before the plane landed. She put the time to good use.

Since May 22, BIA had not advertised troop flights to the public. Responsibility for contacting people to travel to the airport fell to ordinary Mainers, men and women who, like Thompson, had not dreamed six months earlier that they would write history in Bangor. Years earlier, Thompson had graduated from Belfast High School and had later married Gerald Thompson, a Jackson boy who enlisted in the Air Force. He went to Vietnam, returning home to his family at Malmstrom Air Force Base in Great Falls, Mont., on Sept. 25, 1969.

In November of that year, he suffered a fatal heart attack, and Sylvia, a 31-year-old mother with three young children, had suddenly become a widow. She buried Gerry in Jackson, where she and her children lived with his mother until July 1970, when they moved to Brewer.

As the years passed, Thompson devoted herself to raising her children and to performing volunteer work for many elderly people, whether through housecleaning or participating in Meals on Wheels. She never lost her interest in the Air Force and things military. When soldiers started coming home from the Gulf, she turned out to meet them.

"I'm not exactly sure why I came out here," she said. "There was the curiosity, of course, because everyone was excited about what was happening at the airport.

"Maybe it was because I remembered worrying about Gerry while he was in Vietnam," she speculated. "These boys and girls had just been through their own war. Oh, I guess I just don't know for sure."

Thompson vividly described the tears, the joy, the excitement that occurred during her first troop flight. "I watched them as they came into the terminal, and, oh, when you've seen these men come in and be so appreciative because you're here, it was just so worthwhile."

She returned time and again, providing a sympathetic shoulder for one soldier "who just cried and cried" and, another time, ferrying a few troops to a nearby bank so they could get some cash before they reboarded their plane.

During one flight, a grizzled, battle-hardened veteran of Vietnam and the Gulf told Thompson, "I took 16 men over there. I was real tough on them, but I brought 16 men back." Another time, Brig. Gen. Tom Sikora presented her with a medal, and she rewarded him with a teddy bear snatched from a rapidly depleting gift table.

By late May, the troop greeters developed a telephone network to contact people about incoming flights. Thompson became a central figure in this grapevine, which extended well south and east of Bangor. When notified

Sylvia Thompson, an Air Force widow, pins a ribbon on Air Force Lt. Col. Terry Hughey. Thompson and other volunteers made sure people turned out to greet the troop flights after the official welcoming organization shut down.

about a flight, she would call people, leaving a message on an answering-machine here, talking to someone there. She would call a few local radio stations that gladly broadcast the information to their listening audiences.

Thompson would also call the American Red Cross, whose many volunteers proudly staffed the gift table after May 22. "I can't say enough about the Red Cross," she commented. "They've made a big difference."

Besides attending the regularly scheduled troop flights, Thompson often came to BIA to welcome home a Maine man or woman traveling on a civilian flight. Delta, United, and the commuter airlines brought home many Gulf veterans who never enjoyed a fullscale greeting, but who, thanks to people like Sylvia Thompson, still received a rousing reception at Bangor International Airport.

Through the many contacts she developed at the homecomings, Thompson learned when Maine residents were arriving at BIA. Despite a busy schedule, she usually grabbed a few yellow ribbons, maybe an American flag or two, and headed for Godfrey Boulevard. The ribbons she pinned to lapels; the flags she either waved or offered to a grateful soldier.

"I felt they (the troops coming home one by one) should be greeted, and their family members often called and said they'd like their loved ones to be greeted," she said.

Tonight, Oct. 8, marked the seventh month since the first troop flight landed in Bangor. Except for a dedicated core of perhaps 100 people, most area residents no longer expressed interest in the continuing flights. Had Thompson wearied of them, too?

"Oh, no!" she exclaimed.

"It has been well worth it. I'm still hearing the same thing, (that) they're so glad we're here and say they appreciate what we're doing. I'd like to see it right to the end, until the last one (troop) is back. I believe that the troops who are over there now are just as deserving of a welcome as those who were there during the war," she said.

"I don't intend to stop until the flights stop," Sylvia Thompson said.

ADVANCE NOTICE FROM A NEW FATHER

Some tourists came and went before the leathernecks ever landed. At 9:40 p.m. on Tuesday, Oct. 8, the PA system at BIA reported the arrival of Balair Flight 665, headed for Europe from Orlando. For some reason, the PA system always sounded crystal clear from the outside, but fuzzy and faint inside the domestic terminal.

The Balair relief crew arrived 10 minutes later, about the time their plane docked at the international terminal. Mike Stott, American Trans Air rep for Maine, swept into the airport behind the Europeans. He had a plane to meet - AMT Flight 1042 - and passengers to greet - 188 Marines and sailors flying west to El Toro Marine Corps Air Station in California.

Within minutes, Balair passengers packed the domestic terminal, where a few dozen people waited to greet the Marines. Europeans and Americans brushed elbows, but seldom chatted.

When the first Balair boarding call sounded at 10:20 p.m., people remained in the terminal, browsing for a few touristy items inside Mr. Paperback or sneaking a beer or two in the lounge. Another boarding call came at 10:27 p.m. Apparently in no hurry to go home, Europeans still lingered within the terminal.

Monarch Flight 084 touched down at 10:26 p.m. "Definitely Brits, I'd say," George Nye commented.

AMT Flight 1042 landed at 10:35 p.m., just minutes after someone chased the remaining Balair passengers from the terminal. The L-1011 taxied past the Balair jet and rolled up to a jetway.

Marines thundered onto the ramp at 10:48 p.m. They just missed a slacker or two among the Balair passengers.

Name tags, again. Not many, but enough to identify Thompson and Roos, two young leathernecks. Civilians applauded and cheered, as did the AMT relief crew. At 10:56 p.m., the Marines still plugged the ramp and patiently waited while their comrades moved single file along the wire. A tall and smiling Marine wrapped his burly arms around a teen-age girl and swept her off her feet. She squealed in delight.

Marine Capt. Paul Wilson stepped from line to speak with a troop greeter. "My MOS (military occupational specialty) is logistics," the captain said. "Logistics covers the entire gamut from supply, parts, major equipment, food, water, transportation, billeting, all the support items that go along with actually getting the troops from one location to another, helping them to survive from day to day." The happy new father of a five-day-old son named Michael was heading home to Camp Pendleton, Calif., where he was assigned as the logistics officer for the 7th Engineer Support Battalion. "While I was over in Saudi, I was the Combat Service Support Element, Landing Support Detachment commander," Wilson stated. "I had charge of 157 Marines and three officers." A bright light burned through the troop greeter's hazy, tired mind. "Where you at Jubail?" he asked Wilson. "Yes, sir, I was," the captain grinned again, anticipating the next question.

"Did you have an officer by the name of -"

"Lieutenant Willis," Wilson finished the question. "Yes, sir." "Lieutenant Willis! Julian Marcus 'Mark' Willis! He stayed with me when he came home on emergency leave," the troop greeter replayed his family's recent history. "Has he gone back?"

Yes, Willis had returned to the gulf, Wilson said. But he should be coming back through Bangor within a few days on his way to Camp LeJeune.

Wilson said that Willis had told his comrades all about his Bangor visit, even to seeing Stephen King's home. He had remained in the States until his mother felt better, then returned to the Gulf.

"I was glad to get him back. Good, hard worker. Knew his stuff," Wilson said. "I was relatively inexperienced in that type of operation, and he'd been doing it. He was my second-in-command and really kept me out of heat at times."

When asked to describe his detachment's function in Jubail, Wilson explained that "our mission was to retrograde Marine Corps equipment that was sent over to Saudi Arabia for the war; to redeploy the personnel; and to reconstitute the Maritime Prepositioning Force... the ships that float around.

"The CSSE, we provided all of the logistics...that's maintenance, supply, medical, headquarters and postal, food, and billeting," he said.

The landing support detachment loaded outgoing equipment aboard various ships. "On the prepositioning ships, there's a computer program that tells you exactly what piece by serial number goes exactly where," the captain pointed out.

"On the redeployment ships, that was a little more difficult. We were dealing with large, wieldy, in a lot of cases, broken items from the war aboard a ship (where) we might not know exactly what the layout is until the day it pulls up (to the dock)," Wilson stated.

The temperature steadily climbed by late summer, reaching "about the 116-degree range with about 95 percent humidity" at 8 a.m. "By about 3 p.m., the humidity had dropped into the high 70s, and the heat would get up above the 120-degree range," Wilson said. "It's starting to cool off now. It gets down to the high 70s at night and still in the low 100s during the day," he said.

Wilson eagerly anticipated a reunion with his family, especially young Michael. The Marines should land at El Toro about 2 a.m. Pacific time, then endure a long bus ride to Camp Pendleton. He expected that Patricia and Michael would meet him there about 4:30 a.m.

"My wife and I did a deal," Wilson grinned. "She got to carry him the first nine months, and I get to carry him the next nine."

As AMT Flight 1042 approached BIA that night, "we weren't really sure if there'd be a reception for us," Wilson admitted. "We'd heard that Bangor was the Welcome Home Capital of America right now, and we were fairly confident that somebody would be here.

"It's great. I'm a bit of a cynic at times, and I really enjoyed it. I really appreciated it," he said.

Two days later, the Navy sent some personnel home through BIA. World Airways Flight 31038 eased down from a warm, crystal clear blue sky and swirled smoke on the

BIA runway at 12:59 p.m. on Thursday, Oct. 10. The plane carried 149 passengers headed for Mayport Naval Air Station in Jacksonville, Fla.

During the last two days, rumors had circulated among the troop greeters that "we're deciding when to stop meeting the troops." The American Red Cross volunteers had recently announced that they would suspend operations at the gift table in two weeks.

"That seems awful sudden," an older woman commented.

"It's about time," a friend responded. "There can't be many more of our troops over there."

Tom Dean stood with another troop greeter near the passengerservice desk and waited for the troops - probably Marines and sailors - to leave their plane. A few minutes passed, then a moustachioed man sporting an Izod knit shirt and a baseball cap bearing Arabic lettering made the turn from the security corridor. Behind him came other men, all of whom hauled assorted luggage.

"You guys with the Navy flight?" a troop greeter inquired. When a sailor nodded, the greeter blurted, "Welcome home!" and bounded down the ramp.

Sailors clad in civvies poured down the ramp and past the gift table to meet the 100 people waiting for them. Right hands eagerly reached out for a friendly shake, while left hands clutched the teddy bears proffered by the ARC volunteers.

The sailors comprised the crews from two Navy minesweepers, the USS Impervious and USS Adroit. Lt. Cmdr. Arthur Langston, assigned to the Impervious, said that the sailors had left Saudi Arabia at about 4:30 a.m. that day.

The crew from the Impervious had been stationed in the Gulf for more than 180 days, or since April 11, Langston said. The Impervious had swept the Persian Gulf for mines off Kuwait. "We were among the minesweepers (assigned) to clear the mines out with the Multinational Force. There was extensive mining done around Kuwait's offshore waters. After the war, the job was to clear those mines out so they would not be a hazard to shipping," Langston explained.

The Impervious used sonar equipment, acoustic equipment, to find the mines so they could be immobilized, either by divers or with other types of acoustic devices.

The sailors knew that a single mine could cripple or sink the Impervious. "It's very stressful," Langston admitted, "because you're within a live minefield, at times as close as 50 yards to live mines. If the boat moved any closer than that, you would be right on top of one."

The Impervious suffered no damage or casualties during its operations off Kuwait. Neither did the other minesweepers assigned to the task force. "First time that I can think of during any mine evolution in history that has happened," Langston stated.

Some sailors who'd disembarked at BIA had already changed into their dress whites, which led Langston to explain that his crew would "be deplaning in uniform" at Mayport. The Adroit's crewmen would change into their dress whites in Florida before the WOA jet flew them to their final destination in San Diego.

Langston contrasted his warm reception in Bangor with a homecoming from Vietnam. "I met protesters when I got off the plane at Travis Air Force Base," he recalled.

"I'll never forget. I left Travis Air Force Base and (went) over to San Francisco International, and there was demonstrators there, protesting our activities in Vietnam. This is a big difference. This makes me feel good," he said.

"We'd heard rumors (about the BIA receptions) on the plane," the lieutenant commander said. "One of the World Airways flight attendants said that Bangor was still welcoming everybody home who came out of the Gulf, so that gave everybody a kind of a warm feeling, hoping that it would happen, 'cause I don't think anybody thought it would."

When Langston noted that the USS Impervious and USS Adroit were sailing home aboard another ship, the troop greeter asked why. "There are actually three ships," Langston said, "except that one of the crews of the third MSO (mine sweeper, oceans), half of their crew will be coming over with the ships. The other half will fly out at a later date, probably about another week.

"The minesweepers were loaded aboard a large freighter. Our ships really aren't that big, so it made sense to ship them home by ship," Langston said. "Does sound kind of funny, doesn't it, shipping a ship by ship? Saves wear and tear on the engine and electrical equipment, though.

"The nearest comparison I can make is from World War II, when the Navy would ship landing craft overseas in larger ships." he said.

MARK'S RETURN ENGAGEMENT

The last Marines reached Bangor International Airport late Thursday, Oct. 10.

For the last seven months, the troop greeters had enthusiastically welcomed home more than 58,000 Gulf veterans, including thousands of Marines. The civilians particularly loved the Marines, whose uninhibited nature spontaneously combusted into more wild parties, dancing, and celebrating than the other services usually enjoyed.

After tonight, however, the leatherneck-sponsored blowouts would end, and within several weeks, all the celebrating would cease.

Mike Stott, the faithful American Trans Air rep, confirmed that AMT Flight 1039 would land in Bangor at 10:35 p.m. on Oct. 10. He plotted the plane's course as Dhahran to Sigonella to Shannon, BIA, and Cherry Point. There wouldn't be many flights after this, he said.

People slowly straggled into the domestic terminal after 10 p.m. George Nye and Everett Steele wandered into the coffee shop, poured themselves some hot coffee, and settled at a table near the entrance. Uniformed AMT personnel, apparently from the relief crew, purchased snacks for their overland hop to North Carolina and vanished deeper into the coffee shop.

Other troop greeters - Joy and Aubrey Brown, Dick Shaw, and Elthier Sonia - worked the counter for steaming coffee and doughnuts and surrounded a table near Nye and Steele.

"You know, I heard that tonight's flight is bringing out the last of the Marines," Aubrey Brown said. "Aren't any more over there."

The troop greeter who had played host to Marine Lieutenant Mark Willis in August said he expected Willis to be aboard the plane for a second welcome home. He promised to introduce the young Marine to the other troop greeters. AMT Flight 1039 put down on time through a light drizzle, swung off the runway, and rolled after the "follow-me" truck past the domestic terminal. Civilians applauded as the L-1011 slowly rolled to a stop at Gate 5.

Three Marines appeared atop the ramp at 10:50 p.m.

That night, the troop greeter who awaited Mark Willis traded places with people who'd waited for returning relatives or friends on other troop flights. He'd wondered why parents, spouses, and children could not identify a loved one among so many strangers. Now, as he stood beyond the gift table that night, he realized why.

All the Marines looked alike. Skin color separated the races, of course, but in those splotched desert fatigues, black Marines looked the same, and white Marines looked the same. The occasional Hispanic or Oriental features broke the monotony, but all the Marines pouring down the ramp that night resembled a camouflaged tidal wave, where a leatherneck submerged his individuality into the Corps.

And the civilian suddenly realized that just like the snowflakes in Maine, no two camouflage uniforms striding past him were the same. A large blotch over a right shoulder, a smaller blotch over the next right shoulder, then no blotch at all. Whoever wove the uniforms did not sew them with the same pattern, but varied the camouflage.

He shook hands with the incoming Marines and Navy corpsmen, then anxiously scanned the leathernecks backing far up the ramp. "Welcome home, gentlemen," he greeted the Marines, who overran the unofficial "official" receiving line and beelined into the terminal. Even an Army hitchhiker made his way along the wire.

"God bless you, ma'am," George Nye said while shaking hands with a woman Marine. "Glad to have you back." More soldiers strolled down the ramp. Nye beamed and stood slightly taller as he welcomed home a fellow grunt.

Marine 1st Lt. Julian Marcus "Mark" Willis landed in Bangor with Brig. Gen. Gary Brown on Oct. 10, 1991. This was Willis' second homecoming through BIA.

Marines kept passing the man waiting for Willis. He tensed as the line gradually dwindled. Had Willis actually boarded the plane in Dhahran? Had a last-minute glitch bumped him from the L-1011?

No! "Hey! How are you doin'?" the civilian cried, waving wildly to a grinning Mark Willis, who stood a full head above the leathernecks on either side of him.

"Pretty good!" Willis replied.

"Welcome back!" the civilian exclaimed as he edged through the crowded ramp. "Welcome home, sir!"

"How are you doing, sir?" Willis asked, a smile lighting his face. He warmly shook hands with his one-time host, who wrapped his arms around the tall, solidly-built Marine.

"I was telling them, I said, 'I know that you'll be here,'" Willis said, sweeping a hand to indicate his companions.

"I met Capt. Wilson here two nights ago," the troop greeter said before expounding his recollections from the Oct. 8 flight. Willis expressed his surprise that of all the Marines aboard that flight, Paul Wilson had encountered one of the two adults whom Willis knew in Bangor, Maine.

Disdaining to haul Mark from the line, the civilian slipped behind him and viewed tonight's reception from a Marine's point-of-view. He grasped the hands thrust his way, then laughed aloud as startled women cried, "What are you doing here?"

As he turned the corner into the terminal, the civilian imagined how the cavernous second floor had appeared on March 8, when a thousand people packed the airport to greet the afternoon flight. Wall-to-wall humanity, a cacophonous din, ear-splitting screams. What was it like for troops just 18 hours removed from the Gulf?

"I wonder what the troops thought when they saw all those people standing there, shouting and cheering and waving flags?" the veteran troop greeter thought. "How do you feel when 1,000 strangers are going nuts because you're passing through their airport?"

That night, he momentarily sensed the emotions surely felt by so many men and women who'd walked this route since March 8. Civilians' eyes danced in pure joy as non-military hands drew the Marines close for a hug, a kiss, or a shared laugh. The troop greeters didn't care - heck, they'd never cared - if a troop's skin was sun-burnt, black, yellow, brown, red, or white. The civilians didn't care if the troop was male or female, tall or short, Rebel or Yank, thin or fat. Maine residents didn't even care about the troop's service branch.

Not at all. Through 220 flights, only one thing about each troop mattered to the civilians who turned out to meet them.

That sole requirement was that the soldier, the Marine, the Air Force type, the sailor, and, yes, even the few Coasties who slipped unseen past the veteran greeter during all those flights, that every troop had returned home safely from war - and had received a proper greeting.

As they worked their way along the wire, Willis' former host introduced Mark as "the Marine who's coming through Bangor a second time." People warmly responded. "Does it feel any different the second time through?" someone asked.

"Yes, it does. I'm coming home under happier terms this time. My mother's felt very good for some time," Willis responded.

A lieutenant named Van Weaver joined the conversation. Stationed in Jubail with Willis, he'd heard all the stories about Stephen King's estate, the million-dollar baseball diamond that King was building for area youngsters in the park behind his home, and American-made pizza.

"This is the last official flight (of Marines)," Willis said, confirming suspicions. "There are a few people back there, tying up odds and ends, but that's probably fewer than 12 Marines."

"You know, people will be disappointed (because tonight's flight was the last Marine flight), because they love Marines," a troop greeter commented. "I remember. I was the only Marine on the tail end of the Army, and once they (the troop greeters) found out I was a Marine, psssh!" Willis said, imitating a crowd rushing its favorite rock star.

"You know what?" Willis said to his former host. "I want to have you meet the general." He indicated a rugged, square-shouldered leatherneck with wire-rimmed glasses who stood partway across the terminal. A single silver star - metal, not cloth - glistening on each lapel, the general smiled and chatted with the Maine residents who frequently surrounded him.

Willis explained that Brig. Gen. Gary Brown was the senior Marine officer "in charge of everybody over there when Schwarzkopf gave up power." More people suddenly converged on Gen. Brown, so he and his former host waited a minute. A few troop greeters whirled past them, then swept back to pin the typical yellow ribbon on the lieutenant's uniform. "Welcome back the second time!" Hilda Gott exclaimed, her eyes twinkling. When the path briefly cleared toward Gen. Brown, Willis moved forward and stood beside him. "Sir, I'd like to introduce Brian Swartz," he said. The general warmly shook hands. "I'm with the Bangor Daily News," Swartz said. "The lieutenant here was a guest of mine back in August." "Is that right?" Gen. Brown beamed. He listened intently as the two men explained how they'd met.

"Pizza and a real nice tour of Bangor, Maine," Willis said. Gen. Brown had served in Vietnam. "The receptions we received coming home from Vietnam were not good at all. It was pretty bad," he said. He hesitated, then smiled broadly as he looked around the terminal. "This has made up for it here.

"When I started coming through the line tonight and saw how all the people were greeting us and the outpouring of love, and the hugging, I think I lost it for a moment," Gen. Brown said. "I shed a few tears. It was great."

Other troop greeters descended on the last leatherneck general to leave the Gulf. "He gets around quite a bit. He was always down where we were working. He's also a pretty highly decorated Marine, several times over in Vietnam," Willis said, voicing his admiration for the general.

Willis looked across the crowd and chuckled, "I think the general got captured for a little while." Civilians thronged around a smiling Gen. Brown, who penned some autographs and thanked his fans for a job well done.

"Oh, yeah, he's not going anywhere! They love generals!" Swartz said, relating the tale about an Army general who'd landed in Bangor 5 p.m. that day when his C-141 Starlifer developed mechanical trouble. A few people had actually been on hand to meet the Army brass.

Hilda Gott flitted through the crowd, spotted the general, and targeted him for a handshake. Then she swung Gen. Brown into an impromptu dance.

The evening passed quickly. Tom Dean interviewed Willis for a tape on the troop flights, then turned his camcorder on Van Weaver. "I'm from Atlanta, Ga.," the lieutenant proudly said as the videotape rolled.

Marines drifted back and forth to the gift table, where the Red Cross volunteers handed out teddy bears right and left. Suddenly, a boarding call sounded for AMT Flight 1039 at 11:18 p.m., and the return engagement of Lt. Mark Willis drew to its finale.

As his comrades retreated along the wire, Willis said it was probably the first deployment where his unit had gone away and returned to have Americans greet them.

"Although a lot of these guys weren't old enough to experience Vietnam, they've heard how miserable it was for the people coming home, so at least they've got pleasant memories from their visit to Bangor," he commented.

FROM ELMIRA TO BANGOR, WITH LOVE

AT&T urges Americans to "reach out and touch someone," by phone, that is.

Elmira, N.Y., reached out and touched someone long distance, but did it in person at Bangor International Airport.

On Friday, Oct. 11, World Airways Flight A31043 touched down in Bangor while en route from Saudi Arabia to Altus Air Force Base, Okla. With 236 passengers aboard, the DC-10 landed on an exceptionally dark night that did not deter some 100 people from turning out to greet the troops. As civilians formed their imaginary wire, a knot developed near Gate 2. More than a dozen people - primarily men and children whose attention centered on a bespectacled brunette wearing an "I Support Operation Desert Storm" sweatshirt - unfurled a large, white banner bolted to two aluminum poles. Its white cloth divided by a massive yellow ribbon that someone had drawn across its midsection, the banner proclaimed, "We support our troops - come home soon!" A name, that of Pfc. Brian Hatfield, had been printed across the ribbon.

Brian and Gail Hatfield had driven from Elmira, N.Y., to welcome home their son, who'd gone to the Gulf with the 471st Transportation Co. from Fort Sill, Okla. The Hatfields said their son, Brian, had called home about three weeks earlier and alerted them to the fact that he would probably be coming home this week. "So, when he did call, and he gave us the final word, we were really excited," Gail Hatfield said. "We kind of held it all in reserve, knowing they were still sending people over, that he could wind up having to stay."

Brian Hatfield Sr. introduced the New York welcoming committee: "Okay, this is my wife's brother, Hayward Meady, and James Meady, my wife's dad." An uncle, George Meady, and three cousins (George Meady Jr., Lori Meady, and Gim Meady) filled out the family contingent who had accompanied the Hatfields to Bangor.

They'd brought with them a banner that was actually a flag that an uncle had flown over his home in Malden, Mass. "He took it up to the Elks' Lodge that he belongs to, and all the people in the Elks' Lodge signed it," Hatfield explained.

The Elks had penned such messages as "Glad to have you back" and "All right! Bob and Mary Duggan" and "Welcome home, Brian. The Knox clan."

Brian Hatfield said that his Army son had been gone 10 months, shipping out with the 471st on Dec. 18. "He was in Khubar, Dhahran -" "- He was up to the Kuwaiti border," Gail Hatfield interjected. "He was into the oilfields with the transportation unit -" "- taking supplies up, and after the war, he was bringing equipment back down to the port to be shipped back to the United States," Brian concluded. In the last three months, he'd been loading ships.

The Hatfields expressed surprise that people still turned out for the flights. "We knew that you had been doing it in the very beginning. That was on the news at home," Gail recalled. "We had not heard that in months, so we were really surprised when we saw that this was still going on."

A few minutes later, soldiers rounded the corner from the security corridor, and Elmira spread out around its banner as James Meady videotaped the homecoming. Three soldiers bounded downstairs toward the men's room in the international terminal, and two soldiers stood near the passenger-service desk. Question marks etched on their eyebrows, the two men peered down the ramp.

"They look a little lost, the first ones off," Tom Dean noted. Well, I guess that's where we're supposed to go, the troops apparently concluded. George Nye, tonight's unofficial flagbearer, finally suggested that they follow him into the domestic terminal.

Tammy Hatfield cried as she watched the first soldier round the corner from the ramp. He paused a moment, thrust his teddy bear high above his head, and yelled his delight at the reception he'd encountered.

People shouted, applauded, and stomped their feet as patriotic music roared from a tape player. The Hatfields and Meadys stood on tiptoe and searched all those look-alike uniforms for Brian Hatfield. Time passed slowly as more soldiers entered the terminal.

One minute. Two minutes. Three minutes. "Where's Brian? Where's my brother?" Tammy's eyes implored. Then Kim stirred, ducking beneath her sister's shoulder before bouncing on her toes to peer over the desert-fatigued juggernaut.

"Yes! Yes! There he is! Can't you see him?" Kim exclaimed, pointing into the ramp. Her young eyes had apparently glimpsed her brother's face.

Agonizing seconds ticked off the clock as other New Yorkers tried to verify Kim's unconfirmed sighting. Even more soldiers packed themselves into the ramp. How could anyone identify Brian in that crowd?

Then everyone saw Brian.

Somewhere on the jammed ramp, a young, brown-haired man sporting an artillery-man's patch on his left shoulder wormed his way past his comrades and swept into Elmira's outstretched arms. A jubilant Brian Hatfield proudly shook his son's hand as the private rejoined a happy family after 10 months away.

Tears flowed freely that October night. Tammy would not release her brother, who beamed as his relatives touched him and hugged him to convince themselves he was still alive. A cousin cried, too, finally believing that her warrior cousin had returned home safely.

"How does it feel to have him back?" a troop greeter asked a smiling father.

"Oh, wonderful," Brian Hatfield responded. "We sent a boy off to war, and we got a man back."

More soldiers flooded the ramp while Brian and Gail Hatfield and Brian II disappeared into the crowd. Their relatives remained on the wire, applauding the troops and hugging any who ventured their way.

Perhaps four or five yards away, a Pfc. Gosselin entered the domestic terminal. An older couple, a man wearing eyeglasses and draping a small 35 mm. camera around his neck, the woman clad in a light pullover, burst through the wire and overwhelmed the young soldier. Both parents hugged their son tight. His mother kissed his cheek as tears rolled down her face.

Another warrior safely home.

Pfc. Donnell Dowdell, a 20-year-old soldier, hailed from Cincinnati, Ohio. He had gone to war with the 471st Transportation Co., too. He wasn't sure why his outfit had remained so long in the Gulf. "We thought we would get back earlier, but we finished moving people and tanks and equipment from up north, and we started a PSA (a port-support activity)," he said.

"We did that for three or four months," working in Dammam, Saudi Arabia. "They loaded the stuff on, but we tied it down, or sometimes we drove the vehicles onto the boat," Dowdell recalled.

He'd just called his grandmother in Ohio and told her he was in Maine. "She was real happy to hear my voice," he stated. "She didn't know I was in the States. She thought I was still over there, but I wanted to surprise her."

Dowdell hoped to arrive in Cincinnati by the following Tuesday to enjoy a long leave. "I've got about 35 days" accumulated, he said. According to Dowdell, the 471st Transportation Co. was among the last units sent to the Gulf in 1990 to return home. Not all the ships were loaded, Dowdell said, so the Army had sent other outfits to finish the job. "It doesn't matter to me," he said. "We wanted to be out of there by summer, but we're home now. That's all that counts."

ANCHORS AND BEARS AWEIGH

The Navy "dropped anchor" in Bangor for the last time on Sunday, Oct. 13.

World Airways Flight 2500, a gleaming red-and-white DC-10, landed 10 minutes early at 4:50 p.m. The plane had departed Sigonella, Sicily, earlier that Sunday, then had refueled in Ireland. The stop in Bangor would be the aircraft's last before arriving at its final destination in Gulfport, Miss.

Rumors circulated among the troop greeters that Sunday afternoon that the DC-10 contained the remaining sailors assigned to Construction Battalion 133. They wouldn't crash anyone's party today, however, like their comrades had on Oct. 5.

A long delay ensued after the DC-10 reached its gate. "What's going on here?" Dottie Heath asked a friend. "They're getting off here."

"Ah, not quite," a passenger-service rep told some veterans who'd ventured up the ramp and inquired about the hold-up. "Only 19 people are getting off here. Everybody else is staying aboard."

"Great, just great, typical military," George Nye growled. Calculating the odds at 6-to-1 in favor of the troop greeters, Earl Rafuse commented that "we'll smother the 10 with love." Moments later, 10 lucky sailors swept through the doors leading from the security corridor and walked past passenger service. "Welcome to Bangor, guys," Nye said, extending his right hand.

"That's it!" someone yelled into the domestic terminal. "Make do with what you got, guys! This is all you're gonna have!" The civilians broke into wild applause punctuated by whistles and cheers.

A soldier rounded the corner from the security corridor. Clad in their distinctive green fatigues, some more Seebees made the turn, too. Other sailors moved hard on their heels. "Are they all getting off?" a man shouted. "Yeah! I wonder what happened? Yay! Here come the rest of them!"

The crowd went absolutely bonkers.

The "Colonel Bogey March"

The last Navy personnel to return through BIA from the Gulf were Seebees coming home from duty in northern Iraq on Oct. 13, 1991.

echoed from the tape player as a few hundred Seebees inundated the ramp. George Nye directed the traffic passing the gift table. He steered sailors toward the phones, beer, or whatever else they wanted.

The sailors found their fans waiting along the wire.

One sailor wore black dungarees and a black sweatshirt with a "B" emblazoned on its front. A Marine wore jungle fatigues, definitely an oddity among Desert Storm veterans. Everyone carried teddy bears, as the ARC volunteers scrambled to give away as many Ursus Berries as possible before permanently shutting down the gift table. Earl Rafuse, a Navy veteran, mentioned that "originally, they weren't going to let them off because they went through customs already. They were holding them on for customs' reasons. "Then when they found out we were all here, they said, 'Let 'em go.' That's all it was. They didn't realize we were here, and they'd already gone through customs once, so they let them go," he said.

"There's a couple of senior chiefs I just talked with," he said. "They had heard about us, but they'd figured that we'd be long gone by now."

A civilian wearing a brown leather jacket and blue jeans carried a Domino's Pizza through the crowd. He somehow escaped detection by sailors who hadn't tasted American-made pizza for many months. Casting a final look over his left shoulder, the man slipped downstairs. Lt. Andy Trotta reported that the WOA Flight carried Seebees who had been assigned to Suda Bay, Crete; Sigonella, Sicily; and Rota, a Navy base in Spain. "No, this isn't all of us," he said. "We still have a detachment, I believe it's about 20 people, over in Turkey."

He said the sailors realized they wouldn't leave the plane in Bangor. Some sailors left to catch civilian flights to East Coast destinations, Trotta explained.

"Then we heard it over the speaker system that everyone aboard the DC-10 could deplane at BIA. The guys were thrilled. I mean, we are all anxious to get home," Trotta noted, "but we've been in the plane since Spain. We haven't been able to get off. "I'm new to the battalion," the lieutenant reported. "I've been there just five weeks. I'll be the Charlie Co. commander, which is the builders and steelworkers. Just prior to the battalion, I was at the Naval Air Station Oceana, Virginia Beach, with the public-works department there."

According to Trotta, CB-133 should spend the next seven months in Gulfport, completing the stateside portion of a cycle that would take the Seebees overseas again, probably by May 1992. The battalion would deploy to Guam, "stay there for seven months, come back to Gulfport, Miss., and then back to Rota, Spain, for seven months.

"That schedule could change at the drop of a hat. Then there are other battalions that go maybe to Puerto Rico or over to Okinawa. You know, they diversify around," the lieutenant explained.

The Seebees stayed in Bangor perhaps another half hour. They entertained their hosts with tales from Kurdistan, Crete, or Spain. A delighted Rafuse mingled easily with sailors from a younger generation. He'd caught many troop flights that carried strangers. Within the month, Rafuse and his wife, Bernadette, would meet the flight bringing home their son.

About 6 p.m., a boarding call summoned the Seebees to their jet. Troop greeters saw them off, and the ARC volunteers begged the sailors to take every teddy bear they wanted. "Here, take fresh Maine apples with you, too," the ARC women told the sailors.

Earlier that Sunday, the Seebees had left Europe bearless. When their DC-10 put down in Gulfport, they carried about 300 Ursus Berries off the plane. The apples were eaten en route. No one at U.S. Customs even winked an eye. So the plane cleared customs overseas without any bears aboard, and it landed in Mississippi with 300 additional fluffy passengers? Who cares?

The sailors and their children sure did.

GEORGIA AIR GUARD

History played across the national airwaves as the troop greeters arrived at BIA about 6 p.m. on Tuesday, Oct. 15.

The previous weekend, TV cameras had treated Americans to a scandalous hearing into the confirmation of Clarence Thomas as an associate justice on the United States Supreme Court. Tonight, as civilians drove up Godfrey Boulevard toward the terminals, the U.S. Senate voted to confirm the nomination by a 52-48 margin.

Polls indicated that most Americans had listened to the hearings. Among those people who missed most testimony were some personnel from the Georgia Air National Guard.

Tonight capped an intensive 10 days, in which troop flights had ferried home personnel from every service branch. No more flights appeared on this horizon. "Is this the last one?" a veteran troop greeter asked Gary Leighton.

Leighton sighed, then replied that the flight carried 199 military personnel. "They're coming from Balikesir, Turkey. It's going to Marietta, Dobbins Air Force Base in Georgia," he announced.

The AMT L 1011 touched down about 6:20 p.m., slipping past vigilant troop greeters who'd momentarily dropped their watch at the terminal windows. The plane swung around and headed for its gate. At 6:35 p.m., Air Force personnel in jungle fatigues followed a smiling Gary Leighton down the ramp and into the domestic terminal. A crowd estimated at 125-150 people gradually awoke as the Air Force personnel reached the gift table. Then the applause and cheers echoed into the ramp.

A preponderance of older men and women with sleeves stitched with many stripes suggested that these personnel belonged to an Air Guard or Air Force Reserve outfit. Southern accents, far too many for regular Air Force, exchanged pleasantries with Maine residents.

One pilot wore a shoulder patch etched with the outline of an F-104 Starfighter, which the Air Force hadn't flown in years.

Lt. Col. Terry Hughey announced that AMT Flight 514 carried part of the 116th Tactical Fighter Wing. "It's an Air National Guard unit out of Georgia, based at Dobbins Air Force Base just north of Atlanta," he said.

"There's about 200 people in this group who are mostly maintenance, the engineers, the people who support and service the aircraft. The planes are flying separately back to Georgia from Turkey," Col. Hughey explained. The 116th TFW flew the F-15 Eagle, the lieutenant colonel said. "We mostly have the A and B models, so that's the air-to-air superiority."

The wing had deployed to Balikesir, Turkey, and had flown from a Turkish air base where "they fly the '104 as part of their mission. They are about to transition," Hughey commented. "You probably read in the papers that Turkey is making their own, I think it is the F16. They, in fact, will eventually use that aircraft, but right now, they still have the '104," all of which explained the F-104 shoulder patch.

The Georgians "were there as part of a NATO exercise for the last 16 days," Hughey said. "The exercise is called Coronet Freedom. It's a NATO exercise that's quite involved, with Turkey, the U.S., and several NATO nations in different air and sea operations." Of the 1,200 personnel assigned to the 116th TFW, about 280 people had deployed to Turkey.

The wing had not sent any aircraft or personnel to fight in Saudi Arabia. Operation Coronet Freedom had nothing to do with the current situation in the Gulf, the lieutenant colonel emphasized. He said the Turkish air force "is patterned basically after the U.S., and most of the pilots train in the U.S. Their pilots are considered excellent, but their equipment, a lot of it is fairly obsolete.

"They do the best they can with what they've got. Unfortunately, while we were over there as part of the exercise, I think they did have a couple of crashes and a couple of fatalities. That was a little bit on the disheartening side," Hughey said. The American and Turkish air-force personnel traded patches and hats and other paraphernalia while the 116th TFW was stationed overseas. The camaraderie was great, the lieutenant colonel said. People threw parties and invited their counterparts from the other country.

He commanded the civil-engineering squadron, an important component of any air wing. "As we were to go over, of course, these people had to stay somewhere" in less than pristine conditions, so his outfit deployed to provide housing for their comrades.

"They showed us a plot of ground over there and said, `This is where you're going to live," Hughey stated. "We, along with the engineering unit out of Bitburg, Germany, came in, set up tent cities for a place for all the people to live, water production, power production, latrines, showers." He shifted the conversation to the reception that the Georgians had received in Bangor. "We did not expect this. This is a surprise to us. We had no idea this was going on," he said.

About 7:15 p.m., someone blew a whistle, and the Georgians slowly disengaged from the warm greeting they'd been enjoying. The melody from the Colonel Bogey March, the theme song to the movie, "Bridge Over The River Kwai" rebounded into the ramp as the guardsmen gradually bid Maine a hearty farewell. After the last Georgians vanished up the ramp, George Nye, Earl Rafuse, and another volunteer discussed the proposal made by some troop greeters to call it quits at the airport. The three men weighed the pros and cons, then decided that they'd greet the troops until the last Gulf veterans returned. At the time, no one foresaw that the number of remaining troop flights could be counted on one hand, plus a finger.

KEEPING THE FAITH

By mid-October, some Maine residents criticized the troop greetings as a waste of time.

A low-key gripe here, a feigned bellyache there, simmering jealousy from a Vietnam vet: When distilled to their purest essence, the negative remarks melded into a solitary complaint: Why are you bothering to greet the troops when the combat veterans have all come home?

Those troop greeters who fielded protests from friends, family, and co-workers responded diplomatically, if at all. Soft-spoken and inarticulate explanations temporarily shielded many troop greeters from confronting their own doubts.

"Why do we continue meeting the flights?" a middle-aged brunette ask a companion on Oct. 8. "I'm getting tired," a veteran confided. "Do you think all this will continue much longer?"

"I don't know, but if the Red Cross is packing it in, maybe it's time we did, too," a VFWer replied. "Maybe we should set a cutoff date," Paul Tower and George Nye suggested while awaiting a troop flight in mid-October.

The people standing with them that day discussed this reasonable proposal. Like voters in a Maine town meeting, the civilians debated the pros and cons and reached an equitable solution:

They would end it at Christmas.

The suggestion made sense. Nye spoke eloquently in favor of waiting until the holidays ended. "Hey, an airport terminal can be a lonely place when you're a soldier," he said, speaking from experience.

"Let's ask Bob Ziegelaar if we can put up a Christmas tree!" a woman suggested. "We'll decorate it with messages for any troops landing on commercial flights!"

"Great idea!" her friends agreed". Maybe we can write some Christmas cards and leave 'em out here for the troops to pick up. That way, if we're not here, they'll at least know that someone is thinking about them."

Several more troop flights passed into history before the Christmas tree went up at the lower ramp entrance, however.

On Saturday, Oct. 19, World Airways Flight A525RF put down at 1:05 p.m. Notice came late about the flight. Sylvia Thompson reached some troop greeters only an hour before the white DC-10 rolled to a halt at Gate 5.

According to passenger service, the airliner carried troops from Amsterdam to Fort Hood, Texas. A Monarch jet reached the international terminal just moments before WOA Flight A525RF popped its hatch.

A subdued crowd - apparently British tourists from their clipped accents - poured down the ramp five minutes before the soldiers did. A short notice had turned out only scattered troop greeters, who did form a rudimentary wire that separated the Brits and the soldiers.

The American civilians made as much noise as possible. As noise swelled in the terminal, one greeter said to Earl Rafuse, "The Brits must think we're crazy."

"No, we were there first," a pretty brunette smiled, speaking in a cultured English accent.

"Where first?"

"Crazy!" the woman laughed.

As the troops passed along the wire, more British tourists stood and applauded the weary men and women in jungle fatigues. One man in particular, a tall, slim, gentleman with receding gray hair, enthusiastically clapped his hands while standing near the weather kiosk.

A young boy, perhaps no more than 6 or 7 years old, stood beside his father. The child tentatively extended his right hand to passing soldiers and quietly said, "Welcome home." Tall, tanned men occasionally knelt and thanked the British youth.

The WOA DC-10 had brought home troops who had deployed to Europe as part of Reforger '92, a NATO exercise held annually each autumn. "No, this technically isn't a Desert Storm flight," Sylvia Thompson acknowledged. "But I'll bet there are some Desert Storm veterans aboard."

She knew her Army.

When a boarding call sounded for the Monarch flight at 1:30 p.m., the British tourists politely filed from the terminal and exited past the windows. Their generosity left the wire uncluttered for arriving troops.

Sgt. 1st Class James Moody of Beaumont, Texas, found a seat adjacent the restrooms and watched the Brits leave the terminal. He hoped to arrive home in Texas within a few hours, a thought he relished after fighting a war and spending too few months at home.

Moody belonged to the 3rd Signal Brigade at Fort Hood, but he had served as a platoon sergeant with the 147th Signal Battalion, 2nd Armored Division during the Gulf War. He had returned to Fort Hood in April, even as the Army deactivated his division.

Slightly more than four months after he arrived home, Moody headed back overseas to participate in Reforger '92. The exercise ran almost two months, placing Moody and other soldiers in a more pleasant environment than the Gulf.

With Saudi Arabia and Europe behind him, Moody said that he was back in the states "hopefully for a good while." He wanted to spend time with his wife and nine children, "five boys and four girls."

Although Moody had left Texas too soon after returning from Saudi Arabia, his family realized that the Gulf War was a lot different.

"Going to Reforger, you knew the times you were supposed to come back. You knew you were gone just for the training. Going to Saudi, we didn't know the day or time we were coming back," he said.

Like Moody, other Gulf War veterans had volunteered for Reforger '92. He pointed out some comrades who wore the 2nd Armored shoulder patch and mentioned a soldier who'd served in the same platoon deep in the Saudi desert.

On Nov. 15, Bernadine Rafuse called friends to announce that her son, Christopher, would land in Bangor that evening aboard a Delta Airlines jet. Out on the tarmac, a white Saudi DC-8 with green letters sprinkled across its tail glistened beneath the international terminal's exterior lighting. Members of the Saudi royal family were aboard, an airport employee said, reportedly heading home from Rochester, N.Y.

About 20 troop greeters had gathered that warm, rainy evening to meet Christopher Rafuse, as did his family.

The troop greeters viewed tonight's flight as "quasi-official," according to Sylvia Thompson's description. "He's like one of ours', because his parents have been so faithful in meeting other flights," she said.

"His MOS is for mortars," Earl Rafuse said, referring to Christopher's military career. Actually a member of an Army Reserve combat infantry unit in Dexter, Christopher had arrived in Saudi Arabia months after the shooting had ended.

"When he got there, there was no billeting for a mortarman, because everything was all over, so they made a driver out of him for an 18-wheeler," Rafuse said.

"He'd never driven one before in his life. I'd always told him to volunteer for everything. He volunteered, got himself a driver's license, and drove the big rigs."

Christopher Rafuse had driven deep into oil-fired Kuwait with the 9004th Transportation Group, a provisional outfit. He had mailed home many color photographs that graphically recounted the hellfire set by retreating Iraqis. His photos also encompassed shattered Iraqi armor.

The young soldier's plane had landed in Philadelphia that morning, and Christopher had called his mother. "She turned right around and got him a plane ticket from there to Boston and Boston to here," Rafuse said. His son would remain home only for the weekend, then report to Fort Devens, Mass.

The Delta 727 landed at 6:46 p.m. and taxied to Gate 1. Within a few minutes, the first-class passengers started deplaning.

A tall young man clad in desert fatigues rounded the corner from Gate 1 and swept his family into his arms. Troop greeters stood back several paces and applauded. Sylvia Thompson and other women later pinned yellow ribbons on Christopher Rafuse.

Amy Irish, his girlfriend, pinned a big kiss on his lips. Another five days passed before a regular troop flight landed at BIA. Under a warm, sunny sky, American Trans Air Flight 028 touched down at 1:15 p.m. on Wednesday, Nov. 20. The L-1011 was carrying 209 passengers from Europe to Lawton Army Airfield in Oklahoma.

"It's a family flight," BIA supervisor Heidi Suletzki stated. "Soldiers and dependents. They've precleared customs, so they should come right in."

The soldiers who climbed the stairs from the international terminal primarily wore their dress greens and black sweaters. Spouses and children walked down the ramp with the troops. Overwhelmed by all the noise, infants snuggled deeply into a parent's shoulder. Older children, those 3 or 4 years old, either held an adult's hand or clung to a friendly leg.

Civilian clothes camouflaged Theresa George's rank as a specialist. She had served in Europe with the 17th Finance Support Unit. Her husband, Sgt. 1st Class Timothy

George, was assigned to the 3rd Battalion, 17th Field Artillery Regiment, 210th Field Artillery Brigade.

The Georges had been stationed in Ansbach, Germany. "We both went to the Gulf," Theresa said, adding that she'd departed Germany on Dec. 14 and had returned on May 4. The 17th FSU put into Dhahran, set up there approximately for a week, and then moved out to the desert to pay the troopers.

Paydays did not follow a normal schedule in the desert. "We had cashiers that went out and paid soldiers," so paydays sometimes came sooner. "It just depended on when the units requested us. They just get a casual pay, and then it comes out of their pay later on. It's like an advance," George explained.

At various times, the 17th FSU stayed at Log Base Echo and T.A. Thompson Holding Area, a site that defied location on a map. Troops traveled to King Khalid Military City and also flew by helicopter into Kuwait and Iraq. Soldiers who received their pay could spend the money at mobile PXs, which sold quick food items, soda, "some things that you would need for your boots (like Kiwi shoe polish) just the basic little items you would need out there, nothing major," she said.

Timothy George said the 3rd Battalion had gone to war with M-109 howitzers, or self-propelled 155 mm. cannons similar to those used by the 152nd Field Artillery Regiment, Arkansas Army National Guard.

"We went through the 2nd Armored Cavalry Regiment, through the backside through Saudi Arabia, across the berm, and into Iraq," he recalled. "We joined up with the 1st Infantry Division and come around on the swoop from behind with the 7th Corps...We had fire missions (at times during the advance)," he said. A boarding call sounded from the PA system just before the tape player launched into the national anthem. Soldiers and spouses went after children who had wandered into Mr. Paperback or downstairs to ride the escalator. The last soldiers and dependents cleared the terminal by 2:10 p.m., and AMT Flight 028 soon lifted off from BIA.

Only one more AMT L-1011 would pass through Bangor while inbound with passengers from the Gulf. World Airways would send two more DC10s home from Saudi Arabia via BIA.

Still keeping the faith, the troop greeters would meet the three aircraft. No public criticism nor private earbashing deterred the civilians from finishing what they'd started on March 8: Welcoming home every troop flight that landed at BIA.

ICH HATTE EINEN KAMERAD

Wind-swept snow flicked across Godfrey Boulevard on a bitter cold Dec. 5. Bright sunshine reflected off the snow dumped during last Tuesday's storm. Caught by a strong northwest wind, the fluffy snow swirled around parked cars on the highway and parked aircraft on the tarmac.

After edging his car into a slot near the Hilton, a veteran troop greeter tugged his knit hat a little lower over his ears and stepped into the biting wind. Although he had lived in Maine most of his life, a cold wind always chilled him.

Imagine the impression that the wind would leave with the troops coming home today on World Airways Flight A31058, he thought.

Many troop greeters had answered the call to meet the 12:10 p.m. flight. Cars lined the road past the Hertz and Avis garages. The wind whipped and howled across the Hilton's parking lot. It hadn't been this bitter since March 8.

The WOA DC-10 landed at 12:05 p.m. and taxied to Gate 6. According to passenger service, the plane would refuel before flying south to England Air Force Base, Louisiana.

A tall, wavy-haired woman wearing a white EMT's blouse stood beside Lorna Nason near Gate 2. Sandy Snow, a Surry resident, had come to BIA today to meet her son, Pfc. Robert Snow. He'd enlisted in the Army in July 1990, shortly after graduating from George Stevens Academy in Blue Hill.

"He came out of boot camp and went right into the war," Robert's mother said. "He came home for six weeks and went right back over."

When he returned to Saudi Arabia in late spring, Robert was assigned to the 539th Heavy Equipment Maintenance Co. (HEMCO), an outfit normally stationed at Fort Polk, La.

Snow anticipated that her son would arrive home on leave by Dec. 20. He'd called her Monday afternoon to say he would be leaving. "He expected to be in Bangor this evening. I called, and they said this was the flight for that port. They said there were 200 to 250 men, so I'm assuming he's here," she said.

Troop greeters formed their wire at the lower ramp entrance and waited for the soldiers. Minutes dragged past, then multiplied, and finally some people cornered a passenger-service agent and asked for an explanation.

"Half the troops are from Saudi Arabia, and half are from Sigonella," the young man replied. "Well, they lost the customs' paperwork on the guys coming home from the Gulf, so they've all got to clear customs again." "How do you lose paperwork inside a plane?" someone asked.

"I don't know," the BIA rep shrugged. About 12:20 p.m., George Nye entered the international terminal and bounded up the escalator, apologizing for being late. He watched as a BIA maintenance worker erected a Christmas tree just inside the security-screening area. "I promised some of the women that I'd loan them an artificial tree to put up on the ramp," a visibly tired Nye muttered. "We want to set it up before we get more troops coming home for the holidays." At 12:42 p.m., Snow walked up the ramp and stood by the escalator. Three minutes later, four soldiers rode up the escalator and turned into the ramp. When they reached the domestic terminal, everyone waiting for them apparently went nuts. The noise echoed well into the international terminal.

A Spec. McFayden followed a Spec. McFadden upstairs. Another soldier hauled a massive musical instrument, possibly an accordion, and a sailor dropped his duffle bag and hammed for the camera as he rode the escalator. More troops cleared customs behind him. "I hope he's not much longer," Snow whispered, anxious to meet her son.

Then a passenger-service agent learned about Snow's predicament. Activating the PA system, the woman paged "Robert Snow, Robert Snow, would you please, make yourself known to one of the Customs' agents?"

Sandy Snow kept peering down the escalator. "Robert! Robert!" she wildly signaled a young soldier who appeared on the stairs. He wore a Screaming Eagles shoulder patch and a wide smile as his mother enveloped him in her arms.

According to Robert Snow, his flight had originated in Kuwait, and he had been gone "terrible long," and the last few months had been very hot. "You can definitely tell there's been a war (in the gulf)," he said. "The Kuwaitis have cleaned a lot of it up, though."

Sandy said that words could not express how she felt. "I'm just wicked, wicked happy. I hope (he stays) for good this time. I can't handle much more of this."

Mother and son talked for several minutes before Snow returned downstairs to wait until his baggage passed inspection. But before he left, he informed the veteran troop greeter who had played host to a Marine and a soldier in August that Gerry Russell was aboard the plane. "He's looking for you," Snow said.

After Snow vanished downstairs, more troops cleared customs and headed for their reception. A few sailors asked for directions to the ticket counters. "We're catching a flight down the East Coast," one man explained. "Straight ahead and down the ramp," a man replied, steering the unwitting men toward the troop greeters.

Customs gradually opened the floodgate downstairs and poured more troops upstairs. Sailors and Marines intermingled with the soldiers.

Another soldier commented that he'd passed through BIA earlier in 1991. He explained to a nervous woman companion the reception waiting for her, then escorted her down the ramp.

Then a familiar smiling face appeared on the escalator.

"Hey, dude!" Gerry Russell grinned.

"Welcome home to the United States!"

Duffle bag slung over his left shoulder, Russell carried a huge boombox as he made the turn into the ramp. "I heard from Robert Snow that you were waiting up here," he said to the troop greeter.

"We cleared customs over there, but we didn't have the paperwork to show it," Russell said. "They had to do it again. We had a three-hour layover in Sicily, because we had 17 people get on, and when we got to Ireland, nobody got off the plane...We were on the plane about 20 hours straight." World Airways had planned to fly directly from Sicily to BIA, but the plane's heavy weight did require a refueling stop at Shannon International.

George Nye, a Vietnam veteran who fought in the IA Drang Valley, welcomes a home-ward-bound Gulf veteran at BIA. Nye died as the troop flights were winding down.

The WOA DC-10 was bringing home the 539th HEMCO, which had been relieved by another maintenance company. Russell couldn't wait to arrive in Louisiana. "I've been gone long enough," he said. "Get me home!"

He'd told his comrades about the reception awaiting them, yet many soldiers were surprised by the greeting. "We've been staying at Camp Doha since October," Russell said. "The guys couldn't believe that we were going home when we finally found out about it. I guess they really didn't believe anyone would be here to meet them.

"They're making Doha a permanent station now, where they can go out and do field stuff. They have Special Forces up there. It's more of a training center now," he reported.

The Kuwaiti desert made an excellent firing range. "The M-1 battle tank, when they fire that here in the States, they've got a certain range maximum they can shoot. That's it," Russell explained. "Out there, they can shoot as far as it can go."

The oil fires had been extinguished, but the troops hadn't really noticed the smoke "because (it) was kind of in between Kuwait City and us," he said. He had heard reports from other soldiers about morning darkness and oily film deposited on vehicles and equipment.

The civilian mentioned a press report that he'd seen on Nov. 26 that claimed all American ground troops would leave Kuwait within a few weeks. The AP report stated that "about 150 Army Corps of Engineers workers" would remain to help rebuild Kuwait.

"That's not quite right," Russell said. "The unit that just replaced us, the 519th (HEMCO), is going to be there until up 'til June. They are a unit just like us. They're going to be using it (Camp Doha) as a training center."

Russell looked forward to a reunion with his wife, Debbie. Knowing that he wouldn't return to Kuwait raised his morale, and he hoped to remain stateside for a long time. The 539th HEMCO would go on "block leave" soon after returning to Louisiana.

The two men talked through the early afternoon, catching up on the news about Stephen King, the Horror-meister's latest book ("you would love it," Russell said), and the weather.

A soldier, a Pfc. Sprinkler, sprawled in a nearby chair. "Today's his birthday," Russell whispered. "We celebrated it over there, and he's planning to celebrate it in Louisiana tonight."

The troop greeter scanned the terminal for Sylvia Thompson. She answered his summons, listened intently for a moment, then rounded up a few women. Just as the troop greeters surrounded the unsuspecting Sprinkler, the boarding call resounded for WOA Flight A31058.

But the women sang "Happy Birthday" loud and clear, causing Pfc. Sprinkler to smile and leap to his feet. He spotted Russell, pointed, and warned that "you'll pay for this!"

His broad grin betrayed his happiness.

As troops retreated from the terminal, Russell gathered his duffle bag and boombox and followed his companions along the wire. His civilian friend walked with him as far as the security-screening area, where the baggage and boombox went through the electronic scanner.

The men embraced and said good-bye. "Tell everybody I said 'hi,'" Russell said. He waved, then bounded through the doors.

By 2:20 p.m., the DC-10 had closed its hatches and started backing from its jetway. Troop greeters dispersed to their cars. George Nye talked with Russell's friend a moment before wishing him a "Merry Christmas."

"See you next troop flight," the man said.

At 2 p.m. on Monday, Dec. 9, the troop greeter learned George Nye had died quietly in his sleep of heart failure during the weekend. The "family" that comprised the troop greeters had lost one of its own. Nye's family held a memorial Mass at St. John's Catholic Church in Bangor on Saturday, Dec. 14, and interred his ashes in an Ellsworth cemetery. The honor guard from Legion Post 84 provided a military funeral.

In a subsequent column, a newspaper reporter for the Bangor Daily News wrote that "George...might have found the weather appropriate during his funeral. His family and friends said good-bye to him during a driving December rain, similar in intensity to, but far colder than the monsoons he experienced during five years spent fighting communism in Southeast Asia... "All his life, George Nye considered himself a Bangor boy, even when he was fighting for his life in the Ia Drang Valley, prowling with the Special Forces into Laos and Cambodia...or - in the last 10 months of his life - welcoming home the men and women of Operation Desert Storm...

"That's where George made his mark on local history. That's where he made many friends before he died too soon at age 51...

"He once called the troop flights 'a very positive thing, and I'm going to do it until it's over.' Well, he did, and the people who knew him - and his country - are the better for it."

Ich hatte einen Kamerad.

HOLY NIGHT, CHRISTMAS FLIGHT

Scott Schnaible got his Christmas wish. So did another 190 people from the 347th Tactical Fighter Wing at Moody Air Force Base in Valdosta, Ga.

And so did the troop greeters who'd hoped for one more flight in 1991.

Thanks to Kathy Cashin, a Boston-based American Trans Air flight attendant, Lynne Cole learned on Sunday, Dec. 22, about the holiday cheer that AMT would spread in Bangor the next day. "There's a jet arriving about 2:40 p.m. on the 23rd, a troop flight straight out of the Gulf," Cashin informed Cole, who'd met her during Operation Thank You in August.

Cashin flew into Bangor that Sunday, stayed overnight, and caught AMT Flight 1062 Monday afternoon. She and Cole went to supper on the 22nd. Before they did, however, Cole contacted other troop greeters, including Sylvia Thompson, who made her phone calls in turn. If Thompson had announced that "Santa Claus is coming to town tomorrow at two-thirty, sharp," she wouldn't have received a more appreciative response.

A troop flight two days before Christmas? Hallelujah!

Holiday traffic clogged Union Street and its approaches as troop greeters wound their way to Bangor International Airport that afternoon. Consecutive storms late the previous week had dumped more than a foot of snow in the region, but the temperature had warmed on this Monday. Godfrey Boulevard proved wet, but not icy, as vehicles lined the curb past the Hilton.

A United Airlines 727 taxied to Gate 2. Whether relatives waiting for family members on the inbound 727, or passengers waiting to catch its outbound leg, or people gathering to meet AMT Flight 1062, humanity packed the terminal to meet the pre-holiday flight.

The AMT L-1011 descended from the overcast skies as the UAL passengers deplaned at 2:25 p.m. "There it is!" a woman shouted, pointing toward the blue-and-white jet. Her cries immediately separated the troop greeters from the disinterested. Everyone waiting for AMT Flight 1062 applauded and cheered. Everyone else ignored the warning. Despite the chaos created as the UAL passengers strugged through the human wire, Christmas cheer radiated through the terminal. "Merry Christmas! How are you?" troop greeters welcomed friends they had not seen since Dec. 5 or George Nye's funeral on Dec. 14.

Familiar faces appeared on the ramp: Cablevision's Bob Jones and his trusty camcorder; Tom Dean, still determined to tape every troop flight; Everett Steele, who served as today's flagbearer; Hilda Gott and her ribbons; Dottie Heath; and the Rafuses, intent on meeting a flight that brought home someone else's sons and daughters. And there were many others, of course. The crowd numbered about 60 people before the first passengers disembarked from the L-1011. The ramp seemed empty without George Nye, however. "Don't I wish George was here," people commented, acknowledging their loss. Yet in their hearts, they knew that Nye would want the Air Force personnel - for Air Force they were - welcomed home as warmly today as he had greeted the soldiers from the 539th HEMCO on Dec. 5.

More UAL passengers poured from Gate 2, and some troop greeters wondered if the turmoil would subside before the troops appeared on the ramp. As the UAL passengers eased through the ramp, the troop greeters reformed the wire. Dick Shaw stood beside a beaming Sylvia Thompson and her granddaughter, Angela Pfleiderer.

With 24 hours' advance warning, the troop greeters had come prepared for today's

Christmas flight. Joy Brown's red dress contrasted with Lorna Nason's bright kiwi blouse. Women had located and signed more than 150 Christmas cards, placing them in a bin set beside the tree. People launched into Christmas carols, warmly shook hands and hugged, and wished their friends well.

Up the ramp, Steele stood at attention, an American flag held tightly in his hands. Dean and Bill Mason, a cameraman from Channel 2, the local NBC affiliate, compared notes beside the passengerservice desk. Bob Ziegelaar, the head guy at BIA, passed through the ramp and disappeared upstairs to his office.

A white 757 emblazoned with a blue-lettered "Taesa" and some national flag stood parked beside Gate 5. "What flag's that?" asked an inquisitive Bob Jones. "Italy?"

A passenger-service agent identified the airline and the flag as Mexican.

Steele's flag suddenly lifted in the breeze pouring from the security corridor. "Here they come," a troop greeter hissed to Dean and Mason, who hopped to their cameras.

Moments later, two men wearing civilian attire and toting tightly stuffed duffel bags turned the corner from the corridor. Then a desert-fatigued horde appeared on the ramp. Cheers echoed up the ramp as Steele escorted smiling and waving Air Force personnel into the terminal. Civilians broke into "Jingle Bells," and the Christmas party began.

People cheered, applauded, cried "welcome home," and hugged the uniformed men and women who entered BIA that day. Squeezing the welcome into her noon hour, Sheila Dean waited near the end of the wire and extended her arms to the passing Air Force personnel. Embarrassed by her tears, an enlisted woman openly cried as she worked her way along the wire. Attempting to keep his glasses clean, a staff sergeant blinked back his tears as he made the corner by the coffee shop. The emotionally charged atmosphere encour-

In a scene common throughout the troop flights, Bernadette Rafuse of Bangor seeks autographs from returning Air Force personnel on Dec. 23, 1991.

aged the happiness that the man felt, however. By the time he reached Hilda Gott at the end of the wire, a few tears trickled down his cheeks.

"Don't run away from Granny!" Gott implored the young, and not so young, men and women who approached her. She lovingly pinned ribbons on anyone and everyone wearing a uniform.

Air Force personnel passing through BIA that day came from Moody Air Force Base in Georgia. Three officers sporting captain's bars and aviator's wings waved to the crowd, shook hands, and exchanged a few kisses with women standing along the wire.

Then Hilda Gott got her hands on the pilots, and within moments, all three aviators wore ribbons and warm smiles. "I don't need mistletoe!" Gott remonstrated the youngest pilot, who laughed before hugging her again.

An airman asked, "Where's the beer?" "That way," a right arm pointed him toward the Red Baron Lounge.

The last Air Force personnel entered the terminal at 2:52 p.m. With the gift table missing, Maine women improvised on Christmas goodies. One woman passed out cookies, while Joy Brown offered the airmen toward the end of the line some freshly baked brownies. Fred Vardamis of Bangor had stood on the wire for the last half hour. A long-time troop greeter, he had come equipped with a boombox that quietly played Christmas music. He had also brought his canine companion, "a Pekinese with one-eighth poodle" named "Bubby." Usually cradled in his master's left arm, Bubby wore a red Santa cap for today's troop flight.

Bubby soon made friends with a Sgt. Jodray, who settled into an airport chair and patted the Christmas pooch. "No problem," Bubby indicated by rolling his brown eyes. "You can do this all afternoon," he told his sergeant.

"You know, there aren't many pilots with this group," Earl Rafuse commented. "I believe it's a fighter squadron."

Staff Sgt. Lionel Lewis was assigned to the 347th Tactical Fighter Wing, based at Moody Air Force in Valdosta, Ga. Lewis was a Georgian, from historic Chickamauga in the northern part of the state.

He said "we're split into three individual flying squadrons, the 68th, 69th, and 70th. Each one is an F-16 outfit and usually have around 30 aircraft apiece. We've had 12 aircraft over there. They left two days ago." The F-16s, which flew home via Zaragosa Air Base in Spain, had arrived earlier that day.

Lewis was an avionics technician who repaired communications and navigational equipment, as well as radar and flight controls. Though he hadn't been to Saudi Arabia until this recent TDY, the 347th Tactical Fighter Wing had rotated squadrons into the Gulf. One squadron had been on station in Saudi Arabia from January through July 4 and was replaced by his unit.

"On this tour, we're splitting it up," he said. "Each individual will stay three months at a time. My task was for six months, but I only had to stay three of it," from Sept. 20 to Dec. 23.

"Originally, we planned to be home in the middle of January, and I guess somebody with some pull got us home (early)," Lewis stated. "The unit that replaced us got there last week. Of course, they missed their Christmas, but they probably celebrated before that."

Lewis looked forward to rejoining his wife and 3-year-old daughter for the holidays. "She told Santa that she wants her daddy home from Saudi Arabia," he smiled.

Tech. Sgt. Al Carleton came from Evergreen, Ala. Assigned to the 68th Tactical Fighter Squadron, he had been gone 92 days and did not particularly want to go back. In less than another year, he would be out of the Air Force, a veteran of 20 years.

Carleton and Lewis chatted with Lynne Cole until a boarding call sounded at 3:25 p.m.

Civilians and military alike wished one another "Merry Christmas" as the Air Force personnel departed BIA. Dottie Heath, Elthier Sonia, and another woman stood at the lower ramp entrance and handed Christmas cards to the troops as they rounded the corner.

Christmas music wafted from the tape player set beside the dutyfree shop. The visitors smiled, occasionally shed a tear, and hugged the Maine women who told them to have a safe flight home.

As the airmen departed the terminal, they walked past the Christmas tree that the troop greeters had set up on the ramp. A note dedicated the tree to George Nye, who would have really enjoyed this moment.

"Silent Night" softly lifted across the ramp as the last military personnel cleared the terminal. Voices quietly exchanged phrases like "Happy New Year" and "welcome home."

Airman 1st Class Scott Schnaible, a tall, dark-haired young man, trailed his comrades. He mentioned that he came from Indiana and had just got off the phone with his brother. The two men had cooked up a Christmas surprise for their mother.

"My mom thinks I'm still in the desert," Schnaible said. "I told her that they can't call over there. There's no way for them to get through. I told her two weeks ago not to send me any presents, and I made up this great story that they were delaying presents over there because of reduced flights. "I'm going to be home on leave by three o'clock tomorrow afternoon," Schnaible said. "When she (his mom) gets back from church Christmas Eve night, I'm going to walk into the house and really surprise her. I let my brother and sister know so they could meet me at the airport and give me a ride home."

A multistriped sergeant reminded the effervescent Schnaible that "we have to catch a flight." He waved good-bye to the women standing on the ramp and headed for his homecoming in Indiana. "Merry Christmas", a civilian called after the departing airman.

With the last troop flight only a few weeks away, Everett Steele (right) bids "farewell" to an Air Force enlisted man on AMT Flight 1062.

STEALTH FLIGHT, FINAL FLIGHT

The Stealth guys tried to sneak through BIA on Saturday, Jan. 11, 1992, but the troop greeters' radar detected their plane.

Despite a bitter cold breeze that drove the wind chill far below zero, perhaps 60 people had gathered to meet a World Airways DC-10 Flight 31067 - which was headed for Nellis Air Force Base, Nev. A wild rumor suggested that the plane carried Air Force personnel familiar with the F-117A Nighthawk, or Stealth.

And just as their Navy counterparts had done three months earlier, the Stealth guys broke up another Amway conference at the Airport Hilton. When the well-dressed Amway reps arrived in the terminal, the crowd swelled to about 125 people. Not bad for a cold night, Everett Steele commented.

WOA Flight 31067 landed at 7:36 p.m. and immediately taxied past the domestic terminal. Air Force personnel poured down the security corridor and rounded the bend past the passenger-service desk about 10 minutes later.

As the tape player blared Bruce Springsteen's "Born in the USA," the crowd went bonkers. Psyched-up airmen and airwomen rolled along the wire, where they dispensed hugs and handshakes, high fives, warm kisses, and big smiles with Maine residents. In that moment, most troop greeters sensed that tonight was the last time that this would ever happen at BIA.

Yes, the Air Force personnel came from the 37th Tactical Fighter Wing, normally stationed at the Tonopah Proving Grounds in Nevada. A smiling Airman 1st Class Dominque Parker confirmed the Stealth affiliation.

The unit had been gone for a little more than three months, leaving the states in October, Parker said. He had not served in the Gulf with the squadron sent to Saudi Arabia before the Gulf War began, but he had done his time over there.

The personnel from the 37th TFW had actually been a component of the 4404th Composite Wing (Provisional), a hodgepodge of various aircraft and outfits. Parker, who had been in the Air Force for 2-1/2 years, was pleased to be headed home. He planned "to relax a little bit and do some dancing and go back to work, because we're not getting any leave.

"It's good to be back (in the States) with this group," the airman stated. "Everyone here is a great bunch of people, really nice to work with. Ever since I've been with Team Stealth, I've loved it. Everyone has been really helpful. We're a team."

Earlier in the week, an outbound flight had brought other Stealth guys through BIA. "Yes, they were our relief," said Col. Jerry Carpenter, the commanding officer on WOA Flight 31067.

"This is the same plane that flew the (relief) group over there, downloaded them this morning. When it landed...we exchanged the bags and took off about three hours later," he said.

"I noticed your men aren't drinking any beer," a woman commented to Carpenter. "Why's that?"

Clad in a dark brown leather flight jacket, the tall, blond colonel grinned and replied, "Actually, they probably told you what our Rules of Engagement are.

"Our rules were there wouldn't be any liquor on the airplane and none on the final leg going in. I think they know they're not to do that (drink beer)," he said. "And I'm not changing the rules!

"Let me tell you something," Carpenter smiled as he fielded additional questions about the liquor ban from gathering troop greeters. "The last thing I want anybody to do (who has) not had alcohol for 90 days is to walk in, his wife pick him up, and the guy pukes all over the car. Now that would not be a good moment, would it?"

Earl Rafuse cracked up, laughing so hard that he doubled over. "I can understand the ban on booze," another civilian acknowledged.

"We're actually the 37th Fighter Wing now," Carpenter corrected a misconception about the Stealth unit. "Under the new reorganization, they've eliminated the `Tactical' and the `Strategic' and gone to a nomenclature to show the composite structure the Air Force is going to." Carpenter had deployed TDY to Saudi Arabia with the 37th

Operations Group. "That TDY group that just came in here, I was the commander of that group," he said.

"About half the personnel are from the 37th (Fighter) Wing. Our team that supported the 117s and the 117 training actually was composed of people from 33 different bases and about eight major commands," the colonel said.

"We had people from Yakota (Air Base in Japan), Hawaii, a lot of the different states...about half the folks (were) maintenance and operations people," he explained.

"We were down at Khamis Mushait, which is down in the southwest portion of Saudi Arabia, in the Issir range, down towards Yemen," he reported.

"We've been gone since before Halloween," the colonel confirmed Dominique Parker's statement. "This group missed Halloween, Thanksgiving, Christmas, and New Year's. Somebody had to do it. Our folks are proud to do that."

According to the colonel, WOA Flight 31067 was scheduled to land at Nellis 11:15 local Nevada time. The flight would place the colonel closer to Washington state, his childhood stomping grounds. Unlike many airmen who froze as they crossed the jetway that night, he did not mind the cold. "So this is 9 degrees, which is what I think they're advertising, and a wind chill of what, 27 below zero? That's brisk to me; that's not cold. I spent four years in Alaska," he chuckled.

Carpenter had been flying the F-117A for about three-and-a-half years and considered it "a great air plane to fly. It's computer controlled. A pilot makes an input, and the computers control the amount of surface deflection," he explained. "It is very pilot-friendly. You don't know that it is computer-aided or it's not computer-aided. It's just an excellent plane to fly. A lot of fun."

However, "it's the strangest-looking airplane I've ever seen," he admitted. "First time I saw it, I kind of laughed. It's just so odd-looking. Every way you walk around it, it looks a little different. It's been described as everything from an ebony vegematic to a bat-wing, all sorts of things, a Star Wars-sort of machine. I'll tell you, it does its job absolutely wonderfully, as proven from the conflict, and it handles very nicely."

The colonel viewed the F-117A as "only the first step in making an airplane with that concept in mind," an ability to lengthen a defender's reaction time by appearing invisible to radar. "I can't envision an airplane being produced now in the U.S. based on the successes of Stealth that doesn't incorporate some sort of reduced (radar) signature," he said.

With the plane's performance during the Gulf War, the Air Force had removed most secrecy wraps from the F-117A, Carpenter confirmed. After Hilda Gott teased him about Prohibition, Carpenter gladly talked about his family: Janet, his wife; and two sons, ages 15 and 11. "That's the thing you miss the most, especially for this group over the holidays. Missing Thanksgiving, missing Christmas, missing New Year's: The guys on this team have done just an excellent job.

"The real heroes are the families," he stated. "The real heroes are the wives and the kids that miss their husbands or their fathers or their mothers over those kinds of holidays." The initial boarding call for WOA Flight 31067 sounded at 8:23 p.m. Air Force personnel bolted for the ramp, where, for a final time, troop greeters formed their imaginary wire. Women hugged the outgoing airmen and women and quietly bade the troops a last farewell.

"Do you think this is the last flight?" Dick Shaw wondered. "I don't know," a fellow greeter replied. "I'd like to think there are more troops to come home. These guys seem to be on a three month rotation. Maybe there'll be another flight in the spring."

Col. Carpenter, who'd proved such a big hit with the civilians, bounded along the wire and shook every hand he could find. More Air Force personnel followed him. Although undoubtedly tempted by the neon sign hanging outside the Red Baron Lounge, they had observed Prohibition. A woman captain who sported eyeglasses and dark hair whirled as she entered the ramp, then shouted, "Thank you, Bangor!"

Not all the troops reboarded the WOA DC-10. Sgt. Jody Pulsifer of Livermore had deplaned in Bangor to a warm reunion with his wife, Lisa, who'd been staying in Maine with her in-laws until her husband arrived home from Saudi Arabia.

The Pulsifers lingered a while in the terminal, where they chatted with the lingering troop greeters. Pulsifer had immediately shed his desert fatigues for civilian togs, including a non-regulation baseball cap. He beamed as Lisa held his arm. "Hey, this is great, especially since someone said we were going to land in Philly," he said. "When we learned we were coming to Bangor, I called her, and she came up to meet me."

A few minutes later, the Pulsifers disappeared from the domestic terminal, and WOA Flight 31067 vanished from BIA. A last reunion had taken place in Bangor. A last troop flight had greased its tires on the 11,000-foot runway.

After 220 flights flights carrying 60,000 Desert Storm veterans, the epic known as "An American Homecoming" had ended.